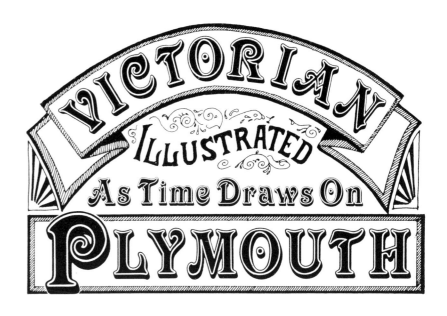

Chris Robinson

Pen&ink
PUBLISHING

British Library Cataloguing in Publication Data
Robinson, Chris, *1954–*
    Victorian Plymouth as time draws on.
    I. Title
    942.358

    ISBN 0–9510747–2–5

Designed by Chris Robinson and Rob Warren
© Chris Robinson 1991

First published September 1991

Typeset, printed & bound in Great Britain
by Latimer Trend & Company Ltd
Estover Close
Plymouth PL6 7PL, Devon

Published by
Pen & Ink Publishing
34 New Street,
Barbican
Plymouth PL1 2NA

for
Brenda Louise Robinson

Acknowledgements

Firstly I'd like to thank my dear departed mother, Brenda, a constant and tireless source of help and encouragement for more than thirty years and who sadly died before this project really got going. Mother, I hope your misgivings will prove unfounded. Secondly, thanks to my father Des Robinson, picture-framer without parallel and whose timely interventions have helped keep 'Pen & Ink' afloat over the last six years.

For the present volume thanks to Rob Warren for his patience and forebearance (I do listen, honest), and for ensuring the smooth running of our New Street operations. Thanks too to his wife Nita whose introduction to word processors was the compilation of this index, a true baptism of fire . . .

From the library thanks are due to the local studies librarian, Jenny Ward, senior assistant librarian John Smith (my godfather), with Margaret Willcocks and Jill McGroarty, and the various other members of staff there who have made my weekly visits there so pleasurable over the last ten years. Still in the library, thanks too to area librarian west John Elliott and in Exeter the county librarian Alison Shute for facillitating the use of the library's material for both the *Evening Herald* articles and the book.

As for the *Herald* itself, thanks to Alan Cooper for keeping 'As Time Draws On' on, thereby ensuring the book's very existence. There is still a lot more to come if that's alright, Alan! Thanks to John Dudley, Lesley Pomeroy, Beryl Clarke, Pat Shapter and Anita Dudley, the promotions team at the *Evening Herald* for their happy countenances and hard work on the book and the calendar. Thanks and apologies here too to *Herald* men Ken Fenn and Terry Scofield who quite rightly can never understand why stories about life a hundred years ago should come in for publication as if they were last-minute news items; I think we've cracked that one now though.

One of the best ways of learning about life a hundred years ago of course is to read any literature published around that time and in that regard thanks to Tony Clement of the Barbican Bookshop and Mark Treece in the Barbican Centre for simply being in the business of selling old books.

Thanks too to Bill Fox-Smith of the Fox-Smith Galleries and Ray Goodey of Peninsula Prints for allowing me access to any old prints that come their way.

The Barbican obviously is Plymouth's focal point for old Plymouth in many ways, especially its streets and buildings, and on a practical note thanks to Peter Stedman, Chairman of the Barbican Association, and his predecessor Jim Woodrow for not only being there in the 1950s to save parts of Looe Street and New Street but who are also still actively involved with the rest of the Association in restoring these valuable properties; including the delightful seventeenth-century building No 34 New Street where our business is based and this book was written.

Crispin Gill is another founder memeber of the Barbican Association and thanks are due to him not only in that capacity but also as author of the most readable formal histories of Plymouth ever published.

On the printing side thanks as ever to John Turner and his team in the Latimer Trend Group, including Chris Pring, Chris Price and Norma and especially Bill Bugler whose ever growing enthusiasm for this venture has been a source of great encouragement as the deadline has approached.

Honourable mentions too for Clive Hooper of Planographic for bits of artwork and various pictures, Kay Cobbledick for all the old books she reworked in her time at 34, for Matthew Webber for his help and for Mike Newton-Perks of Reprocraft for the other Hot Wax.

Last but by no means least my in-laws, Laurie and Patricia Greathead, bog-eyed proof readers whose contribution was co-ordinated by their daughter and my partner, Clare, probably the world's most patient and certainly most pregnant proof reader of all time. Thanks for all the reading, a fair bit of the typing, the support and generally being the 'without which not'.

Plymouth
July 1991

Of the many books referred to in compiling this look at Victorian Plymouth those written in the nineteenth century, not surprisingly, have been the most regularly quoted. Writers whose work has been most consistently plundered include RN Worth, Henry Whitfeld, WHK Wright, Llewelyn Jewitt and John Harris.

As for the artists, the works of two men in particular crop up on numerous occasions, Thomas Allom and Charles Eldred. Allom's drawings were worked up by a variety of engravers and most of them are reproduced here at almost twice their original size; the pictures were first seen in Britton and Brayley's *Devonshire and Cornwall Illustrated*, while Eldred's simple line drawings appeared together with WHK Wright's text in their volume on *The Streets of Old Plymouth* published at the very end of the nineteenth century.

Many of the illustrations reproduced in this book were not credited at the time, however two other artists well represented here are W Hake, whose work was generally published by William Wood of Devonport, and GP Hearder, who drew principally to illustrate the articles he wrote in the 1830s for the *South Devon Monthly Museum*.

With all but a handful of exceptions the pictorial matter used in this book was produced in Queen Victoria's lifetime ... 1819–1901.

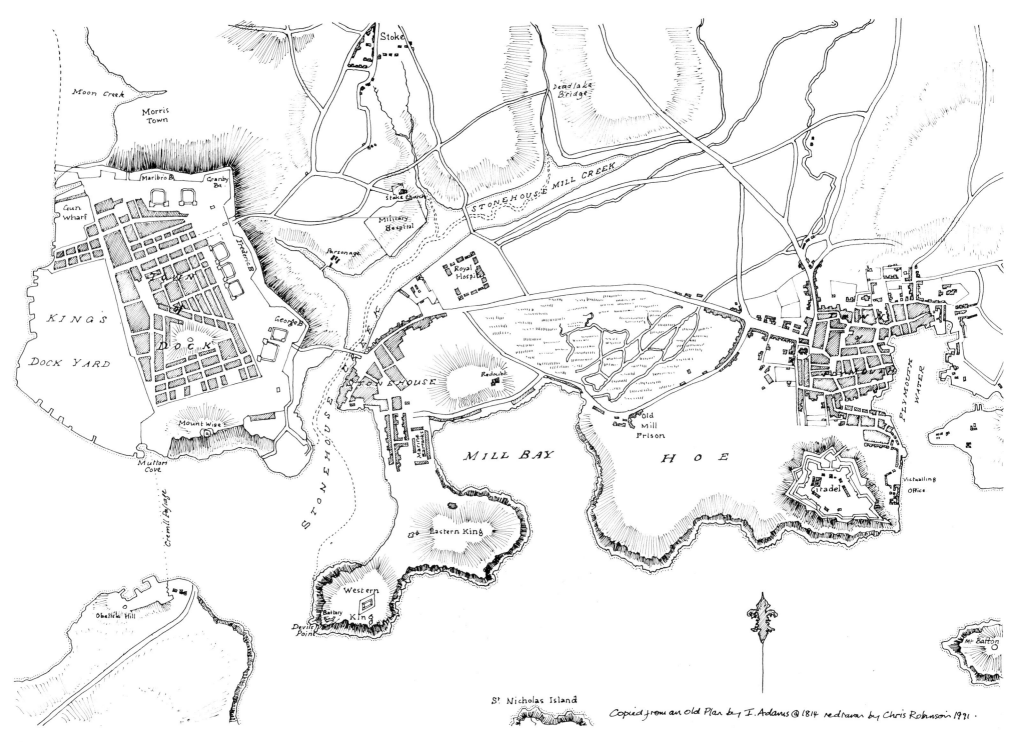

Stoke

Moon Creek

Morris Town

Deadlake Bridge

Marlbro' B.   Granby B.

Gun Wharf

STONEHOUSE MILL CREEK

Frederic B.

KING'S

Stoke Church

Military Hospital

DOCK YARD

DOCK

Parsonage

Royal Hospi.

George B.

STONEHOUSE

Redoubt

STONEHOUSE

PLYMOUTH WATER

Mount Wise

Old Mill Prison

Mutton Cove

Marine

MILL BAY   H O E

Cremill Passage

Victualling Office

Citadel

Eastern King

Obelisk Hill

Western King

Battery

Devil's Point

Mt Batton

St. Nicholas Island

Copied from an old Plan by I. Adams @ 1814 redrawn by Chris Robinson 1991.

vi

The nineteenth century saw Plymouth grow faster than at any time before or since. Scant though the early figures are it would seem that the population roughly doubled in the fifteenth century (from about 1,500 to 3,000), slightly more than doubled in the sixteenth, was fairly static in the seventeenth and doubled again in the eighteenth. At the dawn of the nineteenth century the population of Plymouth was just over 16,000, a little behind that of Exeter, which had always been the bigger of the two. However, by the end of the century Plymouth's population had increased more than sixfold to more than 107,000, twice that of the County Town.

The growth rate of Plymouth also exceeded that of its more immediate neighbours, Devonport and Stonehouse, with whom it was to merge soon after the end of the century. Although very much the youngest partner of this trio, Devonport, whose story really began with the establishment of the Dockyard in the last decade of the seventeenth century, was by far the biggest of the Three Towns in 1800. Indeed with a population in excess of 23,000 it was by far the largest town in Devon and Cornwall. Small wonder then that the people of this town objected to the name Plymouth Dock and generally tended to drop the 'Plymouth' element. Great, of course, were the celebrations when assent was received to change the name to something more befitting their status as the largest port in the county – Devonport.

The very same conditions that created Devonport, however, also constrained it, as a look at this very early nineteenth century map shows; hemmed in on the seaward side by Mount Wise, the King's Dockyard and the Gun Wharf, its boundaries were equally clear cut on the landward front:- the series of defensive lines constructed around the various barrack buildings. Thus the opportunities for expansion were not the same as those enjoyed by Plymouth, consequently its growth pattern was nothing like that of its older neighbour in the nineteenth century and even fell some way behind that of Stonehouse.

Once the Napoleonic Wars had ended Devonport grew very slowly until it breached its boundaries in a big way with the Keyham extension, in the 1850s, when the population shot up from 38,000 to 50,000 in just ten years. An even more dramatic increase occurred in Stonehouse, thirty years earlier, when work began on the Victualling Yard and the local population jumped from 6,000 to more than 9,500 over a ten year period.

As can also be seen from this map the opportunities for expansion in Stonehouse were limited too, once the peninsula had been developed it was obvious that it would not be long before Plymouth's eastern boundary would reach out to stunt any further growth. Indeed in the two decades before the Three Towns merged in 1914 the population of Stonehouse actually fell by over 10%.

But that was at the end of the century when the number of people living in these Three Towns was four times greater than it was when this map was drawn up. Back then there were clear divisions between them; Stonehouse Creek, with little more than a major hospital on each of its banks from the bridge up to Pennycomequick, and the marshes to the east of Stonehouse Hill, above the undeveloped Mill Bay.

In the years that followed, of course, what is shown as Stonehouse Mill Creek was infilled to form Victoria Park, while sometime earlier Stonehouse Hill was excavated, the marshes were built upon and Millbay was developed and laid out as the Great Western Docks.

There were to be other areas where land was reclaimed from the sea, over six acres at Stonehouse for the Victualling Yard and many more at Keyham as the Dockyard expanded along the north eastern banks of the Hamoaze. The stories behind all these developments are to be found in the pages of this book, as are those chronicling Plymouth's urban sprawl over the Hoe, Coxside, Cattedown and northwards beyond 'Old Town'.

Parallel accounts of the progress of the many surrounding communities that now fall within the boundary of the modern city of Plymouth are also given, the stories of growth there for the most part being altogether more modest; Plympton St Mary and St Maurice typically little more than doubling their populations. Morice Town, Stoke and St Budeaux though, as virtual suburbs of the Dockyard which did have room for expansion, enjoyed spectacular growth, St Budeaux's population increasing more than tenfold from 500 to over 6,000 between 1800 and 1900.

It is hard now to imagine the Plymouth depicted in this map, and harder still perhaps to imagine the impact that the developments over the next few decades were to have on those who could remember it this way. But if we feel that an area we might have been familiar with in our youth has changed in later years to a point where it is difficult to picture it exactly as it was, look again at Stonehouse peninsula, the ragged coastline of Millbay and the great open expanse marked Hoe, and try and put yourself in the shoes of someone who grew up knowing this and yet lived to see the Three Towns of the 1880s.

If the Three Towns (Plymouth from 1914) had continued to expand at the same rate as it did in the nineteenth century the population would be roughly three times what it is now as we approach the end of the twentieth century, that is well over 800,000 rather than something under 300,000.

The main element in population growth in recent years came with the assimilation of Plympton and Plymstock rather than with any major baby boom. Admittedly Plymouth has spread its boundaries far and wide, however this is not so much because there are many more people living here than ever before but because the people living here have more space than ever before.

In the nineteenth century it was different, families were bigger, most housing was terraced and the population was much more tightly packed ... and while most of Plymouth's Victorian housing stock remains today, its pattern of use has changed somewhat over the years.

But to return to the map, already much of the modern street plan is in evidence, roads after all tend not to move significantly down the years, curves may alter, streets may be widened but the basic route remains the same. Looking at the earlier map again and picking just a few of those cross country paths we can identify the origins of Tavistock Road (Stoke), Molesworth Road, Alma Road, North Road (East and West), Mutley Plain, King Street and Millbay Road.

By 1880 almost all of Plymouth east of a line from Sutton Harbour to Mutley Plain and south and west of the railway line from Mutley to Millbay had been developed; the Hoe and Hoe Park had assumed the shape and proportions we are familiar with now and West Hoe had more or less taken its present shape.

The development of Millbay was well under way but Stonehouse, as evidenced by its falling population at the end of the nineteenth century, had grown about as much as it could grow. Devonport itself was in the same predicament but, through Morice Town and Stoke, was still stretching out to the north and east.

Plymouth's next great growth areas were also to the north and east as the fields of Peverell and Mount Gould and the newly created parish of St Judes were prepared for the builders. The one 'proposed' road on this map, alongside what was to become Beaumont Park, marked out an important new thoroughfare for non-rail traffic heading north from Friary Station.

The impact of the coming of the railway around the middle of the nineteenth century is also hard for us now to appreciate, both in terms of the effect it had on local commerce and the effect it had on local people, most of whom had probably never ventured across land any further than Cornwall and certain parts of Devon. The graphic accounts of the opening of Millbay Station, Plympton Station and the building of the Royal Albert Bridge help give us some idea of how wonderous the arrival of those early steam trains was here, as elsewhere, in those distant days.

In those days the full weight of the industrial revolution was starting to hit all aspects of life from the factory to the farmyard, from the kitchen to Keyham. As well as what was obviously old, new and attractive to the Victorians we look here at some of the not so obvious subjects around, like some of the small manufactories in the area, including a celebrated local producer of agricultural machinery. It also looks at some of the items people bought for house and home and some of the places that kept them in employment, like the various Service-related establishments in the Three Towns, including the Keyham Steamyard.

While there was undoubtedly a certain amount of new age affluence in the wake of all this so-called progress, which brought many fine buildings and institutions, there was also, of course, a lot of poverty, overcrowding and illness. It was a time when many of the fine old buildings in the very heart of Plymouth became the backdrop for some of the century's more desperate moments as disease and neglect took their toll. This was the legacy that ultimately led to the loss of so many of the city's links with the past, although even then there were critics of those who would abandon our heritage.

Not that the architects of the new Plymouth were what we might call modernists, rather many of them looked to introduce to the Three Towns a classical style echoing the architecture of the Greeks and Romans, a style too old for the area to have ever properly known first time around. Foulston led this movement around Plymouth, Devonport, Stoke and Stonehouse in the early decades of the nineteenth century and in the pages that follow there are many examples of his public and private commissions. Some of them survive today, a great many do not, victims mainly of the blitz but also, in part, of the planners.

The blitz, of course, provided the planners with an unprecedented opportunity in Plymouth and one which they seized in no uncertain terms, as a comparison of the pre and post-war street plans of the city centre shows.

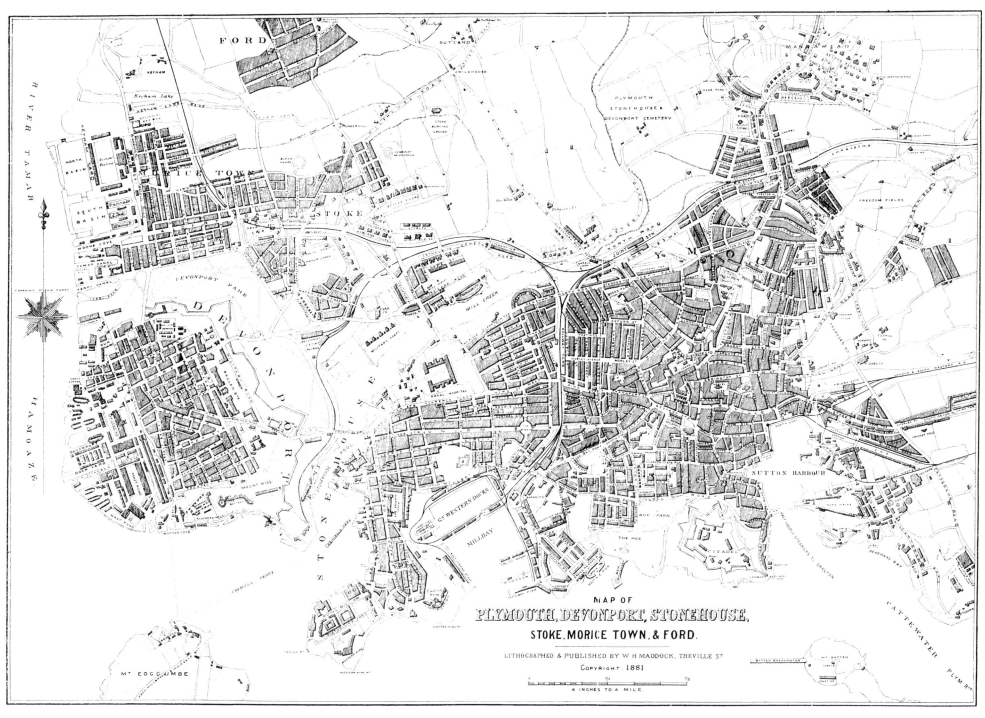

MAP OF
PLYMOUTH, DEVONPORT, STONEHOUSE,
STOKE, MORICE TOWN, & FORD.

LITHOGRAPHED & PUBLISHED BY W. H. MADDOCK, TREVILLE St

COPYRIGHT. 1881.

6 INCHES TO A MILE.

Most of the buildings that stood where Plymouth's modern city centre has been laid out were built in the nineteenth century and doubtless it would be very difficult for any time-travelling Victorian to orientate themselves in today's shopping complex . . . just as it would be for any post-war Plymothian to find their way around the irregularly angled thoroughfares of the old town. Of the pre-war structures that survive today – the erstwhile Royal Cinema, the *Evening Herald* Offices, Central Methodist Hall, St Andrew's Church, Charles Church, the Guildhall and Derry's Clock – only the last mentioned is genuinely Victorian.

The Guildhall, like the two ancient parish churches, survived the blitz only as a shell and, like St Andrew's Church, it was subsequently rebuilt inside; while Central Methodist Hall was itself only a late 1930s restructuring of an old chapel (see the piece on the Ebenezer Chapel). The Royal Cinema and the Herald Offices were also late 1930s buildings, leaving only Derry's Clock and the old bank building next to it as the genuine, intact, city centre survivors of Victorian Plymouth.

Apart from those exceptions detailed above everything else inside the area bounded by Western Approach, Cobourg Street, Charles Street, Exeter Street, Royal Parade and Union Street was either bombed or bulldozed and in the pages that follow you can find many examples of the fine old buildings that were lost in this way.

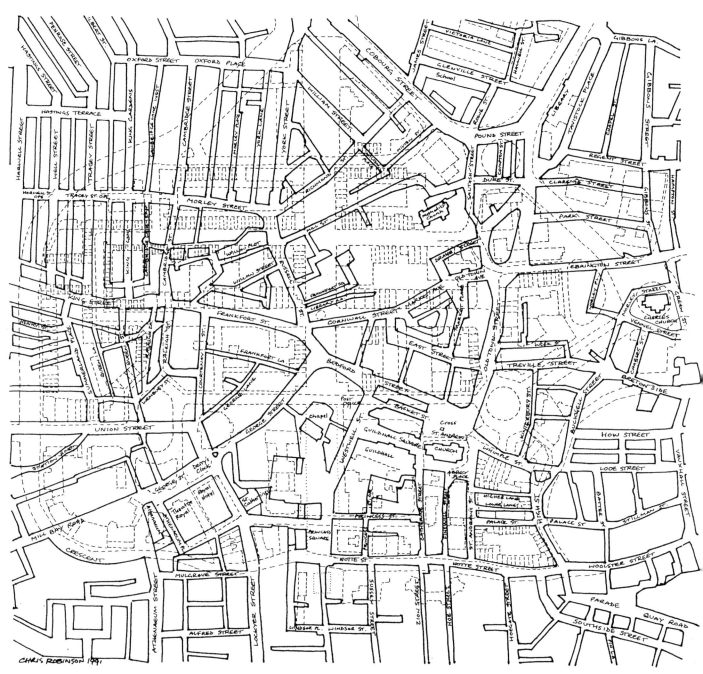

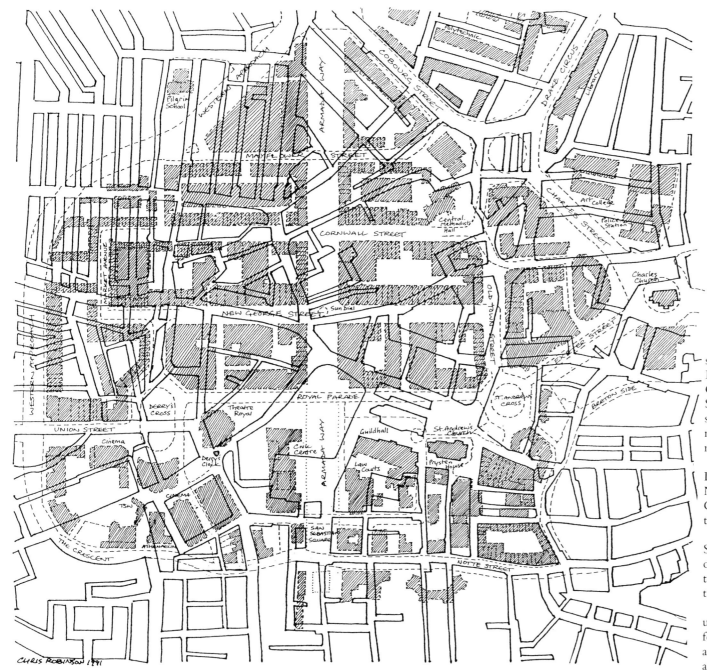

It wasn't just the buildings that disappeared of course, streets and street names disappeared too; among them Bedford Street, East Street, Basket Street, Willow Street, Queen Street, Morley Street, York Street, Richmond Street, Treville Street and William Street. Others, however, survived although in some cases, somewhat confusingly, the new streets did not at any point overlap with their earlier namesakes.

Compare for example Frankfort Street and Frankfort Lane with the present Frankfort Gate, or George Street with New George Street, which perhaps should have been Cornwall Street but was instead moved across a block, or the old Market Avenue with the new.

Other designations were more logical, *viz* Old Town Street, which roughly approximates in line and length to its original counterpart, as indeed does the present day Courtenay Street and Raleigh Street, although there all similarities end.

Hopefully, though, these maps will make it easy to build up a picture of how the various views, depicted on the following pages, relate to both the old and new plans of the area, and those who only know the new will gain a better appreciation of how things were in Victorian Plymouth.

xi

Contents and Illustration Credits

DLS:PCL = *Pictures by kind permission of Devon Library Services: Plymouth Central Library*

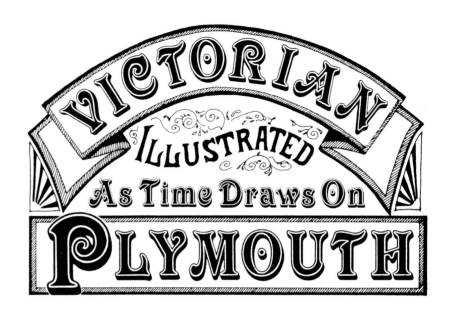

The Cawsey

'Sutton Pool, which opens into Catwater, is the internal Harbour of Plymouth, and the chief seat of the coasting trade and commerce of the town. Except at the entrance, it is completely surrounded by public and private quays, warehouses, shipwright's yards, and buildings connected with maritime interests and pursuits. At the entrance, which is represented in the accompanying View, are two piers of solid masonry, ninety feet apart, which were constructed between the years 1791 and 1800, by means of grants obtained from parliament: the eastern pier is connected with the ancient work called the Barbican, and the western one projects from Teat's Hill. Since the above period, considerable improvements have also been made within the harbour by the Sutton Pool Company . . .'

So ran the text describing this engraving when it was published in Britton and Brayley's *Devonshire and Cornwall Illustrated* in 1832. Thomas Allom it was who produced the original drawing from which this particular view was worked up and it would appear that Allom executed his sketch a year or two earlier for we know that the Barbican Gate, which we can see in the middle of this picture, was pulled down in 1830–31.

'The Barbican Gate or South Gate as its name implies, stood at the Barbican just by the old Fort; it was built in 1602 . . .' (Jewitt 1873). In those days warehouses were built right on to much of the available waterfront of Sutton Pool and so this gate would have been the main entrance and exit for the town for seagoing travellers. Doubtless it was used by the Pilgrim Fathers when they came here 18 years later. A modest affair, originally we learn from early deeds that in 1654 the Barbican gatehouse was leased to Richard Vinson who had 'built it over and by the side'.

It is perhaps difficult to imagine now how Sutton Har-

bour appeared centuries ago, long before any quays were constructed and when the tide was allowed to lap against land, long since reclaimed from the sea. Most of the flat acreage around the harbour today was muddy shoreline originally; indeed, as Crispin Gill suggests in his book on *Sutton Harbour*, it probably looked much as Hooe Lake does today as the two have the same geological history. Clearly, though, there was to a certain extent a natural rocky ridge that ran some way across the entrance to this harbour. This ridge or 'Cawse' was built upon over 500 years ago and in 1511–12 we learn of a new house being put up on it; while 30 years later John Leland wrote, 'The Mouth of the Gulph wherein the Shippes of Plymouth lyith is waullid on eche side and chainid over in Tyme of Necessite.'

In addition to the chains there was also an armoured mast or boom here with iron spikes that could be put across the mouth of the pool at high tide. Quite how negotiable this Cawsey or causeway was for pedestrians at low tide, however, is not very clear, Gill suggests it may have been like the causeway at Noss Mayo.

One thing is sure though, the side running out from the Barbican was more substantial than its Coxside counterpart. The old town records have a number of references to men being paid for carrying stones here and on one occasion there is mention of a considerable sum being spent on ale for the men 'that holpe to slinge the grete stonys at the Cawsey'. This reference coming over 200 years before the 'Admiral McBride' public house was built, as it was in all likelihood, for the men who were working on the construction of the piers that were erected over the top of the causeway.

In order to help finance all the work that was done on the old cawsey it was customary to levy dues on any strange boats that moored themselves to it. 'Cawsey hake' or 'Castle

hake' these dues were known as and the structure boats were most likely to moor themselves to was the Fish House or Fish Cage.

Presumably used as a fish store at some time, it was used for naval stores at the beginning of the eighteenth century. Then in 1742 the Mayor, Launcelot Robinson, moved the watch house here from the guildhall. Ten years later it was moved back again for no apparent reason, although elsewhere we read that the fish house was washed down in a great storm of 1744. Certainly it was described as being in ruins in 1762, when on the night of another great storm, two sons of Mr Collier took shelter behind it only to be swept away to a watery grave by a 'huge bore' which washed down the Barbican (Whitfeld somewhat confusingly dates this incident 1703).

The demise of the fish house clearly removed one of the main barriers at this point to the open sea and in those pre-Breakwater days Sutton Harbour was particularly vulnerable to storms. So it was that the townsfolk were particularly grateful to the MP who represented them from 1784 to 1790, Captain (later Admiral) John MacBride, who helped secure the government grants that made the building of the two piers here possible. Completed by 1800, the harbour was transformed by their construction and as can be seen from the illustration, it wasn't just fishing and commercial boats that took to the water here; as Britton and Brayley added to their account 'boats may be hired at the western pier, to go to any part of the port, or sound'. The story didn't end there, though, as they concluded with a familiar nineteenth-century lament '. . . it is to be regretted that there are no regulations to restrict the charge for fares'.

Watch House

Although parts of this curious old building which stood opposite the 'Admiral MacBride' are thought to have dated from the late eighteenth century, it was substantially erected around 1808 not long after the west pier was completed. Serving both the Police and the Customs over the years it was, sadly, demolished in February 1933 in order that the road running around the front of the Barbican to the Hoe could be improved. The following year the Mayflower Memorial was put up just a metre or so from what had been the front of this building.

Described, in a survey of the ancient buildings of Plymouth not long before its demolition, as a 'highly interesting and picturesque relic of a port building (1760–70, part 1800–25)' this was, in its role as a customs base, also at one time home of the tide survey office.

Records surviving from the late eighteenth/early nineteenth century show some fairly remarkable tidal disturbances in Sutton Pool. Earthquakes in other parts of the world were often the cause of great 'bores' coming into the harbour, such was the case following an earthquake in Lisbon in 1755 and in Quito in 1781. Some 30–40,000 lives were lost in the Lisbon earthquake, all the shipping was destroyed in that port and most of the city was wrecked while the repercussions were felt far and wide.

Further tidal waves are recorded here before the building of the Breakwater, in 1793 and 1795, and in 1811, on 30th June between three o'clock and seven we are told that the tide suddenly fell from eight feet to four feet and rose again several times. One five minute spell in this period witnessing a rise and fall of fully eleven feet.

Such occurrences are, of course, extremely rare and freak tides are unlikely to have ever bothered the children who, by all accounts, used to dive into the water from the first floor window of this building or indeed the lady bathers who had their own bathing place 'under the Hoe'.

In the 1860s these lady bathers were a great attraction on the Hoe and so big were the crowds that gathered to watch them that in 1864 police assistance was required and it was ordered that 'a constable be stationed at the entrance to the ladies bathing place and remain there until 10am.' This would almost certainly have been one of Constable W Fuge's chores. A familiar figure with his high silk hat and great gleaming brass buttons on his coat, Constable Fuge lived at that time in this building, which was then referred to exclusively as a Police Station. One can just imagine this Victorian gentleman standing guard over these women who, although described by some as swimming naked, were invariably clothed in very cumbersome costumes.

For the first eighty years of the nineteenth century women bathers wore heavy pantaloons, with thick frilly flouncy dresses over the top and perhaps a corset underneath, which, when topped off with a head-scarf, oilskin cap or straw hat, made it difficult for all but the most determined to actually do much in the water. Unlike the men who apparently were wont to swim in the nude and there were around this time a number of prosecutions for indecent exposure.

Back on the Barbican, though, much more serious breaches of decency were in question and, just up behind the Police Station in Castle Street, prostitution was another problem Constable Fuge would have been directed to pay attention to. Whitfeld said of Castle Street or 'the Rag' that 'every house was formerly an inn and every inn a brothel', here was a population of the destitute and dissolute, who 'inhaled their own pestilential odours, and vanished with the sunrise.'

In the middle of last century this little street alone contained five beer houses and seven licensed houses; 'Bunch of Grapes', 'Rising Sun', 'Seventeen Stars', 'Fountain', 'Lord Nelson', 'The Jolly Young Waterman' and 'The Welcome Home Sailor'. The Reverend Francis Barnes, who on more than one occasion entered the 'Infernos' of Castle Street and found nude men and women dancing, gave the police particulars of the numbers of different prostitutes harboured there and after their appearing before the committee the police were directed to pay attention.

By the end of the century Castle Street had 'mitigated its character' and the former taverns 'now housed scores of families, and some houses accommodated sixty souls'. By this time too this Barbican building was also serving as the Customs Watch House, and WJ Newell was the Customs Officer in charge here around the time that the first memorial to the Pilgrim Fathers was laid outside its door.

Up until 1891 there was no indication of the point from which the Pilgrim Fathers left Plymouth and that a tablet was placed in the wall of the west pier that year was thanks largely to the efforts of R Hansford Worth and his father Plymouth historian RN Worth. In addition to the tablet on the wall there was also a stone, inscribed 'Mayflower 1620', placed in the roadway. Both are visible in this picture and today the tablet is surrounded by the monument that Alderman Sir Frederick Winnicott helped finance and that City Engineer John Wibberley designed in 1934, and the stone has been moved in front of it.

The Old Castle

'This is situated on the hill immediately above the place which, before the building of the Town Piers, was called The Round, and at other times, The Little Barbican. The Castle to which it belonged and to which it was an outwork is now separated by two houses (from the Barbican) built between them.'

John Harris, writing in 1808, was the first of Plymouth's nineteenth-century historians to try and accurately assess the role of this last surviving fragment of the fortification that gave rise to our Civic Crest and in so doing acknowledged most of the earlier references to the structure.

Leland, who visited here on his travels of England sometime between 1534 and 1543, was one of the earliest sources of information on it: 'on a rokky Hille . . . is a stronge Castel quadrate, having at each corner a great Round Tower, it semith to be no very old Piece of worke.'

No very old piece of work perhaps but what did he mean by 'no very old', subsequent writers seem to think that this could have been anything from around 140–300 years, dating it therefore sometime between 1230 and 1400. Certainly in 1416 we find it recorded that Bishop Stafford of Exeter (who had visited Plymouth in 1411 and who in 1413 was appointed Lord Chancellor by the newly crowned Henry V) granted indulgences to the Mayor and Burgesses to rebuild the causeway and the two towers of the castle which had been all but destroyed in the earlier Breton raids on the town.

Bishop Stafford's arms were used to decorate one of the towers by the grateful townsmen and long afterwards it was known as the Bishop's Tower. Crispin Gill, in his *History of Plymouth* (Vol 1), suggests that this tower 'Probably completed the castle quadrate' and he later adds that the pride in this new castle was reflected in the fact that the four towers or castles were to form part of the first mayoral seal in 1439, following Plymouth's success at becoming the first town in England to be incorporated by an Act of Parliament. This basic design, the four castles between the arms of the cross of St Andrew, still forms the core of the Civic Crest today but back then it replaced the image of a simple single masted ship.

This still does not solve the question of when the castle was begun. Harris states that it 'is supposed to have been built by one of the Valletorts, who were the ancient Lords, and it might have been their residence. It was not an uncommon thing for every great house to be next to a garrison, for protection. Be this as it may, it is very evident that they, the Valletorts, had the Castle, as their Arms remained thereon almost unto this day.'

Certainly the castle was built on Valletort land, the Valletorts having been major landowners in this area since the beginning of the twelfth century, indeed they established an early manorial house on the north eastern bank of the Sourpool (Millbay) on a site now somewhere beneath the bottom of Royal Parade. The castle would not have been built without their consent, the stone for its walls would have come from their quarries and clearly it would have been very much in their interests to protect the town.

It is difficult now to imagine that this castle stood on the 'edge of a precipice, which must have been exceedingly steep', not distanced from the water by a quay or a road with no pier extending from beyond its walls. Southside Quay was not built around to 'Barbygan ynderneath the Castell' until 1572; prior to that the castle was some way out from the town, Southside Street itself just being a rough pathway to the castle.

Sadly of course, little remains of the castle today, most of it was long gone by Harris's time and more disappeared within his lifetime. As early as 1570 it was being described as 'of no strength' but it still had a part to play and in the sixteenth century those who did not turn out to defend the castle when required were threatened with the loss of their freedom, a serious threat for it meant they would be unable to buy and sell goods freely in the town.

The construction of a new fort on the Hoe in the 1590s (superceded by the Citadel 70 years later) diminished the role of the castle yet further although it once again found useful employment during the Civil War. Part of it may have been plundered and used in the construction of the Citadel itself with some of the rock below being quarried as well. The area around Castle Street and Castle Dyke Lane when excavated some years ago revealed evidence of a seventeenth-century refuse tip rather than a castle construction which suggests perhaps that this was what part of the castle site was used for after the Citadel had been built.

During the eighteenth century what was left of its crumbling stonework was pilfered and used in the construction of the small dwellings built around its remains as the numerous little courts constructed around here formerly bore witness. These areas, Horn's Court as well as Cooksley's, Camber's and Martin's, all contained adapted fragments of some medieval structure. So too does the oldest surviving building in Lambhay Street, the 'Fisherman's Arms' and, of course, this structure here.

Believed to be part of the old castle's gatehouse, the rounded detached part is no more and the fragment that still exists no longer sports its strange little roof that was added to adapt this structure into a dwelling house, a role it had in 1890 when this illustration appeared in Worth's *History of Plymouth*.

Emigration Depot

'Plymouth is now the only port for the departure of Government emigrants, and many a tall ship sets sail for the waters of the New World or the Antipodes laden with the precious freight of hundreds of men, women, and children, who, like the pilgrims of the Mayflower, but for more multitudinous reasons, seek in other countries that prosperity which circumstances or their own default have denied them this. The Emigration Depot is at the old Victualling Office, immediately below the Citadel, an exceedingly commodious range of premises. Here the emigrants are collected and housed under due regulation, until the ships which are to bear them away to their new homes have arrived; and many a touching scene have those old walls witnessed.'

RN Worth's above account of the Emigration Depot appeared in the March 1878 edition of *The Graphic*, by which time the old storehouses at Elphinstone Wharf had almost seen 30 years of service as a Government establishment, time in which possibly as many as 200,000 emigrants had had this view as their last sight of England.

Plymouth had, of course, long been associated with the voyages of pioneering colonists but despite the endeavours of the late Elizabethans, the Pilgrim Fathers, and the South Pacific exploits of Cook, there had not been a great deal of emigration from Britain or even Europe in the seventeenth and eighteenth centuries. Rather this had been a time when national power had been equated with population growth and immigration was encouraged while emigration was actively discouraged, sometimes on pain of death. Such is not to say that it did not happen at all but it wasn't until the nineteenth century had dawned that it really became big business. High fertility rates combined with a falling mortality rate brought about a vast increase in the European population and it is estimated that the number of emigrants from Europe in the nineteenth century was roughly equal to one third of the entire population of the continent in 1800.

One of the key figures in the mass emigration of British subjects to the colonies in the early days, was Edward Gibbon Wakefield. London born, Wakefield was appointed secretary to the British minister in Turin in 1814 while still in his teens. Twelve years later, and now on the embassy staff in Paris, he abducted a young heiress and in 1827 was sentenced to three years imprisonment in Newgate. In prison he used his time well writing about the death sentence and studying colonization. Openly critical of what he saw as poorly planned colonization in Australia (the Government were at that time offering settlers 40 acres of land for every £3 or £3 worth of goods that they took with them), Wakefield argued that land should be sold at such a price that labourers could not become land owners too soon and at such a price that some money could be put aside to offer incentives to attract younger immigrants, both male and female.

These proposals soon influenced the developments in New South Wales, but Wakefield was keen to see them put into practice in a new colony and he became involved with the Government sanctioned Association ultimately responsible for founding South Australia in 1836. But he had broken with the promoters of this venture in 1835 and in 1837 he started promoting the formation of the New Zealand Association. This Association soon became a company and on 12 May 1839 Wakefield sailed from the West Pier of Sutton Harbour with the first party of colonists bound for New Zealand in a ship, the *Tory*, which was not unlike the one shown in front of the Citadel here.

On the 25th January 1840 the Plymouth Company of New Zealand was formed by a number of local merchants, notably Thomas Gill and Thomas Woollcombe who bought 60,000 acres from the New Zealand Company (with whom they soon merged) and in November 1840 they sent out their first settlers, 64 adults and 70 children, in the *William Bryan*. Over the next year or so they sent another five ships with an overall total of 897 settlers, mainly from Devon and Cornwall and New Plymouth was founded on North Island.

The biggest boon to local emigration though came in 1847 when the Government took over Elphinstone and Baltic wharves and the old Lambhay Victualling Yard as their Emigration Depot. Victualling operations had, of course, been moved around to the Royal William Yard in the 1830s and although still owned by the Ordnance Board, Thomas Gill is shown as being in possession of this site in 1845 and doubtless it had already served some years as an emigration base.

At first equipped with 500 berths (later increased to 1,118) the Depot was the scene of great activity. In 1847, 26 vessels sailed from Plymouth carrying 1,730 emigrants. The following year the figures were more than trebled and in 1849 some 109 ships left here for Australia bearing over 14,000 emigrants. There were also a further 21 ships which sailed from here that year, half of them bound for Canada, giving a total of almost 16,000 emigrants for the year, that's an average of over 300 per week.

The Irish potato famine of 1847, the arrival of the railways in Plymouth in 1849, the discovery of gold in Australia in 1851 and the general state of the local rural economy all had their effect on the drive for emigration from the middle of last century and while it appears that as many as a third of the Britons who emigrated between 1839 and 1939 returned home it is calculated that somewhere around six million stayed overseas and for a good many of them this would have been their last sight of old Blighty.

New Street

'There yet remained in New Street the survivals of mansions and merchant houses, and under the withered whitewash could be traced oaken panellings, and glorious carvings. Affluent adventurers of the Elizabethan era had dwelt in those reeking tenements, so that, as some of the older haunts were swept away overcrowding had intensified in others to which the evicted resorted' (Whitfeld 1899).

Philip Brannon, who based his painting of this New Street scene on a sketch he produced here in 1841, was clearly aware of the historical associations of these fine buildings but just how much he romanticized his vision we shall never know. However, the restored 32 New Street, seen here on the right in the shadow and the reconstructed No 16 opposite remain today to give us enough information to know that Brannon's picture is certainly very accurate in terms of the actual structures depicted. The recent façade stripping of No 34 (inside of which this article is being written) shows us further that this building too was doubtless accurately represented by the artist.

Underneath the twentieth century covering of render and chicken wire have been found the original seventeenth-century timbers of this building, including at first floor level 'an impressive example of seventeenth-century show carpentry. It is four bays wide. The wider bays are separated by a central post the top of which is turned, baluster-like and divided from the outer bays by large posts' (Keystone Historic Buildings Consultants 1990).

From the middle here, then, projected the oriel window, as shown in Brannon's picture which appears to confirm the notion that No 34 was built as one of a mirror plan pair with No 35.

The painting also shows Nos 14 and 15 New Street which after being refaced in the nineteenth century survived through to the late 1970s when sadly they were pulled down (they have since been replaced with a reasonably sympathetic housing development).

The great limestone warehouses stand little changed from 150 years ago – the lifting block on the nearest warehouse on the right is still in place. The uses of the various warehouses have changed somewhat however, although the work of potter John Pollex and carpenter Trevor Pate, who have their craft workshop in the warehouse on the right here on the western side of White Lane, employ skills as traditional as you could wish to find in our modern world.

Largest of the three warehouses, No 33 New Street, was, perhaps like the others, largely a nineteenth-century addition to the street. It was built and named Palace Vaults in 1809 by John Gotlob Werninck.

During the Napoleonic Wars Plymouth became the major port for auctioning captured ships, their cargoes and other spoils of war and several warehouses were built to store these treasures. Palace Vaults was one such warehouse and it is possible that its name was adapted from that of the wooden warship *Pallas*. Launched in Devonport on 17th November 1804 and subsequently dubbed the *Golden Pallas*, this was the ship Captain Lord Thomas Cochrane sailed into Plymouth, in April 1805, with three golden candlesticks almost five feet high on each of her three mastheads. Among the other prizes stored in the *Pallas*'s hold after a successful month in the Azores was 430,000 dollars. Another time Captain Cochrane brought the *Pallas* back with so much captured claret on board that the price fell below the amount of duty payable and so he poured it into the Cattewater.

JG Werninck, incidentally, also bought the neighbouring No 34 New Street in August 1809. Werninck was clearly having problems, though, as within three months he had to mortgage No 34 to Sir William Elford and others who were partners in the Plymouth Bank. Four years later the property passed over to the bank following Werninck's bankruptcy.

Ironically, in December 1825, the building changed hands again as a result of the bankruptcy of the Plymouth Bank itself and the then Mayor Edmund Lockyer 'and others' acquired the building as assignees of the estates of the partners of the bank.

One other building little changed from the depiction of it here is the modest two storey building known then, as now, as the 'Robin Hood'. In 1841 the 'Robin Hood', now a cafe and private club, was one of five pubs in the street only one other of which, the 'Anchor and Hope', survived into the twentieth century as a licensed premises. Those to fall by the wayside were the 'East and West Country House', the 'Royal Highlander' (at Garrison Steps) and the 'Welchman's Arms', run for many years by Owen Williams and situated, just off our picture to the right, in No 19 New Street.

There were at times yet other pubs in the street too, at the beginning of the nineteenth century we read of the 'Rose and Crown', the 'Gibralter' and in the building now occupied by the 'Green Lanterns' restaurant, just off the picture to the left, the 'Hampshire Hog'.

One thing, however, this picture does not convey is the way of life of the people who occupied these buildings 150 years ago. While that is something you would not necessarily expect of any picture of this kind, the overall impression given is certainly not one of a street no more than 18 feet wide, in which there was no drainage, where over half the houses had no privies or wcs, where 600 people were living in just 43 houses and where, in one year alone in the 1840s, 17 people died of cholera.

It is hard now to imagine life in such circumstances, but to revisit this scene and find so much of it still intact makes it easier to try to travel back through the centuries and imagine the good times and the not so good times this street has witnessed. That we can still do so is thanks largely to the Old Plymouth Society who saved the building, now run by the city as a museum, No 32, back in the 1920s and the Barbican Association who, in the 1950s, saved Nos 34–40 and the 'Robin Hood' from the hands of the demolition men.

Pin Lane

'The most interesting domestic buildings still left in Plymouth are in Pins Lane', so wrote Victorian historian Richard Norsworthy Worth in his *History of Plymouth* published in 1890. Above the text was this illustration of numbers 1–3 Pins Lane by his son R Hansford Worth, one of the many artists of that period to record an image of these dwellings. Indeed ten years later Charles Eldred also drew these buildings for the book *Streets of Old Plymouth* but this time in the accompanying text by WHK Wright we read that these 'quaint little houses . . . had become very dilapidated, and were very insanitary, consequently their removal was necessary. Nevertheless one cannot but regret that so picturesque a bit of old Plymouth could not have been preserved.'

It was certainly a great loss being perhaps the only surviving example in the town of what Worth calls the 'ancient arrangement of cellar and solar'; the cellar here being accessed through the door at street level and the solar being a reference to the upper room. This name comes quite simply from the Latin 'sol' meaning sun and originally a solar room would have been open to the sun.

Just how ancient Pins Lane, or Pin Lane as it is now, is we cannot be sure, certainly it is one of the oldest thoroughfares in Plymouth and, although it now only has buildings on its corners with New Street and Southside Street, it clearly once had buildings lining either side of the lane. Possibly named on account of its steepness – Pin from the ancient British 'pen' meaning hill – there was a small garden just beyond what was No 5 Pin Lane, just before the steps leading into New Street and a larger garden behind the block on the western side of the lane.

That was the lay out in the late eighteenth and early nineteenth centuries, however, as the nineteenth century progressed, so this part of Plymouth became very overcrowded with many more people and animals living in these habitations than they were meant for. It did not by all accounts make a pretty picture . . . 'Rude looking poles from which clothes were hung to dry were extended at every window, and the play of the air was thus obstructed. More especially filthy were Lambhay Hill, Looe Street, Castle Dyke Lane, Castle Rag or "Damnation Alley", Arches Row, Cambridge Lane West, Catte Street and Stonehouse Lane. Without check or remonstrance, pigs and fowl were bred in cellars and gardens, most houses were without water, and there were no facilities for removing offal. White's Lane, Stoke's Lane, Pin's Lane, and Garrison Lane were thick with filthy accumulations; few of the backlets were provided with closets, washhouses or drying places; and drains were considered a doubtful luxury.' (Whitfeld 1899.)

It was, doubtless, in the efforts to clean up this part of town that the buildings on the western side of Pins Lane were pulled down and two new little housing developments appeared on their site – Lucknow Place and Havelock Place; the buildings we see here surviving this redevelopment perhaps on account of their now unique character.

Sadly, though, they did not last into the twentieth century and waterman John Charlick and boatman James Rowe, both of whom had lived here for 20 years or more, were the last to occupy Nos 1 and 2 Pins Lane, while the Herberts, William and Ellen, were the last in the nearest of the houses, No 3. The somewhat taller structures of No 4 and 5 Pins Lane, however, remained and stood well into this century, No 5 being the last to go in the post-war Barbican clear out in the late 1950s.

Pins Lane was, according to Whitfeld, once 'temporarily' called Lucknow Street but he doesn't say when or for how long. Clearly, though, this too would have been in the latter part of the nineteenth century for Lucknow and Havelock are two of the better known names associated with perhaps the most violent uprising in military history, the Indian Mutiny of 1857.

Sparked by a general fear that the British were trying to convert Indians to Christianity, it came to a head over the use of greased cartridges. Before they could be rammed into place in the new Enfield rifles, the ends of these heavily greased cartridges had to be bitten off and the rumour went round that the grease contained cow fat (blasphemous to Hindus) and pig fat (regarded as filth by Muslims) and that this was a plot to force Indian troops into Christianity. Despite orders being sent out not to issue such cartridges to sepoy troops and even though it became no longer necessary to bite the cartridges, the damage had been done and when 85 men were severely punished (ten years working on the roads in chains) for refusing to use the cartridges, by a harsh and foolish British officer, the mutiny began.

In no time at all it spread across 1000 miles of India, not all sepoys turned against their British officers and fellow British soldiers but many did and they were joined by all manner of rogues and vagabonds. The British were besieged in a number of garrison towns in temperatures of around 100 degrees in the shade. At Cawnpore, the British surrendered on the promise of a safe passage from the town. The promise was not kept and the men were executed, and the women and children were brutally butchered. A howl for vengeance went up in Britain and to quote JB Priestly 'It is doubtful if the English have ever been so bloodthirsty as they were in 1857.'

Lucknow then was another of the towns defended by the British this time in a longer, harder encounter, there was a successful moonlight flight from here by the women and children and General Sir Henry Havelock was one of the main heroes of the defence. Struck down there by dysentery, Havelock had joined the army in 1815 and was a true public hero. Sir Colin Campbell and Sir James Outram (hence Outram Terrace, Devonport) were the other two principal figures in the relief of Lucknow.

Collier & Co

The family business of Collier & Co was established in Southside Street by Jonathan Collier in 1676 and for almost 300 years it carried on here, being passed down from father to son in direct line until July 1956 when it was acquired by E Dingle & Co. Jonathan Collier was at that time a shipping agent and a corn and timber merchant and the family had been on the Barbican for many years already.

It is said that members of the Collier family helped to build the Citadel, although it was common for many families to make this claim; a claim which usually was based on the fact that most adults in the area at that time at some stage 'assisted in carrying the stones for the workmen who were engaged in erecting the Citadel, in order to boast that they had helped rear the structure'.

In 1703 tragedy struck the family when two Collier brothers, Thomas and William, who had gone to watch waves crash into the Barbican were swept into the harbour and drowned, by the same storm that destroyed Winstanley's lighthouse on the Eddystone Rock. Later in the eighteenth century Joseph Collier became town steward, a position he held for many years until 1764, the year he died, when he handed all his papers over to the then Mayor Thomas Bewes.

Sixty eight years later the names Collier and Bewes were linked once more as John Collier and a later Thomas Bewes were returned as Plymouth's first post Reform Act Members of Parliament.

John Collier was born in Southside Street in 1769, he put up for Parliament again in 1835 and 1837, both times being successfully returned with Bewes and thereby became Plymouth's first Victorian MP. Like his two sons after him, William and Robert, John Collier was very much the classic nineteenth century Liberal. Well thought of by all classes, he was also a Magistrate, Alderman of the Borough, Deputy Lieutenant for Devon and for nearly 50 years he was the agent for LLoyds for this port. He was also the Vice-Consul for Sweden, Norway and Portugal. When he died aged 80, on the last day of February 1849 at his residence in Old Town Street, the Guildhall flag was hoisted at half mast and 'the shipping for the port paid a similar compliment'. He was buried in the family vault in Westwell Street.

Recalling his father over forty years later, William Collier told the story of a day when John was standing at his door, here in Southside Street, when a man 'pursued by a press-gang, rushed past him into the back part of the house. The

officer in command was pushing by after the man, but my father stood in the way and asked him what he wanted. He said he was taking the man for his Majesty's service. My father said the king himself could not enter his house by force, by the law of the land, and the press gang should not. The officer was aware of this fact' he said 'and left with his gang'. William Collier was John Collier's second son, born in 1824 when John was 55, and he it was to whom the LLoyds agency was passed as well as the Vice-Consulships of Sweden, Norway and Portugal. Very active in consular work, he went on to add Austria, Hungary and Uruguay to that list.

Married to Cycill Christiana Calmady of Langdon Court, William, like his father before him, also became a JP for Devon and for six years, 1848–54, he served on Plymouth Town Council, of which he did not always have a high opinion. He spoke of the Council's 'destructive tastes' with respect to places of antiquarian interest and also denounced many members as 'great enemies of trees .. who have cut down all they could get at'.

A passionate writer on the preservation of Dartmoor, William, who was educated at the old Corporation Grammar School under the harsh regime of the Rev John Henry Coates Borwell, was also outspoken against some of the punishments in education. Nevertheless he was a firm believer in good education and was one of the founder's of the Girls' and Boys' High Schools in Plymouth (Plymouth High and Plymouth College) and was a governor of both for many years.

In one respect William didn't follow his father, though, and that was as a MP, however, his elder brother Robert did, representing Plymouth in the House of Commons from 1852–1871. Robert, or Sir Robert as he became, opted for a career in the legal profession and in later years achieved the distinction of being appointed Solicitor General, Attorney General and Judge of the High Court. In 1885, the year before he died, Robert Collier was made Lord Monkswell, a title that was disclaimed in 1964 by the fourth heir to the baronetcy, Dr William Adrian Larry Collier, who was then in practice in Essex and had just served for nine years on Halstead's Urban District Council.

Ten years after this the name Collier came down from this building for the first time in almost three hundred years, the last hundred of which had seen the name Millman (the celebrated Barbican pawnbrokers, now occupied by Dolls and Miniatures) above the door of the building, immediately to the right of this view.

Today both those names have gone, the buildings, however, have changed little in their outward appearance, that fine old building on the left at the bottom of Pin Lane, No 51 Southside Street, being one good example of the Council reconditioning old housing this century. It was done in 1933 and doubtless William Collier, who died in 1902, would have approved wholeheartedly.

Southside Street

It must have been sometime around 1898 that Charles Eldred sketched this view of Southside Street, for we know from the dates above the refashioned frontages of buildings that appear just under the sign for the 'Custom House Tavern' that these were changed in 1899. These buildings stand on the corner of Pin Lane, opposite the distinctive form of No 51 Southside Street with its late sixteenth early seventeenth century double gabled roof, facing onto the street. The angle here appears to indicate a fair bit of artistic license as the darkened arched doorway is probably the original entrance into Mitre Court and the building to the left of it, here shown as Blowey & Co,

Chronometer Maker and Optician, today houses Tony Clements Barbican Bookshop.

But what of the 'Custom House Tavern' and what would life have been like in Southside Street around this time? Today it is a newsagent-cum-souvenir and sweet shop, Country Corner, and for many years after the last war 'carnival goods' were sold here by the Earls Acre Trading Co. But a pub it was in 1898 and for many years after that; Albert Horn the last licensee here having moved in before the outbreak of the First World War. It had not always been a drinking establishment, though, and in 1830 it was a butcher's shop run, strangely enough, by a Mr Beer. William Beer that was and a few years later we find another Beer, Richard, selling beer in No 46, the building shown on the left of this picture.

The 'Custom House Tavern', though, enjoyed a long innings as an inn, however, unlike the public houses of today this was one drinking establishment where the ladies, seen talking here in the street, would not have been welcome. 'No Women Allowed' was the policy here and certainly no lager drinkers here either, the customers of the 'Custom House' liked their ale dark, Guinness and porter were the favourites. Porter, short for porter's ale or porter's beer, was originally made specially for porters and other labourers and it acquired its colour from being brewed from malt that was partly charred or browned by its being dried at a high temperature. Samuel Fuge was landlord here at the beginning of the 1890s, JW Hooper at the end of them.

The reconstruction of the buildings opposite in 1899 clearly affected the businesses there and so Blowey & Co moved across the road to the premises immediately behind our vantage point here on the opposite corner of Parade Ope, where the Pizzaghetti Restaurant now is.

Bloweys also sold compasses and specialized as marine opticians but originally they were Opticians and Chronometer Makers. In those days, of course, timepieces were quite different from those of today. You would not have found a wristwatch here in the nineteenth century that's for sure, for although such a watch had been devised as early as 1790 they were thought of mainly as items of jewelry until the 1880s, when the German Admiralty ordered a consignment of wristwatches from a Swiss firm for their artillery officers at sea. But still the idea didn't catch on and it wasn't until the fashionable ladies of Paris started wearing wristwatches, sometime around 1908, that the idea really caught

on in Europe. Even then men regarded them as being effeminate until, that was, they were found to be more practical than pocket watches by men on active service during the First World War.

Next door to Bloweys when they moved over to this side of the street, was George Greenslade & Son, mastmakers. George had already been there many years making blocks, spars and pumps and son Syd carried on the business for many years into this century.

In 1898 the next shop along from Greenslade's was Yarmouth Stores Ltd outfitters and today in this street of contrasts, where some businesses count their anniversaries in months not years, they are still there, with the original counters and many original fixtures and fittings combining with the distinctive smell of oilskin apparel to give the shop a wonderful traditional air of continuity, although they cater more for the yachtsman than the fisherman.

Not surprisingly, as the Barbican is the oldest part of the City, there are many names that have survived the passing generations here and some businesses that have survived changing names. Collier and Coates are two of the longest established, Collier's wine merchandising stretching back over three centuries and Coates' distillery, home of Plymouth Gin, first being set up here in 1793.

Meanwhile, still on this side of the street at No 28 was the shipbroking concern of Bellamy and Co.; established as Luscumbes in 1779 and now based at Millbay Docks, they were based in Southside Street for many years. In 1900 the Mayor of Plymouth, Richard Risdon, died in office and the 'portly, stately, imperial-bearded figure' of Joseph Bellamy, later Sir Joseph, stepped into his shoes. A familiar sight sedately going to and from his office here, Joseph A Bellamy was Mayor in his own right the following term 1901–2.

One traditional occupation represented in this street from its Elizabethan origins to the present day is that of the baker. In the middle of the nineteenth century there were as many as seven separate different bakers working here; Spry, Hawkins, Stanbury, Walling, Mitchell, Southey and at No 40, Francis Fone. Today run by Roger Compton, this bakery, known as Jacka's after his predecessors John then Hugh Jacka, has only been sold twice since 1597 and not only is it the oldest surviving bakery in Southside Street but is accepted as the oldest continuously working bakery in the country!

Old Custom House

'On the Parade stands a quaint old building, now used as a store, everything but its substantial walls being in a state of decay. The numerous bricked-up arches indicate that it originally presented a very different appearance. There remain on the level of the street two handsome doorways with lintels and posts of carved granite. This was the Custom House of Plymouth in the seventeenth century, and the immediate predecessor of the building on the opposite side of the Parade . . .'

Such were the opening thoughts of WHK Wright whose text accompanied Charles Eldred's drawings in their book on *The Streets of Old Plymouth*, published in 1901. At that time they had been unable to date the 'New Quay' in front of this building and suggested that when this Custom House was erected 'what is now known as the Parade, was a creek with private houses and warehouses lining both sides of the way, the water flowing almost to the bottom of High Street'.

Evidence now indicates that the Quay was built on land reclaimed from Sutton Harbour in 1572, some 14 years before we find our first reference to a local Custom House. In 1586 in the town's *Widey Court Book* there is an entry 'Work done on the Custom house'. It is of course by no means clear from this if it is this particular building that is being referred to. Plymouth may have had several buildings that served as the Custom house prior to 1820, and certainly we known there was an intermediate premises between the one shown here and the one that stands opposite.

The term Custom-house itself appears to have been first coined in this country in 1490 and we know that the main features of a centralised Customs service had been established by 1300. Indeed even before 1200 feudal lords rights to customs had been transferred to the Crown and the ports placed, for fiscal purposes, outside the control of local government. In Mediterranean countries Custom and Excise Duties existed over 2,000 years ago, while in this country there is evidence that customs duties were levied in Roman and Saxon times.

Local references go back at least to 1400 when Henry IV ordered the searchers and custom-ers of Plymouth to allow Martin de Sensu, the Portuguese Ambassador, to leave the kingdom without his baggage being searched. Customs officials were after all representatives of the king and,

although they were generally nominated from among the ranks of respected local merchants, that didn't always mean they had little travelling to do themselves or that they might always retain respect once in their post. Customs men could often make great fortunes for themselves, but they had to be careful.

In 1423 'customers and comptrollers' of Plymouth were obliged to appear at Westminster with their accounts and in 1537 we learn that Henry Harfam, 'Customer of Plymouth', was executed at Tyburn although we don't know the nature of his offence. Plymouth had by this time experienced a certain lull in its prosperity; the fact that, like many southern ports, it was home to a number of pirates certainly didn't help to foster good trade relations, while the French and Breton raids of the fifteenth century caused considerable havoc in the town.

In order to help pay for improved fortifications to guard the port, Queen Elizabeth, in 1593, granted the town the benefit of the customs and when work was held up because of a lack of funds, the Queen charged the town with not being efficient in collecting their dues. In the event it was the duties on pilchards that went a long way towards paying for the defences. Pilchards, or pilchard curing at least, is said to have made the fortunes of many important local families including the Pollexfens, Trelawneys, Hewers and Rogers.

John Rogers had come to Plymouth with a 'handsome place' in the Custom House, around 1670, in the days when customs officers were still unsalaried and took their rewards in the fees they charged the ship owners they had to deal with. In this way it was possible to make a lot of money and certainly Rogers made himself a vast fortune, although doubtless a large part of it was raised when he left the customs and concentrated fulltime on his merchandising activities. Later an MP for the town and made a baronet by William III, he died of an apoplexy while smoking his pipe in a local coffee house in 1710. Strangely enough tobacco was said to be another major contributor to his fortune; today the family name is most conspicuously remembered in the Ivybridge school, which had its origins in Plymouth and was established by Dame Hannah Rogers.

John Rogers was quite likely to have worked in this building in his time as a Customs official and undoubtedly it was a very impressive structure. Such glory, however, did

not attend the building throughout the nineteenth century. Used for a number of years by tin plate worker William Martin, its primary use towards the end of the 1800s was as a store or as a stables and until 1893 at least its next door neighbour at No 19 the Parade was the 'Coal Exchange Inn'. In 1926 No 18 was due to be demolished and it was only spared by the actions of the Old Plymouth Society and the acquiescence of its owner. Gutted by enemy bombs during the Blitz, it was thankfully rebuilt after the war and remains a fine piece of our local heritage.

Custom House

While no one is quite sure when the old Custom House on the opposite side of the Parade ceased to be used as such, we do know that the present edifice was built in 1820 and that its immediate predecessor was 'a mere private building, having nothing to recommend it for its architecture, accommodation for its officers or the public'.

Thought to have been located on what is now the car park next to the 'Three Crowns' on Guy's Quay and seen here as warehouse accommodation, this Custom House was deemed to be 'more fitting for a place for smuggled goods than for the Collector of such an important port', with the chief officer himself being 'shut up in a dirty hole'.

These were doubtless quite difficult times for the customs men; business being transacted here from ten until four each day with only seven days recognized as holidays each year (the Queen's birthday, Good Friday, King Charles's Restoration, the King's birthday, the Prince of Wales's birthday, the King's Coronation and Christmas day) and smuggling a constant problem.

Within the control of these men was Sutton Pool itself, the Hamoaze, Barn Pool, Stonehouse Pool, the 'Catwater', and all the 'various other small harbours on the coast deemed to be within the port of Plymouth'. These were the days, moreover, when Cawsand Bay, despite being in Cornwall, was recognized as being the head quarters of Devon smuggling and dealing with smugglers was no easy business. Unless Customs officers were prepared to turn a blind eye and accept bribes '. . . wear fog spectacles with blank paper shades', they were quite liable to be cowed or beaten, even in some instances murdered.

In one incident, on 1st September 1784, a large gang of 50 to 60 armed men held Customs officers off while they landed a valuable cargo near Plymouth. All sorts of goods were smuggled; in 1822 a huge haul of salt was captured by Customs men in Mutton Cove, but among the favourite types of contraband were hard spirits. One observer estimated at the beginning of the nineteenth century that more brandy and rum was smuggled into Dorset, Devon and Cornwall than was imported legally into London each year. As many as 40,000 men were thought to be involved in smuggling across the three counties, that's more than the the population of Plymouth was at the time.

Of course the Napoleonic wars didn't help, the drain on manpower all round meant that Customs men were more likely to collude with smugglers than catch them and by the end of the war there were thought to be as many as 50 Cawsand boats involved in 'running goods'. However, the long years of war also put a huge strain on the Treasury and just as Parliament had originally imposed excise duties on 'spirits, hops and beer' in 1643 to help pay for the Civil War, so the government now looked for new and effective ways in which they could combat smuggling and raise their revenue. They also decided to end the situation whereby there were separate boards of customs and excise for England, Scotland and Ireland, thus from 1823 there was one Board of Customs and one Board of Excise for the whole of the United Kingdom.

For Plymouth the major consequence of all these end of war reforms was that David Laing, the newly appointed surveyor of buildings to the Board of Customs was given, as one of his first jobs, the task of designing a new Custom House for the port. Built over a number of years using French prisoners of war, who also worked on the Victualling Yard and the prison that housed them – Dartmoor, the new Custom House was completed in 1820 and first occupied by the Department in 1823.

A former pupil of Sir John Soane, Laing worked on the Plymouth Custom House with his pupil, Devon architect Thomas Lee, and clearly the end product has been a very lasting one. Laing was not so fortunate with his custom house in London, however. Completed by 1817, this building stood to the west of Sir Christopher Wren's structure built some 100 years earlier. The Laing building was constructed upon a certain amount of beech piling and planking which was used as the substratum of the foundation. By 1825 this timber had decayed so badly that the front of the London Custom House fell down along with Laing's reputation. A great deal of legal wrangling followed and eventually new foundations were put in and the building was rearranged. Laing meanwhile was suspended from office and forced to retire from practice.

Such is not to say that the building of this impressive granite fronted pile was without its problems. One of the local firms of contractors involved in the project, carpenters and glaziers Gribble and Hellyer, went bankrupt before it was finished; they claimed to have been poorly paid.

Many hours of many years have since been recorded by the Custom House clock; like so many of the features of this building it is original and still keeps good time although it is no longer allowed to chime. As for the business conducted within these walls, that too has little altered; Excise duties were, though, combined with Customs in 1909 when they moved across from the Board of Inland Revenue, which itself had been established in 1849. While some departments have branched out this remains the local Customs HQ, it also deals with the Registration of Ships for the south-west and acts as Receiver for Wrecks for the Port of Plymouth.

Smuggling, of course, continues to be a major problem for customs officers, with various illegal drugs being the main smuggled item, but with sophisticated land, sea and air resources now available a hard battle is now waged with smugglers. Smugglers no longer have quite the romanticized popular hero image they did of old and in 1988 alone, drugs with a street value of over £185 million were seized by customs men in this country.

High Street

'Few people, perhaps, who pass down High Street towards the quays realise that for centuries this old thoroughfare was the principal street of Plymouth. Long before George Street or Bedford Street were known, centuries before Union Street emerged from the marshes, the High Street of Plymouth was the very heart and centre of the famous old town. Up and down this street the brave men who helped to make the history of Elizabethan days passed and repassed, exchanging greetings with friends and comrades and perchance, holding revel in one or other of the taverns or houses of call with which the neighbourhood abounded.'

Few people, indeed, today are likely to be aware of this street's history, the preceding account was written at the end of the nineteenth century. Now sadly little remains of the street and even its name has been changed.

The basic street line, however, has been preserved for High Street ran virtually from the site of the Unemployment Office in Buckwell Street to the Parade on the Barbican. Curving around past the School of Architecture annex across Palace Street it crossed Notte Street and carried on through the flats that now stand on the south side of the road. Until recently it was possible to follow this route to its conclusion, locked gates now bar public access but the cobbled lower end of High Street can still clearly be seen through the gates.

Two hundred years ago a description of this same short route would have borne little or no resemblance to that above. Starting at the Guildhall, Market Street (as High Street was for some years known) curved south from Higher Broad Street (which later became Buckwell Street) around past Cat Street (later Stillman Street, now Palace Street) across Vintry Street (where Notte Street now meets Vauxhall Street) and down to the Parade. Coming back up the western side of High Street the story was much the same as once again there have been a number of changes in the naming of the streets and lanes.

Notte Street was originally Nut Street, Palace Street, which now leads to the Merchant's House, was Lower Lane 100 years ago and Patrick Lane 200 years ago. Similarly the lane now called Lower Lane was Middle Lane 100 years ago and Linam Lane 200 years ago, while the Higher Lane of Victorian times is still known by that name today, but 200 years ago it was called Loaders Lane.

All this is, of course, thoroughly confusing but it doesn't detract from the fact that High Street, like so many similarly named streets in other towns, was one of the three principal streets of the mediaeval town of Sutton, as Plymouth itself was then known.

At the top of High Street stood, it is believed, the Market cross around which, every Thursday, market stalls were set up and trading took place. The cross would have been erected sometime after 27th January 1254 for that was when Henry III signed a grant, in his winter quarters in France where he then was with his army, allowing Sutton to hold a market. This act thereby conferred the status of 'town' upon Sutton.

The market cross standing at the top of High Street would then have been at the very heart of the town, for here was the junction of Sutton's three main arteries, Whimple Street leading to the parish church of St Andrew, Higher Broad Street (later Buckwell Street) which ran north and east from here to Breton Side and so on to Exeter, and High Street itself running down to the waterside (there is a suggestion that the earliest settlement around Sutton Harbour was near the southern end of High Street).

Given, then, the early history of this location, it comes as no surprise to find in 1606 that the town's new guildhall was built on this triangular site, with its ground floor being primarily used for market trading. There was a good deal of rebuilding and redevelopment carried out in High Street around this time, as the wealth brought into the town during Elizabeth's reign led to a general expansion in the area.

By the nineteenth century, however, the character of the street had changed dramatically '. . . Little do the dwellers in the now squalid tenements and crowded courts imagine that generations of fair women and brave men lived and loved in what were in those olden days mansions, and are now mere backwaters of the prosperous life of the modern progressive town. Here in what are now designated slums, lived the merchant princes and the men of light and leading of their day, and there were many prosperous traders who carried on their avocations in Plymouth's High Street' (Wright 1901).

Still a busy and major thoroughfare at the beginning of this century, with over 40 separate commercial premises with a now redundant guildhall at its top, (the original building was replaced in 1800 by a construction which itself was superceded in 1874), a number of properties (including some of those shown here) were pulled down just before the war to make way for the new flats opened by Viscountess Astor in 1938. The Blitz spelt the end for a few more, and within a few years of the change of name from High Street to Buckwell Street in the early fifties the planners accounted for most of the remaining buildings. All that now remains are three or four properties from the Oldwell Eating House around to the corner of Whimple Street.

High Street

'This town is dearer than Jerusalem
After a year's siege; for they would make you pay
For daylight, if they knew how to measure
The sunbeams by the yard. Nay, sell the very
Aire too, if they could serve it out in fine
China Bottles. If you walk but three turnes
In the High Street, they will ask you mony
For wearing out the Pebles.'

So said Captain Cable to his men who were about to take leave ashore in Plymouth as portrayed in the play *Newes from Plymouth* which was written by Sir William Davenant (1606–68), who had succeeded Ben Johnson as poet laureate in 1637. A favourite of Charles I, Davenant fought on the King's side in the Civil War and was knighted by Charles at Gloucester in 1643.

In 1657, in order to evade the ban on plays, Sir William produced the first English opera, *The Seige of Rhodes* in which Mrs Coleman became the first actress to appear on the English stage. Mainly known for his earlier works, notably a comedy *The Witts*, produced in 1636, Davenant became the unfortunate butt of jokes by the court wits not long after this when, as the result of an illness, the playwright lost his nose.

Thought to have been the godson of William Shakespeare, Davenant was not averse to implying that he was in fact the illegitimate son of the great bard. Certainly Shakespeare was a regular visitor to the 'Crown Inn' in Oxford which was kept by Davenant's parents. One wonders, in turn, what taverns if any Davenant himself might have visited in Plymouth.

In his day Plymouth's High Street was where 'lived the merchant princes and the men of light and leading . . .' and 'many prosperous traders who carried on their avocations'. Doubtless there was an inn here somewhere but it is unlikely that the 'Shakespeare Inn' dates back that far.

Standing at the very bottom of the street on the corner that met the Parade, Wolf Emden ran his hosiery and haberdashery business here in the middle of last century but like a number of properties in the street its history as a

hostelry is uncertain. There were after all as many as eight beer houses here in 1850, however, few survived into the twentieth century.

'The Butcher's', later known as the 'Valiant Soldier', was the last to go in the late 1930s, it used to stand on the street's south eastern corner of what was Woolster Street or Vintry Street and is now part of Notte Street. Further up the hill there was the 'Vintry Inn' itself, just down from where the 'Breton Arms' is now, there was also the 'Britannia', on the western corner of Notte Street, and the one which appears to have changed its name several times between 1850 and 1900, the 'Naval Reserve', formerly the 'Clock' (c1866) or the 'Globe' (c1852). This particular High Street inn became Mitchell's secondhand furniture dealers in the 1930s.

One other pub, across the road and up the hill a little from the 'Naval Reserve' was the 'Napoleon Inn', which stood very close to the High Street house in which Plymouth's celebrated painter Charles Locke Eastlake used to live; there is even speculation that he may have worked on his famous pictures of the prisoner Napoleon on board HMS *Bellerophon* in Plymouth Sound here in 1815.

Eastlake was then only 22 and the larger painting, which was life size, attracted much interest and brought the artist about £1,000, a great fortune in those days. The original Eastlake house stood between High Street's two oldest surviving buildings. Allowed to deteriorate, it was pulled down and rebuilt in 1981 by FR Cross and Sons, who also renovated the two buildings on either side of it. Parts of these buildings are thought to date back to the fifteenth century and the well in the 'Oldwell' building is probably mediaeval.

High Street, once one of Plymouth's most impressive thoroughfares, became just another run-down part of the town as the end of the nineteenth century approached and so it is no surprise to find here, in the middle of our view, the Plymouth Soup Society Kitchen. There were several soup kitchens dotted around the Three Towns last century, the one here operated from about 1888 to the early 1900s and there was another in Green Street which dated back to 1847.

The latter was constructed thanks to the Misses White of Seven Trees and all of them depended on public donations to provide a very worthwhile service to the poor families of the area. The soup was never given away, though, it was sold for a penny per quart. In the winter of 1852–3 alone some 20,836 quarts of soup were distributed and it would have been more had there been more funds available for ingredients.

As well as the soup kitchen there were also several bakers in the street and many were they that trooped out of Luscombe's on a Sunday having paid their penny to have their family dinner cooked!

Notte Street

'Notte Street, or Nut Street as it was sometimes called, was formerly, like all the old Plymouth streets, very narrow and not particularly straight. It was however, graced with several fine old houses, not the least pretentious being the grand old Elizabethan mansion shown in the accompanying sketch. This was one of the finest specimens of Tudor architecture that the town possessed, and was a worthy specimen of the many ancient domestic buildings which existed up to a few years ago to show what a picturesque old town Plymouth must have been.' (WHK Wright 1901.)

Certainly Notte Street is one of the oldest recorded thoroughfares in Plymouth, we find it referred to in 1439 in the town's Act of Incorporation as 'Note Strete' and Crispin Gill has suggested (*Plymouth a New History – Ice Age to the Elizabethans*) that this street then the southern edge of the town, 'in all likelihood looking across a little stream running down to Sutton Harbour, with hazel bushes on the far bank'. Nut Street is still how many locals pronounce it and Whitfeld, writing in 1900, simply states 'Notte Street:

Formerly Nut Street, site of clumps of hazel bushes'. Although it is interesting to note that one medieval, but not local, character was called Algar le Notte because he was bald-headed.

Quite when the tudor-style buildings in Notte Street that survived long into this century were erected we cannot be sure, as Wright went on to say 'What is the history of this old mansion no one can tell; tradition says that it was the residence of Sir Walter Raleigh, but that is doubtful, and there is no evidence to prove it'.

No evidence perhaps, but that did not stop local architect James Hine waxing lyrical about this particular structure in his review of *The Ancient Buildings of Plymouth* published in 1861. 'There is' he wrote 'that noble house in Notte Street! Noble on account of its antiquity and appearance, and noble on account of its present appropriation as the home of the poor and aged widows of workmen who have been in the employ of its present and late proprietors.'

Hine then went into the realms of romantic fantasy '... I fancy I see it in course of erection; the masons and carpenters proceeding cautiously but skillfully with their work; the designer with watchful eye, testing the lines and details, and comparing them with the plan, which he measures with his great compasses. The burly alderman, in doublet hose and ruffs, as he goes to and fro, gives an approving and patronizing glance; and opposite a crowd of small fry is always stationed, looking on vacantly, or wondering how much higher it is going. And when finished how well it looks, with its honest oak doors and windows, its diamond lights and high pitched roof, and inside its bold staircase, its panelled ceiling, and wainscotted walls. It was one of the best houses in the town, and was no doubt fitted with tapestries and Eastern carpets, massive tables, and high backed chairs and settles, cushioned with Utrecht velvet. Here and there a legend might have been written on the glass or walls. The whole interior was sombre yet cheery.

Who knows? Perhaps Sir Walter Raleigh may have been entertained in this house, and (though less likely) Sir Francis Drake would have talked politics here. At Christmastide, its walls would ring with merry laughter, and madrigals and glees be sung around an open hearth.'

Hine's picture, while purely a piece of supposition,

nevertheless gives some idea of the context in which this house was built, Notte Street would have had very few buildings in it of any kind at the time, just a few impressive town houses perhaps. Justinian Peard, Mayor of Plymouth at the end of the Civil War seige, 1644–5, and again in 1656–7, we know had a house in Notte Street (he also lived for a time in St Andrew's Street in the building that survives today as the Merchant's House and he later bought Cann House at Tamerton Foliot).

The following century William Cookworthy opened a pharmacy in Nut Street and later lived in what was described as the finest house in Plymouth of the Queen Anne period, 1702–1714. This house stood some yards back from what is now the northern line of Notte Street and in the 1880s a Mission Hall was built in front of it by a carpenter and builder, who'd come to Plymouth 20 years earlier, from Horrabridge – Isaac Foot.

Isaac Foot established a business in Notte Street on the corner of Hoegate Street on the site of what had been King's Brewery, (a nice twist for a man who didn't drink) situated just to the left of the buildings shown here. This brewery, incidentally, which stretched along Hoegate Street, was established in 1810 and, together with another brewery also in Hoegate Street, was the first business to bring steam engines to Plymouth.

The character of Notte Street had altered greatly by the nineteenth century and indeed the character of these buildings here was also changed in the 1880s when Messrs Bulteel and Company of the Naval Bank oversaw their conversion into an imposing terrace that was to house the Plymouth Municipal Artisan's Dwellings.

In this reconstruction this fine old building was carefully restored, the neighbours to the left were built up to a similar height and the archway, which became the main entrance to the Artisan's Dwellings, was moved to a position directly under the window shown at the top of the building on the right.

Although part of this block survived the Blitz and Isaac Foot's business was still being continued here in the 1950s, today, of course, nothing remains of the southern side of Notte Street and we have just a part of it still standing just opposite this view.

Notte Street

Notte Street in the nineteenth century undoubtedly had quite a different atmosphere to it than it had had in its earlier days. Some of the grand old buildings survived but their grandeur had long since been eroded as the Victorian town of Plymouth expanded and this became an 'inner town' area rather than a street on the edge of the 'green belt'.

The redevelopment of these once exclusive tudor townhouses here as Artisan's Dwellings in the 1880s typified this change. Notte Street was now a busy thoroughfare housing a working population, the yard of the Artisan's Dwellings contained large workshops. Passing through the large arched entrance into an area overlooked by iron and concrete galleries you would have found, 100 years ago, on your right George Lewarne's brush manufactory and on your left the printing works of John Smith (who published the *Plymouth Almanac*).

Some years later the Western Morning News Company occupied these same print works and they in turn were succeeded here by LH Varcoe & Co. Meanwhile the brushworks had also changed hands and in its place in the years leading up to the Second World War were the general salerooms of Frederick J Oats, Partridge & Co.; Stuart Photo Services Ltd also had space here before the war.

On the eastern side of the Notte Street entrance to this yard you would have found around the turn of the century in the building nearest Knight or Mitchell, fish dealers, and next door to them John Herring, shopkeeper, where children would go in for a farthing's worth of sweets (about one tenth of a new penny). On the western side of the archway, No 13a Notte Street, was the tobacconist shop belonging to George Parker above the door of which, at first floor level, was a very fine coat of arms.

This wonderful piece of detailed carving was one of several gestures honouring the families of those involved in the 1883 rebuilding and renovation of these Notte Street properties. The work was carried out under the direction of Messrs Bulteel & Co of the Naval Bank which had offices nearby; most simply reached by going straight up St Andrew Street, directly opposite No 13 and turning right at the top into Whimple Street where they stood at the junction with High Street.

The Artisan's Dwellings were dedicated to the memory of Thomas Hillersden Bulteel, while Thomas Bulteel and Captain Giles Andrew Daubeny (who had married a Bulteel) were the two who oversaw the project. A small

Daubeny family shield and a similar size Bulteel crest could be seen either side of the archway while on the larger shield above the shop was a much more impressive representation of the Bulteel arms. Even so it only occupied a quarter of this bigger crest, the other three sections being taken up by the arms of Churchill, Crocker of Lyneham and Harris of Belle Vue. Beneath this carving ran the motto 'Loyaute passe partout' – loyalty above everything, the reason for the motto being in French is doubtless part of the heritage of the Bulteels; Bracken suggested that members of the Bulteau (hence Bulteel) family may well have come here seeking refuge from the troubles of France centuries earlier).

Interestingly enough, during all this restoration work twelve very much older shields were found painted on the walls of an upper room in the main old house in the block; among them were those of Ward, Lovelace, Lord Willoughby de Broke and Sir George Byng, who sat as a Member of Parliament for Plymouth from 1705 until 1721 when he was called to the House of Lords.

Among the other names associated with this part of Notte Street are those of Cole, Tenney and Sherrell, these names, however, were not associated with crests but rather appeared above the doors on some of the longer established businesses situated between here and the corner of Zion Street. Members of the Cole family had operated a bakery at No 14 for well over 60 years from at least the middle of the nineteenth century although sometime before the last war Francis James Bunker took over this corner spot from A W Minhinnick.

Directly opposite on the other Notte Street corner with Hoe Street was Tenney's the greengrocers. Another old family business, this was run latterly by Kate Tenney who took over from her father Edwin, this shop was one of the few on the south side of the street to survive the war, unlike Sherrell's dairy business on the Zion Street corner of this block.

Today, of course, all these old businesses on the south side of the street are gone those that survived the war not managing to survive redevelopment in the 1950s, and now the new Hoe Approach Road occupies much of the site of this block that was the Plymouth Municipal Artisans Dwellings.

Abbey in Winchelsea Street

In 1806 John Harris of Hoe Lane began writing *An Essay Toward the History of Plymouth*; the manuscript was, he said, written for the use and amusement of his children. There were then appended the following two lines . . .

'Story's the light of time for after ages
And Books are the lanthorns which their light encages'.

The amount of information subsequently recorded by Harris was quite substantial and as such represents perhaps the earliest attempt to write a history of Plymouth and, while not perhaps as scholarly as it could be, it is a useful starting point for those reading in the 'after ages'. Indeed it is largely from this work that our much of our information about the old 'Mitre Tavern' in Woolster Street comes.

The 'Mitre' we know was pulled down to make way for the Exchange building in 1812 and Harris devotes much space to it under the heading 'Abbey in Winchelsea Street'. This building he says 'is now called the Mitre, from its being a Papist foundation. It was once a very respectable tavern, for 100 years ago, the 'Mitre' was mentioned as one of the

first. It extends from the front as far back as Seven Stars Lane and is almost square.' (Winchelsea Street, incidentally, is an old name for Woolster Street deriving from the Old English word 'wincel' meaning corner, hence we have corner by the sea – Woolster Street is said to mark the original shoreline of this part of Sutton harbour before it turns into Vauxhall Street).

Harris continued his account of the 'Abbey' by describing the buildings: 'The outer front of 'The Mitre' is', he said, 'very plain, it seems to have been raised, as the upper storey is set back. The inner part [shown here] consists of a court of four sides or fronts. There are cloisters to it, with rooms above, supported on colonnades, on three sides of the building. These have now been walled-up with rooms made. On the remaining side or front is an ancient chapel, with a cellar beneath (or cellars). The columns are of very ancient workmanship. There is nothing like them elsewhere in Plymouth. At the entrance to the chapel are two piers of squared stone similar to that used in the buttresses and the quoins of the Old Church. Time has now fretted them away. Over the doorway are two niches, and it is said that there were images in each of them.'

There then followed an account of the interior which, says Harris, seems formerly to have been much larger. It appears to have been an impressive sight nonetheless and depicted over 30 separate panels or compartments, measuring about three feet by one foot six, where a number of saints and prophets were '. . . portrayed in full length and in the most ancient and curious costume'.

The presence above of a number of small human figures supporting shields, on which there were initial letters and fleurs-de-lys alternately, led Harris to suppose the ceiling was of French origin and he went on to speculate about who might have worshipped here in Tudor times. Finally he noted that the paintings and the furniture from the chapel were sold to Mr Clark's Chapel at Buckland near Kingsbridge.

Although Harris did not specifically state that this was originally a monastic building, that was the inference taken by most later writers, WHK Wright suggesting in the text that accompanied this sketch, in 1900, that this building was

'believed to have formed part of the monastery of the Grey Friars'. Worth (1890), Bracken (1931), Walling (1950) and Gerrard (1982) were all more positive in perpetuating this notion, however, in her 1973 article *New Light on the Plymouth Friaries* Jennifer Barber quite clearly demonstrates that the order of the Grey Friars, in the sixteenth and seventeenth century at least, was based in New Street.

Was then the 'Mitre' ever a monastic building? Certainly the deeds examined by Jennifer Barber suggest that from 1513 at least it was in private hands, notably those of the Hawkins family for most the late sixteenth century, during which time the premises were said to include 'the mansion house' and a 'tower house'.

In the seventeenth century the property was being leased in two halves, one half being handed on to William Warren 'during whose tenancy the house became known as "The Golden Fleece" and a public inn'. Barber then goes on to say that by 1749 it had become the 'Mitre' and in the next sentence, that the Woolster Street vicinity 'is noticeably lacking in any street names that might connect it with the Franciscans'. This is not strictly speaking true, however, as we know that the 'Mitre' originally backed on to Seven Stars Lane (later Stillman Street) and this itself is a very common medieval religious title. 'The monastic hostels brought into being many signs derived from religion . . . they include : Star, Seven Stars, Angel, Ark, Mitre, Salutation . . .' (Eric Delderfield, *Introduction to Inn Signs*). It is interesting in this context that one of the oldest named inns in Stillman Street was the 'Salutation'.

It is also perhaps worth noting that monasteries really invented large-scale sheep farming and this helped make them quite affluent particularly in the thirteenth and fourteenth centuries and among the inn signs we find adopted in areas where there was this success are 'Woolpack', 'Lamb', 'Fleece' and 'Golden Fleece'. So, maybe there is a genuine pre-sixteenth century link with local monasticism in this area. Certainly the building that became known as the 'Mitre Tavern' was of great antiquity, perhaps it was an earlier home of the Grey Friars or could it even have been the elusive Plymouth home of the Dominican Black Friars?

Ring of Bells

Had the 'Ring Of Bells' not been pulled down in January 1957, it could well have been a contender for the oldest tavern in Plymouth today. Sadly, however, the building had been derelict for a number of years prior to 1957 and had ceased trading as an inn back in 1924.

Thought to have been built sometime around 1580, it stood on the corner of Woolster Street where it turns into Vauxhall Street. Demolished at the same time were two former hostelries fronting onto Vauxhall Street immediately around this corner; known in the nineteenth century as the 'Steam Packet' and the 'Prince George', the latter, like the 'Ring of Bells' had many sixteenth-century features, including an Elizabethan plaster ceiling. The old line of this corner has now, of course, gone as the road here has been widened and given much more of a curve.

There were, last century, two 'Ring of Bells' inns in Plymouth, the other was in Old Town Street, the name itself is said to derive from the 'Englishman's love of handbell ringing' (Delderfield) although other sources suggest it may refer to a set of tower bells. The second suggestion of course could be taken as lending support to the theory that there was once a substantial religious building in Woolster Street but we may never know for sure. We do know, however, that the granite door arch to the 'Ring of Bells', shown clearly here, has been re-erected for all to see on the northern side of the 'Breton Arms' in Buckwell Street. A board telling its story stands close by and makes reference to Woolster Street's most celebrated residents, the Hawkins family.

William Hawkins originally purchased the building that became the 'Mitre Tavern' sometime around 1540 and he went on to acquire most of what was then on the northern side of Woolster Street. Hawkins, the son of a wealthy Tavistock merchant, had come to Plymouth to act as a shipping agent for his father and quickly made a fortune in his own right; by 1523 he was one of the five richest men in the town. In 1532 he became mayor and four years later he bought a new house in Kinterbury Street. Mayor again in 1538, the following year saw him returned as MP for the town and between then and his death in 1553 he sat in the House under three different monarchs; Henry VIII, Edward VI and Mary. After his death the business was divided between his two sons William and John (later Sir John). William, the elder brother based himself in Plymouth in the new home in Woolster Street while John went off to make his name at sea where he soon became one of the most famous sea captains of the age, riding the thin line between pirate and privateer.

Like his father before him, William also served the town as mayor, 1567-8, 1578-9 and 1587-8, while John was returned to serve the town in Elizabeth's parliament in 1571 and 1572. Both sons were seafarers though, as was Sir Richard Hawkins, John's son, who inherited the Woolster Street property (Richard also served the town as MP and Mayor).

Woolster Street was undoubtedly one of the most desirable areas to live in, in Elizabethan Plymouth. The population of the town was less than 10,000 when Elizabeth came to the throne and there was little development south of the line made by this street and Notte Street at that time.

Among the other notable buildings along from the 'Ring of Bells', indeed it was just next door to the Hawkins' 'Mitre Inn' building, was the Mayoralty House which is supposed to have been the residence of one of Plymouth's first mayors, John Paige, in the middle of the fifteenth century. This building would have stood on the site of the recent archaeological dig in Woolster Street and was used as a mayoralty house well into the late eighteenth century. More recently the base of various motor trade related businesses, the old doorway at least was preserved and today is to be found relocated in the Elizabethan Garden in New Street.

The character of Woolster Street altered substantially with the advent of the nineteenth century as the wealthy members of the community moved further out and commercial considerations brought about many changes in the old residential areas. Perhaps the greatest change came with the demolition of the old 'Mitre' in 1812 and the subsequent erection of the Exchange building in its place.

The Exchange was built in 1813 at a cost of £7,000 raised in £25 shares and was designed to 'bring the commercial classes into closer communion', however, the project was a little over ambitious and for the first 30 years or so it was only partially occupied. Originally it sported a large open area surrounded by a colonnade but this was subsequently

built upon and covered with a glass dome while offices were constructed under the galleries. A victim of the blitz, among the last occupants of this building in 1940 were Sanders, Stevens and Co., ship brokers; Pope and Pearson colliery proprietors; Thomas Parsons and Sons the paint manufacturers; the Tug owners WJ Reynolds and the Trinity Pilots.

Tucked away between the Exchange and the 'Ring of Bells' was the narrow entrance to Woolster Court, a curious little grouping of dwellings which included Jubilee House, Drake Villa, Cape Cottage, Devon Cottage and Surrey Cottage. Today this court has been succeeded by Vauxhall Court created behind the new flats erected here in 1970. Renamed Vauxhall Street after the war, Woolster Street was considerably widened in the rebuilding process and now there is nothing pre-war left at all of the northern side of this once illustrious thoroughfare.

Stillman Street

The first recorded mention we have of Stillman Street is in 1412 and in terms of original documentary evidence it is second only in age to Billbury Street in Plymouth. The street name itself is said to have a 'personal' derivation and the origin of the name Stillman is generally thought to be 'dweller by a stile or steep ascent'. Certainly there is a gradual slope here and it is quite likely that there would have been a stile in this vicinity but it is anybody's guess as to whether this would have any bearing on the origin of this particular street name.

What we do know, though, is that this area is near the heart of the very earliest settlement of what was to become Plymouth and in 1881, when a large part of the northern side of Stillman Street was rebuilt, a very ancient grave was found here.

Thought 'in all probability' to have been 'the grave of one who lived in Devon after the Romans had visited our country, and introduced their mode of burial', it took the form of two large flat stones placed at right angles to each other, making a kind of roof underneath which was a large urn. This black-ware urn almost certainly had contained the ashes of the cremated body of 'one of Plymouth's ancient forefathers'. The grave or *kistvaen*, as it should properly be called, was about eighteen inches deep, two feet wide and about three feet in length and the stones covering it were dunstone, doubtless brought here from some distance specially for this purpose.

Sadly the whole lot was discarded by the workmen engaged on the site and that an account of it survives today is thanks to the efforts of a local member of the Devonshire Association, Francis Brent, who, once alerted to the find, visited the site several times a day to monitor further discoveries.

Amongst the other finds were a number of shells, 'mostly of the oyster, periwinkle, cockle and mussel' thought to have been part of an ancient refuse heap or kitchen midden. At the time of their discovery the importance of such a find had only recently been established, for it was in 1860 Professor Steenstrup, a Danish archaeologist, had dispelled the myth that here was evidence of a raised beach. Steenstrup, by drawing attention to the facts that the remains of such shellfish were invariably fully grown, that normally oysters, periwinkles, cockles and mussels do not live together and that there was no layer of gravel here, suggested that these shell accumulations must rather be domestic refuse heaps formed by early man. This observation was supported by related discoveries of flint implements and animal bones bearing the marks of knives, in certain heaps.

Kitchen middens were then discovered in many places all over the world, including Britain and notably in Devon and Cornwall. The Stillman Street midden thus indicating that there was probably a settlement in this area several thousand of years ago, stone age families living principally on shellfish and partly on the produce of the chase.

The construction the workmen were engaged upon on this site in 1881 was the new malt house for Messrs Pitts. Pitts and Co were malsters and had been in business since 1804 and in 1830 William Pitts was running operations from No 1 Stillman Street. Over the years the business expanded quite spectacularly and by 1894 they were advertising themselves as 'the largest manufacturers of malt in the west'. Then, as well as the newly constructed malthouse in Stillman Street (Nos 10–18), they also had stores and mills on North Quay and Sutton Wharf and offices in Southside Street, next to Trinity Church. The King family were also malsters and they too had premises in Southside Street and in 1875 they joined forces as Pitts, Son and King.

It was in 1875 that Thomas Pitts was put on the Commission of the Peace and also that year that his father died, so he decided to sell the business to James King and his son William and his own son Thomas Pitts jnr. Thomas Pitts senior (1816–1911) lived in Hoe Place House and served for more than 40 years on Plymouth Borough Council. He was a real champion of the Hoe and when in the 1880s the Government decided to let 27 acres of land around the Citadel to the Corporation, it was Pitts who oversaw the laying out of the Hoe for the benefit of the public.

Meanwhile, back in Stillman Street, Pitts's had for many years another store around the corner in Hicks Lane which ran up the side of the big purpose-built malthouse, plus additional spreading and steeping premises further down this street just around to the right from this view.

Like so many Barbican streets the character of Stillman Street undoubtedly changed dramatically in the nineteenth century as housing gave way to commerce and industry, the pattern of change continuing well into this century to the extent that even before the last war there were few people actually living where these quaint historic dwellings had once stood. On the north (left) side was John Hounsell and Phil and Charlotte Lang just up from Reggie Kimber's joinery workshop, while on the south Bill Tremayne and Charlie Ferris had adjoining properties next to Pitts's and next door to Burton's fruit store was John Northcott.

Stillman Street suffered a few direct hits during the war, these houses, however, survived well into the fifties. They did not survive the redevelopment of Stillman Street, however, and today there are modern flats lining both sides of the road which no longer meets Vauxhall Street opposite Fox and Haggart's; but although it's now a cul-de-sac it does at least still follow the original line of the street and the cobblestones have thankfully not been replaced by bland tarmacadam.

Stillman Street

One of the oldest thoroughfares in Plymouth, there is now sadly very little left in Stillman Street of any real antiquity. The house shown on the left was pulled down last century to make way for the massive malthouses of Pitts Son & King and like so much of the rest of the street this was in turn razed to the ground by the German Luftwaffe during the last war. Today there are but two pre-war survivors in this end of the street, the early nineteenth-century house on the right, No 40, and in the immediate foreground, No 41, the storehouse next door to it, still with its lifting-tackle in place.

The house on the right was at one time said to be in Seven Stars Lane, although it later became part of Stillman Street (1845), and it was in this building in 1804 that one of Plymouth's foremost nineteenth-century scholars was born, John Kitto.

John Kitto's parents, John Kitto senior and Elizabeth Picken, were Cornish but they had been married in Charles Church in March 1803. John Kitto senior was a mason but he was not very wealthy and liked to drink, while his eldest son was very delicate and was not expected to live. Despite all this the young John Kitto learnt to read and write and developed a love of books, he had very little formal schooling, though, and when he was ten he was employed in a barber's shop.

Blamed, wrongly, while there for conspiring in a theft, John went to work for his father and it was around the corner from here in Batter Street in 1817, working on repairs to a house there, that John Kitto junior suffered a terrible accident. He was carrying slates up a ladder when he slipped and fell 35 feet to the ground. For two weeks he lay unconscious, when he finally recovered he found that he had lost his hearing, a disability that ultimately was to throw him even further into the literary world. First, however, came a spell in the workhouse, his parents were unable to keep him, and he had some unhappy work placements before a paper he had written came to the attention of the Hele Trustees and he was taken in hand by the Rev Robert Lampen, Dr Woollcombe, Col Hawker and Mr G Harvey. Kitto was then put to board with Mr R Burnard, clerk to the Workhouse.

Soon Kitto was befriended by an Exeter dentist who introduced him to the Missionary College in Islington and under their auspices he was sent out to Malta. In the years that followed he travelled widely and, foremost among his many writings, were the *Pictorial Bible* and the *Encyclopedia of Biblical Literature*. Unfortunately, although he enjoyed his work immensely it did not reward him as well as it should have done and he had many financial problems. A well known figure nationally, by 1850 he was awarded a civil pension of £100 a year but despite failing health he refused to give up work. In 1853 after the deaths of two of his nine children, John Kitto suffered a paralytic stroke and his work was finally over. He died the following year in Cannstadt, Germany where his family had taken him some months earlier (it was a German University that had conferred a doctorate upon Kitto).

Thirty years after Kitto's death an institute for working lads was formed by Mr AG Hambly in neighbouring Woolster Street; the following year, 1885, this body moved into the ragged school building in Stillman Street and adopted the name of Kitto in honour of the great man. The Kitto Centre at Burrington is the current base of this worthy organization and its links with the neighbouring school have lead to the adoption of the name John Kitto for the new comprehensive school there.

Meanwhile, back in Stillman Street, well before the end of last century, the Pitts Son & King's malthouse had replaced Kitto's birthplace. As mentioned before, this building was a victim of the blitz as were some of the people who took refuge in the makeshift shelter there on the fateful night that it was hit. An even greater number lost their lives in the shelter on the other side of the street on the eastern side of No 40. John Nichols survived that night sheltering with his mother under the staircase of No 40, the windows of that house were blown out but otherwise it remained intact.

Born in Stillman Street in the 1920s, John Nichols has lived in No 40 almost all his life and no major alterations have been made to the building in all that time, indeed it has altered very little in any respect from its nineteenth-century appearance. The wash-house and the coal house in the back yard are unchanged, as is the outside lavatory with its square wooden seat and round-holed pan. Inside cupboards and cast iron fireplaces again are unaltered, at least one of which is in particularly good condition. A gas light above the

fireplace in the downstairs front room adds to the period atmosphere, as do many fine-framed family photographs some dating from the turn of the century.

It was John's uncle, John Chapman, who last used the stable block and store next door to any great extent; still with its original tiled floor and cast iron drains, there are tethering rings here on the walls. John Chapman, one of the last street traders in Plymouth to sell from a hand-cart, used also to hire out hand-carts. Mainly for fruit and fish, they were stored here with scales to go with them kept at the back.

Lamentably these two isolated nineteenth-century survivors, despite being so unspoilt, are as yet unlisted, but given that the Barbican already has one splendid period house open to the public, the 'Elizabethan' House, maybe one day Mr Nichols' fine house could perhaps be bought and opened as a good example of a Victorian House.

Palace Court

'Palace Court, entered by an arched doorway, is situated in Catte-street, not far from the Old Guildhall, and is, at the present time, so far removed from anything palatial in appearance, or, in fact, that it has simply become the residence – being let off in separate floors and rooms – of people of the very lowest ranks of society. It is, indeed, a place to be but once visited, and that, a visit of but short duration. Still, putting aside all feelings of disgust at the modes of living of its denizens, or of the filth and squalor of the place, it is worth a visit, and some few interesting features will repay examination – especially a carved corbel on the landing of one of the principal staircases. Of this 'Palace Court', denuded of an excrescence, which has been built up in the quadrangle, and so cuts off some portion even of the little amount of free air the inhabitants formerly had to breathe, we give an engraving.'

This graphic description of Palace Court appeared in Llewellynn Jewitt's *History of Plymouth* published in 1873. Within seven years this 'venerable house . . . the most picturesque house in the town' had been pulled down.

A number of eminent figures of the day had campaigned for its preservation, but sadly to no avail, and in 1880 it was demolished and Palace Court Board School was erected in its place. To many, this represented a major improvement, replacing what had become a large slum with a brand new Palace of Education, built in the wake of the 1870 Education Act. In 1941 the school itself was gutted and 10 years later it was reconstructed as studios for the architecture and weaving departments of the School of Art.

Today then the site of Palace Court stands on the northern side of Palace Street and the name Catte Street has passed into the history books. Variously spelt as Katt, Catte and Cat Street, over the years it is interesting to note that one theory (a suggestion by the wags) as to the derivation of the name in the first place is that it comes from Cat-herine; the Catherine in question being Catherine of Arragon, who was reputed to have stayed in Palace Court when she first came to this country on route for London in 1501.

The evidence is by no means conclusive, but undoubtedly the Spanish Princess did stay in Plymouth for some time in October 1501 and according to one Spanish observer, 'had she been the saviour of the world she could not have had a more enthusiastic welcome'. The pages of the town audit book give some idea of the corporation's hospitality as we read of six oxen, twenty sheep, two hogsheads of gaston wine, one of claret, and a pipe of muscadel, being just a part of the fare laid on.

The sixteen-year-old princess was of course on her way to marry Henry VII's eldest son, Arthur. The marriage had been set up because Henry was anxious to secure an alliance with Spain to foil the link between France and Scotland. In the event the fifteen year old Arthur died within six months of the marriage and so as not to lose the 200,000 crown dowry that Catherine represented to the country, Henry made plans for Catherine to marry his second son. This marriage eventually did take place, in 1509, some months after Henry VII's death. So it was that the eighteen-year-old Henry VIII took the twenty-four-year-old Catherine as his first wife.

But back to 1501 when we learn that the Princess apparently spent a fortnight in Plymouth and stayed during this time at the house of 'Master Paynter', John Paynter, who was five times Mayor of Plymouth between 1491 and 1516. Tradition has long upheld that Paynter's house was none other than Palace Court and that therefore Catherine would have been well acquainted with this view in its former glory. Another theory, however, suggests that Palace Court belonged to the Priors of Plympton at this time; that it was the 'convent in Katt Street' that they disposed of in 1539. This at least would give the explanation for the name 'Palace' as it was quite common for prominent religious figures to call their residences 'Palaces'.

Whatever its true status in 1501, it is almost certain that Catherine would have been a guest here, for we are told that she appeared at Palace Court after attending a service in St Andrew's to give thanks for safe crossing to England.

Throughout the sixteenth century and probably well into the seventeenth century Palace Court would have remained a very noble residence indeed, however, as the town gradually expanded its boundaries, so many of Plymouth's wealthier residents moved out and erstwhile large townhouses like these were multi-let. Records show that cellars, lofts and rooms in Palace Court were let out and by the dawn of the nineteenth century this had become one of the worst slums in the town, its proprietors having 'fitted it up with as many miserable rooms for as many miserable people as can be crowded into it'. Small wonder then that some perhaps thought it was a good thing to pull down this historic building in 1880.

Batter Street

'... In 1708 or as some suppose, in 1705, the present Chapel in Batter-street, was built – the Government it is said contributing to its erection in order that after the Union between England and Scotland, (1707) there might be a place of religious worship for the Scotch soldiers who were then quartered in Plymouth in exchange for English Regiments stationed in Scotland, and the chapel was used for this purpose at intervals until the recent erection of the Presbyterian place of worship at Eldad – so that as late as the Crimean War, when the Highlanders then stationed in Plymouth left for Balaclava, the minister of Batter-street Chapel, as their Chaplain, preceded the Regiment to the place of embarkation.'

So said Llewelyn Jewitt in part of one of his longer sentences in his *History of Plymouth* first published in 1873. However Harris writing in 1806 records that it was probably begun in 1702, that date appearing over the principal entrance, and finished in 1704, while the house adjoining, which was built for the minister had the date 1707 on the keystones above the window arches.

The Reverend John Enty was the pastor of the congregation at this time and had been since 1696. Enty had succeeded Nicholas Sherwell and prior to the construction of the Batter Street Chapel, the local nonconformist congregation had been meeting in the 'Green House' in the erstwhile Green Street and the 'Old Marshalls', the onetime Marshalsea or town prison, now the Gin Distillery, in Southside Street.

Sherwell himself had gathered together a congregation in 1662 formed from followers of George Hughes, the vicar of St Andrew's and his assistant Thomas Martyn. Hughes had been one of nearly 2,000 ministers across the country who were ejected from their livings on St Bartholomew's Day, 24th August, 1662 following the passing of the Act of Uniformity.

Sherwell, newly ordained in 1660, had returned to Plymouth from Oxford in 1661 and along with Hughes and Martyn was detained for some time on Drake's Island. In the early years after his release public worship was difficult thanks to the passing of the Conventicle Act in 1664, which made illegal meetings of five or more people, excluding families, in a house, for religious meetings not in accordance with the Prayer Book. Until this Act was repealed, 25 years later with the passing of the Toleration Act, any such meeting had to be very carefully arranged.

After 1689 the climate became much easier, a number of Free Churches were established and many Meeting Houses were erected including, in time, this one in Batter Street.

Batter Street was then known as Pomeroy's Conduit Street and it is interesting to note, in the light of the events that took place on that ill-fated St Bartholomew's Day in 1662, that the most likely derivation for most names beginning 'Batt-' is Bartholomew. The name Pomeroy's Conduit Street, incidentally, probably owes its origin to Lawrence Pomeroy, Mayor of Plymouth, at a time (1623–4) when many of the town's 30 or so public conduits were being erected, in the wake of Drake bringing water to Plymouth in 1592. Pomeroy was doubtless responsible for one of these conduits, just as Walter Matthew had been in 1604, when as Mayor he 'byldyd a newe Cundict by the Great Tree at Brittayne Side att his owne cost and charges'.

The other streets bounding the perimeter of this site were Bull Lane (Peacock Lane) and Seven Stars Lane (Stillman Street). Within a few years of the Chapel being built, a Manse (the Scots word for a Presbyterian minister's dwelling-house) was added.

In those days this site was at the very heart of the town, which then would have had a population of around 8,000, and over the next hundred years the chapel, which was to be capable of accommodating 700 people, prospered.

In 1785 during the joint father and son pastorate of Christopher and Herbert Mends, the Batter Street Benevolent Institution was founded 'for Educating the Children of the Poor'. The oldest local educational establishment to be definitely connected to a religious body, it catered for girls and infants only after 1806.

One local boy who did benefit from Herbert Mend's teaching and books, though, was the celebrated, but then very poor, Stillman Street lad, John Kitto. The Mends's era, which had begun in 1762, came to an end in 1819 when Herbert died and by all accounts almost 1,500 attended his memorial service here and as many more were turned away. The Rev William Rooker who conducted the service was unable to get in through the door and had to climb into the chapel on a ladder that took him from the burial ground outside into the gallery, from where another ladder took him into the pulpit.

As the nineteenth century progressed so this church, which had been mother to Emma Place Church (1787), to the revival of an old chapel in Plympton (1798) and to Courtenay Street Chapel (1848), continued to thrive and around 1870 it was almost rebuilt, 'at a considerable cost'. However, attendances were beginning to decline when the twentieth century dawned and Oliver Searchfield, with joint responsibilties for Emma Place, was the last pastor here in 1920.

In 1923 the chapel was purchased by Lord Astor who wanted to extend the work of the Victory Club and, after considerable reconstruction, the buildings were opened by Lord and Lady Astor on 5th December 1925. The new complex which included the premises formerly occupied by the Victory Club became known as the Virginia House Settlement.

Designed to 'serve the needs of the Barbican people', the Settlement had a busy and happy role until the post war reconstruction of Plymouth and the advent of the Welfare State led to quieter times. More recently, however, a great deal of money, time and effort has been ploughed into the old buildings and the chapel, which, now handsomely restored, are about to start a new lease of life serving the community in ways little dreamt of at the dawn of the eighteenth century.

Looe Street

'The ground rises abruptly, and slippery half worn limestone steps lead to houses more ruinous and more crowded than those fronting the street' wrote the visiting Inspector from the General Board of Health, Robert Rawlinson, in 1853. However, it was to be another 45 years before there was a major slum clearance operation here.

The initiative for this was taken by Mayor JT (John Thomas) Bond in 1890 when he led a slumming tour of the area, which led to the removal of the whole of the north side of the street and its replacement with Corporation Buildings, in 1898. Crispin Gill, in his *Sutton Harbour* book, recounts a 'choice' story related to this. Evidentally Queen Victoria's Diamond Jubilee was celebrated locally with, amongst other things, an enormous bonfire on the Hoe, a bonfire built with timber from the condemned houses of Looe Street and How Street: 'The mayor and aldermen and councillors with their families all had the front seats; when the flames bit into the ancient timbers all their insect population flew for shelter, to the complete discomfort of the civic dignitaries.'

The erection of the Corporation Buildings greatly altered the character of Looe Street, gone in one sweep were half of the small businesses that fronted the street. In the last few years of their existence here these included; William McClonnan's pork butcher's shop, Charles Jones' wardrobe business, Mrs Hancock's pawnshop, Alf Richard's cobbler's-shop, JJ Reeby's bakery, James Popham's dairy and a number of general shops including one belonging to William Edwards, from whose premises this view from the corner of Looe Lane was probably taken.

It is also interesting to note that living in No 1 Looe Street at this time, around the site commonly stated to be the one on which Francis Drake had his house, was a fisherman called Robert Drake. Looe Street it seems was once renown for a certain fishiness in the air, as one account talks of fish-heads falling from overhead garrets here, whilst the wives of hookers made ready for sale large quantities of mackerel freshly delivered to them by donkey cart.

For many years towards the end of the eighteenth and the beginning of the nineteenth century, Looe Street was in fact known as Pike Street, Pike being a name which often has its roots in being the title of one who sells pike, the pike in question being the well known variety of fish with a very pointed, pike-like jaw. As with many other street names in this area that were changed around this time, though, the original returned and stayed and so Looe Street it still is today. It has been suggested that this name came about because of swine running 'loose' in the area, presumably on account of the meat market that was nearby or perhaps the old bull ring. The more likely explanation, however, is that this ancient name refers, like that of its Cornish namesake, to 'an inlet of water, a pool' such as has always been at the very bottom of the street.

For many years after the name changed back, the 'Pike Street Inn', on the north side of the street, on the corner seen here sporting the Looe Lane sign, remained as a reminder of that era. There were at least three beerhouses on the north side of the street in the middle of the nineteenth century, including one called the 'Tavistock Inn', all traces of which, of course, vanished before the century was out.

Another victim of the nineteenth century changes at the bottom of Looe Street was 'a picturesque old house of ancient pattern, the chief feature being that the front was slated; the slates being of curious shapes ... But the most interesting feature was a sign with a grotesque carving of a lion fondling a lamb and the quaint couplet: 'The time will be A Lyon and Lamb will agree'

At the very bottom of Looe Street, at the water's edge was 'Dung Quay', where the profitable business we assume was carried out of trading in 'All the Dung and Soil arising within the Borough belonging to the Mayor and Commonalty', this being let on an annual basis by the Corporation.

The advent of the twentieth century brought yet more changes to the street, the bakery shown here at No 27, though, remained in business until the 1950s. Although it changed hands many times, Nicholas Eade being here when this view was sketched in the 1890s, it had enjoyed continuous use as a bakery for at least 120 years. Unlike the general store next door, it still stands today little altered from the outside.

Looe Street was fortunate to survive the blitz and the post war planning largely in tact, although many buildings were in a sorry state of repair generally and it is thanks largely to the work of the Barbican Association, in the late 1950s and early 1960s, that most of the older buildings on the south side of the street have been handsomely restored. Meanwhile the Corporation Buildings on the north side are currently being restored by the Council.

Looe Street was once one of the most fashionable streets of the town. Sir Francis Drake had a residence here as, later, did Robert Trelawny. Trelawny, whose family had come to Plymouth in 1578, lived here until 1639 when he moved out to Ham House, which he had bought six years earlier when he was mayor. His father, also Robert Trelawny, had previously been mayor of the town on three occasions.

Originally all these fine residences would have had substantial gardens but over the years these came to be filled in with small cottages for the household servants and for workmen, a pattern typical of many of the older, grander streets of Plymouth. By the mid nineteenth century Looe Street infilled to such an extent that it had become one of the town's congested slum areas.

Looe Street

'No 36, Looe-street, is just a house number to many Plymothians. For many years it has been a decaying old house in a cobbled Barbican area thoroughfare. Now thanks to the Old Plymouth Society this Jacobean corner building has been completely renovated at a cost of £3,000.

This marks the first completely renovated old house in the Old Plymouth Society's post-war campaign to restore as many of the city's old historic buildings as possible.'

So ran the opening paragraphs of a local newspaper article from February 1960 about the property shown here, some 60 years or more after this sketch had been made. Since then the Barbican Association, which grew out of the Old Plymouth Society, has indeed gone on to restore many important old properties in both Looe Street and New Street. Without their timely intervention it is doubtful whether many of these buildings would still be standing. Thankfully, however, they are and today this building is occupied by the architectural practice of Bazeley, Miller-Williams & Corfield.

One hundred years ago, though, a very different type of commercial enterprise was carried on here by William Dear the bottle dealer. Here children could bring an empty two pound jam jar and receive a ha'penny in exchange, with which they in turn could purchase half a dozen or so bruised apples. Not that all local children necessarily would have come here, for just four doors down the road at No 32 was another bottle dealer, William Axworthy.

Bottles, despite the advent of mass production, were still quite highly valued at the end of the nineteenth century. After all it wasn't until 1887 that Ashley and Arnall patented their revolutionary mechanical bottle blowing machine that was capable of making 200 bottles an hour (in the early years of the twentieth century this rate was to be increased to something of the order of 2,500 bottles per hour!)

It had been the introduction of three part moulds back in the 1820s that had first led to the production of glass bottles in large numbers and really the nineteenth century marked the beginning of the widespread use of bottles to transport and retail a great variety of liquids. Up until then glass bottles had been used mainly for wine, medicine and perfume, primarily for the well-to-do. The improvements in bottle production, however, soon led to the introduction of new bottle users as breweries, pharmacies, 'parfumaries', distillers, mineral water manufacturers, ink manufacturers and hotels all jumped on the bottle bandwagon.

In addition to glass bottles, of course, there were also hand made stoneware bottles produced by large city based potteries and stamped with a decorative and informative 'transfer'. Moulded glass bottles, meanwhile, for the most part carried specially embossed wording and motifs that would serve in place of a label, describing the bottle's contents, its maker or its owner.

In those days 'most bottles were not disposable but were to be returned to the brewery or the bottling company named on the bottle. Indeed some carried warnings such as; "This bottle is the property of Rundle & Chaplin, Devonport. To buy or sell is illegal" or "Anyone illegally using this bottle will be prosecuted".' (Winfrid Scut *Plymouth Bottles*)

Whether or not William Dear was ever involved in illegal bottle dealing we will doubtless never know, but that he was not always a bottle dealer we do know, as in the 1850s and 1860s at least he was working from these very premises as a brushmaker.

There were around that time several brushmakers in town, George Lewarne, Richard Cornelius, Richard Rilstone, Watts & Co and the Wills Brothers to name but a few. Scattered at various points around the town one of them, the Wills Brothers business, was very near here, just a few doors up Looe Street and around the corner into Peacock Lane.

The Looe Street/Peacock Lane corner, now occupied by the Plymouth Arts Centre, was once famous for housing the town's most celebrated inn, the 'Pope's Head', which only lost its reputation when Foulston's 'Royal Hotel' was opened in 1811. The 'Pope's Head' is the first inn to be mentioned by name in the known records of Plymouth, in 1573. Quite how it got its name we don't know, but it is interesting to note that the market place that once stood at the top of Looe Street was, in 1600, the location chosen for the official burning of the Pope's Bulls and Pardons. This burning had been ordered by 'her majesties Commissioners for Ecclesiastical Causes' and it is possible that it was not the first occasion that such an event had taken place.

Peacock Lane, incidentally, was once known as Bull Lane, however, the bulls in question here are almost certainly those that were baited here at the adjacent bull ring, prior to being slaughtered by any of the local butchers. It was considered that the meat was more tender after a bull had been baited and butchers could face a stiff fine if they

allowed bulls to be slaughtered without first going through this ritual (in 1604–5 butchers William Jerman and John Jope were fined five shillings for just such an offence).

This was the sort of time that No 36 Looe Street, with its fine period window corbels, was most likely under construction; the original Jacobean doorway, incidentally, as shown here is now in the custody of the City Museum while a very good copy of it now stands in its place. The entrance shown here on the Batter Street corner of the building originally led through to three old cottages at the rear of the building, the foundations of which can still be seen in the courtyard at the back, this doorway itself, however, was blocked off in the restoration of the property.

Briton Side

Street names and place names often provide very good clues concerning the history of a particular area and to a certain extent this is true of Bretonside, however, it may perhaps be that in this case more questions are in the end posed than are answered.

One of the town's earliest historians, John Harris, was probably the first to express a written view on this one. 'Now,' he wrote in 1808, 'from Martin's Gate eastward it is still known by the name of Briton's (i.e. Breton's) Side, from the circumstances of the French landing there in the fourteenth century (i.e. early fifteenth century), under Marshall Bretagne, and burning 400 houses.'

Worth, writing in 1890 added more to this story. There were, he noted, in the opening years of the fifteenth century attacks on Plymouth by the French and Bretons 'on sundry occasions' and much damage was done 'but', he said 'the accounts were confused and contradictory'. However, he did add more detail to the account mentioned by Harris of the notorious assault of 1403.

'The attack was made on the afternoon of Lammas-day, August 10th, when large bodies of Bretons, under Sieur du Chastel, Lord of Chateau Neuf, near St Malo, landed about a mile from the town, which they entered at the 'bak haf', and burned and plundered at will until ten the next morning. Upwards of 600 houses were burnt at the spot thence called Briton Side (now part of Exeter Street), but the castle and the higher parts of the town (Old Town) held out; many of Chastel's men were killed or mutilated, while others were captured.'

Plymouth around this time was about the fourth largest town in England but even so its population would only have been around 7,000 which puts the scale of this horrific attack in some sort of perspective. But however devastating the attack itself, it does indeed seem odd, as Crispin Gill suggests in his book on *Sutton Harbour*, to 'call a suburb Bretonside because it had been burnt by the Bretons'.

It remains true, though, that virtually from that day down to Harris's day there was an annual Freedom Day Fight between the boys living on the Old Town side of the town walls and those on the Breton side of the walls. Originally these fights were held near the site of the recently removed 'Burton (Breton) Boys pub' but as the town expanded they were moved up the hill and out of harm's way to what then became known as Freedom Fields.

This has, of course, confused later observers who, aware of the fact that this area was also the scene of the last great offensive during the Civil War in the seige of Plymouth in 1643 (and seen as being the 'Great Deliverance' from the Royalist troops) assume that this was the 'Freedom' referred to in Freedom Fields . . . but it is not.

Could it also be, though, that by a similar misunderstanding the Breton element of Breton Side is also of much greater antiquity than is commonly supposed? After all the earliest spelling of the area is 'Britayne Side' and as Gill again suggests 'there are reasons for thinking that the Britons of Breton Side might have been there before the Anglo-Saxons of Sutton'.

This area may well have been the site of the first settlement on the edge of Sutton Harbour but, like the ancient Britons from Britayne (the Bartholomew Street area) in Exeter, they may well have left when Athelstan pushed into the south-west in the tenth century. Certainly from the third century onwards Britons had been migrating from Cornwall to Brittany to avoid the Saxon pirates and the Breton tongue has much in common with that of the Cornish.

Breton Side, of course, has not always even been called by that name, as from the 1880s through to 1958 this stretch was nominally added to Exeter Street. Furthermore, the Breton Side of today incorporates part of the original Bilbury Street, the oldest named street, in Plymouth and one that almost certainly harks back to the town's Celtic roots.

Bilbury Street ran west from Martyn's Gate, while Breton Side started at the gate, which crossed the road just next to the 'King's Head' and ran as far as the 'Old Tree' at the top of Hawker's Avenue. Martyn's Gate was erected soon after the Civil War and it adjoined the recently purchased property of John Martyn who, following in his father's footsteps, had been Mayor in 1634–5. It had three rooms over, glazed with diminutive window panes and was deemed to be very inconvenient in later years because coaches could scarcely pass through it. It was pulled down in 1789, after a visiting prince lost a servant who died after bumping his head on the masonry when riding under the gate.

Running north from the gate was Green Street which extended beyond Charles Church and which was for a time known as Little Church Lane. Two other thoroughfares ran north from Breton Side one of which, Moon Street, can be seen here coming out between the two blocks shown on the left.

This street ran into another street, once known by a name that undoubtedly harked back to the troubled times of the unwelcome French visitations for it was called Catch French Street, later abbreviated to French Street and renamed Hill Street in 1826. Moon Street itself was originally Moon's Lane and in the middle of the nineteenth century when the local enemies were dirt, disease and overcrowding, 128 people from this street died in the course of one year.

The one other northern route off Bretonside is North Street itself, although again this has been known by more than one name. White Cross Street it was from the associations with the local White Friars and later it became Old Penny Lane. Old Penny Lane was its name in 1797 when the famous copper cartwheel penny of George III replaced the hitherto traditional silver penny; just how old the Old Penny in question was, though, we will doubtless never know for already by then the penny, our oldest coin, was over 1,000 years old.

Higher Street

As you come into Plymouth City Centre today along Exeter Street and carry on just past the turn off to Breton Side and the Barbican, it is hard to imagine that in the middle of last century you would have found yourself here in the middle of one of Plymouth's older thoroughfares – Higher Street.

Parts of this street did manage to survive well into this century but by then most of its heart had been ripped out, a situation that was lamented by many at the time.

'It is not long since, that in Higher Street, on the north side of Exeter Street, and Lower Street on the south side of the same street there could be seen numerous picturesque houses such as those shown in the accompanying sketch. In common with nearly all the old streets of Plymouth the hand of the destroyer has been busy, and these fine gabled houses have been demolished to give place to newer and less picturesque dwellings.' So wrote WHK Wright at the very end of the nineteenth century, continuing in a vein familiar to conservationists of all generations … 'In this way old Plymouth is vanishing and new Plymouth is arising in all the glory of new bricks and ugly stucco to the disgust of lovers of the picturesque on the one hand, but to the joy of the utilitarian on the other'.

In practical terms in Higher Street, for William Wakeham, this all meant that these grand old buildings which, in later years had housed both his marine stores business and his shoemaking operations, were no more. In the middle of the nineteenth century Higher Street had been full of all manner of shops and stores, William Wakeham was not the only bootmaker, there was also William Full, neither was he the only one supplying marine stores, as both Thomas Marshall and Mary Rone were also trading here then.

Higher Street, long ago known as Hawk Street, was for centuries the highest, in the sense of being the most northerly, principal street of the town that ran in an east west direction and being on the outskirts of town was doubtless once very fashionable. Like so many of Plymouth's old streets, however, its character changed significantly in the nineteenth century.

At the beginning of that century there were three inns in this street, as you would expect for a thoroughfare that was almost the first that visitors to the town would pass through. One of these hostelries was later claimed by Exeter Street, this was the 'Burton Boy', another was the 'White Cow' and the third had the intriguing name of the 'Alexander and Roxanna'.

Mr Thomas Copplestone was granted a licence for 'Alexander and Roxanna' on Thursday 11th March 1802. Quite how long it had been known by that name we will doubtless never know but the couple it refers to are undoubtedly Alexander III of Macedonia and his wife Roxane.

Dubbed 'the great', Alexander (356–323 BC) was tutored by Aristotle and showed great promise at an early age. He married Roxane in 327 and a son, Alexander IV, was born after Alexander's death 323. Roxane achieved further fame, or perhaps notoriety, after her husband's death by murdering his other wife Barsine. Exactly what it was about this story that appealed at some stage to a Plymouth innkeeper in Higher Street many hundreds of years later is yet another mystery likely never to be solved.

Apart from the 'Burton Boy', though, these names were not destined to survive here in the nineteenth century and it is quite possible that the 'Alexander and Roxane' and the 'White Cow' became the 'Victoria Inn' and the 'Sportsman's Inn'. Both were listed in Higher Street in the 1840s, Mary Widdecombe in charge of one George Mugford the other.

In time the 'Victoria', which stood almost directly opposite these buildings here on the south eastern corner of Gasking Street, was claimed by that street, while the 'Sportsman's' was on the same corner but further round into Higher Street. Both remained as licenced premises for a number of years into the twentieth century but today the site of these establishments and the whole of Higher Street lies buried beneath the new Exeter Street, just below the new office block being constructed between what is left of Gasking Street and part of North Street.

The junction with North Street originally marked the western end of Higher Street towards which this view takes us, at the other end it terminated at its meeting with the old Exeter Street, now part of the extended Breton Side, and just a few feet beyond that Lower Street.

Lower Street, running parallel to the old Exeter Street, still appears on the map today but apart from the cobbles and the kerb stones there is little that survives here and certainly nothing that serves as a reminder of its Tudor ancestry. Narrower than Higher Street, Lower Street's fortunes fell lower than most in the nineteenth century and

at one time there were over 500 people there living in fewer than 30 houses. The national average for people living in a house was then about 5.5 in Plymouth generally the figure was over 9.0 while in Lower Street itself it was nearer 20, with at least 40 rooms in this street sleeping 4 or more!

The insanitary conditions created by the overcrowding in this street took an obvious toll on the people who lived there, particularly the men, and more than one in five of the women here over the age of 16 were widows.

It is against this sort of background, then, that decisions were taken by the reformers to pull down so many of these ancient and by then dilapidated buildings in an attempt to solve the problems that then existed. It is nevertheless lamentable that we should have lost so much of old Plymouth in this way.

Friary Court

Over the years there have been a number of street names in this area that served to remind locals of the order of Carmelite Friars that settled here, having been granted a 'messuage and orchard', back in 1288. Better known perhaps as Whitefriars (because of the white mantle they wore over their brown habits) they had their origins in an order founded by a French crusader, St Berthold, on the slopes of Mount Carmel in Palestine, sometime around 1155. These Carmelites first lived on this mountain as hermits in separate huts then around 1235 they were dislodged by the advancing Saracens and they accompanied the returning crusaders to Sicily, Cyprus, southern France and England. The Friars that found their way to Sutton, as Plymouth was then known, themselves hailed from Bristol.

Not long after arriving here they started building a church for themselves and in 1314, after a few minor controversies, they were granted an episcopal licence to celebrate divine service and to choose any bishop they pleased to consecrate their church. Fifteen years later they were able to further extend their convent, then described as being on the north east corner of Sutton Pool, beside the small creek that had become known as 'Frerene Lake'. Like all the other names associated with this order, that name has long since been confined to the history books; others include Friary Green, Friary Gate (taken down 1763), Friary Street (Harbour Avenue), Whitefriars Lane (Beaumont Road), Whitecross Street (North Street) and most recently Friary Station.

The Friary itself was a victim of Henry VIII's 'Dissolution of the Monasteries' and the house was surrendered to the crown by Prior John Mellyn on the 18th of September 1538. There were at that time only five of the brethren living there.

In 1539 the Friary site was leased to James Horswell who, just three years earlier, had ended his second term as mayor.

Horswell was no friend of the local religious community and had somewhat unfairly had three friars arrested. For this he had been subsequently banished from the town for a year, but the undaunted Horswell, who was said to be always in debt and to live largely by extortion, had returned and he later was to serve a third term as mayor in 1542.

William Amadas acquired the Friary site in 1546 and through the second marriage of his widowed daughter-in-law Jane, the land passed into the family of her new husband John Sparke in the 1580s. It was to remain in Sparke hands throughout the seventeenth century, eventually passing over to the Molesworth's on the death of William Sparke in 1714. Then in 1785 it changed hands again when Sir William Molesworth sold it to another William, William Clark.

It was not long after this that what was left of the buildings here were converted for a new use as a hospital for sick soldiers and during the Napoleonic Wars thousands of men passed through here, many of them actually dying here.

After the war these buildings saw use as accommodation for some of Plymouth's more colourful nineteenth century characters, as a most wonderful account in the *South Devon Monthly Museum* of 1835 bears witness, the writer spending a very lively evening there for what was deemed to be a typical Saturday night feast. However, in order to feel comfortable in the company he was keeping, he did first find it necessary to borrow a most ancient hat, an old hunting coat and a pair of fisherman's boots with only one sole.

Tom Hynes presided over the proceedings and among the many guests, anything up to four dozen of them, were dealers in cabbage nets and matches ('often blinds to cover the more lucrative occupation of thieving'), bellow makers, knife grinders, and umbrella renovators ('generally gipsies'),

wandering Italians (men in command of gangs of boys who 'perambulate the streets with an organ, a monkey, a white mouse or some other means of amusement'), thimble riggers and prod-in-the-loop boys (gambling con-men), solicitors and booksellers. If the last two mentioned sound almost respectable remember these solicitors were the sort who wrote begging letters and the booksellers sold scandal sheets, typically accounts of 'bloody murders, accidents, offences &c'.

Most of these characters would have slept here too, in straw beds laid out on the floor with no more than six inches between them '. . . Bedclothes there were none, each traveller sleeping in the habiliments which decorate him by day'.

As for the great Saturday night feast itself, this was eaten 'without the aid of knives and forks' off upturned barrels and uneven tables and it consisted of fish, fowl, ham, beef, cheese, turnips, onions, bread and 'an ample tin cauldron holding about a wheelbarrow full of potatoes'. For 'libations at dinner each guest was provided with a pewter pot of Scott's XXX' (from the brewery run owned by Robert Falcon Scott's ancestors).

After the supper came the brandy, 'the best that was ever smuggled from "Guarnsy" island'. Towards midnight we read that Tom Hynes slipped off his chair under one of the tables while Jack O'Diamonds and Billy Brown turned too for a bruising match, the rest of the company pairing off as accessories in the fray, whereupon the writer 'thought fit to evaporate into thin air'.

In time Friary Court itself also evaporated into thin air and within a few years of the arrival of the railways here at Friary in the 1870s all these buildings had disappeared. Last used for passenger traffic in 1958, there is little left today of Friary freight depot even as the twentieth century witnesses the beginning of a new era for this most ancient of sites.

Eldred.

FRIARY GREEN.

Charles Church

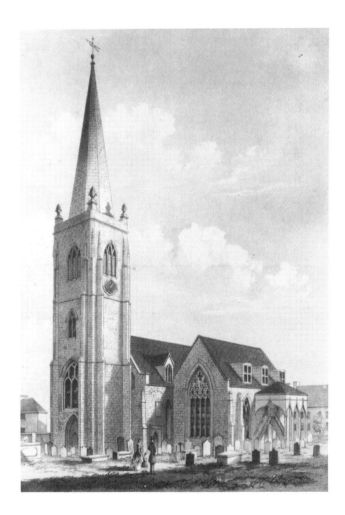

just as St. Andrew's is frequently called 'Old Church'.

In this way in 1879 WHK Wright described the beginnings of Charles Church. The course of events back in the early part of the seventeenth century was, however, far from being that simple. These were the days of religious persecution, the early days of puritanism and non-conformity; in Plymouth those famous religious 'Independents', the Pilgrim Fathers, had but recently been 'kindly entertained and courteously used by divers friends there dwelling'. There was in the town a strong and influential body of Puritans and through their influence, in 1631, Thomas Forde was chosen by the Corporation to be the lecturer at St. Andrew's, while the following year they appointed, as was their prerogative, Alexander Grosse, to the Vicarage. However, both appointments were overruled by Charles I, who would not even consider Grosse for the post of lecturer. Thus although the main argument put forward by the Mayor and Corporation in 1634 for the creation of a new parish was that St. Andrew's was no longer large enough to accommodate the local church-going population, it is just as likely that the new church was wanted so that the local Puritan dignitaries could have their own place of worship. (Plymouth's population at this time had actually decreased somewhat due to the pestilence).

Although Charles I did eventually sanction this 'new' church in 1640, he also insisted it should be named after him and in this climate it therefore comes as no surprise that Plymouth sided with the puritan Cromwell against the King two years later.

When the Civil War began Charles Church, although well under way, was far from being complete and there is a suggestion that the walled structure was used for stabling for the defending force's horses. However, there is also record of a burial here as early as 1646, a baptism on the first day of 1645 and a wedding on 10th May 1644. Iron pegs were said to have been hammered into the walls and great canvasses stretched across the roof space covering the chancel at least.

Francis Porter, appointed in 1658, was the first Minister here and although the church was eventually completed by 1658 there was no consecration until after the Restoration of the Monarchy in 1660. Porter then subsequently conformed, following the Act of Uniformity in 1661 (although curiously enough Bedford and Hughes of St. Andrew's did not). Considered by some to be the finest post Reformation Gothic style church in the country, a degenerate disciple of William of Wykeham is thought to have been the architect. It's also thought he probably designed the old Plympton Grammar School. At this time Charles Church had only a wooden spire which, so legend has it, was later 'knocked away by the broomsticks of a lot of witches, which struck it in their flight' (Worth). By 1708 it had been covered with lead and in 1767 it was taken down and the present stone spire was erected. The year after the tower had been leaded, Colonel Joseph Jory, an eminent local benefactor, presented Charles Church with a peal of six bells and ten years later he further provided a clock and chimes.

Sadly the bells and the four others that later joined them have now gone as has the clock and the many other alterations and additions effected over the years. These were lost as the Church prepared to celebrate the tercentenary of its foundation. Charles Church was gutted by fire following a heavy air raid on 21st March 1941, and so this grand edifice which first saw life in times of war all but ended its service in war time. Memorial services have, however, over the years been conducted in the ruined shell and Charles Church has been left as a memorial to the 1200 local civilians who lost their lives in the Second World War. The human remains of those buried here in the preceding centuries have now long since been removed and a busy roundabout today occupies the old cemetery land. The mid fifties construction of the roundabout also claimed another of its neighbours, the old Sunday School building in erstwhile Vennel Street. One of the oldest in the country, the Household of Faith school had moved here eleven years after its inception in 1787. Today its traditions and those of Charles Church itself are kept alive in Charles with St. Matthias Church, St. Matthias (1887) being the nearest survivor of the eight separate parishes carved out of Charles parish between 1829 and 1910.

'Up until the reign of Charles I, Plymouth consisted of but one parish. In 1634 the Corporation took steps to divide the town into two parishes, and in 1640 an 'Act' was passed sanctioning the same, and for building a new church in the additional parish. The Church is still called 'New Church'

The Jacobean Guildhall

'1606 . . . king of denmark cometh into England. the Guildhall of plimmouth built by the town, and the Old Shambles.' So wrote James Yonge in his diary sometime around the end of the seventeenth century.

The guildhall referred to was the one shown here and it is believed to have been at least the third guildhall Plymouth had known. Worth reckoned that the first 'was probably somewhere in "Old Town"' while a second was thought to have been new built in Southside Street not long after the Act of Incorporation with Sutton Prior in 1439.

Guilds themselves were unknown in this country before the Norman conquest, but after that time references to such bodies start to occur in British records. Initially a guild would most likely have been 'an association of persons contributing money for some common object' as most early spellings take the form *gild*, *geld* or *yeld* – originally meaning payment, money, tribute or offering. (Some guilds were religious bodies.)

Whatever the derivation, there is little doubt that in many parts of England and in the royal burghs in Scotland, Guilds of merchants not only preceded any other municipal bodies but frequently became the governing body of a town. In a similar way representatives of trade guilds often superceded older organizations as the municipal authority. It is therefore no surprise to find that this Jacobean Guildhall was dominated on the ground level by traders; here was the butter and poultry market which was held under the arches and in an 'enclosed court behind it were collected the corn-market and the vegetable market'. Not everyone however appeared to find this arrangement satisfactory as we read of the 'great annoyance of all Passengers . . . there being on market days scarcely a possibility of passing and great was the clamour and dire the confusion that prevailed'. This place was then literally a 'Shambles' but then shamble meant a place where meat or flesh was sold.

After the market on Saturday however this scene was once again transformed when 'the space under the Hall was duly cleaned, in order to prepare it as a fit promenade for all that was dignified and powerful in the corporate body on the Sunday morning, prior to their attendance at public worship [which in those days was compulsory for the corporate body]. . . . Here under each arch stood an Halbadier with his ensign of office extended, whilst the dignified great ones paced up and down until the wonted signal was given for the procession to form itself.' An halbadier was a civic guard carrying a halberd; a weapon which has a spear and battle axe-type fitting at the end of a handle that is between five and seven feet long.

It is hard now to imagine these scenes of chaos one day and pomp the next, particularly as our view here shows no activity at all. Clearly depicted though are the 'seventeen steps', infamous in their day in Plymouth as the prospect facing anyone 'acting illegally either by commission of any crime, or incurrence of debt'. The 'Seventeen Steps' led up into the Hall where sat the 'Mayor and other Magistrates and various members of the Corporation'.

If found guilty by the officials in this Hall, there was at the Western end of the building a debtors prison and beyond it an apartment for the detention of criminals. Below this and entered by the side of the steps were two dungeons one of which was called the 'Clink'. A common enough term in Devon and Cornwall for a lock-up, the Plymouth Clink was described in 1777 as being 'seventeen feet by eight, about five feet and a half high, with a wicket in the door seven inches by five to admit light and air'. (Howard, who concluded the place was unfit for the reception of human beings). Small wonder its reputation 'long survived its existence' and naughty children were long after threatened with 'the Clink'.

Built by Thomas Apsey of Nettlecom; John Martyn and Walter Mathewe supplied the timber, George Sheere the ironwork, John Burden was the plumber, Michael Bountie the glazier, while Pascoe Peppell sold the lime for this fine Guildhall, built in the reign of James I at a cost of £794 8s 1d.

It stood for almost 200 years little changed, apart from substantial rebuilding in 1667, until the very dawn of the nineteenth century when it was pulled down and succeeded

by a new guildhall, in 1800, which in turn stood on the same site – although not always as a guildhall, at the junction of High Street and Whimple Street until the Blitz of 1941.

The Georgian Guildhall

'In 1800 when the "Old Guildhall" was taken down private interest prevailed powerfully to induce its re-erection on the same site, and in an evil hour, a man called Eveleigh who had been Clerk of the Works to some Architect at Bath, undertook in so limited a space to provide room for a Guildhall, all the purposes of a Mayoralty House, as far as regards kitchens and their appendages and dining rooms; prisons for debtors as well as thieves, rogues and vagabonds, a news-room, and withal a Market-place; such a preposterous plan could only be approved by ignorant men who unfortunately at this time governed the affairs of the Corporation; it met with very general reprehension and some feeble opposition amongst the inhabitants, but nothing effectual was done to impede its progress. And thus £7,000 was spent in erecting a structure, which soon was found to be inadequate for the purposes of a prison, but moderately adapted to the purposes of a Guildhall, and totally inefficient as a place for a hall of justice . . . So much for our modern improvements.'

Reading the above account, it is difficult to believe it was written over 150 years ago about a building which had been standing little over 30 years. However, by all accounts, the building shown here was 'condemned almost from the first' (Wright) as being 'inconvenient and unworthy, in every respect, of the important town to which it belongs' (Worth).

Its impact on all the market business which had previously been conducted on this site was mirrored in the readoption of the name 'High Street' for the street which ran up to meet Whimple Street from the Barbican. It had, for many years, been known as Market Street but High Street was its original name. Whimple Street itself, incidentally, acquired its name because the street was famous for the sale of Whimples or womens' hoods. Properly spelt without the 'h', wimples were or are garments of linen or silk folded in such a way as to envelope the head, chin and sides of the face and neck, the sort of headgear worn by some nuns.

Just who the original wimpler was, the local wimple maker or makers is unclear, but around the middle of last century J. Masters was the only hat and cap maker listed in the street, although Spooners' straw bonnet warehouse was also based here.

Bookseller Row was another name given to this street at one time; again, however, despite every address in the street containing a retail outlet, JS Doidge, a name well known in local publishing circles, was the only bookseller listed here in 1867. Here too though was the Post Office, the Naval Bank and the West of England Paper Staining Company. But to return to the Guildhall, with its illuminated clock, by 1869 plan for its replacement were well under way and when in 1874 the new (and present albeit reconstructed) Guildhall was opened, this building lay empty until September 1876 when the newly established Plymouth Free Library was opened here. This new usage quickly proved successful and in its first two years there were almost 250,000 book issues recorded, an impressive statistic as there were only about 10,000 books in the library altogether at the time. The news rooms were also busy. Here many daily and weekly journals were placed on stands with monthlies and quarterlies on the tables: 'These rooms' noted the librarian WHK Wright, 'are very popular, and are thronged at all hours of the day.'

On completion of Plymouth's main Library in 1910, this Georgian Guildhall, the foundation stone for which was laid in May 1799 not 1800, was taken over by the City Treasury and Stores Officer. It maintained this role until the bombing raids of March 1941, when the building was gutted and all the stores records and Rate Valuation lists for the city were lost.

The building itself survived as a shell for a few more years, finally being pulled down a few months before the war ended, in February 1945. Today much of its site is occupied by the Unemployment office in Buckwell Street.

St Andrew's Street

R.H.WORTH del

'St Andrew's Street may certainly be called one of the oldest streets of Old Plymouth. Within living memory it contained some good specimens of Tudor architecture and some of the best examples in the town. With their high gabled roofs, and projecting upper stories, these old houses formed a picturesque feature in the street architecture of Plymouth. Modern improvements and sanitary considerations have, however, swept away nearly all that is picturesque ... one side of this fine old street has been entirely removed, but on the other, or west side, are still to be found some notable examples of ancient buildings, the one depicted here being the best example.'

Since that account was written back in 1901, St Andrew's Street has of course changed to an even greater extent and this fine building, rescued by the City Council in 1970 and restored over five years, 1972–77, now stands alone. The whole of the rest of the west side of the street has been demolished and redeveloped, as has much of the eastern side,

although there are still a few remaining nineteenth-century buildings, to the north and south of the magistrates' court.

At the time this drawing was executed this mansion, which we now call the Merchant's House, was in use, in part at least, as a greengrocer's. Charles Rooks was the shopkeeper. Next-door to him Henry H Bustin was the licensee of the 'Mechanics Inn' and further up again, William Beacham worked as a boot and shoe repairer. At that time Beacham was the only shoeman in the street but earlier in the nineteenth century there had been as many as five boot and shoemakers here; Butcher, Pedlar, Kidger, Lowman and Dunning. Strange that a street that for much of the twentieth century was given over to motor trade should then have catered so well for the pedestrian.

Certain names that ran businesses here in the early 1800s are no longer to be found in the Plymouth area at all and one wonders what happened to the families of Thomas Dunsterville, who was a broker here and William Peagam, a tailor. Other names, while not altogether common, have survived and there are quite a few Curgenvens about, possibly descended from the Curgenvens who had the stamp office here in 1812. That same year John Symons jnr, a builder, was based in the street and one wonders here if he was any relative of the William Symons, three times Mayor of Plymouth (1668–9, 1680–1, 1688–9), who lived for some time in the Merchant's House.

William Symons was the great ancestor of the Symonses of Chaddlewood, having bought a lot of the property that had belonged to the Sparke family who in turn did much of their property acquisition in the days of Elizabeth I, when William Parker also made his fortune. Parker, a naval captain, was also at one time Mayor of Plymouth, he is also the man who is credited with building or at least redeveloping this fine house in St Andrew's Street.

From the various architectural clues found here, it is'-'thought to be certain that there was a house on this site since

the early 1500s, but that in all likelihood this was probably modernised by William Parker either at the end of that century or the beginning of the seventeenth century. Parker was Mayor of Plymouth 1601–2 and we know he was living in this house in 1609, perhaps even earlier. We have no records of any occupants or owners prior to that date.

Said to have been in Drake's fleet set against the Armada in 1588, as the master of the victualling ship *Mary Rose*, William Parker, a proven sea captain, was also a privateer and he embarked upon his first independent venture in 1596. He left Plymouth in November with two ships, the *Prudence* and the *Adventure*, and set sail for Jamaica and Mexico. Away for eight months he and his men sacked and looted Puerto de Cavallos and Campeachy where they were driven off by the Spanish. On the way home however they also managed to capture a Spanish ship with £5,000 worth of silver on board. Although wounded in the course of these actions, Parker was obviously well placed after this and although the dates are not entirely clear, it appears that he was appointed Mayor of Plymouth in September 1601 and set off on another trip in November.

Again he took the *Prudence* and a smaller ship the *Pearl* and a pinnace of 20 tons. This trip proved to be an even richer one for the new Mayor as he and his men sacked St Vincent and took Porto Bello and two frigates from the Spanish treasure fleet. The pinnace however was lost with all but three of its hands.

Parker returned to Plymouth in May 1602 and although he continued to spend time at sea he appears to have settled here as a merchant. He died at sea on an expedition led by Sir Thomas Dale to the East Indies in September 1618, not long after Dale had described Parker as 'unfit for his work being old and corpulent'.

The house stayed in the Parker family until 1632 and throughout the seventeenth and eighteenth centuries remained one of the finer residences of the town.

Turk's Head

'I was designed and put upon my foundations rather more than 400 years ago, and have to thank the Crusaders, who beat the Infidels in the Holy War, for my name. In my youthful days the good town I'm about to quit for ever hadn't as many hundreds as it now has thousands of people, but it had more friars of orders grey, black and white, than there are parsons of every shade in all modern Plymouth. Some of them were early patrons of mine, and ever and anon gave me a call, liking well my sign, but better still my sack and my jovial company. A church, a monastery, and a town cross were my near neighbours, and I thrived well in their company; and of my surrounding contemporaries (solid, gabled, and mullioned, and put together much as I am), there was hardly one that kept its head (or tiles) much higher than mine, for the tall and overhanging timbered houses, like my old friend in Notte Street, had not yet been thought of.'

So ran part of a newspaper article published around July 1861, the time that this building, believed then to have been the oldest house in Plymouth, was demolished. Its silver rag roof slates a beauty to behold in the moonlight, this building was the 'Turk's Head' which stood at the corner of Higher Lane where it met St Andrew's Street on the site since occupied by the 'Abbey Hotel'. Whether or not it had always been an inn has generally been a matter for conjecture '. . . Could we trust the name we might say that the Turk's Head Inn was a relic of the crusading days, but we fear we must not indulge in the romantic visions which that fancied connexion shadows forth. We find it entered as the Turk's Head in the *Picture of Plymouth* (1812) and we can trace no earlier record. But Harris, in his MS. notes on Old Plymouth, written at various times during the early part of the nineteenth century, calls it the Abbot's House . . .' (Charles Eldred, *Streets of Old Plymouth*, 1901).

Despite the doubts of some writers, we do know that 700 years ago there was mention of the 'Turk's Head Inn' in

Exeter, which stands next to the Guildhall. In 1289 the city authorities granted the proprietors permission to lean a beam against the Guildhall in consideration of the payment of one penny a year. The story behind the name of this particular 'Turk's Head' is said to be, that a Turkish prisoner was held captive there and beheaded in the pub's cellars by Exeter's executioner. The story goes that the unfortunate Turk's head was then used as a target on the jousting ground that then existed behind the inn.

All this would have taken place around the time of the Crusades, 1095–1291; the first was probably the most successful (1095–99), but on the whole these military expeditions, sent out by the countries of western Christendom to recover the Holy Places of Palestine from Muslim occupation, did not achieve their main aims. However, Europe did greatly benefit from the growth of East–West trade that followed in their wake and from the eastern ideas and concepts that subsequently made their way into medieval culture.

The Turks, who were first heard of as a tribal group on the frontier of China in AD 595 and went on rapidly to spread their power far and wide, were the principal foe identified by the Crusaders. With their characteristic wavy hair and full flowing beards they were to inspire a great number of inn signs! The 'Turk's Head' is by far the most common but there is also the 'Saracen's Head' and the 'Blackamoor's Head'. Names like the 'Gentil Knight' and the 'White Knight' were also generated by the Crusades as were the names of two famous inns the 'Jerusalem', in London, and one of the oldest inns in the country, the 'Trip to Jerusalem' in Nottingham.

Quite what light this throws on the 'Turk's Head' in Plymouth is uncertain. We do now at least have documentary evidence of the Inn before 1812, for we know that Robert Westlake was granted his licence for the 'Turk's Head', in St Andrews Street, on Tuesday 16th October 1804

and that a landlord called Smith ran the Inn in 1798.

Harris, in his manuscripts, as well as referring to it as the Abbot's House, said that there 'could hardly be a doubt that it is coeval with the Old Church to which it has always belonged'. He then went on to describe how, together with the land to the north east corner of St Andrew's Street by the church door and behind the houses on the southern side of Market Place, this site was held on leases 'paying and yielding certain hie rent to respective vicars' which 'seems as much to say that was the garden ground or backlet attached to it.'

Whatever then the true age of this building though and however many years it saw service as an inn, one thing is sure, in the summer of 1861 it all came to an end; a sad end no doubt for James Stevens one of the last licensees here, but a happy one no doubt for those who like to see change and for TM Tucker, one of the first landlords of the new 'Abbey Hotel' erected in its place.

Abbey Place

What tales of the times would the people in this picture have been able to tell us? Drawn by Thomas Allom and engraved by Wallis, it was published in 1830, the year George IV died, at the age of 67, of alcoholic cirrhosis and dropsy at Windsor and was succeeded by his 64-year-old brother William. It was also the year that the great Whig Reformer, the 2nd Earl Grey, MP for Tavistock, defeated the then Prime Minister, the Duke of Wellington, who was opposed to political reform, in the general election and began a four year term of office.

Here in Plymouth, meanwhile, reform of a different kind was soon to be the subject of heated exchanges as the Vicar of St Andrew's, John Hatchard, opposed the attempts of his Bishop, Bishop Phillpotts of Exeter, to abolish pew rents and to remove signs on the church walls offering 'seats for hire'. Ultimately the pew system was doomed anyway but the congregation that Hatchard had supported him in his attempts to retain it despite being lambasted by the Bishop '. . . I will not come to this place year after year and see the house of God stolen from the poor,' he exclaimed from the pulpit, '. . . You shall not shut yourself in snug pews and cram the poor into the aisles – I'll see to that at any rate.'

Change was slow but it did take place and Hatchard, who was one of St Andrew's longest serving incumbents, 1824–1870, saw much of it. He would also have seen many changes here outside the church. The 'Prysten House' served as Messrs Welsford, Arthur & Rosedew's 'Abbey Wine Vaults' when he first arrived. Known throughout the

nineteenth century as 'The Abbey', by 1850 Daniel Millward junior had expanded his father's grocery business and taken over this building. Daniel Millward senior, meanwhile, continued to operate from 32 Notte Street where he had established the business back in the 1820s. In those days, incidentally, next door to the Abbey was a pub, the 'Duke of York'.

Following the Millward's in 'The Abbey' were another firm of wholesale grocers Brown, Wills & Nicholson, who also dealt substantially in tea and were based here, with some members of the firm at times using rooms for domestic accommodation, until the 1940s. At times too they shared this grand fifteenth-century building with other firms: Cridland's Corn Stores, Hindson & Co (tea growers of Natal), and JC House (the machine ruler). During their time here the building underwent a number of structural alterations. The courtyard was roofed over to gain more storage space and the interior walls became blackened with years of bacon curing.

After the last war the eastern part of the building was used as the local headquarters of the St John Ambulance Brigade and Association. The campaign to see the building become part of the church was well under way by this stage and had been started by the Rev. Arthur Perowne, vicar of St Andrew's 1913–1920. Brown, Wills & Nicholson were well disposed to this idea but inevitably it took a long time, eventually though it was restored to it's present state, Body Son & Fleury overseeing much of the work which was

carried out by the contractors Cooper & Son. Opened initially to the public by appointment only, this fine period piece is now open on a regular basis.

The present view from this vantage point suggests then that there has been less change than there actually has, as far as the church and 'abbey' are concerned, however there is no denying the obvious changes with respect to the old houses shown here to the right. In all, four houses ran from the top of Finewell Street to meet St Andrew Street, Nos 1–4 Abbey Place. Since 1979 the site upon which they stood has been occupied by the new Magistrates' Court but they were demolished many years before that.

Last century they were home to a variety of residents and small businesses; William Couch the bootmaker spent many years in No 1 after moving here from High Street, Walter Cleave, who had formerly run the 'George Inn' in Old Town Street, moved his grocery and tea business into Nos 2–3 in the 1830s, and John Griffin, house painter and glazier moved from St Andrew's Street into No 4 a few years later. Shortly before its demolition, No 1 was again being occupied by a firm of boot repairers, Barker's, the others were primarily given over to domestic use, although Mrs Trench was conducting a business in wardrobes downstairs in No 2.

In 1933 Mumford's opened their new three-story garage at the top of St Andrew's Street, on a site which took in the buildings of Abbey Place, and so another slice of old Plymouth was left to survive only in memories and pictures.

Prysten House

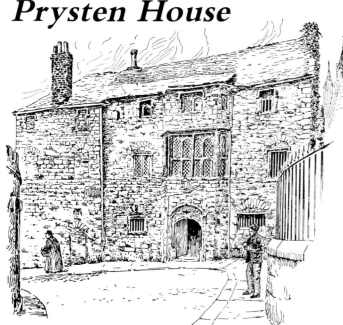

'On the south side of St Andrew's Church are the remains, in a very perfect state, of doubtless another religious edifice, probably of the later part of the fifteenth century. I have been unable to obtain anything like a satisfactory clue to its history, although by some it is thought to have been a house of the Cistercians. It goes by the name of 'the Abbey', and is said to be connected with the crypt under the chancel of St Andrew's Church, by a subterranean passage, now blocked up.'

Such were the thoughts of the architect James Hine, as expressed in a paper he read at the Plymouth Athenaeum on Wednesday the 19th December 1860. The building he was referring to is perhaps best known now as 'the Prysten House'. Bomb damaged during the second world war, it was restored in the late 1950s under the guidance of another distinguished architect, AS Parker.

Parker was a member of the Old Plymouth Society, a body which, in 1942, reported that the house was 'built, or re-erected, in the latter part of the fifteenth century. It is recorded as being in existence in 1490.' The report then went on to add, 'It was the residence of Chantry and other priests of St. Andrew's and accommodated the Preaching Canons of Plympton Priory, to which both Church and town were formerly attached.'

Another nineteenth century historian, J Brooking Rowe, thought it likely that there was a link between the house and the church, but as he stated in his *Ecclesiastical History of Old Plymouth* published in 1873, there was not the 'slightest clue and any opinion is the purest speculation'.

The only clues that had then been unearthed, the reference to a 'domus presbiterorum' in the borough rentals of 1491 and a 'prystenhouse', mentioned in 1538 in the town's Black Book, fail to give any indication of the site of such a building.

Extensive research since carried out by Jennifer Barber and published in 1973, reveals that Brooking Rowe was right to doubt what appeared to be an obvious link. By delving through a number of different archive sources, various rental records and medieval deeds reveal quite a clear picture of the earlier history of this site.

Described as a tenement in Sutton Prior, south of the church and bounded by the church cemetery on the north and an unnamed street on the east, it was granted to William Benteleghe in 1395 by the heirs of William Lecceleghe. Benteleghe sold the eastern part of the property seven years later to another William, William Cheke, whose widow Christina was to grant it to William Grene in 1437. Grene, a chaplain, one of the few religious figures directly referred to in connection with this site, disposed of the tenement within a couple of years. Walter Peterfeld became the new owner and for the next 45 years the property remained in the Peterfeld family. Then, in October 1487, John, son and heir of William Peterfeld, sold it to Thomas Yogge and his first wife, Margaret.

Thomas Yogge was one of three Cornish born brothers who did much for this town, his elder brother William was four times mayor of Plymouth between 1459 and 1470, however in 1472, a few months after William's death the corporation decreed that any 'Foreyn man', any man not born or apprenticed within the town would be deprived of their Freedom. This meant effectively that such 'foreyners'

could no longer compete on equal economic terms with native Plymouth merchants. This decree seems to have prompted the two remaining Yogge brothers to leave the town. John retired to the family home in Duloe, while it appears that Thomas then went to London. His sisters, having married into local families naturally remained, and he continued to hold property here and in 1498 he bought the site immediately to the south of his original purchase here in Finewell Street.

With the acquisition of this adjacent site it would seem that Yogge then decided to build this grand three-winged structure that we see today perhaps intending to live here in his retirement with his second wife Joan. Whatever happened here in those early years of the sixteenth century we know that Thomas died, a little after Joan, in 1509 and that brother John inherited the 'New Place', as it was referred to in 1513. For the next 200 years however it was known almost constantly as Yogge's House. It was by this name it was referred to in 1608 by which time the house was in the possession of the Waddon family, although by 1736 when it finally passed out of their hands it was 'now and for sundry years past called the Old Abbey'.

There appears to be no reason for this at all, but doubtless the fact that the Rev. Thomas Arthur Crew paid the rental on this property for much of the remainder of the eighteenth century did much to keep the association alive.

As to the location of the true Prysten House, the evidence uncovered by Jennifer Barber suggests that this was almost certainly a little further to the south of the church, on a site backing onto Finewell Street, but actually in Catherine Street.

Referred to as early as 1491, this 'prystenhouse' is thought to have been a more modest affair, smaller than this Finewell Street property, which it is suggested, would have always been too big for the few chantry priests and local clergy that the town had in those distant times.

Catherine Street

For the greater part of the nineteenth century this building, the Hospital of the Poor's Portion, otherwise known as the old Workhouse, stood near the top of Catherine Street on the site of that part of the guildhall complex building now occupied by BBC Radio Devon.

Completed in 1630, it's foundation lay in the notion that grew in Elizabethan times that it was a charitable thing to do, 'setting the poore on worke', that is finding or creating work for the poor if they were unable to find it for themselves.

Town records show that a move was first made towards this in 1597, a petition exists that suggests that a serge weaver from Exeter, William Woulfe, was induced by the Corporation to come to Plymouth to instruct 20 poor children in the art of spinning worsted. Nine years later there was a dispute over how much Woulfe was supposed to have been paid for this but essentially it appears there was basic agreement that Woulfe was to have had an allowance for the diet of every child and there also to have been a provision of clothing for each child.

In 1611 we find William Weekes operating with a similar brief and it would appear from the records that the first attempt to actually set up a workhouse proper was in the old castle. The work in question being weaving, knitting stockings and picking oakum. A common task in such institutions well into the late nineteenth century, oakum picking was the retrieval of loose fibres obtained by untwisting and picking old rope, oakum literally means 'off-combings' and this material was commonly used for caulking or stopping up the seams of ships to prevent leaking.

Such, then, was the climate in which the Hospital of the Poor's Portion was established. Catherine Lane, as it then was, running down from the parish church (Charles was yet to be built) was probably an obvious choice for such an institution; there were already long established almshouses at the top of the Lane, just above St Andrew's Church tower and in 1615 that other celebrated charitable institution, the Hospital of Orphans Aid, had been erected on the site just up from that on which the Hospital of the Poor's Portion was to be built.

The Hospital of Orphans Aid was built under the terms of the will of the wealthy Plymouth merchant William Laurence, who died in 1612. The condition being that within seven years of his death, Thomas and Nicholas Sherwill, merchants, should, with £100 left to them for the purpose,

erect and build a 'convenient Almshouse' for 'poore people . . . to dwell and inhabite therein or for the education and bringing up of poore children or orphants of the same borough'.

The word 'hospital' in both these cases of course had a meaning different to that with which we are now familiar, these were not places for the sick and wounded or for those in need of medical attention but rather for the needy, infirm and aged and were invariably charitable institutions. There were, with both of these institutions, close links with the church and above the doorway to the Poor's Portion, seen here below the gable and large window, was the motto 'By God's helpe throvghe Christ' (this doorway stood for some years after the building came down in a garden in Mannamead and can be seen today in the Elizabethan Gardens behind New Street). Regulations concerning the religious teaching and exercises here were evidently very strict.

Management of the Hospital of the Poor's Portion was in the hands of the Mayor and Corporation and one time mayor Abraham Colmer was one of the executors of the original deed. In 1708, however, the Corporation conveyed their rights and trusts to a body of guardians who became incorporated by Act of Parliament.

1708 was an eventful year, Dr Blackett, the new bishop made his visitation and a new gallery was built for the boys. It must have been cold in the workhouse that year for we read in the town records that there was 'a very severe winter, great dearth etc. . . . and a mighty lightening and thunder threw down one of the pinnacles of St Andrew's Tower'.

One of the other consequences of the 1708 Act was that the Workhouse also became a 'house of correction' and among the workhouse records we find entries like these;

'March 15 1727 That Mary Clarke be committed to Bridewell and have six pounds of Hemp to beat everyday and in default thereof be whipt . . . That Diana Weymouth and her Daughter Elizabeth be whipt for not performing the task set them by this house.'

As the nineteenth century dawned the workhouse, which had gradually sunk into a 'nest of vagabonds', underwent a series of improvements; in 1814 it was enlarged, the eastern quadrangle was rebuilt in 1827 and the building was again extended in 1833. Further Acts of Parliament relating to the premises were passed over the years including, in 1813, a provision that the declared House of Correction within the Workhouse be available for lunatics and 'for other purposes'.

In 1849, however, the guardians resolved to build a new workhouse on land the Hospital had been endowed with from the beginning. One of several sites, this was the 'Moore Splatt north of Crosse Downe' (Greenbank) where the new building would come to form with the 'modern' Hospital and the Prison part of the trinity of establishments remembered as Faith, Hope and Charity.

Meanwhile, the site of the 'venerable pile with its quadrangle, its large Bridewell, its pound for hemp beating, its cells, dormitories, hall and numerous offices was eventually sold to the Corporation of the borough (in 1857 for £3,250) as part of the site for the New Guildhall and Municipal buildings.'

Yogge's Tower

'St Andrew, or Old Church, though it has suffered from over praise, is a noble fabric, of which Plymouthians may well be proud; and the massive proportions and simple dignity of its tower – unexcelled for boldness and effect in the county – go far to redeem what may be regarded by some as the faults of the remainder of the building – essentially, however, a typical Devonshire Perpendicular church. The oldest portion of the present fabric is in part the south chancel aisle, which dates from 1385; and there are no means of forming an opinion as to what its predecessor was like, though probably it was Late Norman.'

That is how RN Worth opened his account of St Andrew's Church in 1890. Since that time the main body of the church has been completely rebuilt following the devastation caused by enemy bombing in the Blitz. For several years after the war the church walls stood unprotected from the elements on both sides, the floor area having been laid out as a garden. Unfortunately there appears to have been no attempt made during this period to excavate the foundations and dig up the past of this site. Fortunately,

however, the oldest complete part of the Church, as it stood in 1890, survived the war unscathed and that was the massive tower, together with all its contents, its bells and its clock.

Two dates have been put forward for the building of the tower- 1440: 'The tower of Saint Andrew's Church was built this year at the expense of Mr Thomas Yogge, a merchant of the town', and 1460. Both versions credit the 'Marchaunt' Yogge with providing funds, but one version claims that it was William and not Thomas Yogge. John Leland in his account of the story written around the times of his travels in the 1530s and early 1540s notes that Thomas Yogge 'paid of late yeres for making of the Steple of Plymmouthe Cherch, [but] the Toun paid for the Stuffe'. In other words Yogge paid for the labour, the Town for the materials.

Leland went on to say that 'This Thomas Yogge made a fair House of More Stone on the Northe side of the Chirch Yard of Plymmouthe Paroche Chirch; [he also] build[ed] a fair Chapel on the Northside of Plymmouthe Chirch.'

Despite the fact that Leland's record is one of the earliest references we have on this subject, historians have tended to feel after looking at other sources that all is not quite right with this account.

Thomas Yogge had at least two sisters and almost certainly two brothers, one of whom, William was Mayor of Plymouth four times; 1459–60, 1461–62, 1467–68 and 1470–71. William died, childless, in 1472 just two years after he had been appointed Controller of Customs within the port. His brother John was appointed his executor and he left money to the fabric of St Andrew's (or St Uthu's as Leland Called it), to the town's defences and to the two friaries. William was the most likely candidate for contributing to the tower, while it was undoubtedly Thomas who built the fair house of moor stone to the side of the church, although as Jennifer Barber suggests in her paper on 'Yogge's House or Prysten House', this must 'surely be the Finewell Street house and Leland's use of 'north' one of his not infrequent slips'.

While we may not have all the information we would like about those distant times, one or two curious details have been handed down from this period; we are told, for example, that the Mayor in 1440 was Walter Clovelly, nicknamed Goat's Face, for his extreme long beard, which he made a vow he should never be cut or shaven, after the death of his wife. In 1457, just before we believe the tower to have been built, we learn that the then Mayor, John Carynnick, affecting the custom of his betters 'excited no small diversion by walking to church in a laced bonnet and with silver buckles on his shoes'.

Of William Yogge himself we are told that he was the antithesis of Carynnick, that he was 'a close, thrifty man, proud of no exterior show, but much bent on amassing wealth'. This picture is further coloured when we imagine this four time Mayor not disdaining 'to carry home his little Sunday joint from the Market, and when he was twitted with degrading his office, sourly retorting that it was a poor horse that was ashamed to bear its provender to the stable'. Whatever personal qualities Yogge might have been 'twitted' with or reproached for there can be no denying that his generosity was in large part responsible for Plymouth's most enduring landmark although it is hard now to imagine just how St Andrew's Church tower would have towered above the little town of Plymouth which then stood almost entirely to its south and east, tucked around Sutton Harbour.

St Andrew's Tower

'Thirty years ago Bedford-street was much narrower than it is today, in fact, not wider throughout than its present narrowest part, and its eastern end was even narrower than that. The wall of the churchyard extended several feet further north and east than at present, while against the churchyard wall were some miserable houses. Catherine-street was simply a narrow lane, approached from Bedford-street by a rugged flight of steps.'

In this way WHK Wright, in 1879, unwittingly described the view shown here although Wright was actually in the middle of an account of the view offered from the top of St Andrew's Church tower. Looking down from his lofty vantage point over 100 steep steps above ground level, he recounted how the churchyard was said to have been enclosed back in 1596 when it was then known to have occupied a considerable area. Over the years it was encroached upon 'by building a row of shambles and other houses on part of the churchyard, and on the west side by the building of the Hospital, where the Vicar had anciently a house.' These 'obstructions' were removed in 1813 when the streets and roadways were widened. A tablet, formerly in the churchyard wall and now laid flat in front of the church commemorates these improvements.

Further developments followed, notably the lowering of the ground around the church, the net result being that the tower was now 'thrown open to view in every direction'.

Back inside the tower and thanks largely to the exertions of Charles Norrington, two new bells, trebles, were presented to St Andrew's, in 1874, by the senior MP for the town, Edward Bates. This brought the number in the peal to ten, and those ten bells have rung unchanged from that day to this.

Sadly Charles Norrington died in 1877 at the age of 25. Also still in the tower today is the Carillon and Westminster Quarter Chimes presented to the town by Charles's father, Charles snr, in 1878. The Carillon contains fourteen tunes, sacred and secular, and they were set so that the tune was changed each day in fortnightly rotation. A wondrous thing in its own right, the Carillon has not been heard for many long years.

The bells themselves have an interesting history and although there is no direct reference to them until 1501 it can be assumed that there have been bells in the tower since it was built forty years earlier. In 1594 we know that there were 'fyve newe belles cast at the Townes only charge'. The bells were cast in a furnace built in the town and the total cost was £293 12s. 4d. Drake and Hawkins gave a broken piece of brass cannon towards the project.

In 1631 the peal was evidently recast and the Church books throughout the seventeenth century are liberally sprinkled with references to special occasions upon which the bells were rung; 1639–40, in remembrance of God's gracious deliverance from the Spanish invasion; 1641–42, at the rejoicing for the pacification between England and Scotland; 1643, in memorial of the Sabbath-day fight; 1685, on the news of Charles II recovering ...and so on.

In the severe winter of 1708–9 disaster struck the tower and a mighty lightning and thunder clap threw down one of the great pinnacles. Whatever the consequences were are unclear but we are told that Colonel Jory gave the church a new ring of bells that same year. Part of the church wall was torn down by lightning in 1727 'some with the surprise was struck down backward to ye ground', but this time it appears that the tower escaped unscathed.

One of the bells was recast in 1733 and then, in 1749 as a consequence of the tenor having cracked, the six bells were recast, by Thomas Bilbie of Cullompton, into a peal of eight with the addition of more metal. Quite how well the new peal was housed we cannot tell but three years later two of the bells fell while in full swing and caused great damage to the belfry and the church . . .' the necessary repairs amounting to quite a considerable sum'.

No further changes were rung until 1839 when the tenor again cracked and it was recast, by Thomas Mears of London, this time as a slightly smaller bell.

For over 200 years it was the custom for the bells of St Andrew to ring a merry peal annually on the Saturday night preceding the 25th July in commemoration of the defeat of the Armada, however, as Worth lamented in 1890 '. . . the nineteenth century put an end to this interesting practice'. Throughout the twentieth century too there has been a tendency to ring the bells less frequently in celebration of such anniversaries and royal birthdays, although they were rung for the 400th anniversary of the Armada.

Bill Myers, who looks after the bells today, can remember ringing with his father, George, on Armistice Day in 1918 and together with George's other two sons Tom and Fred, the family have been responsible for the bells and the clock since 1914. Futhermore, just as the bells survived the blitz, so too did the clock, the four faces of which kept good time throughout the war and beyond stopping only ever for repairs and repainting. Electrically wound, the mechanical clock of St Andrew's that we see today was made by Thomas Mudge of London in 1706, the four dials were affixed in 1857 by Frank Goulding of Plymouth.

St Andrew's Church Interior

In 1812 there was a plan put forward to divide St Andrew and Charles into four new parishes, there was, however, no immediate action taken. Six years later there was actually a proposal to divide St Andrew's Church into two places of worship with the construction of a 'Babylonish wall' across the building, fortunately this plan was not acted upon either. However, it had been over 300 years since there had been any major change to the structure of the fabric of St Andrew's, apart from the 'choking with pews and galleries', and the long years of neglect '. . . imperatively called for restoration'.

'Year after year the painter and plasterer had added another coat of whitewash and colour to the granite pillars and sculptured images, already buried in such accretions to the depth of an inch'(Whitfeld). One of the main reasons for this neglect it would appear was the scandalous system of pew rentals under which 'people who did not often visit Plymouth, and had only a remote connection with it, bought the seats as a speculation and re-leased them to parishioners . . . By these means they reaped substantial profits, and the Church was destitute of revenues to meet the deficiencies'.

So it was that in 1825 that celebrated architect John Foulston was called in to draw up plans to 'restore' St Andrew's. In the event Foulston's scheme arranged for; the illegal seat holdings to be abolished, for 100 seats to be set apart for the Corporation, for 500 seats to be made available to the poor and for the remainder to be let at annual rentals.

As for the building itself, the church was cleared from one end to the other in April 1826 with the screens and a number of other valuable items being sold by auction. Foulston, by pulling down the old unsightly galleries and putting up new ones, was able to double the amount of accommodation inside the church, but it meant that the tower arch was blocked and the gangways were narrowed and his efforts by no means met with universal approval.

'Irreparable mischief was then done, for Mr Foulston had no feeling for Gothic art' (Worth). Foulston applied 'his Gothic art with little respect for antiquity and he reduced the church to a mere shadow of itself' (Whitfeld).

Foulston's work is clearly shown in the drawing by Thomas Allom shown here and executed around 1830; it shows the large organ loft and gallery at the west end, beneath which was sited the vestry where parish meetings were held, it also shows the galleries in each of the transepts supported by arches and the 'huge three-decker' pulpit.

The dissatisfaction with Foulston's work was resolved in the 1870s when another more major restoration was undertaken. Sir Gilbert Scott was the architect in charge on this occasion, although much of the work was drawn up by James Hine, who had been responsible for the design of the new pulpit a few years earlier. Hine's 'extremely beautiful' pulpit was constructed by Harry Hems of Exeter. Octagonal and principally made of fine Corsham Down stone on a base of Penryn granite, it cost £150.

The main changes effected in the mid-1870s-restoration were the removal of the galleries which returned the interior to the simple open space it had originally been. The organ was also moved at this time – to the north chapel or transept. Built by James Parsons of the Dockyard in 1737, it had been greatly enlarged in 1859 and improved in 1870 and with its moving it was rebuilt and enlarged once again, as indeed it was just prior to its destruction in 1941.

Sadly, of course, almost all of the non-structural features of St Andrew's were destroyed during the air raid of the early hours of the morning of 22 March 1941, and just as the original ancient glass had been lost 300 years before in the Civil War, so none of the more modern glass survived the Second World War. Indeed apart from the tower, the church itself barely survived – the roof went as did most of the furnishings, leaving only the walls.

For many years left in its skeletal state and laid out as a 'garden church', services continued to be held here from time to time, in order to maintain an unbroken tradition of worship, and eight years after it had been ravaged a service was held here to inaugurate the repair work. Princess Elizabeth, the future Queen, laid the stone commemorating the beginning of the most major restoration the church has ever seen on the 22nd October 1949. Eight years on again – on St Andrew's Day, 30th November 1957, St Andrew's Church was officially re-consecrated and re-opened. The only really significant changes to its pre-war layout being two small vestry extensions on the south side of the church.

Ebenezer Chapel

John Wesley was born in Lincolnshire in 1703, he was ordained in 1728. His father was also a priest. In 1729 he returned to Oxford where he had first gone to study eight years earlier and when there took over the leadership of a religious study group established by his younger brother Charles. This group frequently practised communion, had regular habits of devotion and among their many deeds of social service, they were wont to make prison visits. Before long the group had earnt themselves many nicknames, the most popular being either 'the holy club' or the 'methodists'. After a few years the group went their separate ways but not before George Whitfield had been recruited to their ranks.

In April 1739 John Wesley was persuaded by Whitfield to preach in the open air at Bristol. Recently fired by an enlightening experience in London, the much travelled Wesley wanted to bring new spiritual vigour to the church of England and to this end, the following month, he had laid the foundations for a religious society in Bristol. Complete with a chapel, school and hostel, Wesley alone bore the financial responsibility. Similar developments followed around the country and in 1744 Whitfield visited Plymouth, intending to embark for America. A study class was formed here the following year and by the time Wesley himself first visited the town in 1746 he found several zealous preachers

hard at work. Preaching was conducted out of doors at many different locations around the town; on the Parade, in Catte Street, under a tree in Briton Side, in the Old Mitre in Southside Street and in a Moravian preaching place on the site of the old Exchange in Woolster Street.

Life was not easy for these nonconformists however and 'castigation' of congregations was regarded by naval officers as a 'chartered humour, and their military colleagues despatched regimental bands to disturb open-air preachers'. This only had the effect of making those so persecuted even more determined to assert themselves and in 1779 a carpenter called Redstone and a dockyard quarterman, Nehemiah Jane, established the first Wesleyan chapel in the Three Towns, in Lower Street. In 1792, the year after Wesley died, Philip Shepheard laid the foundation stone of a larger chapel which could accommodate 500 souls. This building was erected in the garden of Mr Prideaux's house in Mud Lane (later to become Buckwell Street) and most of the fittings from the Lower Street Chapel were installed here.

The harassment by no means ended just because services were being conducted indoors, however, and there were regular interruptions. A gang of brawlers were pounced upon in one incident in 1812 by 'the more muscular members of the congregation and transferred to the custody of the watchmen'. They were later released but only on the

condition that they publicly promised to abstain from such conduct in the future. A humiliating apology was subsequently published for their having made 'a great noise, thereby disturbing a congregation of people called the Methodists'.

The congregation had grown considerably by this time and in 1813 the Plymouth Circuit was formally constituted and in October of that year it held its first Quarterly Meeting; new premises were actively sought. On the 15th March 1816 they were found for on that day Thomas Tanner, a baker from Treville Street, and Richard Lethbridge, a baker and grocer from Old Town Street, completed the purchase of this site from Commissioner Fanshawe of the Dockyard (there was a certain irony in this for it was Fanshawe who threatened to discharge Dockyard workers if they continued to attend the nonconformist Unitarian Chapel in Devonport).

At that time this land, which had once belonged to Sir Francis Drake (his name appears on the deeds) was on the outskirts of town, before long of course it was to be surrounded by developments. The foundation stone for this new Chapel was laid on Tuesday 4th June 1816, it was to be called the Ebenezer Chapel. The name itself comes from a Hebrew word meaning 'stone of help' and consequently is often used as a symbol of nonconformity; the Baptists also established an Ebenezer Chapel in 1816, in Union Street. It is interesting to note too that Lethbridge christened his son, born two days after the deeds were signed, Ebenezer.

Originally sited at the top of what was called for a while Ebenezer Lane, and what became Saltash Street, this building was added to in 1858 when a school and minister's house were erected, and was further extended in 1892 and 1908. Essentially however it retained its early appearance both outside and in, until fire destroyed the Wesleyan Chapel in Ham Street in 1937. This congregation had only recently been joined by the Cobourg Street Methodists and so a decision was taken to solve the accommodation situation by reconstructing the Ebenezer Chapel as a more spacious edifice – the Methodist Central Hall. Completed in 1940 and providing a valuable role for the city throughout the war years, that is how it stands today; the side windows and the rooms at the rear of the building still there as a reminder of how it looked all those years ago.

Old Town Street

'There was living in Old Town Street, not more I believe than twenty years ago, an extremely old lady, who kept a tripe shop there, and who remembered the time – probably about when Dr Johnson was here – when most of the houses in Old Town Street were covered with thatch. Could this venerable individual be permitted to revisit the scene of her mortal occupation, and supposing she had a taste for architecture as well as for tripe, she would be rather interested as well as astonished, I think, in noticing in the place of her old shop and other old buildings, (which, if they had no other recommendation, were at least easy to get at when the roofs and chimney tops were out of order) an assemblage of great houses in the Roman-Corinthian, Anglo-Italian, Lombardo-Venetian, and other styles too numerous to mention, constituting a sort of second edition in bricks and mortar of Mr Wightwick's "Palace of Architecture".'

So observed local architect John Hine in his review of the *Ancient Buildings of Plymouth* at the beginning of the 1860s, almost 100 years after the famous Dr Johnson had visited the town. In those 100 years Old Town Street had undoubtedly undergone a great deal of change, there can be little doubt however that were Mr Hine to be permitted to revisit this scene 100 years later it would be he that who be the most interested and astonished.

In 1762 when the celebrated lexicographer came to Plymouth, he would have found at the bottom of Old Town the old Shambles. Built in 1656, this was a narrow range of buildings 200 feet by 12 running northwards up the middle of the street from the town conduit at the junction of St Andrew's churchyard, Whimple Street and Old Town Street. There were at that time no turnings off the western side of Old Town Street until you arrived outside the Old Town gate at the Old Town conduit. Coming back down the eastern side of the street, just before the Shambles itself, you would have encountered Week Street and Butchers Lane.

Butchers Lane was a name given to Treville Street sometime around the middle of the eighteenth century. Quite why the name was changed is unclear but it was a common enough practice at the time; Week Street was known for a time as Duck's Lane. It would seem that the reason for choosing the name Butchers Lane was quite simply that there was, at the bottom of the lane, an inn called 'Butchers Arms' which was evidently 'a great resort for farmers of inordinate drinking capacity'.

On the 18th October 1803 the Improvement Commissioners responsible for Lighting, Paving and Watching decided that this nonsense had gone on long enough and that the 'lane modernly called Butchers Lane in this borough shall in future resume and be called or distinguished by its proper ancient name of Treville Street'. It was originally named after the local family of successful Elizabethan merchants, the Trevills.

In 1804 a new market was opened behind the western side of Old Town Street and the inappropriately named East Street was cut through the bottom half of Old Town Street to meet up with it. Eight years later Drake Street was constructed at top end of the street, thereby creating another access into the market.

As the town developed yet more demands were made upon this area and in the late 1870s Market Avenue (sometimes called Old Town Lane) was created following the demolition of No 25 Old Town Street which stood right next to the building of which only the corner is showing on the left hand side of this view. Once home to the 'Cornish Inn', this corner site appears to have been rebuilt at the same time as Market Avenue was created, nos 23 and 24 subsequently being occupied by the Golden Boot Company and Jacob Best's Ironmongery (which had previously been based in the corner building on the opposite side of the road shown here on the right). By 1897, though, these buildings were added to Stidston's Old Town Street business. Originally operating as Stidston, Moulder and Stidston, linen and woollen drapers, the firm had already been in Nos 21 and 22 for more than 20 years and were to continue here for at least another ten years.

As for the main block shown here, we can see clearly the name of Henry Preston who worked here for some 25 years, until the early 1890s, as a hairdresser and was succeeded in the business by TW Jeffery who carried on as a coiffeur in the same building for a similar duration.

The view here from the corner of Ebrington Street, shows this part of Old Town Street in the middle of its 1880s reconstruction, the delightful-looking corner building here being soon after pulled down and a 'very prominent and attractive' building being constructed on the new north corner of Market Avenue and Old Town Street. The buildings being occupied for many years afterwards by JN Taylor another draper who in 1894 boasted that 'the attendance afforded by the numerous staff is at all times prompt and polite'. The same piece of publicity also noted that 'the terminus of the recent new line of tramcars is within one minute's walk of the shop, which will be a boon to visitors from Mutley, Mannamead, and the surrounding districts'.

At the other end of this block of buildings, just out of sight, where Drake Street turned off Old Town Street, stood, for most of the nineteenth century, an inn which by name remembered one of the great British heroes of the Napoleonic age, Sir Edward Pellew (1757–1833), who in 1814 was given a peerage by George III and was thereafter known as Lord Exmouth. Pellew performed many impressive feats of daring in his time but was perhaps best remembered locally for his almost single handed rescue of 500–600 souls from the transport ship *Dutton* wrecked off the Hoe in the violent storms of the 26th January 1796.

The Rose and Crown

'In the 'Rose and Crown', one of the oldest Plymouth hostelries, we seem to have a survival of the War of the Roses, and certainly the appearance of the old inn, as shown in the sketch, points to it having dated from very early times.' (WHK Wright, *Streets of Old Plymouth*, 1901)

Scant as this information is, it is nevertheless as much as any of the history books have ever had to say about this ancient inn which stood for well over 300 years in Old Town Street on the corner of Week Street. The suggestion that it was a relic of the War of the Roses is based on the fact that many English inns adopted the name 'Rose and Crown' in the aftermath of the marriage of Henry VII to Elizabeth. Twenty-year-old Elizabeth was one of Edward IV's four daughters and her marriage with Henry in 1486 brought to an end the civil wars which had been raging up and down the country for 30 years.

Fought between the houses of Lancaster (red rose) and York (white rose), the first battle was at St Albans in May

1455. Won by the Yorkists, Henry VI soon after became a prisoner, for a second time, of the man who had deposed him, Edward IV. Edward had usurped the throne in 1461 and held on to it (but for a brief period during 1470–71 when Henry was reinstated) until his death in 1483. He in turn was succeeded by his 12-year-old son Edward who was deposed by his uncle Richard III, his father's only surviving brother. Edward was subsequently murdered in the Tower of London. Richard III, meanwhile, carried on the Yorkist regime until he was defeated in battle at Bosworth by the future Henry VII.

This was doubtless a popular outcome locally for, although there was never any fighting in Plymouth, some of the key figures in the drama came here and sympathy generally is thought to have been with Lancastrians. In 1461 the French King had sent troops here to support the Lancastrian cause. Ten years later Warwick, the Kingmaker, turned against Edward IV and persuaded the King's brother Clarence to do the same and together with others they landed here and were dined in the Guildhall, proclaiming Henry VI king once again. Warwick was subsequently killed at Barnet and Clarence returned to his brother's side.

Finally in 1483 the future Henry VII, then calling himself the Duke of Richmond, came 'with a great navy and army of strangers to Plymouth'. He didn't land here, however, and, along with many eminent westcountry figures, spent that winter in exile in Brittany before returning the following year to Milford Haven and success at Bosworth.

The fighting finally over, it is indeed quite feasible that the 'Rose and Crown' commemorated the end of the struggle between the two Royal Houses. However, what is not so clear is whether another old Old Town Street inn, the 'White Hart', also dated from the fifteenth century, for that badge or emblem is traditionally associated with the Yorkist King Richard II.

The 'White Lion' is another Yorkist emblem for that was the badge of Edward IV and was the name of an old inn in Tavistock Street. The Lancastrians, meanwhile, were it seems represented by the sign of the 'White Swan', the badge of Edward of Lancaster who fell at Shrewsbury in 1403, for until recently that was the name of the St Andrew Street inn now known as the 'Pen and Parchment'. Plymouth also once had a 'Red Lion' and that name was usually

chosen in honour of the Lancastrian, John of Gaunt.

But to return to the 'Rose and Crown', in the sixteenth century this would have been one of the northernmost inns in the town, Old Town Street being then a lone street projecting up towards the town wall beyond the main body of the town. In 1585 we find the first mention of Week Street intercepting it, shown here on the corner by the two figures. The name apparently derives from the old English *wic* meaning dairy farm.

For two centuries there was little or no development beyond Old Town Street and Week Street on its eastern side, then came another time of war and a period of great expansion and prosperity for Plymouth. Matthew Lapp was the licensee here throughout the Napoleonic Wars and doubtless many a story was told by soldiers and sailors within these walls during that time.

During the first half of the nineteenth century this whole area became surrounded by development and Old Town Street was gradually 'modernised' and started losing its old town flavour. Henry Hoare was landlord here when the 'White Hart' across the road closed its doors for the last time. As other old buildings fell, still the 'Rose and Crown' survived and E Kissell, with his name bold across the door, continued to serve his customers in the 1890s as further alterations hit the street.

Throughout the First World War it was EW Beck that kept this great and ancient inn open. Sadly, however, it was the local demolition men of the 1920s and not the enemy bombs of the 1940s that finally destroyed this irreplaceable timepiece, which had gradually become almost lost in a street of high buildings that, in the end, towered high above it. Today, of course, nothing survives of even nineteenth century Old Town Street although the present street of that name follows much the same line. Week Street has gone altogether and today the Royal Bank of Scotland occupies the site of the old junction, while the 'Rose and Crown' stood on land now occupied by the Post Office.

Originally it was a Pearl Assurance building that rose up on the site of the 'Rose and Crown', next door to an earlier piece of rebuilding that since 1897 had housed Butland the tailor (Butland and Treloar since 1910). Prior to that Sleeman's dining rooms had been next door and they subsequently moved up to No 86.

The Old Four Castles

'Old Four Castles. 1722. Mr John Codd's Packhorses will set out for Exon on Tuesdays, Thursdays, and Saturdays, and come in on the other days. Goods for London are to be brought to the warehouse at the Inn and 'twill be in London the Saturday sevennight after.'

Quoted in Bracken's *History of Plymouth*, this advertisement appeared in a newsheet of 1722 and gives us flavour of days long gone when a journey to London in under a day was absolutely inconceivable. Even so this doubtless was an improvement on earlier days before the turnpiking of many major roads.

Standing only some ten doors up from the 'Rose and Crown' in Old Town Street the 'Old Four Castles' was another of the street's celebrated ancient inns. Of its early history we know very little save that Thomas Pike was landlord here in 1657, the year Oliver Cromwell was offered the English crown by Parliament under the terms of the 'Humble Petition and Advice'. Fearing the republicanism of the army, Cromwell declined and in Plymouth £3 10s was spent at the 'proclaymenge of his highnes the Lord Protector of the Commonwealth of England'. At the 'Four Castles' Thomas Pike struck a token and ten trees were planted in the New Churchyard.

This was the churchyard of the new Charles Church which, although begun before the Civil War began, was only completed in 1657. Indeed it is said that the half finished walls were used by Plymouth's Parliamentarian sympathizers to stable horses during the Royalist seige of the town. It is to the walls of an even earlier structure that we must look, however, to find the source of the name of this particular Old Town Street hostelry; the 'Four Castles' is named after the same 'castle quadrate' that gave us the town crest – four castles around a saltire. The four castles in question being the towers of the medieval fortress overlooking the entrance to Sutton Pool. Largely rendered obsolete by the construction of the Royal Citadel on the Hoe by Charles II (designed to ensure there was never to be a repeat of the civil war saga in this area at least) only a part of the old castle now survives; of the 'Four Castles Inn' though nothing at all survives.

Closed in 1895, the 'Old Four Castles' was pulled down

the following year as, it would appear, was the 'Old Town Inn' three doors up the street, victims both of the Victorian redevelopment of the area. Interestingly enough as Plymouth was being extended around the middle of the nineteenth century, two of the town's new streets had hostelries that reflected the modernization mentality for there was the 'New Four Castles' in Russell Street and the 'New Town Inn' in York Street, two Victorian thoroughfares now buried beneath the modern city centre.

There were at least a dozen watering holes in 'Old Town Street' in the middle of the nineteenth century, in addition to the 'Old Four Castles' and the ancient 'Rose and Crown' there was the equally venerable 'White Hart'. The 'White Hart' was another favourite coaching inn. Old Town Street was after all the main route out of the town as the main road to London was formerly via Tavistock.

An indication of the ever improving service to London, incidentally, is given in another eighteenth-century advertisement which reveals that in 1760, around the time that the stage coach first reached Plymouth, the journey to London had been cut to about five days.

Other Old Town Street inns included the town's other 'Ring of Bells', the 'Jubilee Spirit Vaults', the 'Commercial Hotel', the 'Golden Lion', the 'Cornish Inn' and the 'Devonshire Inn' (which stood next door to each other), the 'Half Moon', the 'Lord Exmouth' and the 'Bedford'. Of them all, only two really outlived the Victorian redevelopment of the street, although there were three others, including the 'Rose and Crown' that managed to limp into the twentieth century.

At the corner of Bedford Street, at the entrance to Old Town Street was the 'Jubilee', strangely enough renamed the 'Telegraph' soon after Queen Victoria's Jubilee. This subsequently became part of the Spooners site (by 1903) as did the 'Commercial' (by 1909). In later years the 'Commercial' ('Capital family and travellers house' 1824) was better known as Chubb's Hotel; Francis Chubb had taken over the place in the 1840s and it continued to be run by members of his family for the next 40 years or so.

Another look at an old coaching ad shows how far the travel situation had improved by 1830, for it is from then

that we read of the Subscription New Light Coach 'conveying four inside and ten outside passengers' leaving John Hannaford's 'Commercial Inn' in Old Town Street at half past three in the morning, passing now through 'Ridgway, Ivybridge, Buckfastleigh, Ashburton and Chudleigh, arriving at the 'Half Moon Hotel', Exeter, at four o'clock in the afternoon'. It then proceeded at six through Ilminster, Wincanton and Salisbury and arrived at the 'Bull and Mouth', London at half past three the following afternoon.

The two longest standing survivors in the street, though, were the 'Golden Lion' and the 'Bedford'. The site of the 'Golden Lion' was among the first to be cleared after the Second World War although its licence was kept up until 1960 when it was finally surrendered and transferred to the 'Two Trees' in Union Street. The 'Bedford', meanwhile, survived the war Tom Elliott running it through the post war years into the 1960s when as the 'Bedford Vaults' it finally met its end. This inn like so many of its old Old Town Street counterparts had stabling facilities, they backed on to Caxton Mews, and when the 'Bedford' went, a piece of Plymouth's heritage passed into the history books.

Old Town Gate

that 'Old Town' has been fussily modernised into 'Old Town Street', but the memory of the original site is happily preserved.

While not disputing the antiquity of Old Town itself, Crispin Gill, in his *New History of Plymouth* (1966) suggests that the Valletort residence was nearer Sourpool (between Millbay and Derry's Cross) and that Old Town was the name given to the first farm, the original Sutton and that old Town Street ran up to it. 'A detached house in its own garden (it was called Norley latterly, to confuse the issue) stood on the site until, in our times, the telephone exchange was built there.'

Whatever the medieval history of Old Town may be, we do know that until 1809 this gate stood at the top of Old Town Street (roughly on the site of the present C&A building) and that until it was demolished there was very little development 'without it' or beyond it. Quite how long this gate had stood though is another mystery. We do know that his engraving was taken from a 'curious old painting' (Jewitt) and that in 1759 it was rebuilt from plans and elevations drawn up by John Eastridge and Oliver Anstis. Prior to this, in 1656, we learn from the town records that the gate then measured 42 feet east to west and 18 feet north to south and was said to have been 'lately erected by the Mayor and Commonalty'. We are also told that William Yeo had just acquired the lease and that John Watts had '. . . lately there dwelt.'

This, however, would also just have been a rebuilding for the town's gates we know were in place during the Civil War and for centuries before that, the belief being that there was some kind of wall around the town from the early fifteenth century at least.

For a long time, though, this gate would have stood some way from the main body of the town, the population not significantly increasing from the 7,000 or so that it was in 1377 until the late eighteenth century. The original picture here doubtless dates from around this time and shows clearly two developments, one, fairly recent, the other, the old town conduit, which itself was removed in 1834.

'The Valletorts were the first to stimulate the fortunes of Plymouth. King Henry 1 gave the manor of Sutton, with those of Maker and Kings Tamerton, to Reginald of Valletort; and either Reginald or his successors made it a place of residence.' The original site of their garden and park were described in early deeds (1370 and 1373) as 'at the west part of Churcherhull, the way from Sutton to Stonhous lying north, the meadow of William Cole south and the land of Thomas Cok called Romisbury west.' Thus quotes Worth in his *History of Plymouth* (1890). The residence itself

he suggests 'would be nearly adjacent to the church' (Churchull being the hill on which stands St Andrew's Church). 'Here, by the side of the mansion of its Valletort lords, the germ of the ancient Plymouth, for centuries known as Old Town, was planted and grew. The day came when Sutton Prior beat it in the race; but the village of the Valletorts was the real beginning of Plymouth Town; and its superior antiquity was visible at Leyland's visit when he found it "sore decayed".' (1538)

Worth then concluded his piece on this area by noting

Old Town Conduit

'The "destruction" of the Conduit, at the head of Old Town Street, has been lamented . . . Now, it may be consoling to observe that, for "destruction" we may read removal and renovation. The front of the building has been identically re-erected in the wall on the east side of the road to North hill, with the addition of two or three hitherto neglected and valuable fragments of the Drake period, and a tablet in compliment to the present Mayor.'

So wrote architect George Wightwick in a letter to the Editor of the *South Devon Monthly Museum*, in time for the issue dated 1st of March 1834. As the architect behind this destruction, Wightwick had clearly come in for some harsh criticism and he went on to say '. . . If, as an instrument in this work, I lose any portion of any good man's esteem, let me endeavour in a measure to re-instate myself by graphically restoring the revered building, precisely as it originally stood. . . . The annexed view is from an accurate sketch taken about a fortnight before the work of removal commenced . . . Peace to the remains of Francis Drake!'

Since its rebuilding in 1670 this conduit 'house' had stood, unaltered, just a few yards to the north of the Old Town Gate, a site it appears to have occupied since the end of the sixteenth century when it was first erected. The carving running around its top reads 'Made in the Maioraltie of John Trelawnye 1598'. The carving of the King's arms, the arms of the town and those of Drake, however, date from the 1670 rebuilding; mason John Somerton was paid £6 for this work. The Kings arms of course were those of Charles II, in whose honour, ten years earlier, the town's conduits had been made to flow – for two days – with wine, following the 'Glorious Restoration'.

This phenomenon was made to happen again on the 14th of May 1713 after the War of Spanish Succession had been ended with the signing of the Treaty of Utrecht, an

agreement that brought to an end many years of European struggle and set England on to imperial and commercial greatness. Three other conduits are recorded as flowing with wine that day; Martin's, New Quay and Pope's Head, the latter being at the top of Looe Street.

Prior to the construction of the Elizabethan leat, water was obtained from a number of local wells or from one of the earlier conduits, supplied either from a well or one of two streamlets which once flowed through the town. As the local population expanded, however, such sources were far from sufficient and although Drake's leat gave Plymouth one of the first municipal water supplies in the country, it by no means arrived too soon.

For some 230 years the leat, although much repaired and improved, served the town with little alteration, and it was

not until the 1820s that it underwent any extensive modernization. A course of action that was largely precipitated by an extreme water shortage during the winter of 1823. This, combined with the need to supply the new Victualling Yard at Stonehouse, led to the building of Drake's Place Reservoir and a number of other improvements; the remaining public conduits were closed (there had been 27 at one time) and 'the leaden pipes used for conveying water to the houses of inhabitants were taken up, and iron pipes laid through all the principal streets' (CC Whiteford). As a consequence of this then, the Old Town Conduit was deemed to have no further use and in 1827 it ceased to operate.

Not everyone agreed with this situation though and there were long and angry debates about what was seen as the removal of the last free water supply to the poor of the borough. A supply to which it was claimed they had a definite right. The improvements effectively meant that individuals could all now be supplied with water, provided that they pay the appropriate rate. In practice this left many without easy access to fresh water and 20 years later a report revealed that out of 4045 houses in the town, 753 had no water supply and only 437 had cisterns or tanks capable of retaining a 'needful quantity of water'.

For those who were lucky enough to have a direct supply there were still problems, however – the leat was open for most of its length, it was prone to pollution and piracy (people 'stealing' water to power their mills), there was a good deal of wastage and the supply could be intermittent or even nonexistent. In 1855 there was such a severe frost that Plymouth went without water for six days. There were similar problems experienced during the blizzards of 1881 and 1891. Problems which were eventually overcome with the construction of Burrator Reservoir in 1898 and the laying of pipes in place of large vulnerable sections of leat.

Plymouth Public Library

Plymouth Public Library 'originated chiefly in the literary zeal' of Mr George Eastlake in 1810. It started life in the Guildhall in Whimple Street and moved to this impressive purpose-built edifice in 1813. Following the establishment of Plymouth's Free Library in 1876 it became known as the Proprietary and Cottonian Library. Extended in 1853 to accommodate the collection of William Cotton, its frontage was brought into line with the rest of Cornwall Street and it stood little changed until it was completely destroyed in the blitz of 1941.

George Eastlake, father of the celebrated artist Charles Lock Eastlake, was Solicitor to the Admiralty (a post that had been held by the family for several generations) and Judge Advocate of the Admiralty Court. He was well known for his 'literary tastes and acquirements, at a time when intellectual pursuits were less commonly followed than in our own times, the facilities for doing so, prodigiously inferior to those enjoyed by the present generation' (*South Devon Monthly Museum* 1833). He was also always supportive of his son who wrote to him in 1809 from Charterhouse, where he had been sent for schooling, stating, 'when I cease to be a painter I almost cease to live'. Clearly his son had received a good grounding in the arts while just a boy at home in Plymouth. In 1896 his father had written a poem in praise of the heroic efforts of Captain Edward

Pellew, who helped save many lives when the great East Indian sailing ship *Dutton* crashed on the rocks under the Citadel. This eulogy was read at a ceremony which later conferred upon Pellew the Freedom of the Town.

In 1810, then, Eastlake was the leading spirit at a public meeting held at the Guildhall on 20th November, where a number of the town's prominent, and needless to say, wealthy gentlemen agreed to subscribe 30 guineas each towards the establishment of a public library. These gentlemen thereby became the library's first proprietors; among those who made up the first committee – Lord Boringdon (later first Earl of Morley), Sir William Elford Bt, William Eastlake (another of George's sons), William Marshall and Edmund Lockyer.

Eighteen months later, on 19th May 1812, a solemn procession of proprietors made their way from the old Guildhall to this then vacant site in Cornwall Street, where the foundation stone of a new library was to be laid. A band of Royal Marines and the Chief Constable escorted them and when they arrived a porcelain box made at 'the Pottery' was deposited underneath the foundation stone. Later in the year another meeting was called at the Guildhall on Friday 18th December at precisely 12 o'clock to discuss exactly how the library was going to be furnished with books and how the whole enterprise was to be paid for.

In the event the monies raised from 205 subscribers, each paying 30 guineas, paid for the building which cost in the region of £4,000. The building was designed by the man Lockyer had selected in 1811, John Foulston, and so the library was only Foulston's second project in the town. The design, which the architect exhibited at the Royal Academy in 1813, was loosely based on that of the *Choragic Monument of Thrasyllas*. This was an Athenian temple honouring the Greek philosopher of the first century AD and was one of the many ancient remains portrayed in the second volume of the *Antiquities of Athens* published in 1787. Produced by

English architect James Stuart, with Nicholas Revett, the first volume had appeared in 1762 and between them the two books were to have a considerable effect on late eighteenth- and early nineteenth-century architecture. Certainly Foulston found the inspiration for his solo career there and indeed when he finally moved to Plymouth from London around 1813, he came to live in a house on Townsend Hill, which he called 'Athenian Cottage'.

The Greek monument upon which the library was based was particularly popular with architects of the day because its pilasters, i.e. its flat columns against the face of the wall, were easier and cheaper to construct than conventional columns. Records of the early years of Plymouth Public Library were for the most part lost when the building went up in smoke in 1941. We do know, however, that there was an unexpected slump in the affairs of this institution and at one stage the 30 guinea shares could be had for only £10. It was not long before the situation improved again though and by 1833 matters were once more 'in a very prosperous condition', although by this time complaints were being made about the location of the building '. . . We have often wished it had formed a sort of right wing to the hotel and Theatre, the Athenaeum being the left. Twenty years ago, however, it never entered into the imagination of persons in general that Plymouth would have travelled Westward so far and so fast. Instead of so many new streets being added, it was confidently prophesied at the close of the war that the grass would grow in those already built. But how different the fact from that prediction!'

In 1815, when the Napoleonic War ended, the Theatre Royal stood in fields and this library would have stood in the pedestrian precinct just in front of Sherrat and Hughes bookshop. After the last war the library moved to 111 North Hill on the corner of Alton Terrace where it continues to operate today.

Inside Plymouth Public Library

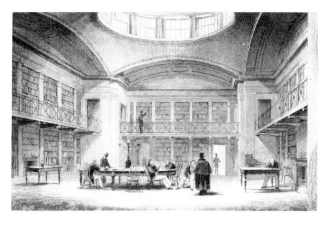

In 1843 the following notice was posted inside this library; 'MUCH inconvenience having been experienced in consequence of the detention of newspapers for a longer time than is compatible with the general accommodation . . . IT WAS RESOLVED at the monthly meeting of the committee of the 6th January 1843, that two sand-glasses, of 15 minutes each, be provided, and gentlemen be limited, in the perusal of a paper, to that time, in case it is required by another member.'

In those days papers were a good deal more expensive in comparative terms than they are now and the library was in great demand for the newspapers it carried; sadly its massive files of early Plymouth journals were among the most distressing losses of the Blitz. There was almost a complete run of papers here from 1805 onwards including such titles as the *Devonport Telegraph and Plymouth Chronicle*, *Plymouth and Dock Telegraph*, *Devonport Independent*, *Plymouth Herald*, *Plymouth Journal*, *Plymouth Mail*, *Plymouth, Devonport and Stonehouse Herald* and others leading up to the 1860s and the birth of the *Western Morning News* and *Western Daily Mercury*.

By this time Plymouth had yet to establish a Free Library and the Cornwall Street venture was very successful. In 1853 it undertook a major extension, primarily to house an important private collection, the 'Cottonian'. This was the property of William Cotton FSA, of Ivybridge who gave his fine collection of books, prints, old master drawings, paintings, manuscripts and *objets d'art* for the 'purpose of Amusement and instruction by the inhabitants of the Towns of Plymouth, Stonehouse and Devonport and their vicinity'. The collection had been started by William Townson who died in 1749 and who left his estate to Charles Rogers who in turn, upon his death in 1784, left it to his nephew William Cotton. In 1816 it was passed on again, to William Cotton jnr, by this time some very valuable items from the collection had been sold but over the years William added to it, his most important contribution being his own collection of Sir Joshua Reynolds' works. Originally Cotton had hoped to found a Reynolds Memorial Institution at Plymp-

ton but it never transpired and so he approached the trustees of the Proprietary Library who agreed to make room for it in Cornwall Street.

It is hard now to imagine the impact this gift would have had on the Three Towns, access to works of art and literature being that much more limited than they are today through books, magazines and television. Of course even then, not all local people could readily use the Proprietary Library's facilities but it was as generous a move as could be imagined in those days and every proprietor did at least have the privilege (among others) 'of nominating one Young Man to the Library, between the Age of Fifteen and Twenty One years as a Reader'. In other words they could come in and look at the material in the Library but they were not allowed to borrow any of it. Nevertheless this was something that many were prepared to pay for; two guineas a year would allow you to visit the Library as a reader only, three guineas would entitle you to use the Newspaper room . . . (in those days one guinea would have been a good weekly wage).

Relying for the most part on natural lighting, readers, like those shown here, were comfortably catered for in this 'lofty quadrangular room'. Thirty-three feet square, there was at each corner 'a massive hollow pier with pilasters, supporting an entableture and cornice, from which spring elegant segmental arches. The whole . . . surmounted by a vaulted dome . . .' A spiral staircase linking the two floors was concealed in one of the piers. Off this main room there was also a committee room and a Law Library.

To accommodate Cotton's Collection a subscription list was opened for the provision of a new room and staircase; Albert, the Prince Consort and Plymouth Corporation set the ball rolling with donations of fifty pounds each. Architect George Wightwick (Foulston's former partner who had taken over the business six months after he joined it, around 1829,when Foulston retired) was commissioned to extend the 40-year-old building. This he did by bringing the frontage of the building out into line with the rest of the street and creating a new entrance with a large room above

it. Fortunately for the city however the Cottonian Collection did not stay in this room – in 1918 it was moved to the newly built City Art Gallery where it can still be found today.

Not so fortunate was the prized 'Halliwell Collection' of Manuscripts presented to the Library by James Orchard Halliwell through the Library's most celebrated Librarian, Llewellyn Jewitt, author of the first published history of Plymouth. This like so many other treasured items was another of the casualties of that fateful night of the 21st–22nd March 1941.

On that night only four of the six fire watchers detailed for Cornwall Street duties arrived at their posts and rather than split up decided to tackle any eventuality together. The alarm soon sounded and of the bombs to fall in this area, a nearby shop fire first claimed their attention and by the time the blaze in the library had been detected the fire had taken it's hold. A passing young naval sub-lieutenant asked if he could help and he made a valiant attempt to save the tin boxes which it was known had been filled with precious items in the event of just such an emergency. Unfortunately these five boxes were upstairs under a table in the committee room and he was unable to reach them. By the time the fire engines arrived the library and its 35,000 volumes were doomed. Only one box kept in the bank and some 400 books out on loan survived.

Relocated after the war on North Hill, the Plymouth Proprietary Library today is open, upon payment of a relatively modest subscription, to anyone keen to find a quiet haven in which to read or borrow any of the books from its substantially replenished shelves.

Freemasons' Hall and Commercial Rooms

'This Building situated in Cornwall Street and contiguous to the Market, holds a prominent rank among the Public Buildings in the Town. It was commenced in the year 1827, by some of the fraternity who were actuated by the laudable spirit of rescuing their order from the stigma attached to it, in consequence of holding their meetings at Inns, &c.' (WPB 1833)

Inns were, prior to the nineteenth century, among the few places that any group of people could meet, other than private houses or religious buildings and so all sorts of organizations were founded in them. The earliest masonic lodge in the Three Towns was formed at Plymouth Dock, in the 'Free Masons Arms', in 1735; 'There was a very Grand Procession from the said Dock to Plymouth Town; a very fine Band of Musick playing before them and the bells ringing at both places . . . They dined at 'Prince Eugene's Head', where a very elegant Entertainment was provided . . . There was such a number of people flocked together on this occasion that was never seen in that country before.' (*St James Evening Post*, London, April 8th 1735)

Originally descended from medieval lodges of operative (ie working) masons, constituted to provide a recognized guild to a group of working men (who because of their work moved around a lot), it appears from the records that from the seventeenth century onwards, 'non operatives' were gradually admitted. Noblemen, landed gentry and men of learning joined lodges 'from motives of patronage and curiosity'.

In 1717 the first 'Grand Lodge' was established in England and in 1786 HRH Duke of Clarence was initiated as a Freemason into Lodge number 86 ('Prince George Lodge' 1748) at the 'Prince George Inn' in Vauxhall Street. In 1813 his elder brother, the Duke of Sussex, helped establish the United Grand Lodge of England with himself as Grand Master. Fourteen years later the Duke of Clarence, now aged 62 and recently appointed Lord High Admiral, was again in Plymouth and attended a gathering of the masonic lodges of the Three Towns. At this gathering he was first congratulated on his appointment and then addressed thus '. . . Under a firm conviction that whatever may tend to the advancement of Free-masonry will receive the unqualified approbation of your Royal Highness, we presume to inform you that a few public spirited brethren are erecting a Masonic Hall, in a central and excellent situation in the borough of Plymouth . . . thereby extending the order, and upholding the respectability of our fraternity in these populous, increasing, and loyal towns.'

The Duke, in reply, thanked his audience, remembered his initiation 42 years earlier and added, 'I shall contribute, with sincere satisfaction, to the erection of the Masonic Hall . . . and thank you for your good wishes towards myself, who will, by a faithful and diligent discharge of my duty, endeavour to obtain the approbation of God and my fellow subjects.'

The hall was opened with great state the following year and two years after that the Duke succeeded his eldest brother (George IV) and became William IV. The Royal William Victualling Yard was completed while this 'sailor-king' was on the throne and he was, in turn, succeeded by his niece Victoria, whose son became ruler of the English craft (of Freemasonry) and who herself not only assisted the society but was one of the largest donors to Masonic Charities, annually subscribing to Funds.

With the walls and ceiling of the Freemasons Hall decorated with many allegorical Greek and Roman scenes, the building was typical of the nineteenth century obsession for the 'classics'. Lodge number 170, 'Fortitude' (1759) was the main one to hold its meetings here and it was represented by a picture of the Roman, Mutius C Scaevola. Other figures depicted characters representing Friendship, Faith, Hope, Charity, Justice and Silence, all being names of some of the lodges of the Three Towns.

One hundred years ago there were 18 lodges meeting in the area, six of whom met here. Today there are over 50 and they meet in one of the six masonic halls in Plymouth today; Manadon, St Aubyn, Huyshe, Davy, Queen Victoria and Mount Edgcumbe in Citadel Road which is the most centrally placed for old Plymouth.

Not long after the turn of the century the Freemasons moved from this building to premises in Princess Square at the same time as the auctioneers Skardon Sons and Hosking, who had also been based in this Cornwall Street building since 1828. From the very beginning there had also been commercial rooms here, with papers from all parts laid on the tables and local information of every kind posted in the room . . . 'the tout ensemble of which is admirable, particularly by night when lighted up with Gas issuing from three splendid chandeliers . . .'

In 1909 this fine old building was taken over by the expanding business of John Yeo & Co, in whose hands it remained until it was completely destroyed in the blitz of March 1941.

The view here, executed in 1832, was taken from the old fish-market while the hall itself occupied the site that today stands between Debenhams and Dingles, in front of the shops in Cornwall Street, half way across the pedestrian precinct.

Plymouth Theatre

Plymouth's first properly documented theatre appears to have been in Broad Hoe Lane (Hoe Gate Street); an improvised structure in which concerts and dramas were presented. Opened towards the middle of the eighteenth century, it would have featured few, if any straight dramatic productions, not because there was no demand for them, but because under the terms of Robert Walpole's licensing act of 1737 such performances were restricted to 'patent theatres' only. In London this meant a virtual monopoly for Drury Lane and Covent Garden, while elsewhere it more or less forced theatres to present only dumb shows and light musical entertainment. However, many regional houses got around this by advertising dramatic performances as concerts... in other words patrons would arrive at the theatre, 'sit through a brief selection of musical items and then be treated in the parts between the music to a free or 'gratis' performance of say, *The Tempest* or *Enchanted Island* with 'the original musick, songs, dances, machinery and decorations proper to the entertainment'. Typically, a hornpipe would be performed between dramatic pieces.

Such is not to say, however, that these evenings were enjoyed in the way we might now imagine. Interruptions, riots and drunkenness were commonplace both in the auditorium and on stage. In 1749 a notorious travelling company of comedians known as the 'Brandy Company' played *The Beaux Strategem* at the Hoe Gate Theatre. Properly known as the 'Bath Players', they achieved their nickname because most of the company drank themselves to death. Banished from Somerset and lately resident in Exeter, they must have felt quite at home in an establishment renowned for fighting and quarreling between casts and audiences.

Before long, though, it became apparent that this makeshift theatre was not up to much more use or abuse as a place of entertainment. So it was that in 1758 the Hoe Gate building was abandoned and Arthur, 'a light comedian of eminence' and one of the more sober members of the 'Bath Players', managed to convert three partly built houses to the far western end of Plymouth (opposite Frankfort Gate) into the early entertainment emporium shown here.

Opened in June 1758, for the first three night's performances there was no roof on the building, such was the hurry to set the new venue up and running. Audiences were undaunted and receipts on the first night were very encouraging (£38) and over the next ten weeks over £1,800 was taken. Clearly the prospects looked good and it did not take long for a similar enterprise to be launched in the rapidly expanding, neighbouring town of Plymouth Dock.

Called simply the 'Dock Theatre', it opened in 1762 and with admission charges similar to those at Frankfort Gate (Box 2s 6d, Pits 1s, Gallery 6d) it meant that Dock theatregoers no longer had to face the inconvenience of an expedition to the ferry crossing at Stonehouse Creek and across the marshy road to Plymouth (Stonehouse Bridge was not begun until 1767 and not opened until 1769).

The attempts to run two theatres in the area, however, soon proved to be a problem for both, quarrels quickly developed and there was even a disastrous attempt to open a third theatre in George Street (the Frankfort Gate Building stood at the junction of Bedford and George Streets, not far from where the sundial stands today). Both theatres weathered the difficulties, though, and before long they had established individual reputations for themselves, Plymouth emerging the slightly more respectable of the two, 'Dock was more popular with the boisterous 'gods' who preferred the 'bluer' jokes' (Harvey Crane 1980). Although James Winston, in his *Theatre Tourist*, published at the end of the nineteenth century, noted that 'The Plymouth taste like that of most other country towns is very far from a refined one, preferring buffoonery to the chastest acting'.

The situation was improving though, thanks, in no small part, to the passing in 1788 of an act which gave local justices the power to license the performance of straight plays for sixty days at a time. This at last went some way to ending the crazy monopoly the two London theatres had on presenting full length plays.

A year later another event was to have a notable effect on the fortunes of the Plymouth theatre, the visit of George III, who was apparently brought here by his local hosts at Saltram. Certainly the visit was a welcome one, particularly as well into the nineteenth century there were complaints that 'private theatricals . . . at local mansions' took a lot of business from the recognised theatres. Following the King's visit the management decided, doubtless unofficially, to raise the status of their establishment to 'Theatre Royal', a title which was to stick, however tenuous.

For all this, though, the theatre was running out of time, it had become structurally unsound.

In 1809 the site was earmarked for the proposed new Theatre Royal. Architect John Foulston, however, had other plans and so the building was left to play out the rest of the century in a variety of other roles. In 1878 it was occupied by GB Eyre, the upholsterer, but it still showed signs of its former uses.

The buildings shown to the left of the theatre, incidentally, were originally part of Frankfort Place and 'among the best houses in the town, residences of some of the wealthiest inhabitants'(Wright).

New Theatre, Frankfort Gate

Theatre going in the early nineteenth and late eighteenth centuries was often much livlier than one can ever imagine it being today. Indeed it was not far from the truth to say that you almost took your life in your hands by simply venturing into such a place. Such was the real threat of dreaded press gangs around the turn of the century, always on the ready to conscript any able bodied man on sight. Small wonder then that in this services-dominated-town the theatre whould be full of drunken Jack tars, rowdy sailors, ready for whatever excitement they could find.

Coupled with this was the fact that the acting profession itself was famous for its low morality. In 1728 the freemen rulers of the Hospital of the Poor's Portion adopted an 'inviolable resolution' that 'in case players or actors of interludes, who by statute law are declared rogues and vagabonds, shall presume to act within the borough of Plymouth,' they should be 'kept in prison to hard labour till the further pleasure of this Corporation herein'. Later in the century, of course, with the provision of a recognised theatre, the situation did improve, the behaviour didn't always though.

Take for example a popular piece of theatre like Shakespeare's *Othello*, although difficult to stage fully and remain within the law, this was a popular work with audiences and thespians alike, but remember these were the days when actors thought more in terms of being heard than in trying to convey a sense of realism and when little attention was paid to set design or historical accuracy.

Therefore picture the scene; Desdemona is discovered by Othello dying on a bed (a plank resting between two chairs) and she is having difficulty staying put:

Desdemona; O, banish me, my lord, but kill me not!
Othello; (Keep yourself up) Down, strumpet.
Des; Kill me tomorrow, let me live tonight. (I shall be over.)
Oth; Nay an you strive. (Lie still you bitch.)
Des; But half an hour! (I'm falling)

They almost finish the scene but then to stop her falling, Othello leans over and trys to keep her steady with his knee whereupon the whole lot goes over and Othello lands in an unseemly position on top of poor Desdemona.

Recorded asides in another production of the same play reveal other aspects of the problems faced by actors in those days. Here we have Mr Hayne playing Othello, unable to

ignore the disturbances in the upper boxes;

'Most potent, grave and reverend seigneurs, my very noble and approved good Masters (I'll tell you what, young fellows, I'll have every one of you in custody before you are aware of it). That I have taken away this old man's daughter is most true. (That young woman with the blue ribbons is as bad as any of you). True I have married her, (What, are you at it again?) She loved me for the dangers I had passed, and I loved her that she did pity them. (Now if there's a constable in the house let him do his duty)'. (Whitfeld)

Discourse between audience and actors was by no means uncommon and constables would often have been too hopelessly outnumbered to be able to assert any real control over the proceedings. Slanging matches frequently degenerated into slinging matches as all manner of items, perishable and otherwise, would be hurled onto and from the stage. There were even occasions when members of the audience would throw themselves onto the stage.

There is a record of yet another production of Othello, this time at the theatre in Plymouth Dock, (which by this time had earnt a reputation for it's rum swilling patrons, with sailors penned apart from 'dissolute women in the hope they would thus be amenable to some decency) . . . Rage and sympathy filled every gallant tar. 'Is the black brute allowed to cut her life lines?' one asked his friend with bated breath, and when Desdemona was seized by the throat as she lay in bed, his companion shouted 'I'm —— if I can stand it any longer.' Throwing himself over the side of the gallery, he called upon his companions to rush to the rescue and in a minute Desdemona was torn from the grasp of the Moor. Othello bolted into the street and rushed in terror through the back lanes to his home, dagger in hand and with warpaint untouched.'

As the nineteenth century progressed, however, so standards on and off stage improved and great advances were made in acting styles, in set design and costume. Following the 1843 Theatre Regulations Act, there was an effective end to the drama monopoly and consequently plays could more readily be presented in their entirety in the provinces, thereby heralding a new era in the theatre.

Westcott's

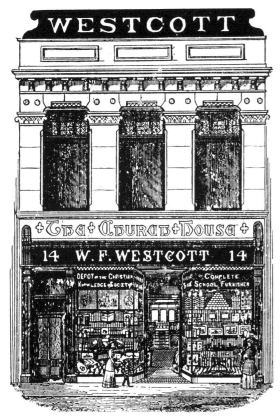

In 1843 William White established an SPCK Bookshop at No 14 Frankfort Street, 20 years later the business was taken over by Leonard Wescott and it remained in the hands of that family until just after the turn of the century. Around 1902, when the western end of Old Town Street was being rebuilt, the Wescott firm was purchased by Underhill's who had previously been based at 74 Old Town Street. Still with the SPCK agency, in 1939 the Frankfort Street premises was completely reconstructed and it re-opened with a very modern, typically 1930s-style frontage; sadly during the air raids of March 1941 the building was totally destroyed .

William PH White was the parish clerk of St Andrew's and he initially advertised his shop as the 'Depository for the Promotion of Christian Knowledge'. The Society for the Promotion of Christian Knowledge had been founded in London many years earlier, back in 1698, by Dr Thomas

Bray together with a group of four laymen (Lord Guilford, Sir Humphrey Mackworth, Mr Justice Hook and Colonel Colchester) its main objectives: to 'consult upon the the best means of promoting religion and learning in any part of his Majesties plantations abroad'; this necessarily entailed supplying and supporting a missionary clergy. Meanwhile, on the home front, in order to 'arrest the terrible decay of religion in this country', they proposed to provide clerical lending libraries in market towns and 'set up catechetical schools for the education of poor children in reading, writing and especially in the principals of Christian religion'.

In pursuing these aims they began publishing their own books and papers, including works by Bray himself and titles such as *The Husbandman's Spiritual Companion*, *The Christian Soldier*, and *Serious Advice and Warning to Servants, more especially those of the Nobility and Gentry*. Chiefly, though, they produced cheap reprints of standard Anglican works and it was these we find heading the list of publications advertised by Leonard Wescott not long after he took over the business in the 1860's.

'For really cheap and well-bound BIBLES, TESTA-MENTS, PRAYER BOOKS, and CHURCH SERVICES, in every large variety inspect the stock at the Christian Knowledge Society's Depot.' Leonard D Wescott, Superintendent. The aforementioned books were all 'supplied to the public at cost price', there was, however, also 'a large assortment of interesting and neatly bound books suitable for presents'. Few books in those days would have had dust-jackets and fewer still pictorial or even colourful jackets.

In addition to selling books, LD Wescott also printed and bound books here in Frankfort Street, indeed they were printers to the 'Ex Libris' Society of London and also did work for authors, publishers, and commercial houses, at home and abroad – they printed the *Commercial Guide to Plymouth* of 1894 in which these two illustrations appeared.

As can be seen from the interior view, Wescott's also had large School and Stationery Departments and they claimed to be the complete school furnishers '. . . exercise books and other material ruled and made up on the premises'.

At that time the Franfort Street premises had only just been rebuilt (1893) and the 60 foot double frontage was a new feature of the shop, which, as it faced road, was somewhat overshadowed by the Winnicott Brother's establishment next door. The shop today would have stood just down from the *Evening Herald* offices in New George Street near WH Smith's. Before the War Garratt's, Ball's, Pengelly's and Lawson's stood between them.

The day after this shop was destroyed in the Blitz, Underhill's, themselves established in 1889, moved to 101 Tavistock Road where, until recently, they continued to operate their retail and stationery business; it is now owned by Ham and Sewell. The SPCK agency was relinquished in the late 1970s and although this particular agency is no longer operating locally (there are still over 50 SPCK bookshops here and overseas) the Christian Literature Centre, established 40 years ago in York Street, has over the years expanded and today, between its two bases in Cornwall Street, successfully carries on the work begun by William White all those years ago.

Winnicott Brothers

The family business of Winnicott Brothers was established in the 1850s by Richard Winnicott snr, in George Street. It was subsequently carried on by his sons Richard W and John Frederick. Frederick was undoubtedly the most illustrious member of the family, serving Plymouth twice as Mayor (1906–7 and 1921–2) and receiving the Freedom of the City in 1934, ten years after he had been given a knighthood. Born in 1855, Sir Frederick lived to see the Frankfort Street business, shown here as it appeared in 1893, destroyed in the Blitz and to moved to a temporary home in Bedford Terrace. He died in 1948.

In 1857 Richard Winnicott had been trading in George Street for over five years and was advertising himself as a 'furnishing and general ironmonger, plumber and gas fitter'. In those days of course plastic wasn't even a distant dream, electrical appliances were still very much a thing of the future and even gas was a novelty to most people. The first modern-style gas cookers, incorporating an insulated oven with shelves and a cooking top, first went into production in 1852 (earlier gas ovens were simply upright stoves with a circle of burners in the base above which a joint would be suspended from a hook in the ceiling). Gas fires, on the other hand, did not reach the market place in a commercially practicable form until 1856. Essentially though, such items were only affordable by the well to do as the domestic front in the Victorian home was generally dominated by the kitchen hearth '. . . what place is more cosy on a cold winter's night than the kitchen fireside' asked Cassell's *Book of the Household* (1890), while Mrs Caddy wrote glowingly of a 'nice bright stove, placed in a recess glittering with Dutch tiles or Minton's artistic plaques, surrounded by burnished pans and pots of well-lined copper or brass, and neat enamelled saucepans' (*Household Organization*, 1877).

This was the climate in which Richard Winnicott flourished and after about ten years we find that the business had expanded into these premises in Frankfort Street. Before long this former private residence had been rebuilt to contain the impressive-faced limestone with red-brick relief frontage which extended over more than 100 feet. The new work was completed under the direction of the architect, Henry Snell, who also designed the Institute for the Blind on North Hill and who had an office in Frankfort Street

around this time. Praise for the development here was high and it was claimed that 'this block of buildings is considered to be one of the most important, and, structurally considered, one of the finest wholesale warehouses in the West of England' (*Commercial Guide to Plymouth*, 1894).

By this time (1894) the business had passed into the hands of Richard's sons and among the items being wholesaled we find: table cutlery, electro-plated wares of every description, japanned travelling trunks, galvanised baths, a large stock of enamelled wares and tin and iron goods of every description.

In the Fancy Department there were all manner of goods including an 'endless variety of Japanese and other useful and fancy articles of general sale.'

Electro-plating was another Victorian wonder, it enabled the less wealthy to imitate the style of the rich, although in a status-conscious society one always knew if one's cutlery was the genuine article or just silver plated. Japanning was also very popular in the dark dull drawing rooms of the nineteenth century. By this process many an item was lacquered with japan to give it a hard black gloss, japan being the name given to the lacquer which imitated the

finish of certain Japanese products. Thomas Neame of Cambridge Street, working around this time based his whole business on japanning. But it wasn't just this aspect of Japanese culture which appealed to the late Victorians. In 1882 WE Henley wrote '. . . the Japanese dado has become almost a household word and the Japanese fan a household essential'. While the clamour for items from the Orient increased noticeably after the publication of two books, *Things Japanese* in 1888 and *Things Chinese* in 1892.

At the end of last century the Winnicott's business empire embraced these buildings, with another main outlet in George Street plus stores in George Lane and Frankfort Lane. Here until 1941, they moved after the war to Ebrington Street via Bedford Terrace and while this business no longer operates in Plymouth today the Winnicott name is remembered in many ways. Sir Frederick it was who provided the Mayflower Memorial on the Barbican and he it was who laid the foundation stone for the Free Library (Plymouth Central Library) and who some years later donated the fine stained glass window in the library in memory of his wife, fine reminders of a man who was one of the great philanthropists of his day.

Bedford Street

'As George-street may be termed the Regent-street, so we might name Bedford-street the Fleet-street of Plymouth, for here again the business establishments are many and important. One drawback exists in the narrowness of a portion of the thoroughfare, but this will shortly be removed by the demolition of the block of buildings known as "The Island".'(WHK Wright 1878)

Bedford Street was indeed the principal banking and commercial street of Victorian Plymouth, along with Old Town Street, it had been the first of the 'modern' city centre streets to be developed. It was originally known as Frankfort Place and it led to the old west gate of the town, Frankfort Gate, which formerly stood at the end of Barrack Street (Russell Street). The ground eastward of the gate was thought to have been occupied by an old pot house, possibly once a guard house (Harris 1810) while extending southward of the gate was the 'Globe Inn' seen here at the end of Bedford Street.

Described as being in a low and feeble state in later years, a plaque on the wall of 'The Globe' told its story, 'Near this place formerly stood Frankfort Gate which, with others, formed the principal entrance into the town then enclosed by a wall erected for the greater protection thereof by the Mayor and Commonalty under the authority of the Charter of Henry VI. But in course of years, this mode of defence ceasing to be of any effect was taken down in 1783 and the street and avenues adjoining were considerably widened and improved. This tablet was put up by order the Mayor and Commonalty 4th of June 1813'.

Around this time 'The Globe' was enjoying a very good trade, it was, after all, on the on the side of the main thoroughfare to Stonehouse, Stoke and Dock. Reconstructed with the popularity of the coach, it had a sign showing a traveller on horseback 'with a Boniface of rotund proportions handing him the stirrup cup with which it was the custom of landlords to bid their guests a safe journey . . . Underneath this fronticepiece was the clearly written legend: 'Huzza my boys, for Doch-an-dorrach' a whimsical suggestion of the parting drink at the door and an intimation that the traveller was now bound for Dock.' (Whitfeld 1899)

In 1800, when there was a proposal that the new Town hall should be constructed in the large space in front of the Globe the proprietors lost little time in extending the building by the addition of a huge block, the 'Globe Tavern' thereafter becoming the 'Globe Hotel', one of the town's most famous coaching centres and in later years, the headquarters of the Conservative party.

'The Globe' did not survive the century, however; in 1899 it was pulled down and in its place was built the imposing plum-red brick landmark, the offices of the Prudential Assurance Company. Identifiable from many parts of the pre-war city, this towering neo-gothic structure survived the Blitz but not the *Plan for Plymouth*; the front of it extended a few metres into the line of Armada Way and so it was removed by the demolition men.

Precious little of the rest of Bedford Street was left standing after the bombing raids like the Westminster Bank operating from the building seen here at the end of the block to the left of the Globe as we look at it, and directly opposite the Union Branch of the National Provincial Bank which had been built on the site of the 'Borough Arms Coffee Tavern'.

Opened in October 1878, the 'Borough Arms' was the first venture of the Plymouth Coffee House Company whose Board of Directors included many leading ladies and gentlemen of the town; JN Bennett was its chairman, RC Serpell vice-chairman, EE Dawe secretary and Frank Short its manager. The 'Borough Arms' was intended 'to supply a want in our social system and as an inducement to sobriety'. It had refreshment bars on each floor, provided with urns for the supply of tea, coffee, and cocoa, and 'solids of various kinds'. The building was well furnished with handsome white marble tables and comfortable chairs in every room; in the basement there were newspaper stands to accommodate the London and local daily papers and on the ground floor was a spacious salon where meetings were held and once during the week a popular entertainment was provided. There were also club rooms, private rooms for ladies and a board room on the upper floors. The building itself was known as London House prior to its conversion to the 'Borough Arms' and in that capacity it had served as the base of Radford and Son, tailor and draper. Established sometime around 1824 by Elizabeth Radford, this was the business which in later years became Popham and Radford and later still just Pophams Ltd (1931).

London House is seen here on the corner of Bank Street opposite the Devon and Cornwall Bank. This had started life in 1832 as the Plymouth and Devonport Bank and in 1906 was taken over by Lloyds. Up until the Blitz, Yeo's and Popham's stood between Lloyd's and Bedford Arcade.

Spooners

In 1844 Joseph Spooner placed an advertisement in a local directory for his business based in Tuscan House, otherwise known as No 26 Whimple Street. In it the said Joseph Spooner begged 'most respectfully to invite the Nobility, Gentry, and Inhabitants of Plymouth, Stonehouse, Devonport, Devon and Cornwall, to his entire new stock of Millinery, Drapery, Shawls, Furs, and Fancy Goods'.

Joseph James Spooner had apparently been in business for some seven years by this time and the decision to open up in Whimple Street was undoubtedly a sound one, for nowhere in the Three Towns was there a higher concentration of similar retail outlets. Indeed of the 30 or so linen draperers then operating in Plymouth, a fifth of them were based in this street, the street which had acquired its very name from the great number of hat or hood sellers based here. The next highest concentration of such businesses, incidentally, was in Bedford Street where Spooners opened new extensions about 15 years later.

In the general sales pitch of Spooner's 1844 advertisement it is interesting to note that great emphasis was put on novelty and cheapness '. . . Every attention', also being paid 'to the taste and fashion of the age, avoiding at the same time, extravagant charges'. Nothing particularly new or startling perhaps in that but there was more to come, for Joseph Spooner was anxious to point out that the following regulations were adopted in the running of the business 'To mark the prices of each article in plain figures . . . To allow no deviation to be made from these prices . . . To exchange and return the money for every article which may fail upon examination, to give satisfaction' and finally: 'To be careful to exclude from the stock all doubtful or bad fabrics, and to keep only such regular goods as can be recommended.'

These 'regulations', while perhaps telling us a great deal about some of his less scrupulous competitors, are undoubtedly among those factors which helped to transform Spooners into one of the foremost department stores in Plymouth. Before the 1850s had drawn to a close, Spooners had opened their first extension at 38 Whimple Street and within a few years the Bedford Street premises had begun trading. Still at this stage, the business was primarily focussed on goods related to the drapery and millinery trades, the idea of branching out into other lines was, however, just around the corner.

In 1851 William Whiteley visited the Great Exhibition in London, and after seeing so many types of merchandise displayed under one roof he was later inspired to break the traditional mould of drapery and haberdashery. In 1867 he opened a jewellery department, then came a foreign department, selling Oriental novelties; an estate agency, a restaurant, a cleaning and dyeing department and in 1876 a hairdressing salon. The department store was well and truly established and Whiteley adopted the slogan 'Anything from a Pin to an Elephant'.

At the same time Spooners themselves started to diversify (as did one of their former managers, Edward Dingle, who left the firm in 1880 to set up his own business at No 30 Bedford Street). By 1876 they had added premises in Old Town Street to their expanding empire and carpet and furnishing departments were opened. As the 1890s dawned Spooner and Co. adopted a new logo or trademark, a ship's wheel inscribed with their name and address. Whimple Street had by now long since been forsaken and the full extent of Spooners in 1890 read: 'The Piazza, 54, 55, 56 & 58 Bedford Street, 1, 4 & 7 Old Town Street and 1–5 Market Avenue'. On the retail side they were now advertising as Drapers and Silkmercers and Complete House Furnishers.

The impression of a number shops all dotted around the town centre is, however, a misleading one as, for the most part, these buildings were all interconnected, forming the bulk of one large block, 'Spooners' Corner', which overlooked St Andrews Church, running approximately from the south-western corner of the present Old Town Street right across Royal Parade and back and around towards the Piazza, which would have led up through the site of LLoyds Bank today.

The interlinking of these separate departments was almost their downfall for, on the night of the 14th of June 1902, fire almost destroyed the whole of the Bedford Street and Old Town Street operations. It was a Saturday evening, most of the 800 or so staff had gone home but remarkably it was thought that some 180 were still in the buildings when one of the assistants was thought to have knocked into a gas pendant in one of the windows of No 4 Old Town Street, thereby setting fire to some inflammable material.

The massed Fire Brigades of the Three Towns played some 21 hoses on the conflagration, which by 2.30am had died down sufficiently for the Devonport and Stonehouse men to return home. The management of Spooners were quick to recover from the tragedy and it was not long before the stores were once again fully operational. In 1910 there was another fire in Old Town Street but it was devastation on an even larger scale, however, which was to prevent the firm celebrating their centenary in quite the style they would have wished, as the Blitz flattened so much of the town centre.

Today the present Spooner building stands a little to the west of its earlier sites. Reopened here in 1953, Spooners is better known today by the name of the firm who took them over back in 1929 . . . Debenhams.

Matthews'

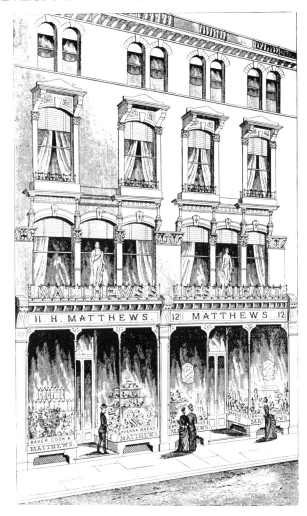

Restaurants, while very much taken for granted these days, were something of a novelty in the nineteenth century. Originally the word 'restaurant' described a particular type of soup made in France which was famous for its restorative properties; a recipe for this soup was published in Lyons around 1550. Two hundred years later the term was being used to refer to French taverns that served this special soup, as well as other foods; although the early 'restaurants' catered more for the invalided customer than the general public as a whole.

Then came the French Revolution and, following the downfall of so many of the great aristocratic families, many household chefs found themselves out of a job and looking to set about cooking for a high class of clientele and at the same time to introduce more people to the idea of eating in public. So was born the celebrated French restaurant, complete with each individual chef's 'specialite de la maison'.

It was not until the late 1830s that restaurants began to take the place of taverns for those eating out in London; then, gradually, the idea spread to other parts of the country. At first there was much resistance to the idea from the established coffee houses and 'chop houses' and it is interesting to note that as late as 1894 this Bedford Street eating house was being advertised as a 'Restaurant and Confectionery Establishment' serving 'Soups, Chops, Steaks . . . and a Choice Selection of High Class Wines'.

British drinking habits changed greatly during Queen Victoria's time. In the early years of her reign it was the tendency of the upper classes to over indulge in brandy and the heavier wines like port, sherry and madeira while the so called lower orders drank a lot of beer . . . and rum . . . and gin. In the 1870s, however, there was a general change, beers, and pubs themselves improved and there was a move towards drinking less. The lighter wines and champagne became popular for those who could afford it, as the French influence spread, particularly in the 'naughty nineties'.

Much of the restaurant jargon was, and indeed still is, French and Matthews themselves advertised their 'Table d'Hote' daily from one to four p.m., the price – 2/6d (just over 12p). This was of course their fixed menu; the word menu itself being lifted straight out of the French language.

Henry Matthews didn't start out as a restaurant proprietor, however, or as a chef (another French word), rather he started in business simply as a baker and pastry-cook, and for the first ten years he was based solely in High Street, taking on extra premises in Bedford Street in early 1860s. Also new to the street around the same time was the well-known local confectionery business of E Tuckett and Son which retained a Bedford Street outlet until the Blitz.

There were no restaurants as such in the street at this time but just a few years earlier Susan Frost had run an 'Eating and Coffee House' at No 4 Bedford Street and at No 17 Mary Biscombe had carried on a similar trade, but that was it apart from the 'Bedford Spirit Vaults', managed in 1864 by Hampden Wotton, the 'Globe' and the 'Boot Inn'.

Restaurants evolved in response to the demands of the new generation of workers and shoppers who, as transport developed and the country became increasingly prosperous, were more mobile and more able to afford to 'eat out' than any of their predecessors had been. Not everyone wanted a heavy meal though and so tea shops also became popular and the traditional coffee house became the café (another French word, it simply means 'coffee').

The 'Borough Arms Coffee House' was opened in the street in 1878, then at the turn of the century CA and WC Goodbody opened up at No 20 Bedford Street. Like Matthews, who they were to take over in the 1920s, Goodbody's were specialist confectioners and many Plymothians were to cherish their memories of the magnificent cakes that would be produced each year for a fantastic Christmas window display only to be cut up as the days went by and be sold by the pound along with the fancy figures used as decoration. Equally well remembered was the enticing aroma of freshly ground coffee that used to waft out of the Central Café into Bedford Street and neighbouring George Street.

In later years Lyons too were to establish a tea shop in the street. This national concern had set up one of the first ever tea houses, in London, in 1894. Sadly, however, like so many of the town's well-known businesses, these Bedford Street buildings were devastated by the Blitz and today no trace of this street remains. The businesses themselves, though, did all survive the war but despite the fact that there are now more restaurants in Plymouth than ever before, there are none bearing any of these well-known old names on their signboards.

Plymouth YMCA

By 1887 the Plymouth operation of the YMCA was doing sufficiently well to undertake the building of a new and impressive headquarters. In Bedford Street, on the corner of Westwell Street, it stood opposite the recently erected Municipal buildings and adjacent to the Head Post Office. Surveying the scene from a lofty pedestal was a statue of Alfred Rooker, the great Liberal Mayor of the town, who held office in 1852 and again in 1874 and who, on the 17th of January 1848, chaired the meeting that made the decision that Plymouth needed a YMCA.

The YMCA is generally said to have been founded in 1844 by a 24-year-old country boy, George Williams, who was working in London for Hitchcock and Rogers, a firm of drapers. Initially, George had just suggested to some of his fellow workers that they should meet with him for prayer and Bible study, however the idea of a club soon came to him and it was proposed that it should be called the 'Young Men's Christian Association'. So it was that on the 6th June 1844, twelve young men met in London (eleven of them worked for Hitchcock's) to form a club whose aim was 'the improvement of the spiritual condition of young men in the drapery and other trades'.

It has since been argued that it was the Scots who really deserve the credit for founding the YMCA, specifically a Glasgwegian, David Naismith. The matter, however, is unresolved, although in his book on *George Williams and the YMCA*, Dr C Binfield wrote 'the chain of coincidence suggests that somewhere the Scottish societies must have had an impact, however indirect, on the London movement'. Whatever it's foundation though there is no denying that the YMCA spread rapidly throughout this country crossing over to America by 1851. Meanwhile George Williams became a partner with Hitchcock's, married the daughter of the head of the firm and ultimately became head of the firm himself and using the money and influence he subsequently gained, helped spread the Association far and wide. He was knighted in 1894 and he died eleven years later at the age of 84.

In 1880, thanks to Williams's generosity and enterprise, Exeter Hall became the headquarters of the movement. While that same year, in Plymouth, the inaugural year of a new president here (Dr Albert Hingston)was marked by a move away from premises in Union Street, not far from Derry's Clock, to a building in Bank Street which stood approximately where there is currently an opening between the two parts of Debenhams. Bank Street thereby became at least the third home of the Plymouth YMCA, for we know that in its earlier years the Association was based at number 13 Frankfort Street, a situation that Crispin Gill described in his account *Plymouth 1848–1958* as being 'between two worlds . . . Above it were nice houses with gardens in front, occupied by surgeons and solicitors. Below, beer houses and small shops became common, and behind the shops across the way were the stews of Willow Plot.'

Devonport YMCA opened the same year as Plymouth, it moved into Fore Street in 1862, later taking space in the Public Hall there until it moved out to St Aubyn Street in 1932. By this time the Plymouth operation had expanded greatly. In 1892 it had taken over the recently established Kitto Institute, founded by Alfred Hambly in 1884 and named in memory of the exemplary Dr John Kitto and in 1916 it had purchased premises in Union Street, as part of the National Council's move to set up a YMCA in every camp. This became of course the Union Street Servicemen's YMCA which carried out sterling work not just during the First World War but right up to the time it was bombed in 1941.

Tragically the Blitz hit the YMCA particularly hard in Plymouth. The main headquarters, which had moved to Old Town Street in 1920, was destroyed on the night of 20th March 1941, as was the Kinterbury Street Kitto base and the residential hostel in Lockyer Street (14 lives were lost in that conflagration). On top of that the Servicemen's YMCA was damaged, along with the Devonport HQ in St Aubyn Street.

In the remaining years of the war a room in Peverell Park Villa served as a meeting place and later, in June 1946, a new temporary HQ was established in Cobourg Memorial Hall. Then on a proud day in May 1958, the new purpose built City of Plymouth YMCA was opened at the top of Armada Way at its junction with Cobourg Street. Described at the time as the most magnificent civilian club the city had ever known, it was closed last year for major refurbishment and is due to open again later this year with splendid facilities on the ground, lower ground and mezzanine floor with the rest being given over to office space. The YMCA in the meantime is concentrating on developing and expanding its sports, social and administrative HQ at the Kitto Centre, Burrington, opposite the new comprehensive school, soon to be named the John Kitto School.

Today the YMCA continues to be guided by its Christian ethic, the most significant departure from its Victorian roots being that a large proportion of its members are female (the YWCA was founded in 1855) and that whole families are encourage to join; the young together with the young at heart.

Basket Street

In 1925 the Plymouth Relay Station of the BBC (which had opened in March 1924) broadcast a series of talks by a local man, Samuel Weekes. Entitled *My Personal Recollections of Plymouth in the late 'Forties'*, these talks proved to be so popular that Mr Weekes was persuaded to have the first two of them published.

In the pamphlet that followed we find Samuel Weekes' memories of this long gone thoroughfare '. . . We proceed through Basket Street, then somewhat further south – the present street being on the site of the quaint old houses of the then Basket Street. A basket factory, the workhouse, a quadrangle, a kitchen garden, a fowl run, a large hall, etc., occupied the space between Westwell Street and the old church. A word or two about some of these.'

'The owner of the basket factory (although I knew his name, for obvious reasons, I will give him a nom de plume and call him Mr Pickwick) – well, Mr Pickwick employed a lot of young women from the lower parts of town, to skin the withes for basket making. They seem to have been so very noisy and rough in manner, so much so, that they were known ironically as "Pickwick's Lambs"!'

'Then, on the new Workhouse being built in 1851 the old building was let out to various tenants. I myself repeatedly went there to get books bound. There appears to have been, long before my time, a foundry here, for I read in an old book, that some of St Andrew's bells were cast here, but of course I could have no personal knowledge of this.' Mr Weekes then concluded his reference to this area by telling

us that 'the Workhouse and all the other buildings were cleared away to make room for the New Guildhall, municipal offices, etc., which were opened in 1874.'

Cleared away they were in the summer of 1870, and on Thursday 28th July thousands gathered on the site of these old buildings to witness the mayor William Luscombe's laying of the foundation stone for the new development. Not everyone had been in favour of the scheme, however, and in 1869 a public meeting had been called in opposition to the project but to no avail. The Corporation had for sometime been buying up lands and houses in Basket Street and Westwell Street and parts of the latter and all of the former were doomed.

The original Basket Street ran from what was the 'Higher Churchyard' on the northern side of St Andrew's, approached by a flight of steps, through to Westwell Street. In todays terms it would have stood just opposite Debenhams on Royal Parade. In eighteenth-century terms it ran into Love Lane for that was the original name for Westwell Street, while Basket Street itself was then called Love Street.

It is hard now to imagine these two thoroughfares being on the outskirts of town but in the 1700s they were, and just as with a later Love Lane at the other side of town (near Beaumont Park), this route was doubtless taken by courting couples on their way to the fields on the northern slopes of the Hoe. In time, of course, the town expanded beyond this area and the names became less and less appropriate and perhaps because of this it was thought that the names should be changed. Westwell indicated the position of one of the towns earlier water supplies and Basket apparently indicated the presence of a basket factory.

Basket making is one of the oldest and most useful crafts known to man and is one of those crafts that can't properly be imitated by a machine. Indeed it wasn't even until 1937 that a machine was introduced from France for stripping the willow from which the tough flexible twigs or branches are most commonly obtained. Despite the willow or withy

being the traditional source of the withes with which baskets are made, it wasn't until 1800 that the willow was grown as a crop in this country. Once it was, however, there was a great boost to the industry and the basket making went on to reach its peak in the nineteenth century.

Certainly in Plymouth there were four basket makers listed in 1844 and this figure more than doubled over the next 20 years. Quite who the Mr Pickwick figure was modeled on we can't be sure but James Mumford had a basket making business back in the 'forties' and in 1867 he was based in Westwell Street.

Standing on the corner of Westwell Street and Basket Street in the distance on the left here was the 'White Horse Inn'. Number 10 of 10 numbered properties in Basket Street, it changed hands many times over the years but what is not clear is whether, like the street itself, it changed its name at the beginning of the nineteenth century. In 1804 we find two inns mentioned in Basket Street, the 'York Inn' and the 'Brick Wall' but no 'White Horse'. The 'White Horse' became a popular inn sign in the eighteenth century during the reign of the first two Georges, when, as the symbol of the Hanovarian Kings, it replaced many 'Royal Oaks' of the Stuart era. So although probably old enough to have been an example of this transition, the directories are inconclusive.

We do know, however, that the 'White Horse' was pulled down in 1870 and that landlord John Short moved down around the corner from the other end of Westwell Street to the 'Princess Inn' in Princess Street. Meanwhile Thomas Geake, hat and cap manufacturer, moved from 7 Basket Street to 43 Frankfort Street and it would appear that Chubb the tailor moved from here to Old Town Street. As for the other late 1860s occupants of Basket Street like last and clog manufacturer John Reed, chimney sweep John Isaac and shopkeeper James Lark, we cannot say other than they must undoubtedly have been amongst those who were sad to see the old street go.

Princess Square

Although possibly incorporating a little bit of artistic licence, this nevertheless appears to be a fairly accurate portrait of Plymouth, looking south from the Municipal Buildings, back in the spring of 1878. Looking at it now, though, perhaps the remarkable thing about this crowded vista is that had it been possible to produce a comparable view from this angle at the beginning of the nineteenth century, you would have seen an uninterrupted stretch of green between the tower of St Andrew's and the Citadel on the left and just a couple of isolated buildings in what became Westwell Street, in the foreground to the right, otherwise nothing between here and the sea.

The original west well from which the street took its name was filled in sometime around the beginning of the century, its location then given as Burying Place Lane (there was a graveyard here until 1950, the trees growing in it are visible in the bottom right hand corner of the picture, some of them survive today as a feature of the landscaping between the Guildhall and the Civic Centre).

Westwell Street proper was the first part of this busy scene to be developed, running as it did into the Foulston-designed Princess Square. Foulston's plan had been to leave the whole square open with a small circular enclosure in the centre surrounding an ornamental structure. Unfortunately, and it is perhaps difficult for us to imagine, this conspicuous central area was privately owned and for many years last century it was 'in a disreputable and dishevelled state' with 'refuse of all sorts pitched in and left there, apparently

without rebuke – it was utterly neglected' (Samuel Weekes).

Later on it seems Princess Square (so named after a visit by Princess, later Queen Victoria) was tidied up somewhat, but it was later still to suffer the ignominy of becoming one of the first, if not the first, car parks (or chars-à-bancs parks) in Plymouth.

Like Princess Square, Lockyer Street, with the Theatre Royal (just out of the picture to the right) and St Andrew's Chapel (St Catherine's) contained many Foulston buildings and essentially much of what fills this view had been laid down by 1860, the most notable exception of course being the Guildhall itself which was completed just a few years before this sketch was made.

Municipal Buildings

'The attention of the visitor is now directed, as a matter of course, to the extensive pile of buildings which graces the opposite side of Westwell-street. Crossing the road we enter the Guildhall-square, in the neighbourhood of which we may now spend half an hour to advantage. The group of buildings now around us is of a very imposing character. In front is the massive tower of St Andrew's Church . . . at our right is the New Guildhall, with police-court, law-courts, prison cells and other portions of a large public establishment. On the left are the Municipal Offices, with Council Chamber in the centre, the various apartments in which we will now proceed to examine in detail.' (WHK Wright 1879)

The date of the illustration shown here is 1876, just two years after the completion of the Guildhall square complex but just before the erection of a statue which stood nearby. This statue was of Alfred Rooker, Mayor of Plymouth when these buildings were inaugurated. Described as a man of eloquence and ability and of unimpeachable character, Rooker was 'a prime mover in the effort to secure adequate accommodation for the municipal government of the town.'

Mounting the steps at the north tower entrance to the Municipal buildings and entering the door, a set of tablets on the wall indicated the whereabouts of all the various departments. The borough treasurer was off to the right, the town clerk's office was upstairs, attached to the committee room of the Town Council; beyond it the office and board-room of the School Board. Dropping down a flight of stairs there was the Mayor's parlour the walls of which were decorated with old maps, engravings and paintings of Plymouth including an original portrait of Drake.

Next came the Council Chamber itself said to be the handsomest room of the whole block. The mayor's seat was at one end, on a raised platform with a canopy, all in carved oak. In front of this was the town clerk's seat and in the centre of the room, the reporter's table plus another table for various borough officials. For the 48 councillors and aldermen there were rows of cushioned seats, with desks, running down either side of the Chamber, while spacious galleries were provided for the public. Lighting was provided by four large stained-glass windows, each with a medallion style portrait in the middle. Queen Victoria, Queen Elizabeth, Drake and Raleigh were the four thus commemorated.

Other notable features included an impressive clock on the front of the gallery, the gift of William Moore who had the unusual distinction of being Mayor of Plymouth for three consecutive years (1874–77), and on the walls a number of full-length portraits: of Charles II, James II, George II, Queen Charlotte, George III, George IV, Queen Caroline, William IV and Prince Albert.

On the other side of the Council Chamber were yet more offices including those of the borough surveyor and the water surveyor, while above these were situated rooms used by the Chamber of Commerce and the Plymouth Debating Society as well as some rooms used as residences by certain borough officials. Having now arrived at the other end of the Municipal Buildings, the exit was by the door in the foot of the Eagle Tower, so named because of the figure that sat at its summit (and which now sits at the top of Armada Way). This Tower housed a powerful light which was trained on one of St Andrew's clock faces so that passing pedestrians might be able to make out the time in the dark hours. The statue which stood at the apex of the Council Chamber roof, incidentally, was a full length figure of Drake.

Sadly, of course, the Municipal Buildings stood for little more than 70 years. Left as a shell after the Blitz, there was no reprieve for this magnificent pile and what was left was pulled down to make way for Royal Parade. The building which ultimately replaced it, the Civic Centre, was opened in 1962 by Her Majesty Queen Elizabeth II, an event commemorated in the design of one of the 14 main windows of the Guildhall. This building was also left as a shell by the bombing, however, after much debate it was eventually rebuilt and reopened in 1959, again an event illustrated on one of the Guildhall windows. The enemy bombing of 1941 is the subject of another window as is the rebuilding of the City which began in 1947. Apart from the images on these four windows the other ten attempt in some way to duplicate the windows they were replacing all showing important scenes in the history of Plymouth; the Civil War seige, the arrest of Raleigh, Drake bringing water to the town, the Inquisition of the Plympton Priors, the landing of the Black Prince, the Breton Raid, the visit of Katherine of Aragon, the Armada, the Pilgrim Fathers and finally Cookworthy's Pottery. As the window to commemorate the opening covered both 1874 and 1959, this obviously meant that three of the original Victorian windows were not 'replaced'; these featured the Proclamation of William of Orange, Napoleon captive in the sound on the *Bellerophon* and the Masonic window.

Undoubtedly one of the most significant changes in the reconstructed Guildhall, however, was the fact the internal focal point of the main hall was now to the east and not as before to the west, the hall was in effect turned completely about face.

The Guildhall

The Guildhall, built on the site of it's Jacobean predecessor at the junction of High Street and Whimple Street, was never really deemed to have met the criteria for which it was designed. It was, it was claimed 'inconvenient as a guildhall, unsuited for a mayoralty house, totally inadequate as a prison, and perfectly absurd for market purposes'. 'Plymothians' wrote Worth in 1890, 'were not long content with this multum in parvo' (too much in too little) and less than thirty years after its completion were looking to build something bigger and better. 'But threatened men live on' continued Worth, 'and so Evelegh's ugly building long continued the centre of civic life in Plymouth'.

It wasn't until the new workhouse was erected at Greenbank in 1858 that it was decided that the most central site for a new guildhall would be to the west of St Andrew's Church. This was where the old workhouse stood, at the top of Catherine Street. So it was that the Corporation purchased this fine old structure, formerly known as the Hospital of the Poor's Portion and which had been built at the beginning of the seventeenth century.

Over the next ten years the Corporation systematically bought up neighbouring properties, the Orphan's Aid Charity buildings and adjoining lands and houses in Basket Street and Westwell Street. Westwell Street itself, as one of the main approaches to this site, was widened at the same time. Not everyone it seems was in favour of the grand scheme going ahead, however, but when in 1869 a meeting was called 'unavailingly' in opposition to the project, it was decided to invite plans from architects and to offer three premiums for the best.

In the event 20 sets of designs were submitted and having called in a professional advisor, Mr Waterhouse, the Council chose the designs of the Plymouth based architects Messrs Alfred Norman and James Hine. The next step was to invite tenders for the execution of the work and in the early part of 1870 twelve were submitted, the Council finding in favour of that sent in by Messrs Call and Pethick. The original quote was for £32,475, Pethick carried out the work and as is so often the case the eventual bill was considerably more than was anticipated. The final cost was about half as much again, almost £50,000.

Having accepted Pethick's tender in June 1870 and having cleared most of the old buildings from the site, on Thursday 28th July at precisely 2.30pm the Mayor and Corporation

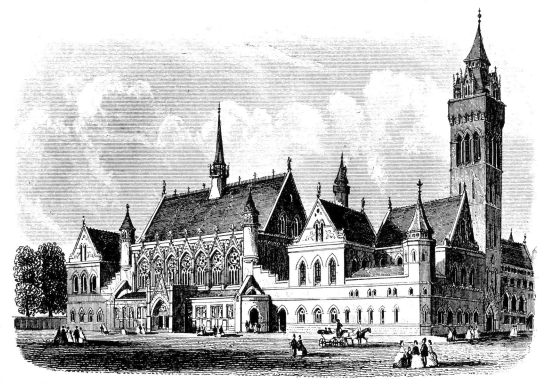

met outside the old Guildhall and walked 'thence in Procession to the spot' where the foundation stone for the new Guildhall was to be laid. At 3 o'clock, they had met up with the Contractors, Architects, Architect's Clerks bearing implements, the Town Surveyor, Corporate Officers, Councillors, Aldermen, Magistrates, Police and Town Sergeants bearing maces, and the Vicar of St Andrew's, Charles Wilkinson, who offered up Prayer. Then the chairman of the Guildhall committee, Alfred Rooker, invited the Mayor, William Luscombe, 'to lay the Stone'. After that the Mayor was given a silver trowel by the Architects and, once the formalities had been concluded, the various dignitaries retired to the Royal Hotel for a Public Commemorative Dinner.

Four years later on the morning of Thursday 13th August 1874 an even grander occasion marked the official opening of the completed buildings. Officiating this time was the Prince of Wales, Queen Victoria's eldest son Albert Edward, Lord High Steward of the Borough of Plymouth and the future Edward VII, then aged 33. Alfred Rooker was now enjoying his second term as Mayor (he had earlier held office in 1851) and this time the celebrations lasted not one but three days.

As the assembled crowds waited for the Prince to be handed the silver key, trumpeters played a Grand Festival March specially written for the occasion by the 30-year-old organist of Sherwell Church, Frederick Lohr. After the formal opening there was a 'Dejeuner in the Great Hall' of the new building and then in the evening there were 'Illuminations and Fireworks'. Over the next two days a Grand Musical Festival was held, the principal works performed being, on the Friday, Mendelssohn's 'Elijah' and, on the Saturday evening at 7pm, Haydn's 'Creation'. A Grand Rehearsal for Inmates of the Charitable Institutions was held earlier on the Saturday. A truly grand spectacle it must have been too with a mixed choir of almost 300 and a band containing over 80 musicians with guest artists including Signor Agnesi, Madlle. Mathilde Enequist and the Prima Donna La Scala, Milan and San Carlos, Naples, Madlle. Elena Corani.

The opening of the Guildhall was later to be the subject of one of the 14 great stained-glass windows that ran down the sides of the Great Hall, while another depicted the reception held here the following day when the Freemasons of Devon and Cornwall met here and welcomed the Prince of Wales as their Grand Master.

The Royal Hotel

It wasn't until the end of the eighteenth century that the word 'hotel' as opposed to 'inn' or 'tavern' properly passed into our vocabulary and prior to the building of the Royal Hotel in 1822 'The Pope's Head' at the top of Looe Street was the principal inn in the town.

Originally intended as one of 'three distinct buildings', a 'tavern, ballroom and theatre', the project was in large part the brainchild of Edmund Lockyer (a local medical man and prominent member of the town council). Sometime around 1809 Lockyer felt the time was right for Plymouth to capitalize on the new wealth in the town, in the wake of the Napoleonic Wars, and to create a grand civic entertainment centre on a scale hitherto unknown in the south west of England. He first approached the architect who, since 1805, had been working on the new prison at Princetown, DA Alexander. Alexander however was too busy to give serious consideration to a scheme he thought would never get off the ground. In the letter he wrote back to Lockyer he said, 'I did not think it at all probable you would build while Timber and Deal are four times the price they should be'.

Lockyer was undaunted and in January 1810 a competition was launched inviting plans for the scheme. By May 15th Lockyer was in a position to write to the then Mayor, Joseph Pridham, with the following recommendations; that John Phillips of Stonehouse be awarded five guineas for his model, while ten guineas should go to Arthur Browne of Norwich, 15 to Oliver Lang of Plymouth Dock and 20 to Cyrus Redding of Plymouth. For the first prize of 50 guineas, however, Lockyer recommended the designs of a 38-year-old London architect, John Foulston. It was a decision that was to have a major impact on the early nineteenth century development of the Three Towns.

The foundation stone of the new complex was laid on the 10th of September 1811 by Lockyer himself who was then serving his second term as Mayor of Plymouth, the latin inscription referring grandly to 'Edmundus Lockyer' and 'Johannes Foulston'.

Within two years the Theatre was open though it was almost another ten years before the Hotel was even tendered for. Money for the building was raised in unusual ways. The council decided to sell its advowsons – its rights to appoint the vicars of St. Andrew's and Charles Church – in order, as one cynic put it, to appoint a landlord and manager. A further substantial sum was raised by a tontine – by this means money was raised in the form of an annuity being paid until the death of the nominee. In other words someone subscribing £10 on such a nominee received a net income of £100 on their death. While this outraged the Puritan element, it quickly proved popular and some £46,000 was raised in three months, Foulston himself subscribing £100 in respect of his wife. The eventual cost of the Theatre was around £60,000, well over £10 million in today's terms.

While the Theatre stood alone for a decade, Foulston, in the meanwhile, was engaged on a number of other works and by the time the Royal Hotel had opened the neighbouring Athenaeum had been conceived and completed and St. Andrew's Chapel directly opposite the Hotel had been planned. Lockyer enjoyed a further two terms as Mayor in the early 1820's and just as the buildings in this scene were being completed, this wide thoroughfare up to the Hoe was named in honour of this 'father and general benefactor of the town'.

Originally the architect envisaged two tetrastyle porticos, entrances, onto Lockyer Street both crowned with elaborate mounted horse sculptures. The completed scheme however was altogether more impressive. 'Important though the building was as an example of the Greek Revival in England – the first as far as Plymouth was concerned – it was of greater significance on purely functional grounds and could claim to have incorporated, if not the first hotel in the modern sense of the word, at least a key example in the transition from Georgian inn to Edwardian 'hydro'. (Frank Jenkins, *John Foulston . . .* 1968)

Here there were 50 bedrooms many with their own dining room, providing suites of rooms for 20 to 30 families. There were also two floors of smaller bedrooms at the top of the building for servants. Further accommodation for servants existed in the basement where there were also laundry rooms, a large kitchen area, fuel and food stores and an ice house which effectively acted as a huge refridgerator. The ground floor, meanwhile, was entered via the two great lobbies and also contained a bar, a large assembly room, a commercial room, coffee room and hotel keeper's room. The spectacular ballroom was on the next floor which also sported card playing rooms, two large haylofts and rooms for the ostlers. In those far off days of horse travel, no trains even, there was stabling for seventy horses and seven coach houses. Today in the age of the car, most theatre patrons have little need for overnight accommodation, just a massive multistory car park which, ironically, covers almost exactly the site of the old Royal Hotel which survived the planners in 1937 but not the bombers a few years later.

Theatre Royal

The original intention of Plymouth Corporation was to site their new theatre on the land occupied by its Frankfort Gate predecessor. The architect they commissioned, however, had other ideas. Such a building as he had in mind would be lost in such a place he said. On learning where the architect had in mind they protested that such a site was too isolated '. . . Isolated! Let me raise the fabric and you will soon see a vast addition to houses in that locality'.

So it was that on 23rd August 1813 the New Theatre Royal, Plymouth was opened with an aptly titled production of *As you Like It* or at least part of it, followed by the farce of *Catherine and Pettrucio* . . . from Shakespeare's *Taming of the Shrew*, the evening's entertainment being preceded by 'An Occasional Address'. The doors opened at six for a seven o'clock start '. . . Ladies and Gentlemen' were 'respectfully requested to send their servants to keep place at HALF-PAST FIVE o'clock'.

We can safely assume that Plymouth Corporation were at one with Benjamin Wyatt, architect of the then newly rebuilt Drury Lane Theatre, when he remarked, 'among the principal objects which call for reform in the theatres of London, no one appears to be more important than that of protecting the more rational and respectable class of spectators from those nuisances to which they have long been exposed, by being obliged to pass through Lobbies, Rooms and Avenues, crowded with the most disreputable members of the community, and subject to the scenes of the most disgusting indecency. The New Theatre Royal originally had different entrances and separate areas for different classes of patrons. Certainly Plymouth had had its fair share of disreputable audiences.

So here we are on this first night entering this impressive new building which, like Wyatt's Drury Lane building, also begun in 1811, and the earlier Bordeaux Theatre of Victor Louis, had its auditorium set in the form of a three quarter circle. Looking up we see an elaborately painted ceiling made to appear like an open dome, adorned with mythical emblems of the Zodiac 'through which Fame with two ariel attendants is seen flying thro' the mimic azure'. There are yet more classical scenes painted on the fronts of the various tiers of seating, tiers which are supported by the then novel means of ornamental cast iron columns (Foulston was undoubtedly concerned to try to minimize the risk of spreading fire which had recently claimed Covent Garden in 1808, and the earlier Drury Lane Theatre in 1809). Finally in front of the stage on one of the great drop curtains was a massive picture showing a magnificent hall with statues and columns, designed by Foulston himself. Foulston's original plans for the building, like those of others he designed, featured many statues, none of which materialised.

The seating capacity of the new theatre was 1,192. On that first Monday night in August, 1,149 persons attended paying an impressive total of £152.14s between them, the most expensive boxes were only four shillings (20p) each and a seat in the gallery could be had for a shilling. However, despite the initial enthusiasm for the venture the theatre struggled. 'It was a big house to fill in a town of moderate size; and to state all the candid truth it was rarely filled. It was exceedingly cold in the winter, and was warmed by the primitive device of burning large fires in the pit . . .' noted one later proprietor, while a contemporary of the 1830s wrote . . .' it is impossible for the actors to dispel the prevailing sadness'.

In the early part of the nineteenth century the theatre changed hands several times as different managers tried to make a go of it. Then in 1845 John Riley Newcombe, actor, manager, sportsman and a man of the world arrived and over the next 42 years, until his death in 1887, was destined to become one of the most conspicuous figures in the public life of Plymouth. Although the theatre was not an overnight success under Newcombe, a success it eventually was, despite the arguments with his landlords, the Corporation and despite the ravages of two fires.

Famous for his plays and latterly his pantomimes, Newcombe was once the subject of a whole page in *Punch*, following his printed exhortations to Plymothians to avoid one of his productions because the acting of the two lady stars was so abysmal.

From 1860 to 1900 there were more than 2,500 different billings at the theatre, generally advertised on gaudy red and yellow posters. However, with the dawn of the moving picture show, the theatre started to struggle once more and such was the impact of the 'talkies' in the late 20's that, according to one contemporary theatre critic, JC Trewin, Plymouth was culturally dead by the mid 30's. Thus it comes as no surprise that in 1937 the Council decided to pull down the Theatre Royal and replace it with a new Royal Cinema (the ABC/Cannon). Originally intended to be but one corner of a massive new Royal Hotel/Theatre complex occupying the whole site of its predecessor, the scheme was never completed – the Blitz not the planners removed the old hotel while the cinema, ironically, survives to this day.

St Andrew's Chapel

After the building of Charles Church back in the middle of the seventeenth century there was a long period of population growth and general expansion but there was no additional church accommodation provided for Plymothians. In 1812 a bill was promoted proposing to divide the town into four parishes with a church in each. However, nothing transpired and the following year another bill suggested building two new churches with funds to be acquired by raising a levy on the inhabitants (the paying of church rates only stopped in 1834).

Strongly opposed by local dissenters, who were nevertheless prepared to contribute towards a new burial ground, this scheme also fell through. However, within 10 years work was under way as first a Chapel of Ease for St Andrew's was built and then a few years later a similar edifice was erected for Charles Church. The former became St Catherine's, the latter, St Luke's.

St Andrew's Chapel of Ease was opened on the 4th October 1823 by its first vicar the Rev Robert Lampen who

earlier in the year, February 1st, had laid the foundation stone. Lampen was one of the four principal investors who helped provide the £5,000 that it cost to complete the scheme. The other three were J Pridham, T Gill and H Woollcombe. Thomas Gill had started an alkali and soap factory at Millbay in 1818, it was one of the first industrial developments in that area, and he later became a leading light in the town, serving as Mayor and Liberal MP. Solicitor Henry Woollcombe on the other hand had already served as Mayor in 1813–14, just after he had founded the Plymouth Institution.

Lampen himself was no outsider having been appointed the town's Lecturer in 1813. One of the last three to hold the title, Lampen's post as Lecturer dated back to 1641, the year Charles Church was begun. Essentially the appointment was for churches where 'there is no preaching in the afternoon' and under its terms parishioners could 'maintain a comfortable lecturer at their own charge and the parson or vicar shall allow this unless he will preach himself'.

In practice this allowed the town to place a Puritan candidate in the pulpit to counter, in the afternoon, the preaching of any Royalist incumbent in the morning. In later years they acted much as any curate would and none were appointed by the Corporation after the Municipal Reform Act had been passed in 1835.

In addition to being town lecturer, Lampen was also a member of the Plymouth Institution and it was he who had the honour of addressing the first meeting in their purpose-built premises, the Athenaeum, in 1819. Situated immediately to the west of Foulston's imposing Theatre Royal complex, the Athenaeum and St Andrew's Chapel were also Foulston-designed buildings.

St Andrew's Chapel or St Catherine's as it was better known this century, was the last of the group to be left standing. Originally facing the Lockyer Street side of the Royal hotel, it remained open until December 1957 and was demolished soon afterwards to make way for the new Municipal buildings. The pews found a new home in the Church of the Ascension, Crownhill, while the seventeenth century black marble font, discarded from St Andrew's in 1850 and given to St Catherine's in 1879, was returned from whence it came when St Andrew's re-opened in November 1957.

Following the bombing of the mother church in the 1941 blitz, the St Andrew's congregation worshipped here and sang to the playing of Dr Harry Moreton, their organist who had served many years in St Andrew's. Little damaged itself by enemy action, St Catherine's had undergone restoration work in 1879–80 under the Rev John Erskine Risk, while during the incumbency of the Rev NN Lewarne, the choir vestry had been added (1907) and the roof was renewed (1912). The original belfry, shown here, was replaced by a much simpler construction.

Seating 800 to 1000, the gallery of St Catherine's, like that of the original Theatre Royal, was supported by columns of delightfully wrought cast-iron and an impressive three-decker pulpit once stood in front of the shallow chancel.

While many were keen to see the reconstruction of St Andrew's, including the Rev William Cooper (appointed vicar of St Andrew's-with-St Catherine in February 1951), many were they who lamented the demise of this charming chapel, one of the last major examples of Foulston's work in the heart of Plymouth.

Hustings

Up until the Reform Act of 1832 few people in this country could vote in Parliamentary elections. In Plymouth at the beginning of last century there were little more than two or three hundred 'freemen' that were empowered to vote. The passing of the 1832 Act meant that now virtually any man occupying a house worth £10 a year rent, whether freehold or leasehold, had the vote. There were great celebrations, however it still only meant that Plymouth had less than 1,500 voters out of a population of some 30,000 (1 in 20). Furthermore it was to be another 34 years before voters could vote privately, by secret ballot, and in the meantime voting went on as it had long done, at public meetings like this one conducted outside the Theatre Royal in 1846.

Plymouth had been sending representatives to Parliament since at least 1298, but for over 500 years here, as elsewhere in the country, the right of election was in the hands of a very few men. Sometimes the matter was determined by the Mayor and Corporation on their own, sometimes by the freemen, either with or without the corporate body. There were four kinds of freemen; honorary, hereditary, apprenticed and purchased. Prior to the Restoration, in 1660, there were very few honorary freemen; the hereditary title was passed on only to the eldest son and similarly the apprenticeship system tended only to apply to a freeman's first apprentice. To purchase such an honour could cost anything from a few shillings to £25. Just before the 1832 Act was passed a large number of these freedoms were purchased but they were to be of little use to the buyers – these new freemen had not voted prior to 1832 and because they had not held the freedom for twelve months the new Act extinguished them. The money thus raised wasn't handed back though, it was put instead into the building of the new gaol!

Of the candidates at this election in 1846, only Ebrington had stood before. First elected in the Plymouth constituency as Viscount Ebrington in 1841, Ebrington, the son of Earl Fortescue, had first captured one of the Devon seats for the Reform cause back in 1818. Not that the nobility had that much difficulty finding seats, rotten boroughs (once populated areas where few people now lived and so there were few voters to win or buy over) and pocket boroughs (where voters were easily bought off) were to be found in all parts of the country. Indeed when Ebrington lost his Devon seat in 1820 the Duke of Bedford gave him the Tavistock seat

that his own son, Lord John Russell, had just vacated. Russell, a leading figure in the Reform movement, a future Prime Minister and grandfather of the philosopher Bertrand Russell, was first returned for the family borough of Tavistock in 1813 when he was just 21. In 1830, following the election occasioned by the death of George IV, Lord John was one of the four ministers entrusted with framing the first Reform bill, it was ultimately his job to compose the document.

So it was that there was great disappointment among the Whigs and their many supporters when, in May 1832, it was learnt that the Reform Bill was being opposed in the House of Lords. In Plymouth flags were put at half mast and a meeting that drew 26,000 people from the Three Towns was held in the Bull Ring under the Hoe (where the Belvedere was later constructed), all supporting the Bill. Great then were their celebrations when on the 4th June the Bill was finally passed.

In Plymouth John Collier and Thomas Bewes, both ardent Reformers, were the first Members to be sent up to Parliament. There was, however, no election on this occasion as both were returned unopposed. Devonport and Stonehouse newly joined together as one constituency which had particular cause to celebrate for, until the Reform Act was passed, there had been little or no recognized representation for the land in these two towns as the land was almost all leasehold (owned chiefly by the St Aubyns and the Edgcumbes) so they not only did not exist as a

constituency but there were few if any inhabitants qualified to vote for South Devon candidates. Plymouth on the other hand had a large percentage of the voters with a say in the South Devon result.

Collier and Bewes fought off two Tories in the election held after the accession of Queen Victoria in 1837 and four years later Thomas Gill and Lord Ebrington held Plymouth for Liberals. In 1846 Lord Ebrington was made a Lord of the Treasury and was obliged to stand again and this time his only opposition was the Chartist, Henry Vincent, whom he comfortably defeated. And so to 1847, three candidates for the two seats, Ebrington, Roundell Palmer (Lord Selborne) standing as a Liberal Conservative, and Mr CR Calmady. Calmady was the chosen replacement for Gill and rather than go out and canvass Mr Calmady decided to trust 'his admitted popularity'. The trust was misplaced and the Liberals lost a seat to the man who professed to be 'free from all party engagements and opposed to all rash and fundamental changes'. The voting was Ebrington 921, Palmer 837 and Calmady 769. At the next election the Conservative candidate, CJ Mare, topped the poll but he was subsequently unseated on a bribery charge.

Influence and intimidation still had its effect on elections and it wasn't until the introduction of voting by ballot that potentially riotous and unruly scenes like this outside the Theatre Royal came to an end. The last ever hustings were used here on 30th November 1868 for the South Devon election – Sir Massey Lopes was returned.

Derry's Clock

At a meeting of the Market Committee of Plymouth Corporation held on Friday 17th January 1862, it was resolved 'that the Surveyor be instructed to prepare a design with an Estimate for building a New Weighing House with an Arch Turret thereon to receive the Clock which the Mayor has announced his intention to present to the Council.'

A fortnight later at the next meeting of the same committee, there was a resolution passed that the Council should be recommended to place from £250 to £300 at the committee's disposal 'to erect a Tower to receive the Clock to be presented by the Mayor'.

Originally it was intended that the clock tower should be erected over Cornwall Street Gate, but when plans were examined by the committee at their mid April meeting, they decided that the tower would perhaps be better off on the south side of the Avenue, on the south side of the Fish Market (this was before the Fish Market was moved from Cornwall Street to the Barbican). Before the month was out, however, the Surveyor, having modified his plans, recommended that the Gate was still the best site.

Tenders were sought for the work and as they were well in excess of the budget set aside for the work (one quote was for £950, others were £568 if the tower was to be constructed upon Arches or £548 if it was put upon girders)

the committee decided once again to look into the possibility of putting the tower on the Weighing House. Within the week revised quotes were submitted and these now came out around £360 and the Market Committee decided to report these figures to the Council with the recommendation that the work could be modified to bring the cost down to within £300.

At the Council Meeting held later that same day, it was resolved, having heard the report from the Market Committee, that really the Clock should be placed in 'some public situation in the Town to be approved of by the Mayor' and furthermore that the subject be referred to the Local Board of Health. Now it just so happened that the Chairman of the Local Board of Health was the Mayor, William Derry, and the whole project, which was intended to commemorate the wedding of the Prince of Wales, was Derry's brainchild. The Mayor was also presenting the clock itself as a personal gift, it was only the housing that the Town was providing.

Before the end of June 1862 the Local Board of Health met and agreed to 'expend the sum of £300 in erecting a Fountain or Public Conduit' on which to erect the clock. There was no scope for this body to allocate funds for building a clock tower and so it had to be a drinking fountain which they could put a clock on top of!

And so to July 1862, the Royal Wedding is still nine months away and the Mayor submits a description and elevation of the tower to the Special Works Committee while the Surveyor produces a plan of the new site – 'at the junction of George Street, Union Street, Lockyer Street and George Place', (a site which at the beginning of the century had been well outside the Town). Everything is approved. At the next Local Board Meeting Henry Hall is named as the London based Architect to be responsible for the work.

From thereon the work seems to have gone ahead without further incident everything was completed on time, the bill for the building work exactly £300 being 'approved and allowed' just eighteen days after the Prince of Wales, Albert Edward (the future Edward VII) married the daughter of Christian IX of Denmark, Princess Alexandra Caroline Maria Charlotte Louisa Julia. The bride was eighteen, the groom was twenty one, they were to have six children three boys and three girls.

In the event the clock cost almost as much as the 'fountain' upon which it has since stood and at £200 it was clearly better value; whatever criticism has been levelled at the old 'Four Faced Deceiver' over the years at least it has continued to see action as a timepiece, the fountains on the other hand, all three of them have been forever dry.

Not so dry however was Harvey's Hotel; at one time owned by Derry and Co., this was formerly the private residence of Sir George Magrath. Described as a clever but somewhat eccentric physician, when Sir George died in 1857, there was evidently great commotion in the area, following the alleged appearance of his ghost! Housing spirits of a liquid variety for many years thereafter, this building, which once had a fountain of its own in its front garden, was later built onto, when the Wiltshire and Dorset Bank was constructed immediately in front of it.

Ironically the later building was converted into a licensed premises, the 'Bank', in 1984, and that same year the old hotel which had become known as the Lockyer Tavern was pulled down. This left Derry's Clock as the oldest structure in this area surviving not just the enemy bombing of the Second World War but also repeated requests for its removal to a more prominent site. Thankfully though this well loved landmark has remained just that, a landmark, enabling subsequent generations of Plymothians to orientate themselves around the many surviving pictures of this part of the nineteenth-century town.

George Street

'One of the earliest attempts to realise the future destiny of Plymouth was the commencement in 1776 of George Street as a pleasant series of suburban residences. Yet so little was that future foreseen by the general public, that it was remarked by one professional gentleman who built a house at its further end that he could never expect his clients to come so far to see him' (Worth 1890).

Prior to 1776 Plymouth had extended eastwards only as far as Frankfort Gate which stood approximately where Armada Way meets New George Street, a little to the south-west of the sundial. So the decision to develop the country lane that ran from here to Millbay was quite a major one.

The choice of the name George Street for such a thoroughfare of grand dwellings was not a particularly surprising one, George had been the name of the country's monarch since George I succeeded to the throne in 1714 and as fate was to have it was to remain so until 1830 as George III, 1760–1820, great grandson of George I, was in turn succeeded by his son George.

Certainly this new area of Plymouth was popular with the local dignitaries and by the time the Theatre Royal and its adjoining Hotel came to be built at the western end of George Street we find a number of eminent citizens living here; among them the proprietor of Frankfort Gate Theatre, Samuel Foote, and three men who served the town as Mayor, William Wellsford, Dr George Bellamy and Edmund Lockyer.

Samuel Foote (originally called Freeman) not only owned and ran the theatre but also regularly appeared in productions there. It was Foote too who retitled the venue the 'Theatre Royal', following a visit to the premises by George III in 1789.

Foote's Theatre Royal was of course later eclipsed by the Foulston designed building of the same name seen here at the other end of George Street. At one time intended to have been built on the site of its predecessor, this supposedly isolated spot was chosen instead and it is perhaps no surprise to find that the man whose brainchild the new theatre really was, was the then Mayor and George Street resident, Edmund Lockyer.

Few if any Plymouth Streets can, however, have witnessed the great changes seen over the years in George Street and within just a few decades of its establishment as a prime residential area new developments were taking place.

By 1823 four small schools had been established here and in 1844 the foundation stone for the George Street Baptist Chapel was laid on the site of the grounds and house of Dr Bellamy; an expansive site Nos 1–15 George Street were also erected on it.

The process of change into a street of commercial businesses was under way by now and when Millbay Station was opened in 1849, George Street naturally became the main thoroughfare to the town and it was rapidly redeveloped. As Worth observed in text he wrote for the issue of the *Graphic Magazine* (March 1878) in which this picture and many others appeared: 'Few communities have progressed so rapidly as Plymouth and its sister towns during the present century. What fifty years since were residential suburbs are now in the heart of the business quarters of Plymouth.'

'And with this growth, as we have already indicated, there has been great change. There are few landmarks which the Plymouthian who had left the town in early boyhood, and returned to it in old age, would recognise. The Tower of St Andrew's would, of course, be a familiar thing, but the sight of the surroundings would puzzle him mightily, for nowhere in the town has so great a clearance been effected. Narrow lanes have been turned into broad thoroughfares, dead walls have given place to handsome palisadings . . . Very lively and crowded are the chief business streets of Plymouth on a fine summer afternoon and George Street or Bedford Street may fairly vie with the leading thoroughfares of any town in the provinces.'

How puzzled would Worth himself now be, were he to stand here and look around him. 'The Bank', to his left, and Derry's Clock in front alone would be familiar. Behind him no George Street and no Bedford Street only St Andrew's Church Tower, albeit out of view. New George Street at no point crosses the line of its old namesake and there is no Bedford Street old or new as no part of it remains. Such was the cost of the Blitz and the post war city centre redevelopment.

But what of the George Street Plymothians would have known in 1878 when this view was published. Still cobbled and gas-lit it contained some of the best shops in town, and opposite the Theatre and the Athenaeum seen here were several popular resorts.

'The Falstaff' was at the end of the street on this side, then coming back towards this vantage point there was the 'Victoria Hotel' on one corner of Athenaeum Lane and the 'Swan of Avon', where Henry Squire had just taken over from William Joce, on the other. Next door to 'The Swan' were the offices of the *Western Morning News* which stood just yards away from the people in the forefront of this scene.

It is interesting to note here that despite the clear shadows implying strong morning sunlight a large number of the women in this picture are shown sporting umbrellas, is it just a coincidence perhaps that the window we see people looking in here belonged to the business of Charles Limpenny, one of the town's foremost umbrella makers? One of many long standing businesses here still trading in 1940 (under Mary Limpenny), the firm had taken over from ER Jago's 'fishing tackle, umbrella, archery and cricket warehouse' in the mid 1870s.

The Athenaeum

'At the corner of Athenaeum Street stands a small but imposing building, the local seat of learning. ... The Athenaeum was built by Mr Foulston in 1818–19, and is a particularly chaste and excellent specimen of the Grecian doric order, with a portico of four columns in front, extending to the breadth of 36 feet, each column being 3 feet 9 inches in diameter. The Plymouth Institution and Devon and Cornwall Natural History Society hold their meetings within its walls. The former society was founded in 1812, for the purpose of promoting literature, science and the fine arts in the town and neighbourhood. More recently, the Natural History Society has been established and amalgamated'. (Wright 1879).

Clubs or societies like the Plymouth Institute were a characteristic feature of intellectual life in the larger towns and cities at the beginning of last century. As the country in general and certain areas in particular witnessed a rapid expansion in population, so 'gentlemen' in industrial Britain found themselves with few places they could conveniently go and so they started forming 'clubs'. In the seventeenth and eighteenth century these clubs tended to form around coffee houses, coffee having then only recently been intro-

duced to Europeans. In Plymouth clubs were formed around the more salubrious taverns, like the erstwhile 'Pope's Head' at the top of Looe Street where the 'Otter Club' met, and the old 'Bunch of Grapes' in Kinterbury Street. The Otter Club's members were so called because they 'bathed regularly on the Hoe'. They met to enjoy each other's society '. . . Polemics and bantering personalities were banished from the club; the object was literary and scientific interchange, associated with the primary aim of good health'(Whitfield). Guests were invited 'to take tea and spend the evening'. The taking of tea was invariably by huge cakes washed down with punch, brandy, port and sherry, while supper would be taken with porter and cider.

Not all clubs were like this, however, indeed some were politically constituted and quite often private houses provided the meeting place. Neither politics nor fitness provided the common ground for the club formed by Plymouth lawyer Henry Woollcombe, though, in 1810. Formed mainly to discuss social problems, Woollcombe's club grew so successfully that on the second anniversary of their beginning he suggested to those assembled in his house that they form a society where lectures on Natural Philo-

sophy and other subjects could be given. Out of this, less than two weeks later, the Plymouth Institute was formed and by the time they came to have their fifth lecture they were meeting in the newly built Plymouth Dispensary, which still stands, in Catherine Street. In 1815 they moved to Frankfort Place and by 1817 the enterprise was successful enough for members to consider building their own premises. Founder member John Foulston, who had come to Plymouth as the architect chosen to build the new Theatre Royal in 1810, offered to plan and supervise the building free. At that time land was not expensive and the site chosen, just next to the Royal Hotel and Theatre, was then on the outskirts of town.

The foundation stone was laid on 1st May 1818 by the now 'Senior President', Henry Woollcombe. Modelled on the Temple of Theseus in the Agora of Athens it was named after the Athenaeum, the temple of Athene goddess of wisdom, in the same Greek city which was used in ancient times as a meeting place for learned men. Started the year after a similar institution in Hereford and twelve years after the London Athenaeum, the Plymouth Athenaeum took forty years to pay for, although in the meantime (1829) a museum, part of the original plans, had been added. Further extensions and developments occurred later. However, all was, of course, lost in the bombing in 1941.

Twenty years later, on 1st June 1961, the present Athenaeum was opened, the new entrance standing some yards back from the original at an angle of roughly 45 degrees to it. Now primarily a theatre, the Plymouth Institution still meets here and a regular series of lectures and exhibitions are still run.

Inside the Athenaeum

In 1832 this view of the 'Interior of the Athenaeum, Plymouth' was published. Engraved by C Moltram, the original drawing was executed by George Wightwick, later described as a 'witty and Scholarly architect' who also enjoyed a certain reputation as a dramatist and was said to be 'the welcome guest at every country house party' (Whitfeld). Born in 1802, George Wightwick appears to have been the epitome of the young gentleman intellectual, attracted by the newly established Plymouth Institution. Indeed in later years, 1848–49, he served as its president. He also belonged to another group, the Blue Friars – 'a select club, whose members dined in monastic garb and espoused the hospitable phrases of local Bohemianism'. However, such were the accepted principals upon which the Plymouth Institution was founded, it is likely that Wightwick's Bohemianism would have been of a fairly moral, as opposed to immoral or even amoral, nature. William Snow Harris, another Blue Friar and one time president of the Institution (1825–26) like Wightwick, had a keen sense of humour but it was in the realms of scientific research that he made his name. Indeed a famous painting commissioned by the Institution's founder, Henry Woollcombe, records Snow Harris surrounded by other leading Athenaeum members demonstrating to the Duke of Clarence his method of using copper as a lightning conductor on ship's masts. The Duke, whose visit to the Athenaeum occurred in July 1827, was undoubtedly interested in the scheme, for in 1787 his frigate, the *Pegasus*, had been struck by lightning whilst he had been on board. However, although the value of these conductors was recognised by the Royal Society and the Russian Navy, it was some time before Snow Harris's 1820 invention received proper recognition from the British Navy, who eventually ordered his conductors to be erected upon every ship, thereby at long last diminishing the catalogue of disasters at sea caused by lightning. In 1847 William Snow Harris was knighted for his work by Queen Victoria, at her own express command.

Essentially, then, the Athenaeum has traditionally been a place for the dissemination of knowledge and for the meeting of persons interested in the acquisition of knowledge and improving the mind. The very first address delivered in this hall at its opening on 4th February 1819, in fact dealt exclusively with the question of the mind and the pursuit of its intellectual and moral improvement. Peppered with Greek and Latin quotations, this discourse, delivered by Robert Lampen MA, harked back to the ancient Greeks and their writings and deliberations and he stressed the need, much as Arts and Social Science faculties at Universities and Colleges do today, for research and contemplation to be carried out for its own sake whether or not tangible results can be identified. 'It cannot' he wrote, 'be at all a matter of surprise that the importance of intellectual pursuits should be under-rated, when it is decided by the fallacious test of comparative utility'.

As he spoke those words Lampen would have stood on the rostrum shown here, directly opposite the president, treasurer and secretary who sat on a platform at the other end of the room. On either side of the large meeting room, 'parliamentary style' were set out benches, later replaced by seats upon which the male members of the Institution sat. The picture here is said to be misleading, as women were not admitted to the membership until the 1870s, although they may have been allowed in for 'conversazione' evenings and also on certain nights during the Autumn Art Exhibition. On permanent display adorning the walls and pedestals were a number of reproduction pieces of Greek statuary. The Duke of Clarence himself, later William IV, gave some casts of part of the friezes of some of the metopes (in the square spaces); the celebrated Plymouth artist Benjamin Haydon gave a cast of the 'tired horse of Selene' while Admiral Sir Byam Martin MP for Plymouth, 1818–27 and 1830–33, presented a replica of the Apollo Belvedere, another copy of which stands in the Italian Garden at Mount Edgcumbe. Replicas of the Elgin Marbles, acquired for the nation by Lord Elgin (encouraged by Haydon) just a few years earlier, also adorned the walls of this august institution.

Today, of course, the new Athenaeum is less elaborately decorated, however, the discourses, and lectures, carry on every Thursday. There are also fortnightly informal meetings of various other societies who now use the building. Membership of the Athenaeum today, meanwhile, continues to be open to all who are interested in the study and promotion of the fine arts, literature, science and technology.

The New Co-operative Buildings

On the 21st February 1894 the first block of Plymouth's new Co-operative buildings was opened in Frankfort Street. It was a day of great celebrations; all the society's rolling stock assembled at Friary Station and then moved on to Treville Street, led by the Town Band. At this point they joined up with a procession of over 500 people on foot who were accompanied by the Devonport Band and together they all made their way through the 'immense concourse of spectators' to this splendid edifice in Frankfort Street. Messrs C Goodanew and T Reynolds took pride of place in the procession. After a formal opening ceremony there was a celebration tea, at 6d. a head, at the Guildhall for the society's 2,500 members, followed by a huge public meeting which spilt over into St Andrew's Hall.

The Plymouth Co-operative Society was then barely 25 years old and its founder members had every reason to feel proud of their enterprise. It had been in a tiny little room in Tin Street (now Vauxhall Street) that ten local craftsmen first came together with the idea of setting up a co-operative society in Plymouth; they met two days after Christmas in 1859. The room was in behind Charles Goodanew's shoe-maker's shop and Charles and William Goodanew were two of the 'ten famous pioneers' who met that day. Fired, by all accounts, by the example of the Rochdale Pioneers whose exploits they had read about in George Jacob Hoylake's *History*, the Plymouth ten were determined to establish a society for obtaining goods in quantity, so that they could buy at a good price and then resell these goods, at a small profit, to members. The idea was that any profit would go partly to building up the business and partly back to members in proportion to what they each spent, this was the dividend or 'divi' as it came to be known. The net result would be that members, the working men of the town, would effectively be paying less for these goods.

That the ten were successful in their endeavours says much for these men, for the idea of the co-operative society was fast becoming a popular one, and although many came to be set up, a great number of early attempts, both here and further afield, failed. Robert Owen's attempts to set up 'villages of co-operation' at the beginning of the nineteenth century also ultimately failed but it was his writings and ideas that introduced many to the concept of co-operation as a way in which the working man could band together and stand against the oppressive capitalist regimes thrown up by the industrial revolution. The basic principles of the Rochdale Pioneers owe much to Owen's work and indeed they remain today at the heart of the Co-operative philosophy. Essentially these are; that membership is open to all regardless of class or creed; that there is democratic control – one man one vote regardless of capital holding; that there is limited payment of interest and further that all surplus or profit is paid back to members in the form of dividend in relation to their purchases, rather than the normal trade practice, whereby profit is distributed in relation to the amount of the shareholders capital investment.

Back in 1860, on the 3rd January, the Plymouth Co-op was established by 18 members who each subscribed one shilling. Within a month £3 had been raised and it was decided that the business could be started; so a shop was rented, an upstairs room above another shop premises in Catte Street and £2 10s 1d was spent on groceries to sell there. Initially only open on Wednesday and Saturday evenings, committee members took it in turn to man the shop. John Webb, another shoemaker and also the first secretary of the society recalled how they all 'vied with each other . . . as to who should be allowed to do the work for nothing . . .' It was not until much later in the year that they could afford to employ a full-time shop assistant. By that time things were going so well that they had taken new premises in Kinterbury Street and Mrs Esther Carter, the wife of a committee member, was paid seven shillings a week to keep the shop open all day.

As well as the trading aspect, one of the aims of co-operative movements was to promote education, Charles Goodanew's shoeshop also sold 'newspapers, pens, periodicals, ink and paper, and all other gear devoted to the spread of knowledge and information for the people' and a reading-room-cum-library was another of their initial achievements.

By the end of the 1860s a bakery business and a butchery department had been added to the Co-operative's operations, in the 1870s a coal store in Vauxhall Street was acquired and drapery and footwear became part of the expanding enterprise. The transport division opened with the purchase of a horse in 1875 and in 1883 the first Co-op dairy was opened in Treville Street.

As the movement went from strength to strength, new shops were opened here and there across the Three Towns and so it becomes easier to picture the excitement that followed in the wake of the eleven bread vans, three milk floats, sixteen hand milk barrows, three grocery vans, five oil wagons and eight coal wagons as they trundled here from the Barbican on the 21st February 1894.

Sadly, of course, this fine building was another blitz victim in the last war, however, the ten Plymouth pioneers would doubtless be amazed to see just how successful the Plymouth Co-operative is 130 years on with well over 100,000 members locally and a turnover approaching £130 million.

Sweets the Tailors

An early advertisement boasted 'ARMY AND NAVY UNIFORMS, LIVERIES, COMPLETE HUNTING, FISHING AND SHOOTING SUITS, LADIES' RIDING HABITS, JACKETS, ULSTERS'. All made 'to order in all the newest styles under my own supervision'.

These were the days when gentlemen could not only afford servants but could also afford to buy them uniforms or 'liveries'. Riding habits were, of course, essential for both sexes as the horse was still the principal means of transport. Jackets, as we know them, were fairly new, appearing for the first time in the late 1840s. However, on this occasion it is the word 'Ulster' that gives us the greatest clue to when this advertisement appeared. Ulsters, long, loose, rough overcoats, first became popular in the 1870s, although they were evidentally somewhat frowned upon by the ultra-smart. Mackintoshes, the first genuine waterpooof coats, were another of Sweet's main lines.

Available for years 'from 21/-', they revolutionised rain-wear in the 1830s when they were introduced. Nowadays most so-called 'macs' cost about fifty times that and are seldom more than showerproof. Such is the nature of inflation and modern living which finds us better able to get dry and less likely to get wet.

Sweet's main advantage over their competitors, however, was not so much that they could make up all the latest fashions to suit their customers but that they were able to suit the – BIG, SHORT, STOUT AND TALL, – generally 'off the peg', or made to measure within 12 hours if required.

'There's a fault in the make of some people's trousers,
That makes you uneasy whenever you bow, sirs;
But the Trousers at Sweet's are so very pliant,
They wouldn't give way to the stretch of a giant.' So ran their famous nineteenth century rhyme, the success of which carried them safely into the twentieth century.

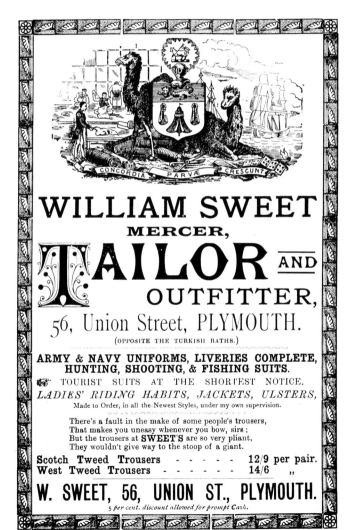

'This business has been established for a considerable period and since its inception has developed into a considerable degree of success and prosperity. The premises consist of a fine double fronted shop, with cutting room and workshop attatched.' The premises described are those shown here and today they are occupied by Cabinet Supplies, however, for many years this was the base of William Sweet, Mercer, Tailor and Outfitter. The description itself dates from 1894 and was written almost 50 years after William Sweet had established the firm in 1835. Originally based in Cambridge Street, he moved into Union Street to No 56 (opposite the Turkish Baths) in the late 1870's. At that time there were a dozen other tailors in the street and over 100 in the three towns.

Doidge's Annual

At the beginning of one of the early editions of *Doidge's Annual* was an illustration of a scene 'witnessed in many happy homes at various seasons of the year'. In this drawing three generations were depicted, the old, the middle-aged, and the young, 'forming a cheerful aspect of domestic life ... the whole enlivened by the visit of a friend who is evidently being received with true English hospitality'. The Introductory Address then went on to say 'While the friend above is being cordially welcomed by all ages, the Publisher rejoices to know that *Doidge's Annual* is cheerfully received into the homes of thousands in the Western Counties as well as throughout the wide wide World, not merely as a visitor, but as a constant resident, highly cherished, and much appreciated. As seen in the illustration, various fruits are to be partaken of, so we invite all to look into this volume, so full of rich and digestible fruit, suitable for every season of the year.' The address was concluded 'by wishing all a happy and prosperous new year'.

Certainly *Doidge's Annual* was a well received companion for thousands, every year, for many years through several generations. Over the years however it was to change in its appearance and content in a number of different ways.

The first twenty editions were overseen by Thomas Sweet Doidge himself who founded *Doidge's Western Counties Illustrated Annual* in 1869. Thomas Doidge was then in his mid thirties having been born in Newton Abbot in 1833. The family moved from Newton Abbot to Torquay when Thomas was six and there they ran a Book and Stationery business. Before long though they had moved again and his father J Sweet Doidge had opened his bookselling business in the Stonehouse end of Union Street. From there they moved to 30 Whimple Street, taking over the bookselling and publishing operations established by George Simms and Edward Nettleton (Nettleton had published a *Guide to the Three Towns* in 1838).

In 1866 Thomas bought the family business and a year later he moved everything here, first occupying just No 170 Union Street. This was the Plymouth end of the street and the site of these premises is roughly next door to the present Post Office there, just along from the 'Prince Regent'. Within a year or two of moving here Thomas launched his fourpenny almanack. It was an instant success and as it grew in size so it increased in price first to 6d, then 9d before becoming by the 1880s the 'largest shilling annual in the world', with a guaranteed circulation of over 13,000.

With all the other interests of the Doidge & Co business, publication of the annual was an 'all hands on deck' affair with various members of the family drafted in to help get everything out on time. Thomas Doidge married twice and outlived both his wives and had four daughters and one son; he was an ardent Christian and for many years ran Plymouth's Young Men's Sunday Afternoon Bible Class. Poor health forced him to give up a number of his interests in later years however, including his position as a Guardian of the Poor. A keen fisherman who 'knew the Sound like the back of his hand' Doidge died on Friday May 11th 1888, of a heart attack which followed a bout of rheumatic fever brought on several years earlier by a chill caught while out all night fishing.

For some years after his death the annual continued to be published by the old firm, then in 1900 it was taken over by Hoyten and Cole who were then based in Russell Street and later moved at the end of the 1920s to Whimple Street where the Doidge business had been working all those years earlier. By this time the price of the almanack had increased to 1/10d, the first increase for many years having come during the First World War when it went from 1/- to 1/3d then to 2/-, before levelling out at 1/10d, a price it was to hold until the Second World War.

In 1940 Hoyten and Cole published *Doidge's Annual* for the last time and the *Western Morning News* took over. The exigencies of war necessitated many changes; a series of three price rises saw the cover charge almost double, although it was to remain at 3/6d until the end; the annual was also reduced in size by 200 pages and in 1943 it had the last of its old fashioned covers. After the war the hard-back red picture cover was superceded in 1950 by a paper cover and then in 1953 by a plain non-pictorial paper cover.

By this time the annual had undergone all sorts of changes to try and keep up with the current fashions; gone were the short stories and the 'fun, wit and frolic' that had been there since Doidge's day, gone to were the colour plates, the pages of abbreviations and semaphore, the household hints and cooking tips and other useful pieces of information. There was, however, still the 'What has happened' look back at the year past, the West Country Pictorial, lighting up times, phases of the moon, market days and a calendar for the coming year. There were also one or two recent innovations like the introduction of potted biographies of local dignitaries and potted histories of local places, plus a comprehensive local sporting review.

It wasn't enough to save the annual though and in 1954 the much loved *Doidge's* made its last appearance, since when only the Plymouth Guild of Social Service's *Christmas Cheer* (published to raise monies for the Lord Mayor's Christmas fund) has come anywhere near replacing it. A slim magazine-like annual, edited for many years by Crispin Gill, this made its first appearance in 1953 and ran up until the mid 1960s.

Doidge & Co.

From their base in Union Street, Nos 169 and 170, the firm of Doidge & Co operated towards the end of last century one of the most successful businesses in town. Famous for the *Doidge's Western Counties Illustrated Annual* which first appeared in 1869, this was by no means the only aspect of their operation which gave them a high public profile.

A typical *Doidge's Annual* of the time ran to around 460 pages, a good 20 or so of which were advertisements reminding readers of all the other aspects of Doidge & Co's work. In addition to their own annual, which they claimed was the largest one shilling annual in the world and was reckoned 100 years ago to have a circulation of around 14,000, there was at their Union Street premises a large book department with some 30,000 volumes in stock.

These books were displayed in their 'commodious shop and four stock rooms' and 'included cheap and expensive editions of the works of the best English and Foreign Authors'. New books not in stock could, it was said, be procured at a very short notice on advantageous terms. Books were then not subject to the Net Book Agreement, designed to protect independent retailers, which currently ensures that new books are sold at a given price in all shops and Doidge's allowed discounts of up to tuppence in the shilling or three shillings and sixpence (about 17p) in the pound off the published price of all new books.

These were the days when only a few titles would have had the modern-style dust jacket but instead you could have the leading works of standard, poetical and prose writers handsomely bound in Morocco, Russia or Calf, making them suitable for birthday and wedding presents and Christmas and New Year gifts. Books for prizes and presentations, for schools and Sunday schools could also be leather-bound here in a variety of special patterns.

If you couldn't manage to get into the shop to see for yourself, that was no problem either for Doidge's would box you up a selection and send them out for you to look at,

thereby avoiding the disappointment many distant customers were wont to experience when ordering from catalogues.

As well as new books there were also a large number of second hand titles available at No 170 Union Street but it wasn't only books that you could buy here, there was also a large selection of novelties in their fancy goods department with the 'Newest and the Latest Games and Puzzles of the Day'. Among the most popular items then were Playing Cards, Bezique, Chess Boards and Men, Draughts and Dominoes.

Writing desks, work boxes, ink stands and stationery cases were other lines carried here as well as various items of stationery itself. 'Old English Scribbling Paper', 'Fine Cream Laid Note Paper', 'Highly Burnished Thick Cream Laid Note Paper', 'Extra Thick Fashionable Delicately Tinted Note Paper' or 'Doidge's Thick Ruled Manuscript' and 'Exercise Paper' were just some of the types of paper available. The ultimate 'marvel of cheapness' being 'Doidge's Monster 6d Exercise Book'. Also good value were their 'Monster Packets of Christmas and New Year Cards', containing 'Fifty Really Good Cards' here was 'more than six shillings worth of fresh good cards' for only a shilling '. . . A Scripture Text Presented with each Packet'.

Doidge & Co also undertook printing, relief stamping and copper plate engraving; 100 Ladies Visiting Cards exquisitely produced for 4/6, Gentlemen's only 4 shillings. They also sold albums for views, scraps, stamps, newspaper cuttings, confessionals and portraits. With photography still very much a novelty, in 1888 Doidge & Co desired to thank all the patrons of their Photographic Art Studio at 169 Union Street and inform them that they had now built this new studio.

'Admitted to be ONE OF THE MOST PERFECTLY LIGHTED, BEST VENTILATED, AND MOST COMMODIOUS GALLERIES IN THE KINGDOM', the gal-

lery was fitted out with all the newest accessories and was deemed by its proprietors to be suitable for taking portraiture of the highest class. These were the days when, among three pages of testimonials about the quality of the studio's work, one of the common recommendations was the fact that photographs from Doidge's bore 'striking likenesses' to their subjects!

This large and impressive studio was also 'peculiarly adapted for taking LARGE GROUPS OF FROM TEN TO FIFTY PERSONS, such as gatherings of the Clergy, Sunday School Teachers, Bible Classes, Church and Chapel Choirs, Clubs, Naval and Military Groups'. In the event, however, the photographic side of Doidge & Co's enterprises was one of the first branches to be dropped although the studio continued to be used for photography for sometime; Henry Yeo then Hedger's were among those who subsequently used it.

In 1900 Doidge & Co gave up the annual and Hoyten and Cole, then of Russell Street, took over the printing and publishing of it. By now Doidge & Co had streamlined their operations and although they still continued to advertise in the annual they had cut the number of their pages to four and had left 169 Union Street altogether. They remained at 170, however, for a number of years but as the twentieth century unfolded, so the name of Doidge & Co disappeared from the local business directories and by the twenties the South Western Dry Cleaners had taken over the old premises. The name was kept alive though until the annual finally folded in 1954 by which time the *Western Morning News* had taken over its publication, but that's another story!

The Royal Union Baths

Bathrooms in the home do not have a particularly long history, their introduction was a gradual one and even in the 'best London houses' they were virtually unknown prior to the 1820s and 30s. Indeed when Queen Victoria came to the throne in 1837 there was no bathroom in Buckingham Palace.

By the 1880s most big new houses in London were built with a bathroom and by 1900 most smaller houses were too; the provinces, however, tended to be a little behind in these developments. In fact even as late as the 1950s statistics show that in Europe and America as a whole, more homes had televisions sets than had baths.

The idea of bathing is an ancient one, often associated with religious rituals but seldom for simple removal of dirt. And the Romans, famous as leisurely bathers, used the term 'sanitas' to describe bodily health rather than cleanliness. Roman baths were enormous; the largest occupying a site estimated to be around twelve times the size of St Paul's Cathedral. However, with the fall of the Roman Empire came the disappearance of their social arts and 'for a thousand years Europe went unwashed'.

Apart from the isolated establishment of Turkish baths, by knights returning from the Crusades, the bathing of our medieval forebears was carried out, for the most part, in a wooden tub in the home; a wooden tub which, it should be said, was not thought improper for members of the family and even their guests to share.

However, right through to the dawn of the nineteenth century, hot water was seen as being an effective luxury and bathing was thought to be something one did to cure an ache or a skin disorder rather than simply to clean. Ultimately though it was precisely the sudden craze for 'water cures', available from spas and 'hydropathic establishments', that led to a revival in the interests of cleanliness.

In Plymouth the first step towards the development of such an hydropathic establishment came in 1828 when 'a charter of incorporation was granted by the King to Edmund Lockyer, Esq., and divers others, his majesty's most loving subjects, empowering them to erect commodious baths for the accommodation, comfort and convenience of the inhabitants and visitors of Plymouth'. Funded by private loans and the issue of £10,000 worth of £25 shares, the foundation stone for the Royal Union Baths was laid on 29th July 1828 by Sir Byam Martin 'acting as proxy for his present Majesty'. The building was opened on the 1st May 1830, less than a year after the first provincial indoor pool had been opened in this country – in Liverpool on 8th June 1829.

The Royal Union Baths which stood in Union Street, on the eastern corner of Bath Street, contained two large swimming baths, each measuring 70 feet by 30 feet (about 21m by 9m) and each had 'twelve neat dressing rooms attached'. Single-sex pools, 'the one intended for the use of ladies' was 'provided with ropes and other tackling' … 'probably', it was said, 'to assist them in the study of natation'. The idea of even an outdoor swimming pool was still comparatively novel in those days, so swimming, or natation, was not a pastime many women or country dwellers would be familiar with.

In addition to these two big pools there were also eight hot baths 'with commodious dressing rooms attached to them', these could be supplied with fresh or salt water. Most of the water used in the Baths was 'conveyed from the sea under the Western hoe, near the spot called the Rusty Anchor'. Shower and Douche baths were also available here and such was the novelty of them that a contemporary description considered it necessary to explain that in this way 'a stream of water may be projected on any part of the body and continued for any length of time'.

Two private cold baths, twelve feet by six, for those who 'swan like, would bathe in perfect loneliness' were also on hand as were two other large baths for children and those with skin complaints, while slipper and hot baths, with hot water were always ready to be sent to any part of the town 'on the shortest notice'.

A dip in the large swimming-baths cost sixpence, while a pound would buy you a course of twelve hot or tepid baths (there were other arrangements for the poor). Open from 6am till 10pm in the summer and 7am till 10pm in the winter, the Royal Union Baths were pulled down after less than 20 years to make way for the then new Millbay railway development. Meanwhile, although other Baths had opened up in the Three Towns, it wasn't until the mass production of cheap fireclay and cast-iron in the 1920s that hot baths became more a part of the British way of life.

The Hoegate

'Hoe gate, of which a view is annexed, is almost the only remaining evidence of Plymouth having been once a walled town, and as such we sincerely hope it may long remain a record of that circumstance. Its situation indeed may lead one to hope that the hand of modern improvement may not reach it; for few are the relics of ancient days remaining amongst us'. So ran the opening sentence of 'The Perambulator's' look at Hoe Gate, as published in the December edition of the short-lived *South Devon Monthly Museum* in 1833.

In the event the Hoe Gate was to stand for only a further 30 years, it being pulled down in 1863 a little over 200 years after it had been 'new built' by Timothy Alsop and leased to him for 99 years 'upon the payment of an annual rent of two shillings per annum'. Although there was much controversy surrounding its demolition, few were really surprised at its passing. As *The Perambulator* himself had observed: '. . . With all our love for specimens of ancient architecture, commemorative as they are of events in our former history, yet we would not carry this veneration so far as not to give way to the increased demands of our modern society for further accommodation in our streets, and the avenues to our town; to satisfy an increased population, using carriages of all descriptions in a way our ancestors neither did nor could use . . .' All this written over 150 years ago, long before the advent on the motor car; what would they make of the traffic that congests Hoegate Street today?

According to at least one Victorian local historian, RN Worth, Plymouth's town wall dated back to at least the early fifteeenth century. Certainly it was rebuilt and added to, at various times, but essentially the wall was made up of the houses and the streets on the edges of the town, and the gates, like this one, tended simply to link buildings and block off the major thoroughfares like this approach to or from the Hoe.

Hoe Gate was the last of the old gates to survive, the others – Friary, Gasking, Frankfurt, Martyn's, Old Town, Coxside and South Gate – were all 'removed' at various times between 1763 and 1863. Demolition of the gate, however, was not brought about entirely by 'a spirit of utilitarianism' for although it did to some extent get in the

way of the Corporation's plans for widening the street in the area, 'decency' was also said 'to forbid its continued existence'. It had, apparently, become a favourite haunt for courting couples. So it was that in 1863 MTW. Fox, then owner of the gate, after reserving some of the architectural ornaments and 'the crook of guineas buried in the basement' for himself, sold off the gate for £44. There is, incidentally, a suggestion that as some of the details of the lower stonework are similar to the Sally port and other gates of the Citadel, Hoe Gate may well have been carved by the same mason.

Timothy Alsop, or Allsop, although credited with its construction, doubtless just paid for the building work. Alsop was a well-known local merchant and member of the town corporation and was Mayor in 1648–49. Possibly one of the most notable figures to be associated with the gate however was William Elford Leach – 'one of the most eminent men whom Plymouth has produced' (Worth) – who was born 'in a room over this structure' in 1790.

Leach, one of the founder members of the Plymouth Institution, studied medicine at St Bartholomew's Hospital in London before going on to Edinburgh where he graduated in 1812. However, after qualifying as a doctor, it was zoology not medicine that he devoted his life to. A pioneer in several fields, his knowledge of crustacea was second to none in his day. Working from the British Museum, where he was appointed assistant librarian in 1813, he published many papers and his 'Malacostraca Podophthalma Britanniae' (or Monograph on the British Crabs, Lobsters, Prawns and other Crustacea with pedunculated eyes) was a seminal work. Sadly his work took its toll and he died in 1836 at his sister's home in Italy after having taken a very early retirement.

Exeter-born Dr Samuel Musgrave was another eminent man of letters who lived in this house. Described as 'learned, honest, talented, impolitic, unfortunate and financially deserted', Musgrave was said to have lived and died poor.

Today a plaque on the wall of Hoegate Street at its junction with Citadel Road marks the site of this celebrated gate.

The Citadel

This picture of the Citadel, sketched by W Hake sometime around 1870, shows the main square as it appeared for much of the nineteenth century. However, significant changes took place in 1895 when the large box-like powderhouse was pulled down to make way for the present officers' mess and the old ordnance range, standing to the left here, was demolished. The main accommodation block, B block, with its back wall replacing an original curtain wall, was erected in its place. A further alteration to this scene was effected in 1903 when the then 175-year-old statue of George II was moved from the middle of the main square a little to the right of, and slightly in front of, the Chapel, where but for a brief period during the last war after it sustained minor damage (the outstretched arm was severed by a bomb blast) it has since remained. The Royal Chapel of St. Katherine the Virgin upon the Hoe within the Royal Citadel, to give it its full title, was the only static element of this arena to undergo any major alteration last century when, in 1845, north and south transepts were added giving the simple little chapel of 1668 a cruciform shape.

Apart then from this and a few of the artist's distortions (the enormous St Bernard type dog looks as though it might have managed one of the 'toy' soldiers on the right for breakfast and a flag that size would have made any sail maker proud ... so who knows what else may not quite be right) this is doubtless how our Victorian forebears would have seen the inside of the Citadel.

The alterations to the chapel were carried out during the command of General the Hon Sir Henry Murray KCB, who presented a font once the work had been completed, the galleries were also added at this time. Sir Henry was General Officer Commanding, Western District from 1842 to 1852, the oldest memorial tablet in the chapel also dates from his time; it is in memory of his son Captain Arthur Murray who died in 1848. The appointment of Sir Henry represented a break with a long standing tradition for until 1842 the overall command of the Citadel had always been in the hands of the so-called Governor of Plymouth, a title which was first conferred upon John, Earl of Bath, in 1665. It is his name you see on the 'foundation stone' of the

Citadel. The Duke of Wellington was one of the last Governors (1820–1826) while the distinction of being the very last went to one of the 'Iron Duke's' right hand men, General Rowland Hill, Baron Almaraz, a veteran of the Peninsular War and the Battle of Waterloo (and not to be confused with the other Rowland Hill of the day, the man behind the penny post). Lord Hill, the soldier, was a popular hero in Plymouth long before his appointment as Governor in 1829, having passed through the Three Towns many times with his troops and having been awarded the Freedom of the Borough after his successful storming of the bridge at Almaraz, which enabled Wellington to advance through Northern Spain. General Hill was also popular with his troops who nicknamed him 'Daddy Hill'. In 1842, the year of his death, he was made a viscount.

General Murray, who succeeded Hill in 1842, was also a veteran of the Peninsular War and Waterloo, where he commanded the 18th Hussars. The alterations to the chapel were by no means the only reminders of Murray's time here in the Citadel; the barracks accommodation was also modernised and there also exists from his regime a set of 'Standing Orders of the Western District', dated May 1850, which give us some idea of life in the Citadel in those days. Men then we learn were expected to parade in heavy

marching order once a week and march some distance in it; caps were to be worn straight and not to one side. Officers were to wear their uniforms and swords at all times within the garrison. Among their other responsibilities NCOs were charged with ensuring that no disorderly women 'should have access to men in the guard room or when on duty as sentinels' (*Citadel*, F W Woodward 1987). Those men with wives and children were given instructions as to where washing could be hung; furthermore wives were not to appear on the ramparts unless they were properly dressed, while children could play in the ditch, then surrounding the Citadel, but not in front of the governors range.

The orders also stated that no strangers were allowed on the ramparts when the guns were being fired. While they were fired ceremonially and for practice quite often, they were never fired in defence at any time last century. Indeed the role of the Citadel as a defensive base was gradually fading, particularly after Palmerston's ring of fortifications had rendered it virtually obsolete.

The firing of the big old guns for practice did not stop, however, until sometime around 1890 when a target attached to a buoy between the Breakwater and Fort Picklecombe was missed and a boat hit instead – killing the man in it.

Regattas in The Sound

'An annual Regatta has been established at this port, called the Plymouth and Devonport Royal Regatta, patronized by his Royal Highness the Duke of Clarence, and supported by the joint subscriptions of the nobility and gentry of these towns; at which boats and yachts of different sizes contend for valuable prizes. This grand national amusement takes place in the Sound, which on such occasions wears a very beautiful and enlivening aspect. Thousands of spectators crowd the Hoe and the neighbouring shores, while an immense number of pleasure boats, filled with gaily dressed gazers, make the waters of the Sound 'instinct with life and motion'. The Regatta continues two days.'

The above account by Henry Carrington in one of the 1830's editions of his *Guides to the Three Towns* perfectly describes the scene captured by artist Thomas Allom and engraved by William le Petit in 1830 which was published under the title *The Regatta Starting*.

Plymouth had staged its first regatta in 1824, not quite 50 years after the earliest known regatta had been held in this country at Vauxhall, and five years before the first Oxford versus Cambridge race had taken place at Henley. Despite a few late eighteenth century roots, rowing and sailing clubs were really a feature of the early nineteenth century and in this part of the world it was the proud boast of Stonehouse that they had been staging such events for some time before Plymouth came in on the act. However, it was the Plymouth event that quickly became, not only the biggest but for some time, one of the most important in the country.

From the very beginning it was a major attraction. In 1824 it was estimated that the crowds on the Hoe were numbered in tens of thousands 'stretched in a deep mass from the foot to the brow of the promenade, and even clustered the edges of those most tremendous precipices at the Western Hoe'. While in the Sound was almost every description of vessel 'from rowing boat to the majestic 74 gun ship . . . Yachtsmen were everywhere in evidence, sauntering over the slopes with their handkerchiefs 'a la Belcher', their blue jackets and flowing trousers giving them a particularly seaman-like air – a compliment to the immortal tars who have in that dress made the four corners of the world feel their irresistable prowess.' (Wearing one's handkerchief 'a la Belcher' was, incidentally, a reference to the popular turn of the century boxer, Jim Belcher, whose habit of wearing a white spotted blue handkerchief around his neck quickly became a national fashion.)

Competing in these great events were racing boats of many sizes from under ten tons to almost two hundred tons. There were, of course, great benefits to be gained from this sport in those pre-steam power days, for not only was there a 'direct tendancy to improve the construction of the Sailing Ship' but it also meant that the nation's stock of sailing craft and experienced sailors was being inreased, which had to be a good thing if there was ever a national emergency. It has to be said, though, that this was very much a rich man's pastime and it wasn't really until the nouveaux riches (those newly wealthy through the industrial revolution) joined the landed gentry in this leisure activity, that it was really able to develop as a sport .

The local development of the sport received a great boost in 1827 when the Duke of Clarence came down with the 'cracks' of the National Yachting Club in his wake. The Duke contributed 'The Clarence Cup' a magnificent golden trophy weighing 92 ounces decorated with the full Clarence arms 'with cable handles supported by dead-geld dolphins, and the sides chased with marine shells and other devices.'

But it wasn't only for the impressive sailing trophies that people competed – the rowing races from the very beginning 'drew a scarcely less numerous crowd'. The men's rowing events, though, tended to be overshadowed by the ladies'. No team wanted to compete against the rowing-men of Saltash and even the Saltash ladies were pretty formidable, they took the eight sovereign prize in 1824. Ten years later a prize of £20 was offered for boats 'manned' by women and again their contest was the object of much attention.

The 1830s generally, though, witnessed an early decline in the sport. In 1830 a gale kept the Cowes yachts at home, then the Clarence Cup was withdrawn and all was left to the newly formed Royal Western Yacht Club to keep local interest afloat. In the event the yachting craze did not fade away and in 1876 the Royal Plymouth Corinthian Yacht Club was instituted. In 1890 the South Western Yacht Club was formed, as the sport gradually became accessible to those outside the monied few.

On The Hoe

The view here was produced for the issue of the *Graphic Magazine* published on 16th March 1878. Around the same time the following account appeared in one of the local handbooks:

'There are few more pleasant methods of spending a spare hour than by taking a saunter on the Hoe on a fine summer afternoon – the liveliness of the scene caused by the assemblage of hundreds of persons of both sexes and from among the most fashionable classes of society; the gay dresses of the ladies, who here delight to display all the adornments which nature and fashion combined, have bestowed upon them; these and many other attractions, contribute . . . a sense of pleasurable excitement . . .'

Difficult as it is to gain any real idea of the gayness of ladies' dresses from the engravings and black and white photographs handed down from those days, the indications are that they were indeed colourful, certainly when compared with the generally austere and drab designs for men then in vogue. Notice too that virtually all the men here are wearing hats, a practice that has only died out in relatively recent years.

With no radios to disturb this pleasant saunter on the Hoe, our guide also tells us of the 'inspiring influence of the music, as performed by a band of musicians – the Royal Marines – scarcely inferior to any in the kingdom'.

Certainly those were the days when the presence of the service personnel in the city was far more heavily felt than it is today, and as we read further we learn that outside the small octagonal Camera Obscura, seen here, was a raised platform and a flag staff, 'around which are wont to congregate some of the semi-nautical and military male-gossips of the neighbourhood . . .' While 'Immediately below the Camera, and approachable by a flight of steps, is a commodious seat, which is usually appropriated by another and not less interesting class of men. Here are wont to assemble (with that regularity for which servicemen are so famous) some of those veterans who in their youth sailed with Nelson to victory at Trafalgar; fought under Wellington at Waterloo – could give a graphic account of the Battle of the Nile, or trod country after country during the Peninsular War – men, whose early recollections are connected with some of the most stirring events of our country's history . . .'

Such men, by the late 1870s, however, were 'alas almost extinct' such battles harking back to 1798, 1805 and 1815, while the Peninsular War was fought between 1808 and 1814. Younger veterans 'who were with the Raglan in the Crimea, with Havelock at Lucknow, Napier in Abyssinia or Wolseley at Coommassie' were now, 'perchance', more likely to be found there instead.

In 1891 this commodious seat was replaced and extended with the construction of the colonnaded Belvedere. At that time, however, it overlooked a series of grassy galleries leading down to the old bull ring. Here in former times bulls would be baited; that is tied to a stake with a long rope which was wound around their horns and then set upon or baited by 'bull' dogs. These dogs would frequently be tossed high into the air, sometimes being caught by their owners. Others weren't so fortunate. However, in the end the bulls came off worst as they were always killed. It was a sport that became popular in this country around the sixteenth century, the same time as bear baiting and cockfighting. Plymouth had two bull rings, the one here and the other near the old Guildhall in High Street. While doubtless unpleasant for the bulls it was a fate few escaped. In 1604 two local butchers, William Jerman and John Jope, were fined five shillings, for killing a bull before it was baited, while 60 years later similar fines received from various butchers topped one pound, which more than covered the sixteen shillings paid to the town 'Smith' that same year for a new stake and 'greate' bullrope for the baiting of bulls. There were times in all this when bulls, mad with pain and fury, would break free and cause havoc in the streets as they charged about pursued by the viewing mob. However, by 1835 all this started to die out as Parliament outlawed both bull and bear baiting (in bear baiting incidentally it was usually the dogs who died as bears weren't quite so expendable in this country).

Along with the old bullring, the Camera Obscura also disappeared with the building of the Belvedere. Popular long before the introduction of photography, the Camera Obscura, literally 'darkened chamber' in Latin, was also 'invented' in the sixteenth century and artists often used this system of projecting images through a tiny hole and a series of lenses into a darkened room to trace images of surrounding scenery.

The top part of the Camera Obscura, containing the hole and lenses, could be revolved like a periscope and for 'one penny' you could witness the entire local vista on the oval table in the middle of this curious little building.

Not everyone knew its function though. One July evening in 1884 two young boys, watching a firework display on the Hoe, climbed up onto the roof only to be sent startled and frightened away when the lady in charge suddenly set the cuppola in motion.

Plymouth Pier

'When some six or seven years ago Mr Lancaster looked for the first time on the grand panoramic sweep of scenery commanded from that historic promenade – the Hoe – he felt that, much as Nature had done for the people of Plymouth, the people of Plymouth had still something to do for themselves. To Mr Lancaster it seemed that one thing was needful; that one thing he set himself to obtain with an energy and a faith which have never forsaken him, and then had the pleasure of witnessing the consummation of his hopes and desires yesterday, when the Promenade Pier which he has been the chief means of bringing into existence was formally opened in the presence of about thirty thousand people, about one third of whom were accommodated on the Pier itself. The weather was splendid.'

So began the account of the opening ceremony of the Promenade Pier in the *Western Daily Mercury* published on the last day of May 1884. The ceremony which had taken place the day before, Thursday 29th, was a great success and was addressed by many local dignitaries and officials, including the Mayors of Plymouth, Devonport and Liskeard – Mr Greenaway, Mr Brickwood-Hutchings and Mr Polkinghorne respectively – and the local MP, the Rt Hon P Stewart Macliver who noted that 'Public piers are now so common all over the country that no surprise need to be felt at one being erected in this borough.'

Certainly the pier was a fashionable item around the seaside resorts of Victorian England. The first had been at Brighton in 1823; originally constructed to unload the Dieppe packet, it soon became a popular place to promenade. Promenading was a principal pastime at weekends and for day trippers, most of whom had little desire to swim and, particularly among the young Victorian misses, little desire to have their milky white skin darkened by overexposure to the sun. Hence the craze for piers, stretching out on long legs of iron over the sea, almost inevitably, as each seaside resort was reached by the railway, so a pier soon followed.

In Plymouth the idea had first come up for serious discussion back in 1865 but nothing came of it until the late 1870s when Mr ES Lancaster had come to the Hoe. Ernest Lancaster was a wealthy merchant, his Victoria Clothing Company in Phoenix Street, which specialised in local serge, at one time employed 'hundreds of hands'. Living in No 1 Lockyer Street on the edge of the Hoe, he was obviously a major local personality and resolute enough to endure the numerous setbacks that hampered the development of the pier.

Apart from the fact that many local people did not want a pier in the first place, the Mayor, John Greenaway included, there were the usual problems of funding and of a change in contractors. In the event, however, sufficient finance was forthcoming, thanks largely to the efforts of the chairman of the pier directors, Baron Albert Grant, and the pier gradually took shape. Chatty Joe, writing in *Doidge's Almanac* of 1881, observed the beginnings of the work and went on to say that 'One result of its completion we hope will be the general lighting of the Hoe either by limelight or gaslight, and we shall then feel a debt of gratitude to the Pier Company in bringing about a result that ought to have been accomplished years ago.'

When it did eventually open the Pier, as can be seen here, only sported some of the attractions by which most Plymothians remember it, for it was not until 1891 that the 2,000 seater pavilion was constructed over the end of it. The original structure, which cost £45,000 (including £17,000 said to have been spent locally on labour and materials) was replete with toll-houses, a gentleman's lavatory and a 'cabinet des femmes' (built to a similar design to the toll-houses) at the entrance and lower down a reading-room, post office, stationery and book stall, refreshment rooms and a look-out house.

'Lighted by electricity', the pier was designed by Mr E Birch of London and it appears always to have been the intention to have a pavilion here but presumably finance was again the problem. It was not until after the pier had been sold by its owners in 1887 that the pavilion was built. Incidentally, had the original plans been followed through completely, an extra stretch of promenade would have been built from the pier entrance over the road back into the bull ring (later superceded by the colonnaded Belvedere) but the town turned that idea down.

The addition of the pavilion made the pier a very popular place; concert parties being a regular summer feature and on winter weekdays the floor was given over to roller skaters. Dancing, boxing and wrestling were other diversions that regularly attracted large crowds. The pleasure boats that moored alongside also were a big attraction although in the early 1920s some of the steamers were shed and as the thirties dawned the directors were again facing financial difficulties – all of which were sadly rendered irrelevant by German bombers in March 1941 when the 'bulbous spoon in the Sound' was wrecked beyond repair.

A lamentable state of affairs for all who loved the pier and, had he known of it, for Ernest Lancaster whose idea it had all been and who, back in 1897, had witnessed the destruction of his own business as fire devastated his unfortunately uninsured premises in Phoenix Street. But who knows, perhaps phoenix-like another pier may one day rise up here again, although once more there will arguments as to its desirability, particularly as part of the attraction of the Hoe is the limited extent to which which it has been despoiled already.

The Breakwater

Work on the Breakwater had been under way for just over ten years when this illustration, one of the first known pictures of it, was sketched by FC Lewis in 1823. Already there had been dramatic changes noted to the state of the sea inside Plymouth Sound and it was already reckoned to have saved many lives and many vessels.

A graphic account of the 'story so far' of the structure was produced by George Granville in 1825 under a title that ran to more than 100 words and began simply enough, *A Companion to the Plymouth and Devonport National Breakwater* . . . Looking at the figures depicted walking across its surface here a passage in the text begins to come to life:

'To him who has the courage to stand upon the massive pile, amid the howling tempest, and contrast with the awful roarings without, the peaceful security within; to view the huge waves, that approach as it were to engulph the helpless victim, suddenly arrested, dashing and expiring at his feet – the effect must be striking beyond conception, and the utility of such a work sufficiently obvious to excite his admiration. But how much higher must that feeling rise, on his being made acquainted with all the circumstances of its history, and the manner of its execution! By a knowledge of these, the national importance of the work becomes manifest. . . .'

Certainly the construction of the Breakwater was a phenomenal undertaking and the celebrations surrounding the laying of the first stone on the 12th August 1812 had been truly spectacular. Ships in the Sound were decorated with colours, crowds lined the many vantage points and the military were 'assembled in gorgeous display'. At the appointed hour of noon the signal was given and the first 'immense block of marble was plunged into the deep; the sparkling spray ascended on high, announcing the event to the distant spectators; the foaming waters closed on its huge mass; and, as it rumbled to its base, some say that Neptune murmured at this invasion of his dominions, and the Tritons howled displeasure. If so, however, the roaring of cannon, and the loud huzzas, that immediately succeeded and reverberated along the echoing hills, quickly stifled the sound and awed the watery gods into eternal silence'.

By the end of the year more than 16,000 tons of stone had 'promiscuously' been dumped along the designated line of the Breakwater and by the 31st March the following year the first part of the structure began to appear above the surface. In all a further 171,198 tons were deposited in 1813, 239,480 tons in 1814 and over the next six or seven years further annual deposits were around the 200,000 ton mark.

The sources of the great bulk of material were the Quarries around Oreston. This area had been chosen after other, nearer, sites had been rejected. Rennie had conducted a petrological survey of the land around the Sound and discovered that there was an abundance of easily procurable and suitable stone. However, the area from Cawsand Bay to Mount Edgcumbe was rejected partly because the Earl of Mount Edgcumbe was unhappy about releasing some of the land and partly because this coastline was a little too exposed for convenient working; as was the area between Bovisand Bay and Staddon Point making it difficult for vessels to load their large cargoes of stone.

A lot of the stone from Bovisand Bay to Mount Batten was simply unsuitable and anyway the problems of preparing a safe berthing in the Bay made the extraction of what stone was available prohibitively expensive. The land from Devil's Point to West Hoe included property in private hands for which a substantial price was being asked, while the Hoe itself, although offered freely under certain conditions by the Corporation, was beset with other problems.

In the end, then, it was in the comparative shelter of the Cattewater that the most suitable site was found and on Leap Year day, the 29th February 1812, a £10,000 lease was signed with the Duke of Bedford for 25 acres of the land he owned in Oreston. Within a few weeks, on the 1st of April, work began there on the construction of quay walls and a light, horse-drawn railway and the quarries were formally opened a week before the first stone was dropped in the Sound.

The only real drawback of the Oreston site was its distance from the Breakwater but the ease of loading the 45 hired and 10 purpose-built vessels that were used in the early years of this project more than compensated. At one time over 300 men were employed on these boats alone, with a further 300 in the quarries and as the structure became workable itself so more and more men were employed on the Breakwater. By 1819 there were over 100 men working there.

By this time the original mooring buoys that had marked the line of the structure had long since been discarded and boats now moored up to the large stones, seen here erected vertically at intervals along the northern side of this approximately smooth surface. Also visible here to left is the square projection which was constructed to offer a 'sheltered debarkation at any wind', there were landing steps on its three water sides.

Here can be seen the flagstaff 'from which the British ensign is displayed on public days and whence floated the Royal Standard, in the summer of 1824, in honour of a visit from His Royal Highness the Duke of Clarence'.

There was, at this stage, still a great deal of work to be done on the Breakwater, although it had gone well past the original six year estimate for its completion, nevertheless its impact was already considerable and 'neat little models of the Breakwater, and a variety of trinkets, beautifully polished, all manufactured from the materials actually used on the Work, are kept for sale at the fancy shops in Devonport and Plymouth'.

Breakwater

In 1832 J Britain and EW Brayley (Fellows of the Society of Antiquaries) published vast quantities of a work entitled *Devonshire & Cornwall Illustrated*. For many people this would have been the first sight they had had of this part of the world and among the many finely crafted engravings there were over two dozen views of the Plymouth area, including the one here of the Breakwater.

The 'Historical and Topographical Description' of this scene began thus, 'Among the great and sublime works of man, calculated either to combat with, or control, the energies of Nature, may be ranked the BREAKWATER, in Plymouth Sound'. In the text that followed the writer went on to describe the reasons for it having been built, the impact that it had made already and how the stone work had been obtained and brought on site:

'The annexed Engraving shews the surface of the Break-water with its recent finishing of squared stones, its crane for landing them, and the contrasted appearance of the water on the outside and inside of the wall; together with the vessel No 1 employed in the conveyance and depositing of the stones. By the aid of some ingenious machinery a cargo of eighty tons can be discharged in about three quarters of an hour'.

There were two basic methods of unloading the stone, one by chain and windlass which took something like three hours hard work and one by the so called 'ingenious machinery', used in conjunction with vessels purpose-built for the project. Capable of carrying loads of 70 or 80 tons, these sloop-rigged sailing boats were designed with two stern hatches, up to which small flat stone bearing trucks could be wheeled, along rails running the length of the boat, to receive and discharge their loads. The two sets of rails ran parallel to each other and each could accommodate eight trucks.

All the boats used for conveying stone had displacement scale gauges at the stern and stem posts and these were used as an acceptable means of determining the weight and hence value of the loads being transported. The first contract issued for conveying stone to the Breakwater was at a rate of 2s 10d per ton (just under 15p), while the original cost of quarrying a ton of usable material was a penny less than that. As the work progressed, fourpence (an amount covered by a single coin, the groat, for much of the nineteenth century) was knocked off the cost of quarrying while the cost of transporting the stone came down by a whole shilling.

After the first ten or twelve years it was estimated that the average cost for each ton of stone sunk at the Breakwater, including the purchase of land, the building of quays, wages and 'every other expense attending the establishment', was eight shillings and a halfpenny (about 40p) per ton. Even at these prices, which inflation today makes look very modest, the initial estimates for building the Breakwater came to well over a million pounds.

The impact of this enormous 'mole', calculated to combat and control the energies of nature, was almost immediate and certainly it was reckoned that havoc wreaked by the devastating storms of 1817 and 1824 would have been many times worse had the partially completed Breakwater not been there.

It was on a Thursday night in January, 1817 that the first really great test of strength came when a terrific hurricane came hot on the heels of a tide six feet above what was normal for a Spring tide. Queen Anne's Battery was swept by waves that threw their spray several hundred yards inland and the *Princess Mary* was driven ashore and smashed to smithereens with all hands and all passengers perishing.

In the Sound itself the frigate *Jasper* and the schooner *Telegraph* were both dashed against the rocks, the former at Mount Batten the later under the Hoe. Despairing men clung to the rigging as the vessels broke up but in no time at all the shore line was strewn with corpses and debris. The newly built road under the Hoe was destroyed and five-ton stones were tossed around like feathers.

Notwithstanding all this, however, it was generally felt that had the Breakwater not been there the damage and destruction would have been many times worse. As indeed it would have been in 1824 when 'the frightful tempest of the 22nd and 23rd of November bestrewed the whole Southern coast of England with wreck and desolation unparalleled in the history of the Island'. On that occasion it was the 'opinion of competent judges' that had the Break-water not existed 'the whole of the lower part of Plymouth would have been swept away and the ruin of shipping in the Catwater have been universal'.

Water two to three feet deep flooded the lower part of Plymouth as it was, while around the margin of Cawsand Bay 'such were the destructive effects of the sea, that houses and other property to the amount of seven to ten thousand pounds were destroyed'. Many ships and lives were lost, the *Coromandel* in particular being lost on the Breakwater itself.

During both storms, the Breakwater suffered itself, in 1817 a stretch 300 yards long, 10 yards wide and 3 feet deep was hurled into the sea and in 1824 some 200,000 tons of stone was shifted, almost 10% of the total dropped by that stage. Needless to say too that all the machinery was lost from the top of the structure and stones weighing as much as ten tons were swept effortlessly from the outer slope to the inner slope.

Overall, however, it was thought that the pounding taken by the Breakwater in these storms was ultimately beneficial in terms of strengthening and compacting the bulk of the deposit and in terms of streamlining and determining the gradients of the slopes on either side of the structure below the water.

Breakwater

Almost 24 years after the first stone had been laid for the beginning of the Breakwater, the first stone was laid for the construction of the lighthouse there. It was on a Saturday, the 16th day of April 1836 and the honour of laying this particular foundation block went to the then Commander-in-Chief of Plymouth, Lord Aurelius Beauclerc.

Plans for a lighthouse on the Western end of the Breakwater had first been drawn up by John Rennie in 1820 (Rennie had been involved with the design of the Bell Rock lighthouse opposite the mouth of the Tay, about 12 miles from Arbroath and so had some experience in this field). The Western end, being adjacent to the main entrance to the sound, was deemed to be most appropriate for a lighthouse. In their original plan Rennie and Whidby had suggested a lighthouse at either end of the structure, now though it was thought best to erect a beacon at the Eastern end.

In the event John Rennie never lived to see the lighthouse or the Breakwater in its finished state, for after a period of illness he died on the 4th October 1821. His son, John, had been touring Europe when he had first heard of his father's condition and, but for being delayed himself by an attack of malaria, would have come straight back to his father's side.

John Rennie did make it back before his father's death, though, and together with his elder brother George (who was primarily a mechanical engineer) he oversaw the completion of the Breakwater and the building of London bridge, a project that had not even been started in his father's lifetime. John Rennie senior was born on a farm in Scotland in 1861 and was buried in St Paul's Cathedral; among the more famous of his other designs were Southwark Bridge (1817), old Waterloo Bridge (1819) and the London and East India Docks.

The lighthouse that was eventually constructed on the Breakwater was not, however, drawn up by either John Rennie snr or jnr, for in 1841 the Admiralty, having reviewed the whole lighthouse question, instructed the Trinity House Engineers, Walker and Burgess, to prepare a design, which they completed the following year. This new plan added two floors to the Rennie design and now meant that the lighthouse was to be furnished with a store room at entrance floor level (eight feet above the Breakwater), a large freshwater cistern below that and a living room above it. This room, 14 feet in diameter contained a stove, a water pump, a sink, a dresser and a cupboard and it was situated just below the sleeping room which was designed to accommodate three lightkeepers. Within the top level of this structure was the 'air room' and finally above that the housing for the lantern itself. At its highest point the lighthouse was 126 feet high, 78 feet above the top of the Breakwater.

Built with fine white granite from quarries in Par, work on the Breakwater lighthouse was completed in two years eight months and eighteen days and the lantern was lit for the first time on Saturday 1st June 1844. This, of course, meant that the 'Light-vessel' which had been moored at the western end of the Breakwater since work had first begun could be de-commissioned after over 30 years service.

A year after the lighthouse had come into use the first stone was laid towards the construction of the Beacon on the Eastern end of the Breakwater. Again the Commander-in-Chief of Plymouth officiated and this time it was Admiral Sir John West who fulfilled that role. Shaped in the form of a truncated cone, the beacon base has a diameter measuring 20 feet while the top of the twelve courses is just over five feet in diameter. Being a relatively straightforward structure it did not take long to complete and by 1st November Sir John West was back on the Breakwater to top it out.

Generally, though, the completion of the Breakwater is said to have been in 1844 when the lighthouse was first lit, although technically the closing stone wasn't added to finish the structure until 1865 and repair work and general maintenance has been ongoing since then. Whichever date we take, however, it nonetheless means that neither of the original engineers lived to see it completed, Rennie having died in 1821 and his partner, Joseph Whidbey, in 1835.

Whidbey was three or four years older than Rennie but he continued to work on the Breakwater, supervising operations from his home, Bovisand House, until March 1830 by which time he had celebrated his 73rd birthday. Buried in Taunton, Whidbey was working as Master-Attendant of Woolwich Dockyard prior to his starting on the Breakwater project. He had been, in his mid-thirties, sailing master of the *Discovery*, under a former mid-shipman of Captain Cook's, George Vancouver, on his exploration of the Pacific.

Both of Rennie's sons, however, survived the completion of the Breakwater, George dying in 1866 aged 75, while John, Sir John as he became, survived into his eighties departing in 1874. William Stuart who, in 1845, was still Superintendent of the Breakwater, was another to see the work through, Stuart had been on the scene since the 1820s at least.

Expenditure on the Breakwater was estimated, by Sir John Rennie in 1847, to be £1,446,963, 'which included every charge' incurred in building this massive 3,620,444 ton structure. That it was money well spent is evidenced today by the fact that the Plymouth Breakwater, which gives shelter to over 1,000 acres of water space, is today one of the oldest, successful, free-standing breakwaters in the world.

Smeaton's Lighthouse

On a night in December in 1755 a fire was discovered in the lantern of the lighthouse on the Eddystone rocks. The duty keeper, 94-year-old Henry Hall, found smoke billowing down from the cuppola in the early hours of the morning, he roused the other two keepers but they were either too late or too ineffectual. The lead roof had started to melt and the framework was giving way. Soon there were burning timbers falling around them together with lumps of molten lead. The men retreated to the lower storey which was of granite and timber courses and at 10 o'clock that morning they were rescued. The lighthouse, built by John Rudyerd 50 years earlier, was by then just a smouldering stump.

Robert Weston, one of the principal shareholders in the old lighthouse, wasted little time in approaching an engineer to design a successor to Rudyerd's construction. The man thus selected was a 31-year-old instrument maker turned engineer who specialised in windmills and watermills, John Smeaton.

Smeaton came to Plymouth for the first time in March 1756, after a journey from London that took six days. It was to be another seven days before the sea state was sufficiently calm for him to visit the site of the lighthouse and a further three before he was able to make an albeit dangerous landing on the rocks themselves.

With a reputation as a highly skilled model maker who believed that experiment 'was the only certain way of coming at the truth in mechanical enquiry' and whose work on wind and water mills is still regarded as a 'paradigm of experimental method in fluid mechanics', Smeaton applied his design approach to this new project. His observations led him to conclude that a lighthouse on these rocks should be shaped more like a tree trunk and built in stone rather than wood.

Winstanley's octagonal tower had stood but five years, it was blown down during a violent storm in the early hours of the morning of November 27th 1703. The architect, who had always said that he would be prepared to stay in the lighthouse during the worst storms imaginable, had come down from Essex especially to ride out the bad weather on the Eddystone Reef and was lost along with his creation.

Henry Winstanley's elaborate polygon shaped tower had been the first light upon these rocks and whilst it stood it undoubtedly saved many lives. Rudyerd's successor to it was in many respects a lot more simple; it was rounded, stone based, but timber clad and topped, and only slightly tapered. Smeaton's decision to erect an all stone tower with an even heavier stone base was clearly designed to overcome the two previous elements of destruction – wind and fire.

The idea of a stone-built structure met with some resistance at first but Weston backed Smeaton and work began inspecting quarries in and around Devon and Cornwall for suitable stone. Granite was to be used for the external work, Portland stone for most of the interior. A large workyard was established at Stonehouse, just off Millbay near the Longroom where all the stone was to be brought, cut in one ton weights and trimmed to match wooden moulds. Smeaton devised an ingenious system of dovetailing, cramping, wedging and cementing his blocks together; the experiments he made in investigating every variable affecting cement in situations where it would be alternately wet and dry are regarded as classics in the history of cement.

In addition to all the work Smeaton did on his lighthouse he also made sure it was firmly rooted to the spot on which it was to stand by carving out a series of steps on the sloping rock itself, to hold the foundation, a block of solid masonry 35 feet high.

Work began on the rock in August 1756, the first stone was laid the following June and on October 16th 1759 the 24 candles in the lantern house were lit for the first time. In all that time there had only been 421 days when the weather was good enough for the men to work on the rock and not

all of those could be used. It was estimated that in all 'the whole time really spent in the erection of the building did not amount to sixteen weeks'.

Smeaton's lighthouse became the prototype for nearly all the sea-girt, wave-swept lighthouses that have been built since and might indeed have been still standing, complete, on those rocks today were it not for the waves' erosion of the foundation rock itself. So it was that the decision was taken to construct another tower on the adjacent reef and after a suggestion put by Mr FJ Webb FGS a subscription was raised to rebuild Smeaton's tower on the Hoe, where it came to replace the old Trinity obelisk in 1882–4. The old base was left on the Eddystone Reef, however, and a new one was given by the local builder, John Pethick.

Today it still stands as a permanent reminder of the Yorkshire born law student, instrument maker and astronomer, famous for his many contributions to the science of engineering. It was not, however, his only lighthouse for Smeaton was also responsible, in 1766, for the construction of the harbour and lighthouse of St Ives, a structure which has undoubtedly fared better than the two he built at Spurn Head in Humberside 1771–76. Never an easy place for the lighthouse architect, one of these was washed away the following year, leaving only a low hut like circle, while the other was in use for 100 years until it became the victim of a storm and now stands, a little forlornly, without its top.

The Eddystone Lighthouse

John Smeaton revisited his lighthouse on a number of occasions. In 1761 he found it clean and in good order inside while outside an accumulation of limpets and marine vegetation around its base made it almost look as though it were growing out of the Eddystone Rock itself. Smeaton had taken every measure he could think of to make his structure permanent and it was showing no signs of being anything else, well . . . almost no signs.

Just four months after Smeaton had left Plymouth in 1759, the youngest of the three lighthouse keepers had written to him after twelve days of gales and described how 'the house did shake as if a man had been up a great tree'. Now whereas Rudyerd's lighthouse had regularly required work on it's timbers for worm, rot and storm damage, Smeaton's tower always looked to be alright after a storm. Indeed it emerged unscathed after a particularly violent storm in January 1762, a storm that had been so fearsome that many local skeptics did not expect to see the tower survive the night at all; but it did shudder.

It also shuddered in 1766 when Smeaton again came down and inspected his light. The problem lay not in the tower but in the house rock upon which it stood; there was a cavity in its steepest face which the waves bore into and seemed to shake the heart of the stone. This was the 'cave' which the keepers took refuge in when Rudyerd's tower burnt down. Smeaton was uncertain as to just how much of a problem this cavity would prove, 'all that can be said is that hitherto it does not seem to have been of any hurt thereto'. He then added 'I could undertake to fill it up and make it solid at the expense of about £250 besides my own attendance if it was thought worth the charge'.

Neither Smeaton nor the proprietors of the lighthouse seem to have taken the matter any further though and it would appear that another fifty years elapsed before the matter was raised again. In 1813 and again in 1818 Robert Stevenson (architect of the Bell Rock Lighthouse and the first of the great dynasty of the Scottish Stevensons associated with lighthouses) visited the Eddystone and expressed concern about the cavity. He reckoned that were the cut to be undermined any further, the tower could be in considerable danger and although there was no evidence to show erosion had taken place, the keepers constantly spoke of the terrifying shake when the seas crashed in hard from the south west. Stevenson reported that he 'considered the

importance of the subject to be such as to require the immediate attention of the Trinity Board', but once again no action appears to have been taken.

In 1835 more alarming reports of the Eddystone shake were received and Trinity House issued a notice to seafarers that it might be necessary to abandon the lighthouse in the near future but nothing further seems to have been done.

Trinity House records have unfortunately been destroyed in three major mishaps down the years but the constitution of this body goes back at least to 1512 and Henry VIII. Successive monarchs, however, have had different attitudes to the powers of this body and it wasn't until 1836 that an Act of Parliament compulsorily transferred all English and Welsh lighthouses to Trinity House. The Scottish and Irish lighthouses were also transferred to their respective authorities and the whole process cost the Government £1,000,000.

At long last it spelt the end of privately owned lighthouses and meant a national programme could now be planned.

Still, however, little was done about the Eddystone shake; although in 1837 the inside of the tower was strengthened with iron clamps and ties from top to bottom and the projecting cornice at the top, designed to stop waves breaking over the light, was reduced in size in case it was actually doing more harm than good by giving the sea something substantial to strike against. Thus fortified, Smeaton's tower came to celebrate its centenary, a year later it was added to the image of Britannia on the reverse side of Britain's bronze coinage (it disappeared in 1895 but a lighthouse was reinstated, on pennies at least, from 1937 until decimalization).

Strengthened again in 1865, there was, of course, by this time another weakness with respect to Smeaton's lighthouse and that was in terms of its lighting. Although the power of the light had long since been increased from its original 67 candle-power to over 1,000 candle-power, with the introduction of Argand lamps in 1810 and then with subsequent advances to over 7,000 it was still only about a tenth of the strength of lights then available but these were too big for Smeaton's tower.

So it was that in 1877, following a Trinity House survey which found definite evidence of erosion of the House Rock, the decision was taken to build a new lighthouse on the reef. It was to be designed by the Engineer-in-Chief of Trinity House, James N Douglass.

There was only one problem, where on the Eddystone to site it, the House Rock was the only major one completely exposed at low water. Stevenson had encountered the same difficulty at Bell Rock, and as he had done a dam would have to be constructed to create a 'dry' area which could be excavated and built upon. This was to be the hardest and most time consuming part of the operation; work began in July 1878 and even with all the advances available to them since Smeaton's Day it took almost a year to construct the dam and to see clearly the ground they had to excavate.

Work then steamed ahead and on the 19th August 1879 the Duke of Edinburgh (the then Master of Trinity House) accompanied by his brother, the Prince of Wales (the future Edward VII) laid the foundation stone of Douglass's lighthouse on the Eddystone reef, as seen here from the top of Smeaton's tower.

Douglass's Lighthouse

When it came to the construction of the fourth Eddystone Lighthouse there was no more obvious candidate for the job than James Nicholas Douglass. Son of one of the principal lighthouse engineers of his day, Nicholas Douglass, James and his brother William had been all around the country's coastline with their father from one inaccessible point to another. Their schooling had come from whatever tutors or institutions were in the area they were in at the time and not surprisingly the boys grew up with a great knowledge of lighthouses.

When he was just twenty one James, after having served an orthodox engineering apprenticeship, was made chief assistant to his father in the task of constructing a lighthouse on the Bishop Rock, just off the Scilly Isles. A few years later he was commissioned by Trinity House to build another lighthouse in his own right. This was another difficult rock tower, the Smalls, off the coast of Wales and was immediately followed up by a more problematic one still, the Wolf Rock off Land's End.

In 1862 Trinity House appointed James Douglass their Engineer-in-Chief and so it was that when he came to undertake the Eddystone project, sixteen years later, he had had a wealth of experience that few men, if any, have ever matched in the field of lighthouses. A marked contrast to the three men who had tackled the reef before him. He also had at his disposal equipment that his predecessors had doubtless barely dreamt of; pneumatic rock drills, mechanical cranes, winches and pumps, and a steam boat.

This boat was the twin-screw tender *Hercules* which had recently returned to this Country from Ceylon where it had been employed in the construction of the Great and Little Basses Rock Lighthouses. Especially built for Douglass to assist in lighthouse building, the *Hercules* was capable of steaming at ten knots, it could carry 120 tons of stone and was fitted with railway tracking for the speedy conveying of blocks from its hold to its stern. A far cry from the craft available to Winstanley, Rudyerd and Smeaton, the *Hercules* also served as a floating workshop and accommodation block.

These many advantages, however, did not mean that the construction of the fourth lighthouse upon the reef was an easy matter. Because the only practical site available was largely under water, it meant that men had often had to work waist high in the water, with lifejackets on and ropes around them in case they got caught by a wave or by the rising tide. Douglass himself was away a lot of the time the work was being done, engaged upon other engineering concerns with Trinity House, and consequently left much of the work to his son William Tregarthen Douglass. As Fred Majdalany observed in his entertaining book *The Red Rocks of Eddystone*, the work 'was difficult, dangerous, and extremely uncomfortable, and James Douglass, who had started his own career assisting his father, no doubt felt that it would do his own son Willie no harm to have a similarly rough introduction to the family calling' (Willie's uncle William Douglass was Engineer-in-Chief to the Irish lighthouse authority).

Thomas Edmond, another Trinity House man, also assisted with the building work and after the base had been fashioned and the foundation stone laid, in August 1879, work progressed rapidly. Again because, unlike their predecessors, they were not reliant upon either sail or oarsmanship, Douglass's men scored the great advantage of being able to extend the working season on the reef from July to October, to between February and December. Within two years they were ready for the last stone to be laid and this was done by the Duke of Edinburgh who landed on the rock when passing up the Channel in HMS *Lively* on 1st June 1881.

The lantern was fitted before the winter set in and William Douglass was left in sole charge of the internal arrangements. During that winter of 1881 William had opportunities to watch the action of heavy seas on both towers. From the lantern of the new structure he observed that 'the waves, striking the old tower at its foundation, ran up the surface with great force, unimpeded by any projection until arriving at the lantern gallery, where they were partially broken up by the cornice, and then expended themselves in heavy spray over the lantern, entirely excluding from view, for the space of half a minute, any portion of the tower or lantern'. By contrast 'at the new tower, the heavy seas striking the cylindrical base were immediately broken up, and rushed round to the opposite side, the sprays only ascending to the height of the lantern gallery'.

The new lighthouse was after all twice as tall and four times as large as Smeaton's, it had nine rooms as opposed to four and it contained 2,171 blocks of granite weighing 4,668 tons. Benefitting from the pioneering work of Smeaton the new tower had indeed been designed to last.

On the 18th May 1882 the new light was lit for the first time, again the Duke of Edinburgh officiated, and a few weeks later James Douglass received a letter from the Prime Minister, William Gladstone, telling him that the Queen proposed to confer upon him a knighthood.

Meanwhile the light in the old tower had been extinguished back in February and William Douglass was given the task of overseeing the dismantling of the old tower for re-erection on Plymouth Hoe in place of the old Trinity House sea mark there.

Manned by three keepers for 100 years, in 1982 the Eddystone became the first rock lighthouse to be fully automated. To mark the tower's centenary HRH Prince Philip, Duke of Edinburgh, was flown out to the tower and landed on its new helicopter landing pad above the light. He then had a tour of inspection of the now deserted lighthouse which is now controlled from new quarters at Penlee Point, quarters which do not have a direct line of vision with the light!

Drake's Island

'The annexed View represents the western side of Plymouth Harbour, as it appears from the Hoe. Its chief features are the Isle of St. Nicholas, and the picturesque grounds of Mount Edgcumbe'.

In this way the many thousands of readers of Britton and Brayley's *Devonshire and Cornwall Illustrated* living outside the West Country were introduced to what was probably their first ever glimpse of this grand scene. The account continued by describing the island: 'Commencing with its name, we remark, that at different periods it has been called St Nicholas's, St Michael's and Drake's Island.' They also mentioned that Risdon in his sixteenth century review of Devonshire had suspected that in Saxon times (when the Tamar formed the boundary between the land occupied by the last Britons and the rest of Saxon England) that the island may have been known as 'Tamarworth'.

Certainly by 1135 it was called St Michael's Island and there was a small chapel on its summit dedicated to the archangel, the great prince of all the angels and leader of the celestial armies. The cult of St Michael was very popular in the middle ages, the annual festival in his honour being instituted as long ago as 287. His day, Michaelmas Day, the 29th September has long since been established in England as one of the four quarter days, days fixed by law and usage for payments of rent due and for the beginning and termination of contracts between landlord and tenant. It is also the day that, traditionally, magistrates are chosen and the lord mayor of London is elected.

Customarily celebrated with the eating of goose, the poet George Gascoine wrote of Michaelmas in 1577, 'At Christmas a capon, at Michaelmas a goose. And somewhat else at new Year's tide for feare the lease flies loose.'

Christmas of course is traditionally associated with St Nicholas, the original Santa Claus (although his day is somewhat earlier in December – the 6th) and while we still do not know why it was in St Nicholas's honour that the chapel on St Michael's Island was rededicated in the late middle ages, the fact remains that it was.

Confusingly though, both names survived for some time, indeed throughout most of the nineteenth century St Nicholas's Island tended to be the most common appellation, even though the chapel itself was pulled down in 1548 and the island's associations with Drake began only 30 years or so later.

The chapel was pulled down in order that the island might be properly fortified against an enemy attack and over the next 400 years the story of the island is almost exclusively the story of its use as a defence post, although one or two notable prisoners were held here during the civil war, when the garrison was considerably strengthened.

'Since that period the fortifications on this island . . . have been greatly augmented, and it now constitutes the chief defence of Plymouth Sound.' So continued the Britton and Brayley account written in the late 1820s, at the end of a decade which had seen various comings and goings on the island. In 1822 we know two officers and 72 men were stationed here while a barrack return for 1825 suggests there was accommodation for as many as three officers and 96 men of the 32nd Foot (Duke of Cornwall's Light Infantry) here.

The arrival of the 1830s heralded a major building programme for the island, notably the commanding officer's house and a new barrack block (which was to obscure the view of the ablution block, built of finely cut limestone in 1790 and seen here overlooking the rocks which themselves form an island at high tide). But the writers weren't to know all this and at the time of their review the only other comment they had to make about the island's resources was that 'in addition to its other defences, it contains furnaces for heating balls red-hot'.

This was, of course, written unwittingly towards the end of the age of the wooden fighting ship and the story of Drake's Island over the next hundred years or so was the story of its defences ever being updated to deal with successive generations of war machinery. Big guns here and elsewhere around the Sound became obsolete at an unprecedented rate as steam powered ironclads replaced the old wooden sailing ships . Faster ships, of course, necessitated the faster reloading of guns and so on.

In the 1860s threats of a French invasion occasioned a frenzy of fort building around the Sound and the Three Towns, including the construction of massive casemates to house big new guns on the island.

Towards the end of the century there was even a station here for launching underwater Brennan torpedoes. However, at no point in the nineteenth century were the defences here or anywhere else around the Sound used in earnest, guns only ever being fired for practice.

Essentially, the silhouette of the island has changed little and the headland of Edgcumbe and Penlee Point even less since Thomas Allom provided his sketch for the engraver Heath to work on. However, the entrance to Millbay is barely recognizable and you'll seldom see a square-rigged ship in full sail slipping gently out into the Sound these days.

Millbay Station

The band of the Royal Marines, 'seated in an open truck embowered with flags' were playing 'See the Conquering Hero Comes' and the assembled multitudes were joining in. The local dignitaries were there, some happier than others and all around there was a sense of history in the making. It was the 2nd of April 1849 and the railway had at last penetrated the heart of Plymouth.

A source of great wonderment and excitement, the 'Iron Horse' had first come to Laira in May of the previous year, stopping all onlookers in their tracks. Out beyond Plympton, Paul Ourry Treby interrupted his hunt to watch the first 'steamer' go down Hemerdon Bank. Initially however, it had not been the intention of the South Devon Railway and especially its great engineer, Isambard Kingdom Brunel, to bring steam trains to Plymouth. First authorized to construct this line in 1844, this was originally going to be the first of the great atmospheric railway lines. Under this system, carriages were to be propelled 'by means of the pressure of the air upon pistons to which they were attached'. The pistons being worked in huge tubes laid between the rails; the pressure to work the pistons coming from stationary steam-engines. Sound in theory, practical difficulties, which in later years could have been overcome, hampered the scheme which ultimately proved to be a costly failure, and the nearest such trains came was Newton Abbot.

However, while Brunel's belief in this system bore no fruit in its day, his glorious bridge over the Tamar certainly did, although it too was dogged by financial problems. Consequently, despite the fact that work began on it in January 1849, it was ten years before the scheme was completed. Then overnight the principal route out of Cornwall was changed from that via Launceston and Tavistock to the quicker route through Plymouth. Here again the authorities would have been well advised to heed the word of Brunel who suggested that a station for the Three Towns should be located near the present North Road site. Not all agreed and despite the misgivings of Devonport's Mayor, the Plymouth terminus was sited at Millbay where great things were being planned. In the long term, however, the Millbay site proved inadequate and was also costly in terms of those buildings that were sacrificed in order to make way for its development.

At the time, though, the arrival of the train itself was the important issue. No longer would three and a half to four hours be the shortest time you could travel from Plymouth to Exeter. No longer would it take twenty one and a quarter hours to get to London by the fastest coach on the road, the *Quicksilver*. However, such is not to say that the railways represented a rapid increase in social mobility. Such changes were, after all, quite slow. Most railway companies assumed that the masses could not only not afford to travel but didn't even have the need to travel. Third class carriages were not always provided and when they were, they were invariably just open trucks with wooden benches and holes in the floor to allow rainwater to drain (the Marines are pictured in one). Second class accommodation was similar but it was covered with a roof but with no glass in the windows. Of course such conditions were not as draughty as they would be today as the trains then travelled much slower; although an 1844 Act of Parliament stipulated that trains carrying third class carriages (often just goods trains) should not average less than 12 miles per hour, while the fares should not exceed one penny per mile.

First class travel on the other hand was particularly luxurious, especially in the early days when the broad gauge, favoured by the Great Western Railway (God's Wonderful Railway) allowed really quite sumptuous carriages and accommodation.

In 1856 Queen Victoria, blown of course on a sailing trip, made an unexpected visit to Plymouth and returned to Windsor by rail, leaving from this station 'crowded with municipal officials'. It is unlikely, however, that Millbay Station itself was ever deemed fit for a Queen in the nineteenth century – indeed one guide said of it in 1874 'there is no greater libel on Plymouth than Plymouth Station as it stands'. Long regarded as a 'shabby shed', improvements carried out by the Great Western Railway, after it absorbed the South Devon Company, did little to improve Millbay in the late 1870s and once it had been opened in 1877, North Road Station began gradually to eclipse Millbay.

Situated directly opposite the Duke of Cornwall (built in 1865) Millbay Station saw its last passengers in 1941, but it was worked as a goods line for another 30 years. Today only railings and gate posts survive and the site, long since cleared, should soon be occupied by the exciting Millbay Pavilions Project.

Duke of Cornwall Hotel

'This has been described as a hotel-building age. Plymouth could supply its quota of evidence in support of this definition. Few towns in proportion to the population are better provided in this particular. The most characteristic hotel of recent date is the 'Duke of Cornwall' adjoining Millbay railway station. It is an excellent example of freely-treated Modern Gothic, differing in style from any other building in the town, and exceedingly picturesque. The sky line is remarkably effective, thanks to the happy way in which the roof and chimneys have been treated. The architect was Mr Hayward.'

So wrote local historian RN Worth for *The Graphic* magazine in 1878, in an edition that featured one of several drawings of the hotel produced last century. At that time the hotel, which cost about £40,000 to build, had only been standing some 13 years having been commissioned by the Railway Directors to accommodate travellers using Millbay Station (seen to the left here) and the Great Western Docks (Millbay).

The station itself was opened in April 1849 and within a few years of the 'Duke' being completed the Railway Commissioners also ordered the erection of the 'Albion Hotel' (which has since become the western wing of its later neighbour, the 'Continental').

Prior to all this development there was very little built in the area west of Derry's Clock and east of Stonehouse. Millbay was still a rough edged inlet with the Marine Barracks on one side and the Old Mill Prison (later used as a barracks itself) on the other. Among the first developments around this corner of Millbay in the nineteenth century were the Millbay Soap Manufactory and the Gas Works.

Long-established thoroughfares connected this neighbourhood with Stonehouse and Plymouth, however, the line of Millbay Road itself, running into the old George Street, marking one and Citadel Road and New Street marking out the other. Apart from some relatively new structures in George Street and a hundred yards or so of old buildings in New Street these were very much country paths, there being just a dozen or so other properties in this immediate area.

As Samuel Weekes recalled when reminiscing about life in the late 1840s there was a '*foot path only* running in front of the houses', that is the few houses that made up the delightfully named Mount Pleasant Grove, 'a very charming row of houses, with a pretty little garden in front', all of which would have enjoyed unbroken rural views from Stoke to what was to become Central Park.

According to Samuel Weekes, Mount Pleasant Grove 'was exactly the site on which the 'Duke of Cornwall' Hotel was built'. This suggests that it was synonymous with Millbay Grove (and earlier just Grove) and that one of the houses, in later years at least, had become a licenced premises known as the 'Saracen's Head', for that is how WHK Wright writing in 1878 described the site of the 'Duke'. John Taylor Wellsford was licensee of the 'Saracen's' in the 1850s and its address was given as '5 Millbay Grove'.

Immediately next to Millbay Grove was Mount Pleasant Terrace, with at its western end what became the 'Mount Pleasant Hotel'. This Weekes recalls was, in his early days, a school house, one in which he was himself a pupil '. . . I had a happy time there for some four years. The headmaster was quite kind, despite the fact that he *always* had a cane in his hand during school hours. If he were not using it on boys' backs, which was his easy way of *emphasising* certain words in the course of his instruction, he always kept it in motion by tapping his own leg – it was never still!'

This school then became an Hotel, the 'Mount Pleasant', a more modest affair than its neighbours but one whose proud boast in the 1878 was that its proprietor '*parle plusieur langue*'; certainly an ability to speak several languages would not go amiss in this neighbourhood today. It may well have been quite useful still to have a railway terminal in this neighbourhood today too but all possibility of that has long since passed, as the construction of the Pavilions complex, completes a programme of redevelopment of this area that began when Millbay Station finally closed to traffic in 1971. Just as many buildings were lost before the railway arrived, especially some comparatively new buildings in the erstwhile Buckland Street (which ran from Buckland House, where the 'New Continental' now stands, to Union Street) so were others lost as all traces of the railway have been removed.

A victim of the Blitz rather than the planners, however, was the church seen here behind the 'Duke of Cornwall'. This was St James-the-Less, constituted in 1847 and designed by the man responsible for several new churches built in Devonport around the same time, including St James-the-Great, J Piers St Aubyn. Not consecrated until 1871 St James-the-Less was described in 1879 as being 'a handsome building, but imperfectly finished for lack of funds', it was we were told 'noted chiefly for the "height" of its services'. Rebuilt at Ham after the war, St Andrew's Primary School now occupies this site.

Cornwall, incidentally, was the first English dukedom and since the fourteenth century the title has been vested in the sovereign's eldest son, and when the hotel was built that was Prince Albert Edward (afterwards Edward VII).

The Great Western Docks

'The borders of Millbay a century since were occupied by the local Vauxhall or Ranelagh, a place of public resort and entertainment, with gardens and a great dancing hall, known as the Long Room. The first practical effort made to develope the capabilities of Millbay was the construction of the Union Dock, now filled up'.

So ran part of the account which accompanied this illustration when it was published in *The Graphic* in March 1879. Prior to the construction of the Union Dock in the first half of the nineteenth century, John Smeaton had undertaken the cutting of the great blocks of stone used in the first really successful Eddystone Lighthouse in a work-yard established here in 1756. For three years there was a buzz of activity as great deliveries of stone arrived by sea from Portland or Falmouth and were off-loaded on to a purpose-built jetty that alone broke the line of this natural inlet. Originally far more extensive than it is now, evidence of earlier usage was corroborated last century with the discovery of ships' anchors in the area where the Octagon now stands. Eastwards it probably extended as far as Derry's

Cross Roundabout, a situation that made it easily the safest sea access for the besieged town of Plymouth during the Civil War. Royalist forts surrounded the northern land approaches while guns positioned at Edgcumbe, Oreston and Mount Batten made Stonehouse Creek and the Catte-water vulnerable approach routes.

However, 300 years passed after the Civil War before Millbay was fully exploited by the town. Thomas Gill set the ball rolling in the 1840s with the construction of Millbay Pier. Gill, born in Tavistock in 1798, had started an alkali and soap factory at Millbay in 1818. An iron foundry had also been opened here a few years earlier and by 1839 there were a large number of factories surrounding the bay. Mayor of Plymouth in 1832 and Liberal MP here from 1841 to 1847, Thomas Gill also owned the West Hoe Estate and it was he who quarried West Hoe, hacking away the high limestone ridge to form the flat area known now as West Hoe.

Within two years of its completion, Gill's pier was taken over by the Great Western Dock Company, who had been

established by an 1846 Act of Parliament to 'develop the docks with full facilities for shipping'(Langley and Small, *Millbay Docks*).

Isambard Kingdom Brunel was engaged as engineer to plan the new dock development. Brunel had already produced plans for Sutton Harbour but these were vetoed by the Admiralty. Brunel was responsible for much of the Great Western, South Devon and later Cornwall Railways, and his wonderful ocean-going screw-steamer, the world's first, the *Great Britain* had pulled alongside Millbay Pier on its first voyage in 1845.

The new docks with their new rail link with Bristol and London quickly put Millbay and Plymouth on the map in an exciting new way. Steamships and the lack of a railway link had seen Falmouth eclipsed as a port of importance after 150 years as the country's chief overseas mail packet station. Southampton had been first to capitalize on the new transport era but now Plymouth came to the fore.

Millbay Docks

'Until the formation of the Docks, Millbay, being practically valueless, was not considered in the local municipal and parochial arrangements' (RN Worth *History of Plymouth* 1890). It thus appears that Millbay, for some time, existed independently of the Three Towns.

Certainly, Millbay was the last of the inner harbours of the Three Towns to be developed, however, once underway, progress was very swift and in no time at all Millbay had become the first of the area's docks to have a main-line rail connection. Not surprisingly this drastic change in fortunes saw the question of ownership become a major issue.

It was Plymouth's claim that the borough boundary included a place called Eastern King (which for the last hundred years or so has been the western boundary of Millbay), however, when the case came for trial in 1859, the Millbay Dock Company argued that the original Eastern King had been 'on the Western Hoe'. They also argued that the 1439 Act of Incorporation had a proviso that Plymouth 'should not extend aught to the water of the Tamar' and that in compliance with this the Corporation of Saltash, to whom the ancient jurisdiction of the 'liberty of the river Thamar' belongs, had always exercised rights over the waters of Millbay.

The judge, Sir Alexander Cockburn, found in favour of the Dock Company. And so it was that Millbay enjoyed 'independent' status until 1868 when, like all other such extra-parochial places, it was compelled to either become a parish in its own right or be annexed to an adjoining parish. A subsequent attempt to constitute a Millbay parish failed and after turning down an offer of annexation by Stonehouse, Millbay was united with the parish of St Andrew.

Although the development of Millbay was quite spectacular around the middle of the nineteenth century, it wasn't all straight forward: the first dock, the Union Dock, promoted by Messrs Derry and WH Evens, and constructed in the 1830s, was filled in as Brunel's plans for the harbour materialised. No trace of this dock, which once occupied the southern angle between Martin and Phoenix Streets, survived.

A variety of delays and financial anxieties blighted the progress of Brunel's work itself, and when the new docks

did finally open, on the 11th February 1857, it perhaps should come as no surprise that celebrations surrounding this long-awaited event were somewhat muted. The *Illustrated London News* noted a fortnight later that the occasion had been 'allowed to pass with little of the ceremonial observances with which the completion of works of such a magnitude are sometimes honoured'.

The main happening that marked that nevertheless historic day was the admission into the dock, 'without the least difficulty', of the 1100 ton, fine screw-steamer *Elba* under Captain Hammill. 'Considerable interest was manifested upon the occasion, the *Elba* being dressed in colours, and the docks being visited during the day by hundreds of persons.'

On the morning of the 12th February 1857 the *Elba* was brought into the graving dock for repairs and was here captured for posterity by the *Illustrated London News's* on-the-spot artist. The ship had been on its way from London to the Mediterranean with a general cargo when it developed a defect near its sternpost. Owned by Mr Newall of Gateshead, 'the well-known manufacturer of wire rope', the

Elba had been built expressly for the laying of the then still novel electric wire cables.

Today this graving dock lies buried under the approaches to the Britanny Ferry terminal, but for over a hundred years, from 1857–1969, the marine and general engineering firm, Willoughby Bros Ltd, had their works alongside here. Indeed this dock, 'where Willoughby's accepted Board of Trade surveys, refitting and extensive repairs, soon proved to be a major asset of the port' (Langley and Small *Millbay Docks* 1987).

Willoughby's also built ships (including the Torpoint Ferries), as did their neighbours, Bickle & Co Ltd, who set up in 1887 a little to the right of the view here, and Ellacot & Son who were across the other side at East Quay. Now an up-market marina development stands on that particular site and although Millbay now operates somewhat differently to way the way it operated earlier this century, it is undoubtedly enjoying a healthy new life as an international ferry-port.

Royal Marine Barracks

'From 1664 until 1755 troops who served as Marine regiments were frequently quartered in the town of Plymouth or at Dock, now known as Devonport. When the Admiralty raised 50 Companies of Marines in 1755, a group of these companies formed the Third, or Plymouth Division. The first order of the Division is dated 7th May, 1755.' (Col RD Ormsby, CBE, RM, *Globe and Laurel*, 1930)

The Marines, soldiers employed in naval service, were first called into service by the Admiralty in 1664. Prior to that troops had only ever been put to sea for temporary duty on board ship. Locally, at first the Marines were billeted on the Barbican, their Orderly Room was in Southside Street, their parade ground the area still known as the Parade, the then New Quay, in front of the old Custom House. The Hoe was also used, for drill and ceremonial parades, and on the 12th May 1755 they held their first parade there.

This was the month, of course, that the Third or Plymouth Division had come into being, there were only two other divisions in the country, at Chatham and Portsmouth, all three being created in 1755.

For the next 25 years or so the Plymouth Marines were variously housed in Plymouth and in Dock, where Military Barracks had been built in 1765, and in 1779 a detachment of 30 men were sent to garrison Drake's Island. Two years later work began on the building of these Barracks at Stonehouse and on Monday 8th December 1783 the Plymouth Division moved into their new purpose-built accommodation for the first time.

Originally, as you can see behind the main block which still stands today, there was an open area now covered over as the drill shed. This in turn was enclosed by a sea wall, broken by a gate leading to steps and a landing place for boats arriving in Firestone Bay.

At right angles to the main block and at either end of it were two wings for the officers. At each end of the south wing were the Commandant's and 2nd Commandant's house with 24 single or 12 double quarters in between. This block too still survives but the view offered from those windows has long since changed. Back in 1783 Durnford Street extended no further than the line of this wing and so the Commandant and his fellow officers would have enjoyed uninterrupted views of the Hoe, the Sound and the mouth of the Tamar. Other than the Barracks at Millbay and the fashionable functions hall, the 'Longroom', just out of view to the left of the picture, few buildings would have interrupted their vista.

The north wing was not quite as well disposed. Similar in construction, this had a Field Officer's house at either end of it and other than its outlook over the parade ground it faced directly across the bottom of 'Bunker's Hill' from which this scene was sketched. In the 1860s the Hill was substantially excavated and a new north wing was built, over twice as long and a building's width behind the earlier structure which was then demolished.

'Properly called Stonehouse Hill, it is quite likely that the nickname "Bunker's Hill" comes from the term "bunk" long since used to describe the "sisters" sitting-room at the end entrance to a hospital ward' (Eric Partridge, *Dictionary of Slang*), for at the north eastern corner of the Barracks at the foot of the hill the Infirmary and Surgeon's quarters were built.

Originally the hill was approached by a winding road which lead up from the gap between the main block and the eastern end of the north wing and it was on this hill in the summer of 1797, just a year or so before this picture was drawn, that a young marine, a drummer, sleeping under a furze bush was woken up by two marines in 'earnest conversation'. One of these marines, an Irish protestant named Lee, was heard to administer an oath to the other 'pledging him to a treasonable uprising on a date to be fixed'.

The young lad ran down to the barracks and informed a sergeant who in turn went to tell the commandant. This was a time when a certain amount of dissatisfaction among United Irishmen (a body founded six years earlier) was combined with general unhappiness at very poor levels of pay in the lower ranks of the services on top of which came the revolutionary fervour from France with whom we were then at war.

The commandant, annoyed at first at being disturbed, was soon to appreciate the gravity of the situation and he went into the mess where the officers were having dinner, ordered them to see that the gates were locked and to follow him with pistols at the ready. The assembly was sounded, the men were all brought out onto the parade ground where they were told to ground arms and were then deprived of ammunition. Arms and ammunition were then placed in the guard room until the extent of the conspiracy was revealed.

It subsequently emerged that Lee was in fact the ringleader and together with a number of enrolled conspirators they were intending to seize the barracks, free themselves and the French prisoners held at Millbay, and not rest until they had overturned the Government. After a court martial Lee and two Irish Catholic marine conspirators were executed on the Hoe in front of some 10,000 servicemen and thousands more local civilians.

Royal Marine Barracks

'Towards the end of 1801 the mail coach dashed into Plymouth, the horses decorated with laurels, and the driver, guard and passengers resplendent with gold and blue favours. Joy pervaded every class when the news was promulgated. Traders of all nations displayed their colours in Sutton Pool and the Catwater; the *Extraordinary Gazette* was read to teeming audiences at the theatres; civilians embraced each other in the pit; and females danced with sailors and soldiers in the galleries. On learning of their approaching release the prisoners were thrown into transports of delight, and the sick left their berths to participate in breakdowns on the decks. Transparencies testified to the exhilaration at Stonehouse, the Naval Hospital and the Marine Barracks; and 800 barrels of tar, oil and pitch were consumed in a monster bonfire on the Hoe.' (Whitfeld, *Plymouth and Devonport: in Times of War and Peace.* 1901)

Britain had been involved in the 'Revolutionary Wars' since 1793 and as news of the peace agreement was confirmed so the rejoicing continued. All manner of men who had served the country during this time were congratulated as were the reserve and volunteer regiments. These men were given a cockade, a rosette for their caps, fixed with a sprig of laurel.

The Marines themselves were to receive a special distinction as, in 1802 the year the Peace of Amiens was signed, in recognition for their services, Major General Bowater

announced to the men on parade that the king had issued 'a most gracious warrant' which meant that they were now 'Royal' Marines.

'When the Marines assumed their new uniforms for the first time, the Barrack Square was thronged and the windows were radiant with toilettes. Salutes having been fired, the battalion presented arms, and the veteran, Colonel Eliot, exclaimed in a loud voice: 'Royal Marines, here's God Save the King, and long life to him.' The sentiment ran through the lines like lightening, and heartier cheers than those raised within and without the barracks were 'rarely heard'. Always regarded as 'a family and constitutional corps', the Marines were surrounded on this occasion by the aristocracy of the West, and 'a most brilliant ball' was held in honour of the event at Pridham's Long Rooms.'(Whitfeld)

Sadly, however, the Peace was short lived. Napoleon who by now had become the sole ruler in France following his election as first consul for life in August 1802, two months after the Amiens agreement, soon provoked a resumption of the hostilities with England. This followed an appeal by the Maltese whose island Napoleon seized in 1803. There ensued another twelve years of intermittent warfare until Napoleon was finally defeated at the Battle of Waterloo on the 18th June 1815.

The state of war of course meant that large numbers of men had to be pressed into service and one point the number

of serving Marines reached 31,000. Such was the strain on resources that a fourth division of Marines was created at Woolwich in 1805 (it was disbanded in 1869). In Stonehouse itself the barracks was bursting at the seams and in 1803 negotiations were opened to purchase the Longroom and the area to the south of the barracks for the Crown. In the event it was bought through Mr Pridham from the Edgcumbe estate for £4,450 and the Longroom became the new Officer's Mess and in 1805 a wooden barracks was built on the site of what is now known as the Upper Battery.

With Napoleon safely out of the way at last there was large scale demobilisation across the services, nevertheless decisions were taken to further extend the barracks. In 1818 the Officer's Mess building was expanded and they moved out of the Longroom which then became a school for the children of NCOs. Meanwhile there was expansion in other parts of the main barracks including the construction of the colonnade seen here on the west side of the Parade Ground.

The colonnade ran between the railings and had the Guardroom cells and duty officers room on the ground floor with the Orderly Room, Library and Paymaster's Office above. Outside the railings and opposite the colonnade stood a lane at least as old as the barracks itself and called Barrack Street. This street backed onto the eastern side of Durnford Street, however it shared little of the latter's elegance and over the years it degenerated into 'a most unsavoury area', sporting twelve pubs, a brewery and innumerable brothels; a veritable 'rookery' as one nineteenth century commentator put it (a rookery then being defined as a cluster of mean tenements densely populated by people of the lowest class).

It was therefore a relief to some when in the wake of the pressure of war once more, this time in the Crimea, it was decided once again to expand the barracks, this time westward. In 1861 the Admiralty began negotiations for the land upon which Barrack Street and the neighbouring eastern side of Durnford Street stood and, once successful, promptly pulled the whole lot down. Down too came the old colonnade, and the new impressive West Block with its high arched entrance was built at an angle onto Durnford Street, thereby increasing the size of the Parade ground and completing the now familiar quadrangular form of the Stonehouse Barracks.

Royal Marine Barracks

One of the strange features of the Crimean war, which indirectly produced the incentive to extend the Barracks here at Stonehouse, was that this conflict saw the British fighting alongside the French who had themselves been the enemy during the last great period of expansion here fifty years earlier.

Fought against Russian interest in the Balkans originally by Turkey and Sardinia in 1853, British and French involvement came the following year. The principal military operations subsequently proved to be the invasion of the Crimea, the seige of Sevastopol (from September 1854-September 1855) and the battles of the Alma (hence Alma Road), Balaclava (including the infamous Charge of the Light Brigade) and Inkerman. All in all the French lost 62,500 men, the British 19,600 although of these 15,700 died of disease. This was of course the scandalous state of affairs that prompted the formation of a proper military nursing service by Florence Nightingale. The Crimean War was settled by the Treaty of Paris in February 1856 although there were no real hostilities after 14th November 1855.

1855 proved to be a significant year for British troops in another way too, for it was then that the use of muskets was finally abandoned altogether. Rifles, themselves a form of musket, had been gradually replacing the traditional and far less accurate musket for some years and soon became a much more effective weapon especially when coupled with the development of the Minie Bullet after its adoption by British Military authorities in 1851. The Minie rifle was used in the Crimean war, although before the fighting had ended its replacement, the Enfield, was being introduced.

This new gunnery required new practice ranges and about this time the marines obtained a range on the sea shore at Mount Batten. Prior to this it is thought, ball practice with muskets probably took place in the ditch of the Citadel. To get to Mount Batten, however, meant that men had to go to and from the barracks here in boats. This was an inconvenient arrangement that was ended around the time this new part of the barracks was constructed and when Millbay Barracks were handed over to the Admiralty in exchange for barrack rooms at Fort Stamford.

Soon after this a new range was built on Staddon Heights which was used jointly by the garrison and the marines. Gun development by no means stopped then though and in less than 20 years with the introduction of the Lee-Metford rifles

(Mk I in 1888, Mk II in 1891) a great number of ranges across the country were condemned as being unsafe and Staddon was one of them. 'The wall for retaining the butts on Staddon Heights still remains as a very prominent landmark, and a fruitful source of varied explanations as to the reason of its existence' (Col RD Ormsby 1930).

By this time developments at Millbay had significantly altered the waterfront of the Stonehouse Barracks, the old sea wall had long since been pulled down and the existing wall was built on land reclaimed from the sea by the Great Western Docks Company. A little to the east of the old wall ablution rooms, a cookhouse and officer's baggage stores were constructed and in 1873 the space between these buildings and the original east block was roofed in to form the drill shed. The cookhouse was opened in the same year, prior to that all meals had been cooked in the barrack rooms.

Such would have been the state of affairs six years earlier when this new entrance block was completed, this view of it from the Parade Ground being sketched soon after its completion in 1867 by W Hake. An impressive twin towered development it was then, like the other side which fronts onto Durnford Street, finished in stucco, a fine plaster, as was the fashion of the day. From that day to this the major change in this view has been the removal of this

surface to expose the fine stonework underneath.

Dress, uniforms and usage to which parts of this building were originally put have of course also changed over the years. The greatest change here being the conversion of what was the lecture room above the main archway into the Chapel of St Christopher, a process that was formally completed on 21st October 1934 when it was dedicated by the Bishop of Exeter.

The Commandant's Lecture Room, as it was known, had been serving in a church capacity many years before that, having been authorized for Divine Service by the Admiralty as early as 1878. It did not at first enjoy exclusive service in that capacity, that did not come about until 1922 and in the meantime it also acted part time as a venue for 'penny readings, dances and matinees musicales, and at a later date work parties'. However it appears that a reredos, a covering at the back of an altar, was erected here in March 1894 and five years later we learn that Parade Services at nearby St George's Church were discontinued, because, it was said, there was a dispute with the vicar over fees paid for attendance.

Thereafter services were held in the chapel in the barracks and until 1906 a new routine was established of two Parade Services a day at 0930 and 1115 hours. The first wedding was held here on the 5th September 1936.

St Lawrence's Chapel

'Valuable information on the extent and character of Stonehouse in the early part of the sixteenth century is afforded by the bird's eye map of the Cornish and Devon coasts in the British Museum. . . .'

'There is no church visible in the map in the town itself, but one is shown on the high land of Devil's Point, on ground since cut away for the Victualling Office. It is a little structure of distinctive character, quite unlike other churches drawn – simply a nave and chancel, with a spired bell-turret at the west end, and standing in an enclosure.'

So said Plymouth's Victorian historian RN Worth in his *Notes on the early history of Stonehouse*, read in lecture form to the members of the Plymouth Institution on the 11th November 1884. He went on to add '. . . With the exception that the latter has a transept of Perpendicular date, this fabric corresponds very closely to the drawing of the church of St Lawrence by Payne, reproduced by Mr Brooking Rowe in his *Ecclesiastical History of Old Plymouth*' (1874). It is that picture we see here and although it is undated we know from Payne's other published works in the area that it was most likely to have be drawn some time between 1788 and 1810. This fits in comfortably with the fact that the Chapel would have been pulled down by 1826 at the latest for that

was when work began on he Victualling Yard.

The situation, however, is by no means as simple as that as Brooking Rowe's description of the history of St Lawrence's is exactly what Worth sees as the history of the original chapel of St George which he states was pulled down in 1787 to make way for the church of St George which was destroyed during the blitz (1941). Brooking Rowe on the other hand believed that it was St Lawrence's which was 'displaced' by St George's in 1787. In an attempt to resolve the matter, Worth claimed that he was the first to cite contemporary evidence of the existence of two chapels. The first being the reference to St Lawrence in 1472 when Magister Johannes Stubbes, the perpetual vicar of 'Plympmouth' was granted a license to appoint a priest to celebrate divine service in 'CAPELLA SANCTA LAURENCIJ APUD STONEHOWSSE'; the second being a grant of 1497 which referred to the 'CAPELL SCI GEORGII MARTII DE EST STONHOUS'.

East Stonehouse quite simply was the area we know today as Stonehouse, the Mount Edgcumbe estate, then under the same ownership, was West Stonehouse. It is quite likely that there was also a chapel at Edgcumbe and indeed that the Durnfords had a private chapel in their East Stonehouse mansion in 1414.

Whatever the situation was over 500 years ago, however, there seems to be little doubt that the remains of the building we see here were used to build the 'ruins' at Mount Edgcumbe, despite the fact that some authorities believe the ruins to date from the middle of the eighteenth century. Standing by these ruins today one can easily see why Devil's Point was such an obvious location for a chapel in ancient times, as in addition to their uses as a place of worship, where congregations could pray for those out at sea, we also find them serving as kind of mediaeval lighthouses. This helps to account for their often being located some way away from the homes of the worshippers, like the chapel at Rame Head, the original chapel of St Katherine upon the Hoe, St Nicholas (formerly St Michael) on Drake's Island and St Lawrence at Devil's Point. The location of the latter not only being important for those returning from distant journeys but also as a place for those who had just completed a successful trip across the mouth of the Tamar on the perilous Cremyll ferry (which used to cross from Devil's Point) to offer their thanks for a safe delivery.

In later years the Cremyll ferry was to cross from a point along the banks of Stonehouse Creek by which time St Lawrence's had been pulled down, which brings us back to trying to establish a date for it's demise. Looking carefully at another of Payne's drawings, a general panorama of Stonehouse, published in 1790, we find there is a small building shown on what we take to be this site so perhaps it wasn't pulled down in 1787 and perhaps it was the Stonehouse chapel which we know was extended in 1639. Certainly it fits the description given by Worth himself of a building standing in a yard planted with trees, 'enclosed by a wall wherein were stiles, which had to be mended to keep the hogs out.' It also has a western bell turret and an added south transept, but who knows if evidence will ever come to light to properly unravel the story of the two Stonehouse chapels.

One thing we do know though, St Lawrence, to whom this chapel was dedicated, was martyred in Rome in AD 258. A deacon to Sixtus I, he was a victim of the Emperor Valerian's purge on Christians and was led off by soldiers one Sunday morning after the bishop had been teaching. Because he was subsequently broiled on a gridiron, Lawrence became the patron saint of curriers. His day is the 10th of August, and because that is a time when shooting stars can often be seen in the sky, such meteors have in the past been dubbed St Lawrence's tears, or the fiery tears of St Lawrence.

Mount Edgcumbe

'Perhaps there are few among the 'stately homes' of England more widely known than that of the Earl of Mount Edgcumbe.' So began a lavishly illustrated article on Mount Edgcumbe written for the *Pall Mall Magazine* in 1897. Its author was Lady Ernestine Edgcumbe, sister of the then Earl, the 4th, William Henry. The detailed account that followed shows that the gardens and grounds have changed little from that day to this, only the house itself, gutted during the Blitz, has undergone any major alterations.

There is, however, one important departure from the situation that prevailed back then and that is that the house is now open to the public and that visitors today enter the house by the Royal Entrance. Mount Edgcumbe House had many Royal visitors in the nineteenth Century and all would have been received by either Lady Ernestine, Emma, Horatia's brother, father (Ernest, the 3rd Earl 1839–61) or grandfather (Richard, the 2nd Earl 1795–1839).

Of course it must be said that Royal visitors did not just come down here to call in on the Edgcumbe's, as Lady Ernestine's article explained; the reasons for Mount Edgcumbe's great reputation arose 'not only from its own beauty, but from the fact that it is situated close to one of the chief naval ports in the country.' She then added '. . . The wooded peninsula called Mount Edgcumbe forms the western side of far-famed Plymouth Sound, and the largest man-o-war when entering the Hamoaze [the inner harbour where are the Royal Dockyards] must pass within a stone's throw of the gardens.' Little could she have known then that two years later, in March 1899, she would launch the biggest warship the world had then ever seen, the second of William White's great and mighty ironclads, 'HMS *Implacable*'.

But that is another story, as indeed is tracing back the history of the Edgcumbe family whose presence on this peninsula goes back to the sixteenth century. The Earldom itself however dates back only to 1789, to the 31st August 1789 to be precise, which was just ten days after King George III had enjoyed a 'sumptuous and elegant, dinner and dessert' at Mount Edgcumbe. It was a Friday and the King and Queen Charlotte, were greeted upon their arrival at Mount Edgcumbe by 'sixteen young maidens dressed in white, strewing roses, carnations and myrtles; and when they came to the steps that lead to the grand arcade, each maiden, on her knee, presented a curious flower to their Majesties, which was graciously received.'

The King had particular cause to be grateful to the Hon.

George Edgcumbe, bred, it was said, to the naval service. He it was who captured the *Jason*, with her rich consignment of silver, off the Cornish coast; he it was whose gallant actions at Minorca had done so much to retrieve the credit of Admiral Byng's expedition; and he it was who was first to bring back news of the fall of Louisburg which helped ensure that by 1760 Canada had been won by the British not the French.

For this last feat, the King had presented George Edgcumbe with 500 guineas. Twenty years later, though, an even bigger prize followed the felling of a great number of trees on the coast of Mount Edgcumbe. This had been deemed necessary in the face of a potential French and Spanish invasion, to deny them concealment should they attempt a landing. The threat was thankfully never realised, the loss of the plantations was nevertheless much lamented and during a visit to the Estate in 1781 the King showed his gratitude by conferring upon Baron George Edgcumbe the title Viscount, a title which he surpassed eight years later, after his second visit, when he awarded George an Earldom.

Such honours were by no means the only positive aspects of the great tree sacrifice as George's son Richard worked on developing the various formal gardens that the felling had made ground available for. By 1815 this work was almost complete and there has been very little change since that date. Richard, incidentally, although well regarded as an artist and a wit, also managed to carve out a reputation as

a gambler and a rake, so as luck would have it when the house was ravaged by fire during the Blitz his portrait was not on display with those of other generations of the family and so it survived unscathed.

As Richard approached his 70th year, Mount Edgcumbe was paid its first visit by the 'future Queen of England', Princess Victoria, who worked up such an appetite when she took in the local air that she asked for a crust of bread. The 14-year-old Princess then eating 'with infinite relish the most modest fare the house had ever afforded.' Victoria later made several return visits to the area as Queen while other nineteenth-century Royal visitors included Grand Duke Michael of Russia (1818), the future King, William IV (1827), Emperor Frederick of Germany and Emperor Napoleon III of France (both in 1871) and in 1865 the Prince and Princess of Wales (Edward VII). The Prince was then 24 and 22-year-old Richard Edgcumbe, a cousin of the then Earl was later to serve Edward as his Sergeant-at-Arms. William Edgcumbe, who had succeeded to the Earldom in 1861, was ten years older; he also held positions at court and accompanied the Prince on many of his travels abroad.

Today Robert, the 8th Earl of Mount Edgcumbe lives in idyllic surroundings in Empacombe around the coast from Cremyll while the family seat, rebuilt under the guidance of architect Adrian Gilbert Scott in 1958, is open to the public Wednesday through to Sundays from the beginning of April to the end of October.

The Government Victualling Establishment

'At Devil's Point is now constructing an extensive Government Victualling Establishment which is intended to unite the business of the Victualling Office at Plymouth and the King's Brewery at South Down. This national undertaking will, it is calculated, require several years for its completion. The various works are on a very grand scale and well worthy of the inspection of strangers'.

In this way Henry Edmund Carrington encouraged readers of his 1828 *Plymouth and Devonport Guide* to visit this spot and see for themselves the remarkable undertaking at East Stonehouse, only the base of which was underway when Henry Worsley came here, to Mount Wise, to sit and draw 'from nature onto stone' this view of the Sound and the as yet incomplete Breakwater.

The idea of moving the victualling operations from Lambhay had been mooted by the Victualling Board back in 1821, and the decision to use this site was doubtless influenced in no small measure by the fact that one of the Board members was the 2nd Earl of Mount Edgecumbe who owned a great deal of land in the area, including this particular site.

There had been talk of moving the victualling operations away from Plymouth from time to time ever since Charles II, suspicious of the loyalty of a town which had proved so troublesome to him in the civil war, considered making Falmouth the south western victualling port for his fleet. In 1678 there were even plans to shift all existing victuals to Falmouth, but they ultimately came to nothing.

A dozen or so years later, however, once work had begun on establishing a dockyard at Point Forward in the Hamoaze, the threat to the Lambhay victualling arrangements started to get more serious. Indeed on the 6th March 1708 there was an Order in Council decreeing that the office be removed from Plymouth and for a new victualling operation to be created at Empacombe (Mount Edgecumbe

land then and now currently home to the present Earl). Thanks, however, to a petition presented to Queen Anne from many of Plymouth's leading citizens and merchants, praying that she would not give leave for this to go ahead, this plan too was thwarted; although in 1707 the resident agent had already begun the work of establishing a 'Victualling Office at Enty Comb'.

The determination of the Plymouth people ensured that the Lambhay Victualling Office was the main local base throughout the eighteenth century. The freehold for the Lambhay site was acquired in 1734 and in 1743 a new bakehouse with adjacent wharf was built between the Victualling Office and the main body of the town. There was, nevertheless, a certain amount of development away from Lambhay.

Unhappy with the quality and price of contract beer (sailors then had a daily ration of a gallon each, to help wash down their none too palatable biscuit and salt meat) the local Commissioners had their own Brewhouse built at South Down on the opposite side of Millbrook Creek to Empacombe in 1733. Originally capable of producing 80 tuns of beer a week, the whole operation was expanded in 1741. Two years later, however, when the question of finding 'a commodious place at or near the Hamoaze' was again raised, both the South Down and Empacombe sites were ruled out, not just because of the objections from Plymouth but also on account of the logistical problems ferrying Devon cattle across the water and of getting orders across quickly. There was no telephone, telegraph or Torpoint Ferry in those days.

Consideration was also given at this stage to creating a victualling base on this side of the water, east of the dockyard, however, this notion was also dismissed, on the grounds that the only suitable land was too far from a convenient freshwater supply and that the seaward approach

was difficult because of mud flats. So instead, as we read in LWM Stephens *History of the Royal William Yard*, it was decided to extend the Lambhay Depot and over the next few years another bakehouse was added and a slaughterhouse, storehouse and wharf.

After all this new investment, of course, the idea of moving became even less practical and the Lambhay site steadily grew. By the turn of the century there were some 86 parts making up the whole, including the granary and bakery and related storehouses, lofts, cellars etc. The problems and pressures associated with equipping the King's Navy during the Napoleonic Wars once again raised the question of finding a suitable site to bring all the victualling operations in the area together.

As Sir John Rennie himself recalled in his autobiography (1875), 'about this time the several victualling departments of the navy at Plymouth were very inefficient, and divided into three or four establishments – one at Southdown, opposite to Devonport, another at Cremill Point, near Stonehouse' – the animal slaughtering had been moved here – 'a third at Plymouth, and the fourth in Plymouth town – being several miles from each other, so that the expense and delay in provisioning vessels of war was considerable. Upon this being represented to the Admiralty by the Victualling Board ... they determined to make an entirely new victualling establishment ...'

'After much discussion Cremill Point, being the nearest to the dockyard at Devonport, and being in other respects, as to depth of water &c., possessed of peculiar advantages, was finally selected as the best place for the new establishment, and I was ordered by the Victualling Board to prepare the necessary plans, specifications, and estimates, and to see them carried into effect.'

New Victualling Office

'The magnificent establishment, now forming by order of Government, on the northern side of Devil's Point, at Plymouth, under the general appellation of the NEW VICTUALLING OFFICE, was commenced in the year 1826, and is to be finished in 1832.'

So began the text accompanying this view in Britton and Brayley's *Devonshire and Cornwall Illustrated*, published in 1832, the year that the Yard was scheduled to have been finished. It wasn't to be, however, and although the transfer of offices and stores from the Old Victualling Office at Lambhay Hill had started in July of the previous year it wasn't until 1835 that all the buildings, complete with the machinery and equipment necessary for baking, brewing and so on, were finally finished.

The project ran well over time and as one might therefore imagine, well over budget. The site itself, partly belonging to the Earl of Mount Edgecumbe and partly to Viscount Valletort and covering roughly seven acres of land and six acres of waterfront (subsequently infilled), had cost the 'Commissioners for Victualling His Majesty's Navy' £16,168 back in 1824 and Sir John Rennie's original estimates for the design and construction of the full Yard had come to £291,512. This was the figure Parliament had sanctioned in 1825. The original contract for the building work alone was won by Hugh McIntosh with a tender of £106,530.

Before long it was obvious that these estimates were inadequate. Both the Treasury and the Admiralty were becoming anxious and so Parliament, then led by the one time MP for Tavistock, the second Earl Grey, called for an inquiry. A special Select Committee was set up and its report was published on the 13th March 1832. Meanwhile, the work carried on and 1832 saw the appointment of the first officer in charge of the New Victualling Yard, Captain Phipps Hornby.

Phipps Hornby was also the first to have the title of Captain Superintendent for prior to that time Plymouth had had a Commissioner, Sir JA Gordon and an Agent Victualler, T Miller; after 1832 the Agent Victualler post ceased to exist. There was also a Clerk of Check, R Bulcock, and a separate Storekeeper, J James, but after 1832 these two posts also merged. All this had been under the general umbrella of the Admiralty's Commissioners of Victualling and a system which had been instituted almost 150 years earlier in 1684, not long after the first office and storehouses had been built at Lambhay.

During the period of transfer from Lambhay to Stonehouse, major reforms were being carried out nationally under Sir James Graham, whom Earl Grey had appointed First Lord of the Admiralty in November 1830. As well as being a member of the four strong committee who prepared the 1832 Reform Bill itself, Graham was responsible for merging the two controlling bodies of the navy, the admiralty and the navy board. Thus the navy board commissioners, including the Commissioners of Victualling, became the administrative heads of departments in the combined admiralty.

The New Victualling Yard here in Stonehouse was very much at the forefront of these new reforms and represented then the most advanced thinking available for victualling a modern navy. This yard, because it was being built from scratch, was necessarily more 'state of the art' than the Weevil (Royal Clarence) Yard at Portsmouth which was being redeveloped around the same time.

New to both establishments and also that at Deptford, were the latest 48 horse-power Boulton and Watt steam engines which were used to drive the Mills and Bakery machinery. It was the responsibility of Sir John Rennie and his brother George to obtain all the machinery employed here and it is interesting to note that their father, John

Rennie, (from whom they had taken over the construction of the Breakwater after his death in 1821) had worked under Boulton and Watt after studying at university in Edinburgh and had made improvements to flour milling machinery while with them.

In addition to these bigger engines there was a steam engine ordered to power the malt grinding plant, another, a 14 horse-power machine from the Horsely Iron Company for the biscuit plant, plus a number of other machines supplied directly from the Rennie Brothers own manufactory.

To give some scale to this machinery and the new victualling arrangements here, the Mills and Bakery were said to be capable of converting some 270,000 pounds of flour into ship's biscuits each week. The Mills themselves were five storeys high and the corn, wheat and meal were hoisted up to the top floor and sieved ground and cleaned before ending up on the ground floor as biscuit meal to be prepared for transportation across to the Bakery block.

The building shown in the engraving here was originally just called the *Long Storehouse* although after the naming of the wharf it became the Clarence Wharf Storehouse. It was the first block to be started here and was, like the Gosport Yard, named after the Duke of Clarence, the future King William IV who in that capacity was later to be honoured with the naming of this yard too.

Today this view stands little changed 160 years on, the contours of the rock face appear much the same although it is a pity that the engraving does not show the landing steps in their true splendour. Undoubtedly the most notable feature of these steps has always been the way each granite step was so very finely dovetailed into its neighbour, lending support to the contention that these are among the most securely constructed flight of steps in the world.

Royal William Victualling Yard

Originally the New Victualling Yard in Stonehouse was to be named in honour of King George IV in whose reign the project was begun. In the event, however, George died aged 67, of alcoholic cirrhosis and dropsy, when blood vessels in his stomach ruptured, on 26th June 1830, well before the yard was completed. So it was that the yard was named after George's successor, his brother William, who was himself 64 when he came to the throne. George's only child, Charlotte, had died in child-birth in November 1817.

Prince William was the third son (of six) of George III and Queen Charlotte, he also had six sisters. William's only other elder brother, Frederick, Duke of York, had died three years earlier in 1827 and that is how, in 1830, William became the oldest prince ever to succeed to the throne (the previous holder of that honour strangely enough was his brother George who had succeeded to his father's throne at the age of 57).

Of all of Britain's Monarchs, William IV was undoubtedly one of the most popular with the people of the Three Towns and he almost certainly had a better knowledge of the area than any ruler before or after him.

The first record of his being here occurred in 1786 when, as the fledgling Prince William Henry, this lively 21-year-old accepted the freedom of Plymouth from four senior Aldermen and Common Councilmen. Diggory Tonkin was then mayor of Plymouth and the ceremony took place on Thursday 23rd May in the very grand residence of a wealthy local merchant, George Winne.

Prince William clearly got on well with George Winne for the following year, two days after Christmas, when he returned from a voyage to America as Captain of the *Pegasus*, Prince William 'took up his residence at Mr Winne's'. William, later to be known as the 'sailor king', had entered the navy as a midshipman when he was just 14 and served off the coast of America and in the West Indies; indeed he was the first prince to visit the New World. It was while off the coast of North America in 1781 that the teenage prince first encountered the high flying Horatio Nelson, already in command of his own ship at the age of 23. Prince William and Nelson were subsequently to maintain 'most cordial relations'.

It was, however, a relationship of another kind that was to bring William to Plymouth, for his father had ordered him here to get him out of the clutches of a young woman. The move was not altogether successful, though, for William promptly fell in love with George Winne's daughter Sally. This further upset the family peace and when William's two elder brothers came to visit him in 1788 they did so in defiance of their father. There can be little doubt, however, that the three princes were unworried.

'Plymouth, January 14th – Last Tuesday evening at eleven, arrived here, in a coach and six (horses), their Royal Highnesses, the Prince of Wales and Duke of York, accompanied by Prince William Henry, who went to meet them. The concourse of people was astonishing, the illuminations splendid, and the demonstrations of joy on every countenance pleasing beyond expression. The carriage proceeded slowly through the town to lodgings prepared for the royal guests in Fore-street.'

After a busy round of social engagements the brothers returned home and in July Prince William once again sailed for America 'accompanied by the most fervent wishes for his safe return from the inhabitants of this town, who had been so highly favoured by his presence; indeed, his politeness and attention will never be forgotten.'

So ran a contemporary account in the town records and certainly it appears that this sentiment has well stood the test of time. Prince William was made Duke of Clarence and St Andrew in 1789 and in Plymouth today we have a Clarence Place in Stonehouse, Devonport and Torpoint (where there is also a Clarence Road) and also a 'Royal Clarence' pub in Albert Road.

Additionally, of course, there are several streets and a public house named in honour of his wife Adelaide whom he married at Kew in 1818 (prior to this William enjoyed a long relationship, 1790–1811, with the actress Dorethea (Mrs) Jordan, who it is said bore him five daughters and five sons, the eldest of which he made the earl of Munster in 1831).

As the Duchess of Clarence, Adelaide opened the Laira Bridge in 1827, the same year that her husband and his 'cracks' came down to add some prestige and a trophy, the Clarence Cup, to the local yachting calendar.

As the Duke of Clarence, William also laid the coping stone of the sea wall of the victualling yard and, of course, as well as being remembered in the naming of the Clarence block, as King William IV, it is in his honour that the yard itself was named and it is his statue which has stood since 1835 above the entrance here to the yard. Reckoned by a contemporary account to be a good likeness, it is a fitting reminder of a king who was undoubtedly better known to the people of this area than any other monarch before or since.

King for only seven years, his reign was notable as being the first for many years to produce really liberal policies. The Reform Act was passed in 1832, slaves were emancipated across the Empire in 1833, the same year that the Factory Act was passed, and a large number of offences previously punishable by death were amended. There was also help for poor schools and a reduction in the invidious stamp duty which had effectively confined the circulation of news to a comparatively small section of society.

News of the King's death came after a short illness in 1837, which perhaps mercifully cut short fears many had that the king might have gone insane, in the event he fell victim to the same disease that claimed his eldest brother, alcoholic cirrhosis.

The Royal William Victualling Yard

'The design and execution of the Royal William Victualling Establishment, at Stonehouse, near Devonport, I claim entirely as my own, with the exception of the machinery, for which my brother George is entitled to an equal share of credit with myself. This establishment, including the cost of the land, amounted, I believe, to between £600,000 and £700,000.' Only one man could have written that and indeed it was Sir John Rennie in his autobiography, published posthumously, the year after he died in 1875.

The cost of Rennie's work here had been the cause of a great deal of concern in Government quarters but as Jonathan Coad observed in his book on the *Historic Architecture of H.M. Naval Base Devonport, 1689–1850*; 'The yard was built with confidence of durable materials and if its original cost caused questions to be asked in London, there can be little doubt that it proved to be an excellent investment.'

To give some scale to the financial aspects of all this it is worth putting one or two prices in context. There was very little inflation throughout most of the nineteenth century indeed the salary of the Captain Superintendent of the Victualling Yard remained unchanged on £800 a year from 1835–1865. This was of course the best paid post in the Yard and Captain Phipps Hornby who first occupied it was also in charge of the Royal Naval Hospital and it was there that he lived. His Second-in-Command, Mr Anthony Brady, officially the storekeeper, lived in No 1 residence in the Victualling Yard and he received an annual salary of £500.

These were both very handsome wages, after all a Cooper in the yard was then earning a little under £60 a year while unskilled labourers would have been on something around £40 a year. Labourers wages appear to have ranged from about 2/2d (11p) per day to 2/9d (14p) per day which certainly isn't a lot by today's standards and wasn't really that impressive in those days either when families tended to be bigger and consequently there were more mouths to feed from a wage packet.

Bread and cheese was the working man's basic diet back then and 1lb of cheese would cost him about 4p and a 4-lb loaf of bread just a bit under that. Meat then was about the same price as cheese while you could have got a pint of milk for an old penny (about 1/2p) and a gallon of beer for a shilling (5p). Small wonder that children were sent to work at a very early age.

A working week back then, incidentally, would have been a six day affair and the working day a good ten hours in the summer and eight in the winter, with annual leave only on public holidays of which there were only four up until 1871 when, under Lord Avebury's Bank Holiday Act, two more were added. Also as the century progressed the idea of Saturday being half a working day became more widespread and in conjunction with it came the growth and development of sporting activities notably football and rugby.

The nineteenth century witnessed a great deal of change generally and in the Victualling Yard changes in the demands on the Cooperage saw the shrinking of what had originally been the largest section here, employing over 80 coopers, to a situation whereby only a dozen coopers were needed to handle the workload. So the Cooperage was moved out of the massive block that housed it into more modest premises. Contract-packed, cased provisions like corned beef led to the decline in demand for casked provision and this, coupled with the adoption of copper, tin and enamel mess utensils, in place of the traditional cooperage-made items, was what sealed part of the cooperage's fate.

Originally tucked in behind the brewery block, shown here to the right, part of the corner of the old cooperage can be seen at the back of the basin to the right of the Melville Square Storehouse. As its name suggests, the Melville Square Block goes back as far as it stretches widthways along its frontage with the huge back wall of the yard running most of the way along its rear elevation before turning out towards the Sound. One of the features of the Victualling Yard is the amount of land and buildings that lie inside the wall behind this sea frontage so spectacularly dominated by the clock tower on the Melville Block.

Lord Melville was First Lord of the Admiralty between 1812–1827, his father, the first Lord Melville had also held the post but only briefly, for he was removed after a year in 1805, and impeached for misuse of public funds as treasurer of the navy in Pitt's first administration. Subsequently acquitted on all charges, the first Lord Melville was the last person in British history to have been impeached. Lord Melville nevertheless retired from public life and died a few years later in 1811, the year before his son came to occupy the same post.

To the left of the Melville Block as shown here is a block that housed the granary, mill and bakery plus stores behind which lay what was originally an open storage area and is now a pleasantly laid out grass square with gardens beyond. This area is overlooked by the two principal residences that were for the commanding officers and again, being 'invisible' from the outside, is a further example of how difficult it is to get a complete impression of the great scale of this enterprise from this vantage point.

Admirals Hard

'We turn into Durnford Street, and pass along the front of the barracks . . . One of the turnings opposite the barracks leads us direct to the Hard, and as we now approach we soon become aware of the holiday state of affairs. Groups of pleasure seekers are congregated, some awaiting the arrival of friends to make up their party, others awaiting the return of the ferry, but all full of excitement and fun. The variety of costume is a matter of remark, more particularly among the ladies, who from time immemorial have called in the artful aid of dress to fascinate the sterner sex. Here we may no doubt find the perfect representation of the famous "Girl of the Period". Here too the little slipshod urchin, whose savings for many weeks past have been appropriated towards this expected trip. Here we have family parties of most alarming extent, from the white headed grand-parent to the toddling grand-child . . . Aunts, uncles, and cousins (including the country cousin) help to swell the family party, and very merry they are, and fine jokes they pass about, which all seems taken in good part, for they have made up their minds to enjoy themselves, and rightly too,

for this trip to Mount Edgcumbe is looked forward to by the families of the labouring classes, something like an annual gathering, very similar to Christmas. . . .'

This graphic description of the scene here at Admiral's Hard appeared in Duprez's *Visitors Guide to Mount Edgcumbe*, published in 1871, not long after this view was recorded by W Hake.

Mount Edgcumbe park was one of the first in England to be opened to the public, albeit on Mondays only, and was receiving visitors for well over 100 years before the formation of the National Trust in 1895. Licence to impark lands (and enclose a deer herd for the pleasure of the chase) in West Stonehouse, had been granted to Piers Edgcumbe by Henry VIII in 1539. Piers had acquired these lands and those of East Stonehouse by his marriage to the heiress to these estates, Joan Durnford and it was their son, Richard, who was responsible for the construction of the house. It was at this time that the area first became known as Mount Edgcumbe.

A ferry service to Barn Pool from Devil's Point (or Cremyll Point as it was also known) had, however, been operating for well over 300 years by this time; it being the main link from Devon to the southermost of the three principal mediaeval routes through Cornwall. Indeed from at least the middle of the seventeenth century until it was eclipsed by the establishment of the Torpoint ferry in 1791, it appears that almost all the mail for Cornwall was transported via the Cremyll ferry.

Although apparently short as the crow flies, the passage was by no means an easy one. Celia Fiennes, an experienced and hardy traveller, recorded her journey thus in 1690: '. . . From Plymouth I went one mile to Cribly Passage, which is a very hazardous passage by reason of three tides meeting. Had I known the danger before, I should not have been very willing to have gone it, not but this is the constant way all people go, and saved several miles' riding. I was at least an hour going over; it was about a mile, but indeed in some places, notwithstanding there were five men rowed and I set my own men to row also, I believe we made not a step for almost a quarter of an hour, but, blessed be God, I came safely over; but those ferry boats are so wet and then the sea and wind always cold to be upon, that I never fail to catch a cold in a ferry boat, as I did this day . . .'

And dangerous it was too; ten years after this was written, the deaths of six women and one man are recorded in the registers of the parish of Rame, all seven drowned at 'Crimble' on 26th July 1701.

It was around this time that the landing on the Cornish side was moved from Barn Pool to Cremyll itself; although Cremyll was then, along with rest of Maker, part of Devon a situation that prevailed until 1844. Then after the completion of the Royal William Victualling Yard, Maker was formally annexed to Cornwall. The establishment of the Victualling Yard also meant that the East Stonehouse landing place for the ferry had to be moved from Devil's Point and in 1824 the Navy bought the old site and made available a new site further along the Stonehouse peninsula where they also constructed this sloping stone landing-jetty known forever since as the Admiral's Hard.

From here people were rowed or sailed across to Mount Edgcumbe and back, sometimes with their horses and carriages, until eventually the decision was taken to intoduce a steam launch into the service in 1884 after almost half a century of campaigning on the part of the steam lobby.

St Paul's, Stonehouse

'The inhabitants of Stonehouse, a town daily increacing in population and importance, had long been greatly inconvenienced for want of church room. The parochial chapel does not furnish accommodation for more than one eighth of the parishioners, while there is lamentably undue proportion of free sittings for the poor. His Majesty's Commissioners therefore determined to erect a chapel capable of containing nearly one thousand persons within the presincts of the parish.'

This new chapel was St Paul's which was built as a chapel of ease to St George's, which itself only dated back to 1789; it having been built on the site of an earlier church building to serve the increaced population following the late eighteenth-century expansion of Stonehouse. St George's was completed just a few years after the Royal Marine Barracks had opened and not many years after the Stonehouse Bridge, the Royal Naval Hospital and Longroom Barracks had been developed.

St Paul's, on the other hand, was opened in 1831 just four years before the Royal William Victualling Yard was completed. Up until 1820 there had been very little development beyond the Royal Marine Barracks and although the 'increace of buildings' in the area was not as great in the early 1830s as was anticipated when the site for this building was chosen, development around 'lower' Durnford Street, as it was then known, soon stripped the chapel of its rural surrounings. The impressive square of neighbouring terraced houses, originally conceived by architect John Foulston, however, was never completed.

Foulston would doubtless have had much cause to be disappointed about this particular part of his work in the Three Towns, coming as it did towards the end of his most productive period. The design of St Paul's has been described by one contemporary critic (Frank Jenkins, *Journal of the Society of Architectural Historians*, May 1963) as being 'a rather meagre swan-song' to his career. In his defence, however, Foulston was working within a very limited budget – his brief was not to exceed £3,000. In the event St Paul's was completed at a cost of only £2,630. As one commentator noted at the time '. . . We might be disposed to criticize some of the features of the building, did we not know that the means were strictly limited . . . We are rather disappointed to wonder, considering the expense of wrought stone, that he could have raised a fabric which forms so pleasing an object . . .' to which there was but one

footnote '. . . though we should nave been pleased had Mr Foulston's means allowed him to raise St Pauls tower about twenty feet higher'.

Whatever the objections, the Gothic style St Paul's was opened for divine service on 5th July 1831 (some accounts say 1832) and consecration by the Bishop of Exeter on the 27th September 1833. Capable of seating one thousand, although pew rents had still not been abolished by this time, over half of the sittings were reserved for the poor 'a large portion of which are in the very best situations'. Long before pew rents were abolished, it was not unknown for pews in some churches to be boxed in and provided with desks, cushions and even fireplaces! Gradually though, the nineteenth century witnessed the elimination of such status symbol church seating.

Such is not to say, however, that the new pews in St Paul's were held in high regard for very long. In 1885 a report in the *Western Daily Mercury* noted that 'Pitchpine seating had now taken the place of the high and uncomfortable pews' in St Paul's and further that the lighting had been improved by the removal of two side galleries. This work was all part of a major internal restoration undertaken by the Rev AA Toms and his committee, presided over by the Earl of Mount Edgcumbe, whose ancestor had provided the land upon which the church had been built. The then present Earl also promised to supply a pulpit to replace the two (a separate pulpit and a reading desk) which despite criticism had for so long preceded it.

James Taylor, a builder from Battery Street, and Samuel Yeomans, a house decorator from Clarence Place, carried out most of the physical work, while Mr Goodfellow, the architect responsible for the changes, was true to his name and made no charge for his services.

While the impetus for the restoration undoubtedly followed the creation of a separate parish of St Paul's in 1883, the bombing of St George's during the last war led to St Paul's merging with its mother church. Latterly, however, even as a combined parish, numbers tended to be declining, although in recent years Foulston's last public work has enjoyed something of a renaissance.

Stonehouse Town Hall

'The last visual memorial of the independent Township of East Stonehouse is now vanishing in the demolition of the large building which was successively 'St George's Hall' and 'Stonehouse Town Hall'. A factory will ultimately stand on the site.' So began a newspaper report accompanying a photograph showing workmen hacking away at this fine old building in August 1946; the Town Hall was just four years away from celebrating its centenary.

Foundations had been laid in 1849, the funding for the scheme was raised in £1 shares and the total cost of the project has variously been quoted as being somewhere between £3,700 and £4,500. The building was completed in 1850, the year many Stonehouse residents died from the terrible cholera epidemic. Centred mainly around the 'notorious' Stonehouse Lane (King Street), this neighbourhood was described as being a 'mere conglomeration of alleys, courts and backlets, all of them badly drained and unventilated.'

The Town Hall was some distance away from this area, it stood in St Mary's Street at the eastern end of Emma Place and when it was built Battery Hill rose up behind it. Plundered for its stone over the years, the hill has not only disappeared but the ground there now dips and Battery Street runs across it. A number of industrial units now cover most of this site.

One of the first descriptions of the new building here appeared in William White's *History, Gazetteer and Directory of Devonshire*, published in 1850 and read as follows . . . 'A large and handsome TOWN-HALL, with accommodations for the County Court, and weekly Petty Sessions, and apartments for the 'Stonehouse Library and Scientific Institution' was erected in 1849–50. It is in Italian style, and contains, besides the court room, the police station, and the apartments of the Institute, a handsome Ball Room, 85 feet by 45.'

The Earl of Mount Edgcumbe was the patron and president of the Institute, he also gave the stone for the building. His two daughters are remembered in the naming of Emma Place and Caroline Place, built in his time and overlooking Millbay near where the Royal Western Yacht Club was then based, at the corner of Hobart Street and Buckingham Place. The Earl was commodore of the club.

For many years the seat of local government in East Stonehouse, there was as early as 1885 talk of incorporation and, in 1896, of amalgamation with Plymouth. Although originally in the parish of St Andrew, it had long since attained its own parish status and in municipal terms it was part of the Roborough Hundred, however, with the passing of the Reform Act in 1832, in electoral terms it was added to the Parliamentary Borough of Devonport.

The consequences of this state of affairs produced some odd situations as one example from the policing of the area shows. The County Police took care of the parish from Ha'penny Gate to Manor Street, while the Borough Police were responsible for the patch east of Manor Street. Legend has it that in the heyday of Union Street's disorderliness, when the Police had more drunks than they could deal with, each force would surreptitiously 'transfer its dead drunks over the border when the other fellow was not looking!'

In 1914 of course the Three Towns amalgamated and East Stonehouse Council was formally dissolved. Dr WEM Corbett was chairman at the time and was mid way through his last term in office. A number of Stonehouse's eminent citizens had sat in the chair over the years, including the Earl of Mount Edgcumbe, Isaac Pearse and Aaron E Lyons the brilliant Jewish barrister. A look through the names of other council members indeed runs like a veritable who's who in Stonehouse in the late nineteenth century. In the earlier records names like Bulteel, Bayly, Taylor and Wills occur often while later we find mention of Lancaster, Vosper and Blight.

After Stonehouse Council had been dissolved, the Hall served for many years as the Head Quarters of the County Court Circuit and the County Court offices, it also housed the staff of the Registrar in Bankruptcy. Over and above all these administrative uses, however, the Hall was also formerly important as a one time cultural centre of Stonehouse social life. In the great assembly room theatrical entertainments were staged, balls were held and concerts promoted. Here Messrs Froenhart and Winterbottom, musical directors of the Royal Marines, conducted not only straightforward military band concerts for large crowds, but also major Symphony Concerts 'which attracted all music lovers and were social occasions as well'.

The Stonehouse Permanent Building Society was yet another organization to have had its base here at some time and in later years the building was handed over to the Medical Officer of Health's Department. In 1940 many of the survivors of the German air attack on the troopship *Lancastria*, were fed and kitted out in the old Town Hall. Indeed generally before it was itself a victim of the German bombers, the Hall performed valuable services for rehabilitation.

The end came on the night of the 19th February 1941, when between 50–75 bombers on their way to South Wales dropped about a dozen high explosive bombs in the areas of Valletort Road, Stoke and the Town Hall here in Stonehouse. Although the shell of the building survived the war it was not to be spared and in the event it became one of the first to go after the war had ended.

Valletort Sanitary Steam Laundry

'The exigencies and requirements of modern civilisation have called into existence, or more greatly developed many new and important industries, and undoubtedly one of the most useful developments of domestic industry is the modern steam laundry. The above establishment has supplied a want long felt in the town.' So began a brief piece of publicity material published in a local commercial guide in 1894, by which time the Valletort Laundry had been in business less than ten years.

Opened in the late 1880s, it was originally called the Stonehouse Bridge Steam Laundry Company and it stood just north of the Bridge, on the edge of Stonehouse Creek, in Water Lane off High Street. Here many had their washing done and another of the firms advertisements featured several quotes from satisfied customers: 'I had occasion to send my washing to the Valletort Laundry, Stonehouse when the Royal Yacht was at Penzance. The washing was well done and finished at a very short notice', this was signed 'R G, Commander *Victoria and Albert* Royal Yacht, Portsmouth' and dated Sept 19th 1891.

Another quote stated that the Marchioness of Ormonde was much pleased with the washing done by the laundry, while the Master of the *Star of Persia* said that the work done by the laundry was the 'best I have ever had done'.

It will be noticed, however, that these customers and the others quoted were not exactly typical of the man in the street, who for the most part continued to have his washing done at home. However, despite the fact that the introduction of pressurised water into many homes made domestic washing easier, the Victorians, while undoubtedly cleaner than their predecessors, changed their clothes less frequently than we now do. They also repaired their clothes regularly and aired them whenever possible rather than clean them. In 1865 we find Mrs Beeton advising her readers that 'Warm skirts and cloth jackets should be hung out in the air, and well beaten with a light cane, and stored with plenty of camphor in presses or boxes'. While 'All cloth, merino, and stuff dresses which are worn daily should be hung out for one day in each week in the open air, beaten lightly with a cane, and well brushed and folded and put away. . . . This cleansing and rest', she added, 'keeps the dress fresh and pleasant, and makes it look better and wear longer than if this little care is neglected.'

The idea of regularly washing clothes with soap became much more realistic around the middle of last century when the very heavy soap duty, which had been imposed back in 1712, was finally lifted in 1852. Although commercial laundries had existed in Rome and Pompeii they did not really become part of British life until Victoria's time. From the middle ages, though, in this country, professional 'fullers' had trodden and beaten cloth – for the purpose of cleaning and thickening it.

The first public laundry opened in England in 1842, prior to that the trade was generally advertised 'Dyeing and Cleaning'; in Plymouth one of the pioneering laundries was begun at the start of the century by John Mortimer who in the 1820s styled himself 'Dyer and Fuller'. Originally based in Drake Street, the Mortimer family concern went on to become one of the biggest laundry businesses in the area, their chocolate and black vans being driven around the streets of Plymouth in the early years of this century by uniformed men in brown top hats.

In 1932 Mortimer's extensive works in Cobourg Street were taken over by the Millbay Laundry. This enterprise had been started by Harold Roberts in Millbay Road in 1885 and it soon went on to become the most successful laundry venture in the area. Formed as a limited liability company, the Millbay Laundry, Cleaning and Dyeing Co, in 1896, by 1904 it had acquired the Valletort Laundry.

Plymouth at this time still had a number of independent laundresses, ladies who took washing in and returned it, on foot, in great wicker baskets, the increased mobility of the big laundries though and the improved efficiency and capability of their machinery made them more and more successful. In 1922 Plymouth's Central Laundry was taken over by Millbay and in the years leading up to the war the firm was serving 20,000 customers a week through its 50 West Country branch offices.

On 21st April 1941 the original Millbay works were destroyed by enemy bombing, the neighbouring Eddystone Works building survived, however, and after the war the site was redeveloped and the Millbay Laundry continued to expand. In 1972 though the firm was taken over by Kneel's of Exeter, a firm which had been established by Alexander Kneel in 1910. This situation lasted just a few years for Kneels themselves were soon bought out by the huge multinational Johnson Group. Then in December 1986 it was announced that the Millbay operation was surplus to requirements and this was then taken over by Dukeimp or Laundrywise, as they are now called. A consortium that has laundries here, in Torbay, Buxton and Cheshire, Laundrywise are once again running the Millbay Laundry along the lines for which it is traditionally known.

Stonehouse

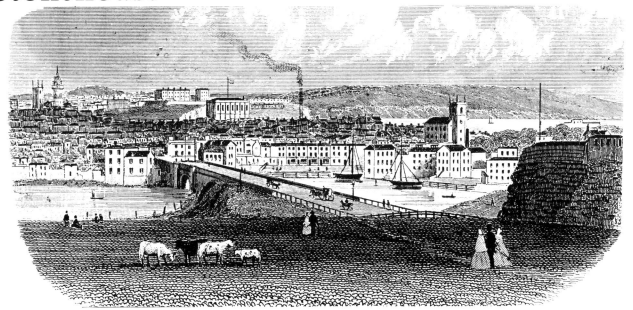

'Till about the commencement of the reign of George III, Stonehouse was but an inconsiderable village, and inhabited chiefly by fishermen and people of the lower classes . . . but during the present century it has risen rapidly, and is now a well built and populous town, the growth of its importance being, in a great measure, attributable to the successive erections of the Royal Navy Hospital, for sick and wounded seamen and marines, to which patients were first admitted in 1762, the Royal Marine Barracks, the Victualling Yard, &c. Most of the land is held on leases, subject to renewal on payment of small fines. The lord of the manor (the Earl of Mount Edgcumbe) holds Courts Leet as well as Courts Baron.' (*Devonshire Directory* 1857)

George III succeeded to the throne in 1760 and certainly by the end of his reign, in 1820, the character of Stonehouse had become very much one dominated by the services. However, in the years that followed the writing of the above account there was to be yet further change as the development of shipyards, breweries, malthouses and warehouses gave an increasingly industrial slant to the area. By the end of the nineteenth century, Stonehouse, the second oldest of the Three Towns, was left with little land undeveloped and nowhere to grow; Plymouth and Devonport had extended their boundaries to meet each other above that peninsula that was Stonehouse and thereby sealed its fate.

At the beginning of the nineteenth century, though, it must indeed have had quite an impressive aura about it, concentrated as it was around its four original thoroughfares; Passage, which became Newport Street, Chapel Street which became the northern end of Durnford Street, a narrow little street which was widened and became the recently demolished Edgcumbe Street, and Fore Street, which later ran into High Street and is now known only as High Street.

Emma Place and Durnford Street, both begun in 1773, were the two new fashionable areas, Durnford Street extending no further than the first phase of the Marine Barracks in 1820. Meanwhile Fore Street ran up to the main gate of the Naval Hospital and beyond that there was just a lane, Stonehouse Lane, the main link road to Plymouth. Patients for both the Naval and the Military Hospital, on the other side of the Stonehouse Creek, were mainly ferried in by boat. In the Naval Hospital alone between 1st January 1800 and 31st December 1814, 'no less than 48,452 seamen and marines were received, a great portion of whom were returned as effective men'. This was of course the time of the Napoleonic Wars, when the concentration of service personnel in the town would have been particularly high.

In 1812 there were at least ten Captains living in Durnford Street plus several other high ranking officers including Admiral De Courcy and Sir Richard King. In Emma Place a few more Captains resided as well as the Admiral and Member of Parliament, Sir Edward Buller, Bart. The directory for that year also listed 18 married women living in the two streets who were presumably either widows or women whose husbands were off fighting for their country.

By contrast there was only one senior ranking serviceman living in Fore Street, this street however sported almost half of the licenced premises of the town, that was nine out of twenty three. There were also three practicing cordwainers in the street, Thomas Field, Barnard Thompson and John Keast; a cordwainer was simply a shoemaker, cordwain being the term for Spanish leather which was fashionable amongst the wealthy for shoes from the middle ages onwards. It is of course still used as the name of the trade guild of shoemakers. There was another cordwainer in Chapel Street where there were a further three licenced premises and a mantua maker and a slopseller. A mantua originally was a silk garment, a gown or a petticoat, though it came to mean dress-making generally. John Russell, the slopseller, on the other hand, would have supplied ready made clothing to seamen, hence the still familiar service term 'slops' for clothing issue.

Stonehouse had a population of around 5,000 at this time. There were two schools for ladies, one in Emma Place one at Cremill Point. The records also show one schoolmaster, one writing master, one dancing master and a musician living in the town, the last two, Edward Ashwick and Philip Fleming both residents of George Street.

George Street took its name from the parish church of St George which was built by public subscription in 1789, on the site of the ancient chapel. Seating some 700, it can be seen towering over its neighbours to the right of this view. Built to the same plan as the Dockyard Chapel, it was damaged beyond repair during the Blitz and was pulled down. Sadly that has been the fate of so much old Stonehouse, the various Government Establishments survive, some in new roles, but the rest has all but disappeared. A great deal of the development seen in this picture was new to the nineteenth and late eighteenth centuries but it has already been cleared away. Durnford Street and Emma Place survive as do some of the later housing developments beyond them, but the heart of old Stonehouse has vanished almost without trace.

Parsonage Field

'In the early decade of the nineteenth century, a stray farm dwelling was to be seen in the Mutley or Mannamead district; there stood a solitary farmstead on the site of the Five Fields, and pasture land stretched to the bottom of Cambridge Street. Eldad, Stoke and Morice Town were scattered hamlets, and there was no inn near Millbridge for the convenience of travellers, or for belated husbands to assure their wives they had been "No Place".'

In this way Henry Whitfeld described part of what we see in the picture here published some years later, in 1859. Millbridge, seen here at the end of the first big expanse of what was then called Mill Lake, was gated 'for the first time within the memory of man' in 1807, by the Edgcumbes who had built the bridge in 1525. It was not a popular move and the Mayor and Corporation of Plymouth marched in state to the site and with the help of a body of carpenters demolished the gate and threw it into the stream. This in turn upset the miller who 'swore roundly at the Mayor, and his Worship fined him on the spot for his rudenesss'.

The Edgcumbes who were legitimately receiving toll money for the more recently erected Stonehouse Bridge decided not to press the claim and chose simply to neglect the bridge which by 1829 had become dilapidated and dangerous. The road itself was avoided by many anyway 'because of the dread of footpads and 'pitch-plasters', and the most favoured thoroughfare to Devonport was via Millbay the Marine Barracks and the Halfpenny Gate' (Stonehouse Bridge).

Eventually, however, locals became unhappy once more and said the bridge should be repaired and in the legal wrangles that followed it was eventually agreed that the Edgcumbes were within their rights to levy tolls and following the recognition of that right they undertook to rebuild the bridge. This work was duly begun in 1830 and the result was 'the reduction of a hill on the Devonport side of the bridge that had hitherto been too steep to admit of the ascent of animals; and Stoke, Newpassage and Plymouth were brought into closer communication'. In 1832 a table of tolls was set up.

Before the end of the nineteenth century the Mill Lake to the east of the bridge had been filled in to form Victoria Park and before the second world war there had been a certain amount of infilling on the western side, which, after the war, housed a number of prefabs as Millbridge Place and Millbridge Gardens were created here. Now gone, the whole of Mill lake has now been infilled and now rugby pitches dominate this view from Parsonage Field.

The parsonage itself, belonging to Stoke Damerel Church, can be seen in the trees to the far left of the foreground. Today the development around Rectory Road and the Rectory Ground of Devonport Services Rugby Club occupy much of this tree lined area. The wall around the Military Hospital, built in 1797, is as prominent today as it was then, however, as is the tower of the church.

Other features which stand out in this view include Wingfield Villas, to the left of the church, newly erected when this drawing was done. Here lived, in the 1860s, Thomas Bulteel, Charles Mallard, John Fullerton and three senior servicemen including Admiral Harper Lowe. The neighbouring Osborne Villas had an even higher concentration of servicemen, the eight properties being occupied by three captains, a lieutenant-colonel and a general, Mrs M Molesworth and William Scoggin. It was a similar story too at Penlee Villas, as these three impressive developments stood surrounded by greenery. A little below these grand buildings stood Arguam Villas, homes of George Rundle and Colonel Robert Yolland.

An impressive sight they doubtless made facing south in the sunlight, but on one occasion at least one of the group had the misfortune to become a spectacular sight at night too. It was during the infamous blizzard of March 1891, several inches of snow had fallen on the Three Towns, uprooting trees and unroofing houses. In the middle of it all the house in Wingfield Villas then occupied by the local rector, lost its large chimney stack which came crashing down through the drawing room; while at No 4 where Devonport's town clerk, JJE Venning lived, a falling chimney stack led to a major fire. 'Crowds of persons endeavoured to reach the scene by way of Millbridge, but the force of the hurricane rendered it impossible to pass.' Meanwhile the Devonport Fire-Brigade, under Captain Burns, struggled with the 'huge tongues of fire' as the thick flakes of snow fell around them.

It was not long, however, before the area around Millbridge was filled with new terraces of smaller houses but still as the beginning of the twentieth century dawned they had yet to cross the railway line or extend north above Alma Villas, seen here above Hotham Place (named after Lord William Hotham, Admiral of the White Fleet who had been Captain of the guardship *Hero* in Plymouth in 1767).

Today housing covers most of this view, a thin green strip, part of Central Park, can still be seen as can some of the trees in the distance around Mutley Park and Thorn Park. In 1859, though, there was little but green fields here. The railway bridge was but a recent mark on the landscape, as was Arundel Crescent, seen just to the right of the bridge and built over part of the Five Fields.

Also on the right of the picture, nearer the foreground, we see the corner block of the Royal Naval Hospital with its Landing Jetty and North Gate on the water's edge. Here patients were brought in for some 150 years before motor transport had developed to such a point that all patients were conveyed through the Main Gates. Just as well too; in later years the lake or creek had not always been easy to navigate and many a boat had found itself stuck and forced to wait for next tide before getting off.

Stonehouse Bridge

Before the building of Stonehouse Bridge the way from Stonehouse to Plymouth Dock (Devonport) was by no means an easy one. There was a footpath along the marsh at the top of Millbay to a ferry, here operated by a 'pilot', who pulled the boat from shore to shore by ropes laid across the creek. But it could only be used by those on foot because of 'the narrowness of the avenues and approaches to and from the said ferry, and other obstructions'.

Difficult by day and 'very desolate and dreary by night', indeed it was 'the custom for those who had to go from one town to the other after sunset to wait until a little party had collected, sufficiently strong to repel attack' before setting off on their journey across the marshes. Some pedestrians forded the creek, when and where possible, others went round by way of Millbridge, this being the usual route for those travelling with pack horses. Here again precautions were often necessary and traders travelling between Plymouth and Dock with 'treasure and merchandise' would supply each man with a case of pistols 'to confront the irrepressible highwayman'.

It is worth remembering that even where there were so called 'frequented ways', they would never be more than ten or twelve feet wide and generally had great lofty hedges at their sides with overhanging bowers and branches which, although affording some protection from the rain, also made them dark and gloomy even in the daytime. Many mounted travellers did their best to avoid such routes, wherever possible, in case they should meet a wide load coming the other way. Pack horses then were well and truly loaded up with all manner of things projecting from extended crooks used to carry merchandise.

Not surprisingly, wheeled carriages were a rare sight and 'even a jolting waggon was an unusual spectacle in the town' (Whitfeld). Nevertheless when George, Lord Edgcumbe and Sir John St Aubyn applied for an Act of Parliament, in 1767, to enable them to bridge the creek and link their two estates, there was allowance made for every conceivable modern mode of wheeled conveyance. The Act empowered them to demand as tolls – 'before any passage over the said bridge be permitted' – for every chaise, chair or calash drawn by one horse the sum of twopence; for every cart, dray, car, sledge or other carriage drawn by one horse, mule, or ass, the same amount; for every coach or chariot drawn by two horses, the sum of threepence, sixpence if there were more than two horses. The toll for pedestrians was fixed at a halfpenny, hence the name by which many people still know it over two hundred years later – Ha'penny Bridge.

The bridge was in use by 1769 although it wasn't actually completed until 1773. Overnight there was an improvement in the communications around the Three Towns; in 1775 hire carriages first began travelling between them and by 1800 there were 41 of these 'Dock diligences' running. In 1828 there was a brief hiccup as the imposition of a coach duty curtailed their activities, however, in April of that year the foundation of the old bus system was laid with the introduction of six hackney coaches planned to run at stated times. This was later replaced, in 1871, by the tramway system.

The construction of the bridge had meant major changes on the Stonehouse bank, for it necessitated the demolition of several buildings and the replanning of the end of High Street and its junction with Edgcumbe Street and Chapel Street, the very heart of eighteenth century Stonehouse. The ferry itself had crossed the creek a little below where the bridge now stands, from the bottom of Newport Street to the old ferry house seen in the picture here.

In June 1767 John Smeaton, more famous locally and nationally as the engineer of the first stone-built Eddystone Lighthouse, produced designs for this bridge running from 'Mr Croal's quay to the opposite shore'. The original bridge was as we see here, a simple single stone arch construction with a long causeway on either side. It has since been widened a couple of times, most recently in the 1960s, but the original fabric can still be seen.

Smeaton built a handful of bridges around the country, all of which still stand, although one was rebuilt and one is no longer in use, but it was unusual for him to work this far from the Great North Road between Edinburgh and London. His family home was in Scotland but doubtless he was very familiar with this area too as he'd lived for some time in Stonehouse when he was working on the Lighthouse between 1756 and 1759. He too fell foul of local undesirables, living somewhere near his stoneworks and Stonehouse Chapel he made a note in a letter dated June 27 1758 '. . . Two or three weeks since some villains in the night broke all the windows of the Chapel and much about the same time our dog that lay in the yard was poisoned'. He then went on to add that he had placed a porter on guard there with a musket!

For over 200 years, then, this bridge crossed Stonehouse Creek which in turn ran up to Millbridge and beyond, originally extending as far as Pennycomequick. Gradually everything north of these bridges was filled in and since 1972 the bridge has marked the end of the Creek. Long gone now the era that recalls the great logs of timber merchants, Fox and Elliot, which were towed under the bridge and chained together and left there to season. Although when this picture was sketched in 1830, Fox and Elliot had yet to occupy the site of the old ferry house that was still just a part of the future.

Richmond Walk

In 1675 Charles II made his illegitimate son, Charles Lennox, Duke of Richmond. The title itself was an old one dating back to the days of William the Conqueror, however at various times through the centuries heirs to the title had died without issue and the honour had been revived a number of times by subsequent monarchs. Lennox's mother was Frances Teresa Stewart (1647–1702) who was educated in France and had come to England as a maid of honour to Catherine of Braganza who Charles II had married on 21st May 1662. It is thought that the 33-year-old king took the 16-year-old Frances as his mistress in 1663. A noted beauty, Frances Stewart was the original model for the figure of Britannia who made her first appearance on British coinage around this time. Charles II had no children by his marriage to Catherine and in time he created Charles Lennox Duke of Richmond and Lennox.

Two hundred years later the Duke's great grandson was in the area as the Master-General of the Ordnance and under his authority, in preparation for a war with the French, a second wall was built around the growing town of Devonport. It wasn't a particularly popular measure with the locals, neither was his decision to move the seat of the Governor of Plymouth from the Citadel to a new and impressive purpose built house, Government House, at Mount Wise. The Duke was criticised for using public money in this way especially as the first Governor to occupy this splendid dwelling was Richmond's brother, General Lord George Lennox. So it was that in 1809, in order to appease those who were angered particularly by this new wall which cut them off from what little foreshore that was left around here, the Duke had Richmond Walk constructed. It ran, as it still does, from Mutton Cove below Mount Wise right around to Stonehouse Bridge.

At that time there was very little development of this stretch of waterfront, a fair amount of limestone had been quarried from the side of Stonehouse Creek but that was about it. By the end of the nineteenth century though, Richmond Walk had become a veritable hive of activity. Here were boatyards, timber merchants, coal merchants and a London and South Western Region Goods Station on what was described as Devonport's New Docks. Here too were a number of private residences, including Victoria Cottages, Marine Villa and Baker's Place. There were three public houses here too and public baths.

Much of this development came after Captain GR Sartorius had sketched this view around 1830, although we can see a group of buildings where Ocean Court now stands and among them was the 'Richmond Walk Inn' which was probably built soon after the walk had been built. Certainly we know that Richard Harris, who was licensee here in 1830, had been here since 1823 and that he was by no means the first publican here having taken over from William Ryder at that time. If that inn was indeed built around 1809 it would have just failed to celebrate its centenary as we last find mention of it in 1906. The other pubs, both in Baker's Place, fared a little better, although one was demolished in the late 1920s along with numbers 1–10 Baker's Place and the other finally closed it's doors during the last war. This was the 'Fisherman's Arms', Edward Steele Baxter was the landlord here when war was declared, and it stood just four doors down from where the railway cut across Baker's Place. The other pub, at number nine, was only two doors from the railway and 100 years ago William Yandle (Yandell) was the licensee there. William Charles Yandell, a boat builder by trade, had been at Richmond Walk for many years and had also been Quay Master here.

Today a few slate hung properties in Baker's Place still stand and the railway lines are still to be seen, although they now cross the road and run straight into a concrete wall. The character of the area is changing here and there but there is still Blagdon's boatyard around the corner, there before the war when next door was Clara Fleming's sweet shop. Clara was born in 1859, she married George 'Tich' Fleming and inherited, from her father, a boat hire business, which he had started from Bromley Cottages, Mount Wise, and which was subsequently run as Fleming's boat hire business.

As well as boat businesses there is a long tradition of timber firms based here; Bayley and Fox, William Clark and Thomas Reslarich were among those here in the nineteenth century with Fox and Eliott surviving well into the twentieth century, while the James Brothers were here by the 1920s. Today Jewsons carry on that business. Meanwhile, among those businesses to have a base here while the trains were still running were the structural engineers Blight and White.

Ocean Quay Station had opened in 1877 and for many years passengers from ocean liners would be landed at Stonehouse Pool and taken by the LSWR up to Waterloo. At the turn of the century there used to be races between the LSWR, who carried the passengers from the liners and the GWR (Great Western Railway) who carried the mails. The first race, held on 9th April 1904, was won by the GWR by 15 minutes with a Plymouth to Paddington time of 4 hours 18 minutes. A terrible accident in 1906 saw the loss of 28 lives on the LSWR route and after that boat trains stopped at Exeter and Salisbury and then followed normal express schedules. In 1910 LSWR stopped running boat trains from here altogether although goods trains continued to run from here until 1966. In the 1970s the station area was redeveloped with the building of the luxury flats at Ocean Court and where once passengers from great liners were landed, sailors on exotic yachts now pull into the marina.

Mutton Cove

It was sometime around 1830 when Captain GR Sartorius RN sat down 'on the spot' and sketched eight views of the local waterfront, all of which were subsequently worked up on stone for litho printing by JD Harding and then published by Byers and Saunders of Devonport. One of these illustrations was the one shown here of Mutton Cove looking towards Mount Edgcumbe with the 'Mount Edgcumbe Inn' in the foreground, where doubtless the good captain would have encountered John Jenkins who was then the landlord. One can easily imagine the licensee acquiring one of the prints and hanging it in the bar.

Although only ever a small community of twenty or thirty substantial buildings, by no means all of which would have been lived in, Mutton Cove at one time sported four pubs, the oldest of them apparently being the 'Mutton Cove Inn' or Hotel as it later became. As well as being the oldest, in all probability it was also the largest, and stood just down from the little building with the pyramid shaped roof. Richard Horrell was the landlord of this hostelry in 1830, while in 1844 we find that Elizabeth Wall was in charge there. Records for this period are by no means complete and it is quite likely that Ms Wall was here for some time prior to that for 1844 is the first year that we find a reference to the 'Waterman's Arms' at Mutton Cove. This Inn was almost right on the water's edge, next door but one to the 'Mutton Cove', and there, in 1844, Richard Wall was recorded as licensee. Richard was succeeded six or seven years later by Ann Wall who most likely was his wife.

The reason for all these watering holes in such a small place of course was that Mutton Cove was one of the principal gateways to the west. In 1750 the ferry across to Mount Edgcumbe, which had previously run from Crimhill (Cremyll Point or Devil's Point) was moved here, because of the growing importance of Plymouth Dock (Devonport)

and by the end of the decade a new road had been made down to Mutton Cove, alongside the land that had recently been appropriated for extension of the Dockyard.

A petition from the Mayor and Corporation of Plymouth appears to have been instrumental in improving this road, and others leading west from Plymouth, in 1784. On arriving here in those days visitors would have found a horse boat and two boats for passengers, which were 'constantly employed in passing'. They would also have found 'a great many watermen plying for hire'. These unofficial ferrymen were 'not put under any direction', nor were their rates regulated and although many people felt they were often over-charged there was no shortage of customers. As well as taking day trippers across to Edgcumbe, the watermen also took sailors back to their ships.

Although the ferry here was eclipsed to some extent by the launching of the Torpoint Ferry in 1791 and despite the Cremyll Ferry (as it was known even when it was based here) moving back to Stonehouse with the construction of the Admiral's hard in 1824, there was still a good living to be had here for the watermen.

One hundred years ago there were half a dozen or so men living in Mutton Cove itself who described themselves as watermen, among them John Dooley, Henry Turner and Thomas Wilkey.

Of course the position and arrangement of the this little harbour, so named 'by reason of the leg-of-mutton formation of the creek' (Whitfeld) meant that it was ideally suited to another popular waterbased activity of the time ... smuggling. There was by all accounts 'a considerable retreat at Mutton Cove' which was long ago excavated into stores. Cave or no cave, however, it is unlikely that illegal trafficking here stopped altogether and on 27th February 1873 Messrs Kendal and Neptune, watermen of Mutton Cove,

were sentenced to six months imprisonment for smuggling 'tobacco stems'.

In time however work for the watermen did dry up and while regatta day here continued to pull the crowds, rowing became more of a sport than a means of employment; there was a thriving rowing club that operated from here based in nearby Pembroke Street. The 'Waterman's Arms' closed before the end of the nineteenth century and in its later years saw service as Sibley's Stables.

Sibley's Wagonettes travelled all around the area; fine coaches drawn by handsome horses with shiny coats. Just before the Second World War, during the last few years that Mutton Cove enjoyed as a distinct community, the firm had become Sibley and Son, funeral furnishers.

The other main business to have been conducted here though centred mainly around the discharging of coal. George Willcocks worked from here, as did for many years the Goodman Brothers, while just around the corner, at Bullock's Dock, William Bennett had his coal merchant's business. As this century unfolded however the business with the largest presence here became the wine and spirit merchants Saccone and Speed who used many of the buildings here simply as stores. Then in 1938 the bonded area was cleared to make way for the 'New Park', a small boating pond.

During the last war further change came in the wake of the arrival of a balloon barrage crew, complete with balloon and attendant vehicles and the site of the old village of Mutton Cove once and for all ceased to bear any resemblance to its eighteenth century roots. Today, although still a public landing place, it is hard now, walking down the old cobbled main thoroughfare, to imagine this as a once bustling little port.

Mount Wise Signalling Station

'The new Telegraph, the one fixed within the Higher Lines, Dock and the other fixed on the heights above Saltram, are nearly completed; the telegraphs themselves are complete, and the lodges for those men that work them are almost finished. They have communicated a message to the Admiralty, and an answer has been returned in a space of time from 28 to 30 minutes. A short message has been conveyed, and an answer returned from London, in a space of time from 10 to 12 minutes; a celerity of conveying intelligence hitherto unknown in this part of the country, and will be a great saving in expenses from this port to the Admiralty and different public offices' (Naval Chronicle 12th July 1806).

In the early nineteenth century the term 'telegraph', as used in the above report, referred to the relaying of messages by semaphore, a process which had just revolutionised the business of communications. The military, for whom speed in conveying information has always been a major consideration and advantage were, not surprisingly, at the forefront of this development. Way back in 1666 the second Marquess of Worcester had devised a system of communica-

tion based on the clock face and although this was similar to modern semaphore it wasn't until 1792 that system of mechanical semaphore was introduced anywhere.

It was a Frenchman, Claude Chappe who installed the first long distance semaphore network – across 22 stations stretching 130 miles between Lille and Paris – the first ever to be called 'telegraph' (the word itself is a combination of two Greek words meaning 'far off' and 'to write'). Four years later Lord George Murray, Archdeacon of Man, invented a mechanical device which was so successful that he was invited to become the admiralty's first director of telegraphy and soon afterwards a chain of stations was set up at three mile intervals between Portsmouth and the Admiralty.

At this stage, however, the semaphore – literally 'signal bearing' – was based on discs and shutters in a framework and it wasn't until 1806 and the installation of the Plymouth to London chain of stations that a new system, based on Admiral Sir Home Popham's simple two arm semaphore, devised in 1803, came into use. Instantly successful, a test

message was acknowledged by London within three minutes, it was much the same as the semaphore still used by the navy today.

Although this system was infinitely more sophisticated than the chain of beacons set in place to warn of the Armada in 1588, it is interesting to note that even then it was reckoned that it would have taken less than twenty minutes to convey such a warning to London. The Plymouth fire beacons were on the Hoe and at Pennycross (Beacon Park), the decision to site the new Telegraph Station here reflected the removal to Devonport of not just the naval base – the dockyard – but also the military headquarters following the construction of Government House at Mount Wise in 1795.

The new signalling system, conveyed across 32 stations before it reached the Admiralty (it went via Portsmouth) was, in 1849, temporarily superseded by the electric telegraph of the South Devon and Great Western Railway. However, within three years the Admiral's Office at Mount Wise had its own 'immediate and direct' communication with London via the new Electric Telegraph.

This new system of electric telegraphy was more in line with what we now understand as telegraphy and employed instruments based on those devised in the late 1830s by Wheatstone and Cooke in England and the celebrated Samuel Finley Breese Morse in America. It was of course Morse's code of dots and dashes that was generally taken up by telegraph users.

It wasn't just the Admiralty who found the Signal Station here useful, though, for following the abolition of local time in 1860 it was the practice to indicate Greenwich time at one o'clock each day at Mount Wise. Folklore records the story of two Devonport locals, 'Titch' and 'Corky', who would stand outside the Old Chapel and look down St Stephen's Street (it's the spire of the bombed church of St Stephen that can be seen here to the left of the flag pole) to the signal station where a large black ball would be hoisted then dropped at one o'clock precisely, whereupon they would 'hurry inside the Old Chapel and check the time'.

With the improved communications of the twentieth century, the role of the Mount Wise signal station gradually declined. although it was in use until at least 1939, with its weather cones and its flags – giving warning of ships moving up and down the Hamoaze – the arms of the semaphore could also often be seen moving. By 1957, though, it was all just a memory as the demolition men moved in and took down what, in the nineteenth century had been one of the area's most important little buildings.

Mount Wise

'Mountwise, the Champ de Mars of Plymouth and Devonport, commands a fine variety of natural objects. The parade itself is a level expanse of gravel, pleasingly skirted by patches of refreshing green sward. On the side towards Devonport is the residence of the Port Admiral and nearly opposite is Government House, originally intended for the occupation of the military Governor of Plymouth. Mountwise presents a joyous scene on the day of a grand review, when the troops in the garrison are mustered to celebrate some national holiday. The towns and villages then, for many miles round, send forth their streams of human existence to swell the great sea of population which collects on the parade. The fields on the banks of the Tamar, Plym and Tavy are deserted, and even the lonely glens of Dartmoor hear the voice of rejoicing. And it is in truth a spirit-stirring sight to gaze on the military spectacle with all its concomitant 'pomp and circumstance' – and to behold so many thousands of smiling happy faces, though the mind is apt to recur the Persian who, in contemplating his vast army from the height 'which looks o'er sea-born Salamis', wept at the thought 'that ere a century should elapse not one of that immense multitude would be living'.

Published in 1828 in Henry Carrington's *Plymouth and Devonport Guide*, it is strange to think that nearer two hundred than one hundred years have elapsed since that account was written, although the picture here is a little later and dates from the 1880s. There were not many major changes to this view in the intervening years, however, although a print first produced in 1859 shows grazing cattle where there were soon after grass covered magazines just below the signal station.

In contrast to this, the twentieth century has witnessed great changes to this scene although the three principal buildings still stand and from the outside at least appear much as they did then.

The house on the left here is that described above as Government House. Completed around 1795, this was the building that Parliament had sanctioned in May 1789 when they had voted in favour of providing £4,743 (a great deal of money then) for the construction of the house especially for the Governor of Plymouth. Prior to this the Governor of Plymouth (a role that had been created in Elizabethan times) seldom if ever stayed in Plymouth and when he did his residence was in the Citadel. The change in circum-

stances was prompted by a piece of what locals termed 'nepotism of the worst order' as the Duke of Richmond, who was Master General of the Ordnance, pushed this measure through in the interests of his younger brother, Lord George Lennox, who had been appointed Governor. Lennox lived here from 1796–1803, after him came a number of notable occupants including, in the 1820s the Rt Hon Earl Grey who was to serve the country as Prime Minister (1830–34) at the time of the Reform Act in 1832.

One hundred years later negotiations opened between War Office and the Admiralty concerning the future of this building, prompted by the imminent move of the headquarters of the General Officer Commanding Wessex area to Salisbury (the position of Governor of Plymouth had been dropped in the 1840s). In 1935 arrangements had been sorted out and the house converted and, on 9th June, Government House became Admiralty House with the appointment of Vice-Admiral the Hon Sir Reginald Plunket-Ernle-Erle-Drax as the new Commander-in-Chief; today it is home to the Flag Officer, Plymouth, Admiral Sir Alan Grose KBE.

The original Admiralty House, meanwhile, seen here second from the right, which was built, we read in the Flag Officer's history of Admiralty House, at the beginning of the nineteenth century, became Hamoaze House when the C-i-C moved out in 1935 and then served as an administrative centre for the navy until the Headquarters of the Plymouth Group Royal Marines was moved here in 1966.

The third major building shown here is in fact the oldest of the group. Built as a private house on the St Levan estate at the bottom of George Street in 1784 it was, with its neighbour No 38, erected the following year, rented from the estate until 1899, when, as Mount Wise House (a name given to it by its last occupant Capt NH Henderson RN), it was purchased for £1,730 and subsequently converted for use as offices for the C-i-C and accommodation for his secretary.

So much for that which remains little changed, as to the rest, the parade ground is taken with tennis courts, a garden for Admiralty House and stretching across the middle ground of this view staff offices; these stand partly on the old courtyard and stables. Beyond them the signal station has been replaced by the Onslow Court married quarters, the base of the old Mount Wise fort still discernable beneath it.

One of the most interesting changes here, of course, is the one that saw the removal of the statue of the military hero, John Colborne, Lord Seaton, from its position on the skyline here, first to a site in front of what was then still Government House in 1904 and then, after the arrival of the C-i-C here, out to the barracks named after him at Crownhill. A move that was all the more remarkable in that less than ten years after Seaton left his original site one of Plymouth's few other statues was erected nearby, the statue commemorating that great British naval explorer Robert Falcon Scott.

Devonport

Devonport Town Hall 'forms a noble termination to the avenue made by the buildings of Ker-street. No spot could be more judiciously chosen for this edifice, as it is situated on an ascent fronting the principal entrance to the town from Plymouth, and is seen with great effect from the draw-bridge rising with a noble portico above the surrounding buildings, the wondrous Parthenon crowning with its glorious front the steep of the Athenian Acropolis.'(Rowe c.1830)

The Town Hall was designed by John Foulston who drew his inspiration from the famous Parthenon temple in Athens. Dedicated to the goddess Athena Parthenos ('parthenos' being Greek for a virgin), this temple was erected about 490 BC and measured 230 ft long and 100 ft wide. Foulston's building is then about half that size and was begun in 1821 and completed the following year. The building contractor was JL Rickard of Devonport and the cost of the whole project was £2902. The monies for this were raised by public subscription, in shares, the land itself having been given by Sir John St Aubyn. Unfortunately, however, the monies raised were insufficient to complete the scheme as the architect had hoped and his proposed figure of Justice never did appear above the portico, although some time after this view was executed around 1829 the existing figure of Britannia was installed in its place.

Prior to the building of this Town Hall the public business of Plymouth Dock, as it then was, had been conducted in the old Workhouse in Duke Street erected in 1777. In those days the population of Plymouth Dock would have been around 10,000–12,000, about the same as that of Plymouth itself. Plymouth though wasn't expanding at anything like the rate of the town that housed the King's Dockyard. Before work began on the Dockyard there was no significant development here at all, indeed it's said that

the first house here was built in 1700 at North Corner. However, by 1733 we find a population of over 3,000 here, which was then not quite half that of Plymouth and by the time work on the Town Hall had been started the number of people living in Dock had risen to 33,578, a figure that was some 12,000 higher than that of Plymouth.

It comes as no surprise therefore to find the inhabitants of Plymouth Dock petitioning the King to grant them the privilege of changing the name of the town, a request that he sanctioned in 1823. So it was that on the 1st January the new appellation of Devonport 'was proclaimed in many public places, with every demonstration of rejoicing'. A major procession set off from the Town Hall at precisely 10 o'clock that morning.

In order to commemorate this great event, Foulston was commissioned to produce a grand column next to the Town Hall. This location was significant in more ways than one for it was aligned with the new road out of Plymouth, which Foulston had also been involved with. The road linked the three towns Plymouth, Stonehouse and now Devonport, it was of course Union Street, and what better way for the fledgling town of Devonport to draw attention to itself than with this well sited monument. A monument which was inspired by the Column erected in Rome in 114 AD in honour of the Emperor Trajun. Like Trajun's Column the Devonport construction, although less elaborate, is around 120ft from ground to crown and has a spiral staircase lighted by small openings running up its shaft. Also, just as the Roman column has a statue of Trajun at its top, so the Devonport column was intended to have a colossal statue of George IV, the King who granted the name change, surmounting it but once again because certain people who promised to subscribe to the cost of the project were not forthcoming the statue never appeared.

It is perhaps remarkable to note that the column was built without the use of any form of scaffolding, stones of granite from Holman's Hill quarry weighing as much as 4 or 5 tons being lifted up to the top by means of a series of tall spars, joined together like the mast of a ship with a crane and winch arrangement to lift and pull. The whole operation taking, it was said, 'a short time'.

In comparative terms, all the main structures in this view were completed in a short time and all were the work of John Foulston. The Mount Zion Chapel, a Calvinist establishment, was begun in November 1823 and completed in July 1824 at a cost of about £2,000. The column itself cost nearer £3,000, while the Oddfellows Hall, 1823, costing some £1,500 was the least expensive of the group.

Originally used as the Devonport and Stonehouse Classical and Mathematical Subscription School, it became, within a few years, the Devonport Library, complete with a 'highly valuable collection of books, both ancient and modern, and a constant supply of the London, provincial, and local newspapers.'

Inspiration for these two buildings most likely came from Thomas Daniell's 'Oriental Scenery' (1795–1815) and Denon's 'Voyage dans la Haute et Basse Egypte' (1802), respectively. The Oddfellows Hall, now the Ker Street Social Club, is one of the few surviving examples of the Egyptian craze that followed the publication of a work entitled 'Description de l'Egypt'(1809).

The Hindu-style chapel helped make up what Foulston called 'a variety of Oriental Architecture'. Today this is the only one of the four not standing, Ker Street Infants' School was built on its site in 1904. This too is no more, while the Town Hall itself, robbed of its original function with the merging of the Three Towns in 1914, has only just managed to survive redevelopment.

Plymouth Dock from near Mount Edgcumbe

The view of the Dockyard from Mount Edgcumbe is one that has attracted many artists over the years, several of whom have produced pictures from around this particular vantage point, none more famous than JMW Turner, the man who was responsible for this image in 1813.

Joseph Mallord William Turner was 38 in the summer of that year, as a young topographical artist he had already toured extensively around England and Wales and he had made his first tour of the Continent, following the Peace of Amiens, back in 1802. By 1851 when he died, Turner had become one of the most famous and most travelled artists the world has known and yet in 1852 Cyrus Redding, writing in *The Gentleman's Magazine*, recorded that Turner had said to him 'he had never seen so many natural beauties in so limited extent of country as he saw in the vicinity of Plymouth. Some of the scenes hardly seemed to belong to this island. Mount Edgcumbe particularly delighted him; and he visited it three or four times.'

The actual engraving reproduced here was executed in 1816 by William Cooke, under Turner's supervision, and it was based on the watercolour Turner had painted here. Turner had first visited Plymouth back in 1811, when he undertook a tour of the west country for the Cooke brothers who had commissioned him to contribute twenty four drawings for a publication called *Picturesque Views of the Southern Coast of England*. The artist had left London in the second week of July and was back by the middle of September. Bearing in mind the difficulties of travelling then it is remarkable that Turner was later to produce over 40 works based on the sketches he made on that trip.

In 1813 the Cooke's project had still not been completed and Turner came west again, this time basing himself in Plymouth for three weeks. While here he stayed with John Collier, the wealthy Southside Street merchant, Ambrose Johns, a local painter and Cyrus Redding a young journalist Turner had met in London the year before. Redding was then editor of the *Plymouth Chronicle* based at Frankfort Place and he lived in a well-situated cottage just up from Mutley Plain. Turner's visit was one clearly he and the artist enjoyed, as evidenced by Redding's account of one of Turner's visits to this very location;

'There were eight or nine of the party including some ladies. We repaired to the heights of Mount Edgcumbe at the appointed hour. Turner, with ample supply of cold meats, shell-fish and wines, was there before us. In that delightful spot we spent the best part of a beautiful summer's day. Never was there more social pleasure partaken by any party in that English Eden. Turner was exceedingly agreeable ... The wine circulated freely, and the remembrance was not obliterated from Turner's mind long years afterwards.'

Turner and Redding also sailed around to Burgh Island from Plymouth and, fearing evening gales, stayed overnight in Kingsbridge, walking back almost all of the 20 miles the following day. For his watercolours Turner was paid the princely sum of seven and a half pounds per picture, the Cooke brothers themselves receiving twenty-five guineas for each plate they engraved. To put this in some sort of perspective, although the engravings took a long time to execute, it would then have taken a dockyard shipwright almost six months to earn that sort of money.

The good time Turner had here at Mount Edgcumbe doubtless induced him to include the group of revellers shown in the foreground: 'Here Turner has replaced his friends with some sailors and some women. They are accompanied by a fiddler with a peg-leg and are waving to a couple making their way up the drive on the right. The carousing men and women seem well-matched by the equally rhythmic and lively beech trees.' So noted Eric Shanes in his book on *Turner's Rivers, Harbours and Coasts* (1981), he also observed that Turner made some adjustments to the image for the engraving 'giving a somewhat bawdier clarity to the waving gestures of the figures.'

By the time this view eventually did find a wider audience via the engraving, changes in the dockyard were already starting to date the picture, not the least of which involved the covering over of the various building slips, first mooted by Richard Pering, who was then Clerk of the Cheque in the Plymouth Yard.

The creation of covered building slips was begun in 1815 with the roofing of Number 1 slip, the northernmost slip on which the first-rate *Britannia* was then being built. Slips 2 and 3 were completed soon after and eventually all the building slips and dry docks, except the New Union Dock, had large roofs erected over them.

These alterations were to have a major impact on the appearance of the dockyard from this vantage point as was the rebuilding of the dockyard chapel. In 1814, the year after Turner's last visit, the condition of the original chapel, built in 1700, had deteriorated to such a dangerous state that the decision was taken to pull it down and erect a new one on the same site. On the 11th November of that year ropes were tied around the upper part of the old chapel tower and it was brought crashing down to the ground.

James Adams of Stonehouse was the architect responsible for the design of the new chapel and the first stone was laid on 19th January 1815. Problems with the ground held up operations a little but then, on almost the third anniversary of the old chapel going, the new chapel was opened for Divine Service, on 9th November 1817.

Built at a cost of around £24,000 this now became the only Dockyard Chapel to have a peal of bells and services were held here for a further hundred years and more until this fine building, like so many of the old survivors in South Yard, became a victim of enemy bombing during the last war.

Devonport from Mount Edgcumbe

JMW Turner's view of Plymouth Dock from Mount Edgcumbe, drawn by him in 1813, was engraved by WB Cooke in 1816 and published that year in London by John Murray who was a major part of a syndicate that Cooke had set up. Cooke put up the initial capital and was one of twelve members of the syndicate, which included Turner, although the artist himself appears not to have made any financial contribution.

John and Arthur Arch, who had a print shop in Cornhill, were also members of the syndicate. Print publishing in those days was big business and Turner's view was subsequently reissued twice, in 1849 and 1860. By then there was quite a range of engravings in print of this view, including at least three others from a very similar angle; one based on an original drawing of Thomas Allom's, which appeared in Britton and Brayley's *Devonshire and Cornwall Illustrated*, another produced for Henry Besley's *Views in Devonshire* after a drawing by George Townsend and this one by T Prior after E Duncan which was reproduced in the *Stationer's Almanac* of 1856.

As they were all executed at slightly different times, they provide a fascinating insight into the growth of the Dockyard and of Devonport itself, or Plymouth Dock as it was when Turner visited and when the first of a number of eighteenth century artists produced views from here.

Prior to the development of the Dockyard, this would have been an almost unblemished rural scene, however, all that was to change after 1789, following a recommendation made by Edward Dummer, Assistant Master Shipwright from Chatham. Dummer was already familiar with this area, having at one time been in charge of the facilities at Teat's Hill, and in the autumn of 1789 he came here at the request of the Admiralty who had decided that there should be Government docking facilities west of Portsmouth.

In his report, Dummer suggested the area just across the water here which was then simply known as Point Forward, the actual site in question being made up of three fields, mostly belonging to the thirteen-year-old Sir Nicholas Morice. The choice was quickly approved, negotiations were begun over the land and, despite complications work was soon under way.

Initially, there was just to be a single dry dock capable of receiving a third-rate man-of-war to be built, taking advantage of the natural contours of the available land, but as soon as the formalities were completed, Dummer submitted plans for a more ambitious scheme including a wet dock and a bigger dry dock. In the event the revised plan was approved, King William himself insisting that the dry dock be big enough to hold a first-rate vessel.

One by one the new posts were filled here, including the appointment, on the 18th January 1691, of Elias Waffe as the first Master Shipwright of the Yard. By the January of the following year the first muster was held and the workforce now totalled seventy four.

William III came down to inspect the yard for himself in 1692, the year both the wet basin and the dry dock was completed. Built on part of the site that had been reclaimed from the sea, the new facilities represented a great advance on anything previously known in this country and doubtless pleased the new king.

Plymouth had been one of the first towns in the country to declare for William and Mary after they had landed at Brixham in 1688 effectively ending the tyranny of his uncle and her father, James II. William was in Plymouth in the spring of 1689 and it is thought that it was probably then that he authorised the scheme for new naval dockyard. Certainly the enthusiasm with which the town greeted the king must have left him well disposed to the area.

Over the next few years the dockyard grew with the addition of a number of related buildings including storehouses, yarn houses, malthouses, a thousand foot long ropehouse and perhaps the most architecturally impressive of them all, 'The Walk' or 'The Terrace'. Built to accommodate the senior dockyard officers, this has been cited as one of the earliest terraces to have been designed to have an architectural unity – sadly only a little of it survived the 2nd World War – but nevertheless that which does still stand represents the oldest piece of dockyard architecture in the country.

By 1700 the site had spread over 24 acres, 25 years later this figure had more than doubled and in 1761 over ten more acres were added. The fate of further expansion programmes was severely affected around this time by the leaving of the two common ways or passages to the water at Mutton Cove and North Corner.

Another stumbling block to the expansion of the yard was the original ropehouse which, running east to west, effectively formed a barrier across the yard. So it was, after a particularly bad fire in the ropehouse in 1761 when about 500 tons of cordage, 700 sails and 1,000 tons of hemp went up in flames, the decision was taken to pull the old building down and replace it with two new longer (1,200 feet each) ropehouses at the top of the yard running north/south. Ropemaking was a major concern in the dockyard, at one time almost half of the Navy's ropes were made in here.

As the yard and its workforce expanded, of course, so did Devonport itself and conspicuous among the features depicted on this engraving are three newly erected church spires, St Paul's 1851 (in Morice Square), St James's 1851 (in Duke Street), St Mary's 1852 (in James Street) and halfway between St Mary's and Devonport Column, the Italianate tower of Devonport Market, which ironically now, stands inside the current boundary wall of South Yard. The three churches and the market were, incidentally, all the work of the architect J Piers St Aubyn.

Alongside the Dockyard

In 1829 when this view was first published the Dockyard was still growing, however, it was then still all contained within the area that became known as South Yard; the scene here showing the Anchor-wharf and the Jetties at the entrance of the Camber. The impressive block of buildings were the sea-facing part of the huge Quadrangle complex of storehouses.

The Dockyard then, of course, was geared up to construct and service the wooden sail-driven men-of-war of the Royal Navy, the vessel partly visible on the left of the picture being the *Sheer-hulk* which was used for fixing the masts and rigging of other vessels. In a description designed to impress the reader with the efficiency of the yard, we learn from a contemporary account that 'such is the order in which every mast, rope and sail is kept, that the largest ships may be rigged for sea within the space of three or four days'.

The same account also informs us that the vessel on the right hand margin of the picture was the one 'employed in taking up and fixing the mooring chains in the harbour'.

The great wooden jetties themselves were constructed in such a way as to 'project from the harbour wall to a greater or less distance so that vessels of every size may be brought within floating distance from the shore, and receive their ballast and stores without the interposition of boats or rafts'.

Of the boats seen here around this time, few would have had a more interesting story to tell than the one we see the hulk of in the centre of this view. Stripped of its rigging, this imposing 74-gun third-rate man-of-war was the erstwhile HMS *Bellerophon*, the ship upon which Napoleon finally surrendered himself after the battle of Waterloo.

Built by Graves of Frindsbury (Chatham) in 1786, it was named in that age when so many people were turning to the classics, after the 'Joseph' of Greek mythology, Bellerophon.

He it was who was tempted by Anteia, wife of Proetus, and afterwards falsely accused by her causing Proetus to send him Anteia's father, the King of Lycia, with a letter praying that the bearer may be put to death. The King, Iobates, was reluctant to slay Bellerophon himself so he set him a number of hazardous tasks including the killing of the Chimaera, the fabulous monster born in Lycia which had a lion's head, a goat's body and a dragon's tail. Bellerophon not only succeeded in all these tasks he also survived an ambush the king set for him and so Iobates decided to let Bellerophon marry his daughter and become his heir.

Bellerophon later attempted to ride off to heaven on Pegasus, the winged horse, but Zeus sent a gadfly to sting the mount and Bellerophon was thrown. For the ordinary seamen Bellerophon's mythological credentials cut little ice and the ship was more popularly known as *Billy Ruffian* or *Bully Ruffian* in just the same way as the contemporary mythologically named *Agamemnon* was called *Eggs and Bacon* and the *Polyphemus* became the *Polly Infamous*.

HMS *Bellerophon* was a busy ship; it was present on the Glorious 1st of June (1794) when Lord Howe with the Channel Fleet scored a decisive victory over the French, it was involved in two blockades of Cadiz (1797 & 1805), it took part in the Battle of the Nile in 1798 and the Battle of Trafalgar in 1805, indeed the *Bellerophon* escorted the *Victory* back to England with Nelson's body. Undoubtedly its most famous moment came ten years later at six o'clock in the morning of Saturday the 15th July, when cruising in the Basque Roads off Rochefort the *Bellerophon*, under it's commander Captain Maitland, took the surrender of the Emperor Buonaparte.

On the 26th July 1815 the *Bellerophon*, with Napoleon on board, dropped anchor in Plymouth Sound and there he remained for several days '. . . thousands upon thousands of visitors flocked to the place, and swarmed in boats of all kinds upon the Sound, surrounding the ship and doing their utmost to obtain a glance at the man who had so long been a terror to Europe, but who was now a prisoner of war. The Emperor frequently came on deck, and placing himself in the gangway gratified the curiosity of the crowd' (Jewitt 1873).

Napoleon was here on the *Bellerophon* until the 7th of August before he was taken away bound for eventual imprisonment on St Helena where he died in 1821. Strangely enough, not long after housing it's most illustrious of prisoners the *Bellerophon* itself became a prison ship and in October 1824 it was renamed the *Captivity*. It was fitted up as a convict ship at Sheerness and first moored alongside Dockyard here in June 1826.

At that time there were only 80 convicts on board but three years later, when Thomas Allom produced the original sketch for this view, the number had increased to around 450 with a potential to house 600. The convicts weren't left idle by any means, rather they were 'constrained to work in the Dock-yard from seven o'clock until twelve, in the mornings, and from a quarter past one o'clock until half past five, in the afternoons. This ship has three decks, the upper-deck being an additional one, with ports cut to admit light.'

The *Captivity* as she now was had a captain and three mates, plus a surgeon, a chaplain, a number of 'inferior officers' and 19 guards. After more than ten years as a convict ship, however, the 50th anniversary of this grand old vessel was to be no jolly affair for those who had affection for the old ship for, in January 1836, she was sold and broken up, her figure head going to Portsmouth to serve as a reminder of the golden age of the *Bully Ruffian*.

Fire in the Dockyard

On the 20th May 1834 the Admiralty started using a Dockyard Police force here at Devonport. The Dockyard Police Force had first been instituted the year before in the wake of Sir Robert Peel's creation of the modern Police Force in 1829. Formed by remodelling the existing collection of Warders and Watchmen in the Dockyard, they received 'good pay', 19/- (95p) for a seven day week. Previously without uniform, they were now equipped with stove piped hats and silver buttoned blue frock coats, cut away at the front from the waist downwards. They carried an ornately decorated truncheon with the Sovereign's Coat of Arms and their own number and a rattle to raise any alarm.

Six years later, in the early hours of one Sunday morning, the 27th September 1840 a Dockyard Police Officer on duty near the three northern docks, noticed smoke pouring through the portholes on the bow of the *Talavera*. This 74-gun man-o-war, was originally to have been named the *Thunderer* but launched as the *Talavera* in October 1818 (in recognition of Sir Arthur Wellesley's famous Peninsular War victory there in 1809, a success which was followed by Wellesley being created viscount Wellington). Laid down at Woolwich Dockyard, the *Talavera* was lying in the Head Dock just in front of the Joiner's and House Carpenter's Shop, the clock tower of which is barely visible here through the flames.

Various cries and shouts induced the guards to fire their muskets in the air and within a few minutes a large force of military and police had been assembled. By this time, however, the insides of the *Talavera* were ablaze and the flames were lighting up the surrounding docks, workshops, jetties and ships, including another 74-gun vessel the *Minden*, which was just to the rear of the *Talavera* in the stern dock

and is seen here slightly below and to the left of the tower of the Dockyard Chapel.

The potential of the horror now realised, the Dockyard bell rang out, more shots were fired and fire engines were summoned from various stations around the Three Towns (including the West of England Insurance Company's engine from Plymouth). Meanwhile '. . . the hissing timbers of the *Talavera* strained and parted with explosive gusts, and all expectation of saving her was abandoned'.

Next in the line of fire came the Adelaide Gallery; one of the newer Dockyard structures, it had been erected in 1826 as a shipwright's shop but was not used as such. Named after Queen Adelaide, it had been turned into a great feature of the yard by Captain Ross, the Yard Superintendent who had set it aside as a Museum for housing various naval trophies. Amongst its many treasures were 'scores of figure-heads of ships that had borne the brunt of some of the most famous naval actions in British History. At one end hung the flag under which Nelson fought and died at Trafalgar; and at the other, the banner which streamed from the poop of the *Queen Charlotte* during the bombardment of Algiers' (Whitfeld).

There was also a sphinx here, thought to be three thousand years old and recently rescued from the sands of Egypt and intended for the British Museum.

Sadly almost all of this collection was lost as the flames from the *Talavera* '. . . darted from under the coping of the shed in terrific volumes, ran along the paper covered top, and engulfed the entire gallery with its combustible contents. Roaring like a furnace, the fire shot into the air; and thick masses of smoke rolled over the yard, now brightened to a dull red colour, as some portion of the building crashed, and then settling like a funeral pall into the surrounding

darkness.'

'From the roof of the Adelaide gallery the flames spread to the covering of the south dock in which lay the *Imogene*. The frigate itself was ablaze, and the fire attained such dimensions that the safety of the entire yard was seriously questioned.'

Fortunately the fire reached its peak by 5.45 am and Condy's painting on which this print is based is probably based around that time. Needless to say the *Talavera*, the flame wracked skeleton of which is shown, and the 28-gun sixth-rate *Imogene* were lost but by 'superhuman efforts' the *Minden* was saved, thanks largely to the men on board ignoring an order to abandon ship. A number of dockside sheds and large quantities of timber were also destroyed.

'Shortly after six o'clock the *Talavera* and *Imogene* were burnt to the water's edge, the pyramids of fire settled down for want of fresh fuel and bare and discoloured walls alone remained of the sheds and stores.'

The cause of the fire was never established '. . . The disaster was variously attributed to dockyard discontent, official parsimony, and the plot of a foreign power whose spies were 'seen gloating' over the devastation. The view that was finally obtained was that the presence of combustibles was sufficient to explain the calamity, and that the use of coal tar to prevent the *Talavera's* timbers from contracting dry-rot accounted for her sudden envelopment' (Whitfeld).

The *Minden*, launched in 1831 and by some years the newest of the three ships at centre of the scene, happily survived the conflagration well enough to have been converted for further use and consequently was relaunched as a Hospital Ship 18 months after the fire in April 1842.

The *Hindostan*

At 5pm on Monday 2nd August 1841 in heavy summer rain the 2,050 ton, 78-gun third-rate *Hindostan* was launched in the Plymouth Yard. A teak-built ship, her frame timbers had been converted in India and sent over to the Dockyard where she was 'laid down' in 1828. Meanwhile, the fifth-rate teak-framed *Tigris* was under construction elsewhere in the yard. Begun in 1822, around the frame of an earlier 46-gun ship, the *Tigris* was never finished for, on 31st August 1832, the Admiralty decided to discontinue work on her and use her teak materials for the *Hindostan*.

So it was that Mrs Ellice, wife of Major-General R Ellice, Army Commander of the Western District, came to name the completed *Hindostan* at its launch on that wet August afternoon. Great were the crowds and loud were the cheers despite the weather, as the Navy's newest fighting ship hit the waves. It is doubtful, however, that any of those present would have been aware that they were witnessing the launch of the last third-rate wooden fighting ship to be launched from this yard.

A familiar enough sight over the years, the *Hindostan* was the twentieth third-rater to have been laid down here since 1703, launches of these big wooden men-o'-war were soon to become a thing of the past. Between 1694 and 1854 almost 100 such wooden warships were launched here and although ten of those were launched after the *Hindostan*, their days were undeniably numbered. Indeed the very last of them, the fourth-rate *Phoebe* was launched in April 1854

but was never commissioned as a sailing ship, for after five years of inactivity she was taken to No 4 dock and fitted for steam with a screw propeller and engines. The same fate also befell the last great first rate man-o-war launched here, the 120-gun *St George*, which was launched in 1840 and converted to steam in 1859 and also the last second rate, the *Aboukir* built on the slip, No 1 slip, the *St George* had vacated in 1840. Launched in 1848, the *Aboukir* was converted to steam at No 5 dock six years later having never left Devonport in the meantime.

Such a future was not to be the lot of the *Hindostan*, however, for although she lay idle at Devonport for more than 20 years she was never converted to steam. Instead in 1865 she was moved to Dartmouth as an auxiliary for the training ship *Britannia*, a covered sliding walkway connecting the two vessels. After serving naval cadets at Dartmouth in this way for 40 years she was then towed to Portsmouth where she became part of the training establishment for boy artificers. 'By an Admiralty Order dated 12 October 1905, her name was changed to *Fisguard III* forming part of the establishment of HMS Fisguard, which consisted of 4 ships, viz *Audacious*, *Erebus*, *Hindostan* and *Sultan*' (KV Burns, *Plymouth's Ships of War*).

For a further 15 years the *Hindostan* remained in service at Fisguard. The following year, 1921, she was sold to a London firm, to be broken up, 80 years after her launch.

To go back to the early 1840s, it's interesting to note that the ship shown here was not the only *Hindostan* on the water back then. Although this man-o-war was never converted to steam, the year after she came down the slipway P&O launched their 2,017 ton *Hindostan*, a cargo carrying paddle steamer that could only carry 200 tons of cargo as it needed 500 tons of coal.

Hindostan incidentally, was often used as the old name for India. Formerly applied to the whole of the country, it has now largely fallen into disuse and if used generally refers to the central Gangetic plain. Literally Hindostan means

country of the Hindoos (Hindus) where stan means country, as in Afghanistan, Pakistan etc. It was perhaps appropriate that the wife of a military man should have christened this particular *Hindostan*, as an early nineteenth-century nickname for the 76th Foot Regiment was the Hindustan Regiment, in the wake of their distinguished role in the Hindustan campaign of 1803–5.

Among the first visitors to this wooden warship in the Dockyard were Queen Victoria and Prince Albert. In August 1843 they included the port in their 'marine excursion' and despite all official attempts at secrecy, when the royal yacht approached Plymouth 'the heights were swarmed by devoted subjects, and a flotilla of pleasure boats sailed out to accord the fair young monarch welcoming cheers. Peals of artillery awakened the echoes as the yacht passed towards Barnpool, and Victoria, who remained on deck, pleasantly acknowledged the salutations of her subjects' (Whitfeld).

With most of our images of Victoria showing an older woman dressed apparently in black, it is illuminating to read further that the 24-year-old Queen was simply attired in 'a straw bonnet with pea green ribbons and a small rosette of flowers, and an apron trimmed with lilac satin thrown over a violet silk dress.' Her husband, also 24, was wearing a frock coat with grey trousers with a gold lace band ornamenting his cap. The *Hindostan*, we are told, was 'minutely inspected' in the Dockyard.

It was an important royal visit for the Dockyard, for it was then that for the first time it could officially be called Devonport Yard. Prior to that time it had always been the Plymouth Yard despite the fact that since the 1st January 1824 the town itself had been called Devonport and not Plymouth Dock. So it was that in August 1843 Queen Victoria sanctioned 'the substitution of the name of Devonport for Plymouth Dock "in every bill, warrant or quittance," and official letters were for the first time authorised to be addressed to "Devonport" instead of "Plymouth".'

Hulks in the Hamoaze

... Noiseless now
Is each forsaken structure, save when sounds
The listless keeper's foot: nought else invades
The deep impressive silence of those decks,
Where lately trod a thousand gallant men!
Flown in the hour of triumph! Hamoaze lifts –
Still lifts its flag, wild streaming on the gale,
But all the gallant show of war is passed.
Unheard the note of preparation now:
How silent, where so late equipping fleets
Sent up the incessant din! The deaf'ning shouts
Of conquering crews are heard no more: the gun
Peals not, save that which roughly greets the morn,
Or bids the sun farewell: the sounds
Roll on the echoing gale – a moment roll
Startling the tranquil bay, and all is – Peace'.

Thus did Devonport's Nicholas Carrington describe such a view as here in his epic poem *Banks of Tamar* first published in 1820. Not everyone, however, perceived the scene in such romantic tones. 'Rotten row' some called it, while others deemed these relics of the past to be no more than 'costly encumbrances – impediments to navigation'. And although it was undoubtedly true that here lay 'Old England's Wooden Walls ... many an old hulk of historic

fame and well known name' there were also those which were 'in truth, instances of 'jobbery' or official carelessness of the most expensive kind, for they have never marched over more mountainous waves than can be found in Hamoaze'.

Much of this, however, was to do with the introduction of steam and the way in which wooden ships, after centuries of service, all of a sudden became unsuited for 'modern warfare'. And indeed great wooden ships that had never been to sea were sold, broken up or sent to swell the procession in the Hamoaze. Incidentally, when they were broken up Government inspectors supervised the work and all the copper bolts were returned 'by arrangement'.

The foregoing, however, is not to suggest that these old wooden vessels were all useless when left in the Hamoaze. In 1878 when this view was recorded there were over 30 craft of varying sizes in 'Harbour Service' at Devonport. Nine were employed as coal depots although over half of these were just old sloops – *Favourite, Fly, Harlequin, Nimrod,* and *Racehorse*. Three others had been refitted as cooking depots 'for the Reserve'; two of these were former gun boats, the *Procris* and the *Skipjack*. These were the days when a permanent land based barracks was yet to be built and so it is no great surprise to find that an old fifth-rate hulk, the

Monmouth was being used as a Roman Catholic Chapel or that another old sloop, the *Perseus* was used 'For scrubbing hammocks etc.' The *Hound* meanwhile, a former Brig, acted as a 'Breakwater for boats' while the *Leda*, another former fifth-rate vessel, served as a Water Police Vessel.

Fifth-rate was the term then used to describe a fighting ship that carried somewhere between 32 and 60 guns, the hulk in the front of the group pictured here was probably just a bit smaller. Three of the others look to be somewhat bigger, probably fourth- or fifth-rate vessels. In 1878 most of these hulks in the Hamoaze that were in Harbour Service were simply described as 'Receiving Hulks'. The *Picque* and the *Cambrian* were two such fifth-rated ships, the *Kent* and the *Vigor* two third rates and the *Vengeance* the biggest, a second-rate.

Launched at Pembroke in mid 1824, HMS *Vengeance* served in the Crimea in 1854 returning to Devonport in mid 1855, its active service almost over. The *Vengeance*, like all other old hulks striped of its useful masts, sat in the Hamoaze as a receiving hulk for almost 40 years until it was finally sold and broken in half in 1897.

If only any one of these wonderful old ships had stayed here but a few decades more what interest they might have excited today.

Fore Street

In the early years of last century 'The Royal Devonshire Cheap Coaches, with six horses,' were in the habit of setting out from the 'London Inn', Dock, every morning at six and eight o'clock (Sundays excepted) calling at the 'Globe Inn', Plymouth, the 'Oxford Arms', Totnes and the 'Golden Lion', Newton Abbot before arriving at the 'New London Inn', Exeter. There three days a week, it would meet a coach bound for London. Across the road meanwhile, 'cheap and expeditious travelling' was offered by the Royal Clarence Coach which set out from the 'Prince George Inn' and called at the 'Commercial Inn', Plymouth, the 'Seven Stars', Totnes, and the 'Globe', Newton Abbot, before arriving at the 'Half Moon Inn', Exeter, around 7pm. For the man in the street, however, these fares were not particularly cheap, only the well to do could readily afford to spend eleven shillings and sixpence for an inside seat or even seven and six for an outside seat.

Similar fares were offered by F Goude, whose 'light balloon coach' set off for Exeter from the neighbouring 'King's Arms', every morning at six o'clock. The scene then would not have been greatly different to the one shown here, for just a few years before this engraving was made the name of the 'King's Arms' was changed to the 'Royal Hotel'.

The 'Royal' was one of the principal inns of Devonport and later in the century it was refaced and improved and equipped with new dining rooms where many a banquet, ball and dinner was held. The 'Prince George' and the 'London' were also major hotels and together with Weakley's prestigious establishment, complete with its 'powerful recommendations of excellent beds and stabling', it meant that all of Devonport's principal inns were situated in this street. As were a number of other notable institutions.. 'to the liberal spirit of private individuals we are indebted for some handsome houses in the town, particularly in Fore Street . . .'(Sandford 1830). There followed a list of banks, jewelry shops, draperers and various drug stores plus wine vaults and Mr Shaw's saw manufactory. As another guide noted, 'being the grand avenue to the dock-yard, Fore-street is the chief street for business in the town.'(Rowe)

It was, of course, the Dockyard that gave birth to Devonport in the first place and Fore Street, as one would deduce from its name, was developed before the rest of Devonport. A plan of 1731 shows North Corner (Cornwall) Street, Prince's (Princess) Street, King's and Queen's Streets, about half of Granby Street and Fore Street. Leading as it did straight up to the main gate of the South Yard it comes as no surprise to find that there were a number of smaller inns situated just outside the gates. Here we find the 'Fountain Inn', referred to as the 'naval rendezvous', the 'Oxford Inn' and the 'Dock-Yard Gate Inn', its sign a pictorial representation of the gate with a man ringing the bell. This bell was rung, until the introduction of a siren, to indicate the start and finish of the working day. Seen here to the left of the gate, the bell stood 60 feet off the ground and was supported by the mainmast of an East Indian Merchant-man. The bell itself was a prize from the French ship *Tonnant* which Nelson had taken at the battle of the Nile, although the French themselves had stolen it from the Church of St John in Malta.

The Napoleonic Wars were a boom time for Devonport and especially Fore Street and towards the end of the fighting a whole host of inns sprang up around the bottom of the street. There was the 'Ring of Bells', 'Peace and Fame', the 'Navy', the 'Phoenix', the 'Jolly Bacchus' and several others including later the 'Dog and Pot', whose sign was 'repeatedly stolen by frolicsome sailors'.

At one time at least fifteen hostelries were situated here; many of them, however, were removed as a consequence of the widening of the street near the end of last century. By this time sailors had a much loved alternative to these licensed premises- the 'Sailors Rest and Institute' complete with its 'very cosy restaurant with settles, bright colours, mirrors and a little gilding . . . I was competing against the public houses' wrote its proprietress Agnes Weston.

Aggie Weston came to Devonport in 1873 working for the temperance movement among sailors and on Monday 8th May 1876 she opened her first 'public house without drink', near the dock gates, in a building formerly occupied by the Co-op. As the success of her venture grew so did the size of the building, to the extent that with its later extensions 'Aggie Weston's Sailors Rest' became the biggest building in the town, its cabins able to house up to 900 men.

Like so many of Fore Street's finest buildings, the 'Royal Sailors Rest' (as it became in 1890) was destroyed in the Blitz. Very little was left standing, gone was the Post Office (1849), the impressive Public Hall (which later became the Electric Cinema), JC Tozers and many other stores and banks and pubs: 'Prince George', 'Golden Lion', 'Two Trees', 'Military Arms', 'Lifeboat' and half a dozen more, only the 'Western Hotel' survived.

Today most of what was Fore Street lies behind the Dockyard wall and there is little left to convey the dignity and importance of what was for two centuries Devonport's finest thoroughfare.

Raglan Barracks

In 1854 Britain was in the grip of an almost hysterical clamour for war. The Prime Minister, Lord Aberdeen, and his cabinet were not really in favour of it neither were a small group of Liberal pacifists or the Quakers, public opinion, however, was unequivocable, the majority of Britons, whatever their class, wanted war.

There had been almost forty years of comparative peace and it was felt that a test of the nation's manhood was long overdue, it was time to push profit-seeking aside, forget comfort and consider instead self-sacrifice and heroism. War was not seen as bad but rather something that generated excitement, great deeds, much glory and national pride. There was, it hardly needs to be said, no thought of losing or even of losses.

So it was that primarily on the pretext of asserting public law against a transgressor, Aberdeen and his chancellor Gladstone, took Britain into a war, over three thousand miles away by sea, in support of Turkey, who had actually turned down terms we had agreed with their aggressors Russia. In addition to this we were to fight alongside the French, our old adversaries, who only a year earlier had been generating rumours of a British invasion.

But it was what the people wanted, the working classes clamouring for comic-strip-style heroes, the officers them-selves looking towards a great jamboree, a military picnic in some exotic far off place. They had little idea of the circumstances that they would find themselves in, in the Crimea. Had they done so one could hardly imagine that so many commanders would have allowed their wives, together with their personal maids, to accompany them to the war zone. Neither was it just relatives who wanted to witness the sport, there were even some wealthy civilians who cancelled their holidays elsewhere to follow the Army and see all the fun!

Meanwhile, Lord Cardigan, whose enormous wealth had already secured him rapid promotion, and who spent £10,000 a year of his own money ensuring that his regi-ment, the 11th Hussars, were the smartest in the country (short jackets and ridiculously tight plum-coloured pants better suited to female hussars in a ballet according to a contemporary edition of the *Times*), he and one or two of his peers decided to go out to the war in their personal yachts.

It wasn't just the British who adopted this party-like attitude to the war, however, and William Russell who was reporting on the war for the *Times* sent back the following account after speaking to some deserters after the first major encounter: 'They said that thirty Russian ladies went out of Sebastopol to see the battle of Alma as though they were going to a play or a picnic. They were quite assured of the success of the Russian troops and great was their alarm and dismay when they found themselves obliged to leave the telegraph house on the hill, and to fly for their lives in their carriages.

The Battle of Alma was fought on the 20th September 1854. Leading the British forces in the allied attack was a man ten days short of his 66th birthday, Lord Raglan.

Created Baron Raglan of Raglan, Monmouthshire in October 1852, Lord Fitzroy Somerset was commissioned when he was only 15 and had gone to Portugal in 1808 as aide-de-camp to the future Duke of Wellington. Present at all the battles in the Napoleonic Wars at which Wellington was himself in command, Raglan was standing next to the Duke at Waterloo. It was then that Raglan was struck in the elbow by a bullet necessitating the immediate amputation of his arm.

In the years after those wars, Raglan, who had married Wellington's niece in 1814, held a succession of posts under Wellington who served in a number of distinguished posi-tions including three terms as Prime Minister (although taken together these lasted just under three years). In 1852 Wellington died, aged 83, and Raglan, who then became master-general of the ordnance, was, with his distinguished record and all his associations the ideal figure to lead the British forces in the Crimea two years later.

This then was the backdrop against which work began on improving the barrack facilities in Devonport in that same year, 1854. First it was necessary to pull down four of Devonport's six original barrack blocks; *George, Cumber-land, Frederick* and *Ligonier* which had been erected almost 100 years earlier in 1757.

In all eleven acres were cleared for the construction of the new barracks with well over a third of this space left to be laid out as a parade ground. As to the barracks themselves, it has been said that the buildings were originally earmarked for India but due to some kind of mix up they ended up here. Whatever the truth, these flat-roofed, yellow, brick-built buildings did look a little odd in Devonport, particu-larly with the seemingly incongruous verandas (a word itself which is of Indian origin), which with their fancy ironwork ran along the length of the men's quarters. The whole effect was one which came to be described as 'Ordnance quadran-gular no-style'.

Raglan Barracks

Raglan Barracks were completed by 1858 by which time the Crimean War was long since over and Lord Raglan long since dead.

In fighting terms the Crimean War had ended in September 1855 when Sebastopol eventually fell to the Allies, or rather the weary Russians at long last gave up their defence of the besieged port and abandoned it after destroying anything of value that was left. The French were most jubilant because their last action the day before had been markedly more successful than the British offensive that day which had left the troops decimated and dispirited.

General Simpson was then in charge of the British forces in the Crimea, following the death of Lord Raglan a few months earlier, on the 28th June. Sir James Simpson was not a popular choice and was not particularly keen to take the job but the appointment came from London made by those who were somewhat out of touch with the situation at the front.

Raglan's death, although met with characteristic grief at home, doubtless saved his reputation from an even more torrid attack from critics than he was already receiving. The Crimean War had not been the glorious episode in British history that its protagonists had hoped for, quite the opposite in fact, with more men dying through incompetence and disease off the field of battle than on it. As the leader of the operation, Raglan bore the brunt of the criticism for the planning and handling of events. Some of the mismanagement was indeed his fault but essentially he was 'a victim of England's unreadiness for war' (Sir Evelyn Wood), a war she should perhaps have never become involved with in the first place.

Raglan was nevertheless rightly remembered as a hero, 'Spite of all that has been said and written against him, an irreparable loss for us!' (Prince Albert), and so it was that these barracks were named after him.

Built at a cost of £120,000 Raglan Barracks were constructed to 'accommodate two entire regiments of Line, or 2,000 men and 80 officers. The officers' barracks are built, one at the north, and one at the south end, each for a separate regiment. The soldiers' barracks form a line of buildings between but thrown back to admit of the Parade in their front, which extends along the whole line from one officers' barracks to the other, being 860 feet in length, and 240 feet in breadth; each block of soldiers' barracks is for a

separate regiment to correspond with the officers' blocks, the building between them common to both regiments, or rather divided internally between them. It contains sergeants' mess-rooms, with kitchens; orderly-rooms; staff-sergeants' quarters, for each; besides which there is a regimental store and a spacious reading-room, with library and librarian's quarters, for the general use of the garrison. In the rear of this building is the Canteen.' (Wright 1879.) Amongst the other buildings on the site there were also laundry drying closets, cooking places and two limestone fives courts; the one at the south-west corner of the barracks almost backing on to the old 'Exeter Arms' in Cumberland Street.

There appears to be no formal record of an opening ceremony of the barracks but we do know that on Christmas Eve 1858, before the impressive main gate had been completed, the 96th Regiment of Foot, one of the first units to be posted here, marched through the Chapel Street gate in full dress preceded by the regimental band. The men were resplendent in their scarlet tunics faced with yellow trim and they were led out by Lt-Col EW Scovell, while the band was conducted by Signor Tamplini. (It was not unusual in those days for regimental bands to be conducted by a civilian, even a foreign one!)

The 96th Regiment of Foot founded in 1824 later became the 2nd Battalion of the Manchester Regiment when the numbering system was abolished and the county titles,

which had first been given out in 1782 to help with recruiting, were extensively revised. Devonport, however, was essentially the head-quarters of the Western district for the 'localisation of forces' and that included Brecknockshire, Cardiganshire, Carmarthenshire, Cornwall, Devonshire, Glamorganshire, Gloucestershire, Haverfordwest, Herefordshire, Monmouthshire, Pembrokeshire, Radnorshire, Somersetshire, Trowbridge (as far regards the regular forces) and Worcestershire.

As well as men from these and other visiting areas there were home grown outfits like the Devonport Rifle Corps which held its first muster here on the new parade ground in 1860, the year the Rifle Volunteers were instituted. After assembling, the men marched through the town in their dark green rifleman's kit led by the more colourful band of the 36th Regiment of Foot (later the 2nd Battalion Worcester Regiment), who wore a scarlet uniform with grass green facings. By then Captain Fowke's Doric styled limestone gateway was complete and today it stands alone as the only surviving part of the nineteenth century barracks, although its clock tower no longer houses a 'clock tower with four dials, for use of the garrison'.

The rest of the original barracks, together with the additional buildings erected nearer the gates at the beginning of the twentieth century, were pulled down in the 1970s to make way for the naval married quarters opened, here in 1976.

Garrison Chapel

Built for the fighting men of the new Raglan Barracks in 1856, this Garrison Chapel was destroyed by airborne enemy bombers less than 100 years later in a manner that would have been inconceivable to the first men who worshipped here.

Accommodating some 1,000 worshippers, this large early english style red brick building with bath stone dressings housed a nave with aisles, transept, turret, side chapel and vestry. It was an imposing interior with tall graceful columns supporting moulded arches, while a small flight of steps led up to the chancel at the eastern end.

On the south side of the chancel a fine organ was installed in 1888 at a cost of £300, the money being raised by subscription. Messrs Hele & Co. of Plymouth (then based at Wyndham Street East) built the organ and on 30th August 1889 when the chapel was reopened, after considerable refurbishment and restoration, it was played at a packed evening service by Mr George Hele jun. who accompanied a massed choir of some 150 voices. This choir was made up of that of the Garrison itself plus that of Stoke Damerel; St James', Torpoint; and St Paul's and St Stephen's of Devonport. Both of these last two mentioned churches fell in the Blitz, St Paul's on the corner of Morice Square and St Stephen's in Clowance Street, with its slender spire seen here

rising high behind the barracks of Mount Wise off Pembroke Street.

The reopening in 1889 was a very grand affair; a brass altar desk, made and donated by James Harrington, was dedicated at a special celebration of the Holy Communion in the morning (Thomas Harrington, James's father perhaps, was then clerk to the Garrison Chapel). In the evening over 1,000 people turned up for the special service. Prayers at this service were intoned by the Garrison Chaplain Rev FG Wright CF, while the Rev C Cardew of St James' and Rev E Read of St Paul's read the lessons. The sermon was preached by the Dean of Exeter, Dr BM Cowis, who 'dwelt upon the necessity of making God's house glorious and beautiful, which he considered one of the strongest evidences of man's love and reverence for his God', and he concluded by 'appealing to his hearers for their liberal contribution on behalf of the restoration fund'.

Largely cleaned and painted by Mr Marshall of Plymouth, the gilding and detailed repainting was carried out by Messrs Fouracre and Watson of Chapel Street, Stonehouse. John Fouracre specialised in gilding work while Henry Watson worked mainly in stained glass, much of which he stained himself.

One of the most interesting items in the chapel was the

bell in the turret; this was cast in Flanders in 1783, ten years before Britain joined the Revolutionary Wars against France, and is thought to have been taken from a French ship sometime between 1793 and 1815.

Built essentially for the Military in Devonport, civilians 'were allowed in, in the nineteenth century at least, by the south door and permitted to fill seats unoccupied by troops at the morning parade service. On Sunday evenings, however, it was a different story and the chapel was free and open with only officer's seats in the chancel being reserved. These Sunday services were very popular as a surpliced choir, mainly composed of soldiers and soldier's sons, led the singing, which on festival days would be accompanied by the military band and drums. Together with the powerful organ this made for 'a very grand effect'.

Not so grand perhaps was the exterior of the chapel '... it somewhat lacks height, and will be improved by a steeple, for which a small tower has already been built'. So read an account written in 1990, sadly, however, such a steeple failed to transpire.

The view of the chapel seen here was sketched by W Hake sometime around 1870 and, as well as showing us the spire of St Stephen's, we can also see Devonport Column rising to the right of the view of the figures in the foreground. As well as the boy pushing his barrow, it is interesting to note the woman pushing her child in an early perambulator.

Originally, of course, a perambulator just referred to someone who perambulated – went for a walk on foot; later it came to be associated with a machine for measuring distances, then later still, in the 1850s, a hand carriage for young children (the abbreviation to pram came in the 1880s).

Although little carriages for children had been produced in the past, it was not until 1850 that there was any regular manufacturing of perambulators. Two rival firms started up that year in London; John Allen in Hackney Road, and A Babin of New Street. Both broke away form any previous design in that both produced prams that had push chair bodies mounted on three wheels, just like the one outside the chapel. Prior to these machines all perambulators had been pulled not pushed.

It wasn't until 1876, some years after this picture was drawn, that regular production began of the classic and now unfashionable style of pram, with the 'basinette' in which young babies could lie full length.

St Stephen's

Situated on the corner of Clowance Street and George Street, St Stephen's Church was the fourth of four new parish churches to be built in Devonport in the 1850s, the other three being St James' (1851), St Paul's (1851) and St Mary's (1852). All four were designed by J Piers St Aubyn and all four have now gone. St Mary's was the only one to survive the Blitz intact but that was later demolished when the church authorities decided that one church was enough to serve the area. So it was that the older St Aubyn Church (1771–2) became the anglican parish church for the old part of Devonport.

The decision to create four new parishes in the growing town of Devonport was made effective in 1846 and the sites for the new churches were given by the Lord of the Manor, the head of the St Aubyn family. The St Aubyn's had acquired the Manor of Stoke Damerel, upon which Devonport is built, in 1749 when the last male member of the Morice family, Sir Nicholas Morice, died leaving the estate to his elder sister Catherine's 23-year-old son, John St Aubyn.

Originally a French family who came over in the wake of the Norman Conquest, the St Aubyn's had lived since about 1380 in an ancient manor house near the Cornish mining village of Praze-an-Beeble. Apparently called 'Clunewic' at the time of the Domesday survey, this became Clowance and was for many centuries the family home of the St Aubyn's (the more recent family seat, St Michael's Mount, was bought in 1659).

John St Aubyn (1726–1772) was the fourth baronet and his son, also Sir John St Aubyn was just fourteen when he came into the family inheritance. Reckoned to have fathered some 15 children, most of them out of wedlock, this Sir John was a popular figure and in his time Plymouth Dock, as Devonport then was, continued a programme of expansion that had begun under his father. Practically all the land in the area was then leasehold and the St Aubyns appear to have been more generous in granting leases than their predecessors (they still hold the leases of hundreds of properties in Devonport today).

Not long after 1775 George Street was 'begun to be built . . . and the Rage for extending the Buildings, or the Speculation of Mechanics, being at that Time very prevalent, Liberty-Street and Clowance-Street on that Side, with Mount-Street, and the cross Streets which connect them and

Windmill Street, trod so fast upon the Heels of each other, that they quickly occupied the full Limits of the Town' (Hoxland 1792).

Open land prior to this, it appears that part of Clowance Street backed on to 'a court for the playing of the game tennis', which later gave its name to a group of private dwellings, which were purchased by the government in a case of emergency, presumably during the Napoleonic Wars, for use as a barracks. Hence the name Racket Court Barracks, although Rowe writing in 1824 says they were never used for troops.

As well as all this accommodation, Clowance Street in 1824 sported two pubs and a bakery. Of the two pubs only the 'Clowance Tavern' at No 42 on the corner of Stanley

Street, survived into the twentieth century, Alfred Brown was its last licensee in 1957, the other, the 'King's Head' at No 31 called last orders in 1867. Meanwhile the bakery next door at No 32 also carried on trading into the 1950s, being run for over 60 years by various members of the Davey family.

St Stephen's Church itself was erected in 1852 at a cost of £7,000 which was raised chiefly by subscription with the help of grants from church building societies. Designed to seat 764 persons, this decorated Gothic style church with its tall spire had particularly attractive windows 'filled with elaborate geometric tracery and the terminal exterior crosses, and the interior decorations are elaborately ornamental'. So wrote WHK Wright in 1878 who went on to add ' The present vicar is the Rev A Dixon, MA, and the service may be designated as 'high'.'

Arthur Dixon had been at St Stephen's for many years by this time, indeed he'd been the first to move into the new vicarage at 27 George Street, opposite the church, in 1864 and was to stay there into the 1890s.

The vicarage like the church was designed by James Piers St Aubyn who was also responsible for Devonport Market in 1852 and who was made a Fellow of the Royal Institute of British Architects (a body which had become 'Royal' in 1834) four years later.

The Church was dedicated, like the Chapel of the Palace of Westminster where Parliament sat for almost 300 years, to the first Christian martyr, St Stephan, and was consecrated on 21 September 1858. Sadly only its tower came through the Blitz unscathed and this, together with the shell of the main body of the building, stood until its demolition in 1959.

The character of the street had by this time been long since altered from its eighteenth-century foundation. Many of the original dwelling houses had been pulled down and replaced, the 1943 *Plan for Plymouth* describing the pre-war 'slum clearance' here as a 'good example of three-storey flats'.

Little else now survives of 'old' Clowance Street, the Blitz also claiming the only other major public building here, the school. Opened in 1870, this was St Stephen's National School, originally for boys, girls and infants it latterly took only girls and infants. Miss Hosking who succeeded Miss Bailey was the last headmistress here.

Royal Albert Hospital

'It always gives us pleasure to draw public attention to such a Philanthropic Institution as the Royal Albert Hospital – an Institution that is alike an ornament to Devonport, and a credit to the nation in which it exists. To look on the outside fills one with a species of awe, for it is a noble pile of buildings. To think of the amount of good such and other kindred institutions have accomplished, causes our hearts to overflow with gratitude.'

The above was written to introduce an article about the Children's Ward of the Royal Albert Hospital in the 1881 edition of *Doidge's Almanac* and towards the end of the piece there was an appeal for contributions ... 'Many persons who cannot spare a pound can spare a shilling (5p), and many who cannot spare a shilling can spare a penny, and pennies amount to pounds in the course of time'.

The Royal Albert Hospital relied heavily on voluntary donations, it had been built in 1862–3 at a cost of £11,500, a sum which was raised partly by subscription and partly by grants from the Admiralty and the War Office; the east wing of the complex, the Lock Ward, had its own entrance and was erected and maintained by the Government.

Prior to the construction of this hospital, Devonport's only recognized medical centre was the Public Dispensary which had been established in Chapel Street. Plymouth itself was little better off. Apart from the Royal Naval and the Military Hospitals in Stonehouse and Stoke there was only the small South Devon and East Cornwall Hospital in Notte Street, which had opened with twelve beds in 1840.

If all this seems almost primitive to us it must be remembered that this was a time when going into hospital was deemed to be a social degradation, suggesting that you either had no family to take care of you or that they couldn't afford, or even didn't want, to nurse you at home. Those for whom money was not a problem never considered going into hospital. They would stay at home and be nursed through any ailment or illness (even infectious ones like scarlet fever or smallpox) by servants or relatives. Women had their babies at home and surgical operations would also be carried out there, even though the doctors and surgeons perhaps came from a nearby public hospital.

Florence Nightingale was undoubtedly one of the main figures responsible for changing the image of the public hospital from the middle of the nineteenth century. Convinced that care in hospital should be better than care by well meaning but perhaps ignorant servants or relatives or

even hired nurses, she set about instituting organized hospital training for nurses. And not only did she succeed in establishing nursing as a recognized profession but she also, with the help of a wealthy Liverpudlian, William Rathbone, set up the first training centre for district nurses – in Liverpool.

Having experienced the atrocious conditions of the hospital in the Crimea at Scutari, Florence Nightingale also became a passionate advocate of the virtues of cleanliness, fresh (but not cold) air, sunlight and wherever possible stimulating views for the patient. Whenever her advice was sought on the planning of new hospitals, these conditions were invariably drawn upon and even new hospitals today to some extent bear some mark of her influence.

Certainly the Royal Albert was one of the first. Plans for it were made public in 1860 but in the event work did not begin until March 1862, three months after Albert, the Prince Consort after whom the building was named, had died. The architect for the new buildings was Alfred Norman of Devonport (the Norman Ward was named after his wife) and the foundation stone was laid by the Earl of Mount Edgcumbe on Tuesday 17th June 1862.

It was a colourful occasion, some 500 people joined the procession from Devonport Guildhall to the grounds of the site. There were a large number of commissioned officers in uniform as well as many members of the neighbouring Lodges of Freemasonry (there was to be a masonic Ward in the Hospital). There were also Mayors, magistrates and the Deputy Provincial Grand Master, the Rev John Huyshe,

Grand Chaplain of England.

A little over 18 months later the Hospital opened, on 1st December 1863. There were then 10 beds available for general patients. Within a few years this number was increased to over 60, including the 20 or so beds in the children's ward which opened in 1865. Named the Emma Ward in remembrance of Viscountess Templeton, Lady St Aubyn, these beds were described in 1881 as 'neat iron cots, covered each with a dainty white quilt', while the nurses here were 'dressed in brown holland tastefully piped with red, and spotless cuffs and collar.'

True to the ideals of Florence Nightingale, the Hospital enjoyed panoramic views, looking out over the Hamoaze and the newly laid out lawns of Devonport Park. For many years it was separated from the park by a great trench or moat which originally formed part of the defences of Devonport. When built, the Royal Albert was right on the northern-most part of Devonport, there was no road behind it and its front entrance, at the top of Passage Hill, was one of the principal meeting places in the town, outside the Marlborough Hotel where the trams curved around by an ornate lamp-post.

Today the Hospital has gone. Renamed the Prince of Wales Hospital, Devonport in 1934, the South Devon & East Cornwall Hospital Devonport in 1948 and the Devonport Section of the Plymouth General Hospital in 1963, it was demolished in 1983. Two towers have, however, been preserved in the housing development that now stands on its site.

Devonport Park

'Rented by the Corporation from the War Office', Devonport Park 'is being gradually laid out, with walks, trees, shrubs, arbours, seats, &c., and affords at once a splendid recreation ground, and fine promenade, with a beautiful view of the surrounding scenery. Here the grand review upon her Majesty's birthday is held, when all the troops in the garrison and volunteers from many towns round assemble, the sight being brilliant, and the concourse of people very great.'

So began an account of Devonport Park in an 1874 *Guide to the Three Towns*. The park was then quite young, its trees were little more than saplings and the paths and public places still being developed, but it was nonetheless impressive, there being little else then like it in the Three Towns (Parks like those at Mutley and Beaumont were both then in existence but both were at that time still attached to private houses).

The idea of a park as a public area within or on the edges of a town or city, as opposed to a tract of land planted with trees surrounding a large house, was very much a Victorian one, and although the seeds were sown in the 1830s it was really the reports on social conditions of our towns in the 1840s that led to direct action. Edwin Chadwick's reports on the sanitary conditions of the poor and on interment in towns in 1842 and 1843 and the 1844 commission on the health of towns brought about the Public Health Act of 1848. This, among other things, gave local authorities the power to establish 'public walks' and 'means of exercise or amusement for the middle or humbler classes'.

There were in those days few opportunities for recreation, and parks were seen not only as somewhere that exercise could be taken but also they had potential as entertainment centres and provided a much needed alternative to drunkenness. They also afforded an opportunity to play some part in education as areas could be set aside for botanical gardens and arboreta – tree gardens (the first of which was opened in Derby in 1840).

Devonport Park itself was begun in the late 1850s, the little Swiss Lodge seen at the entrance here being erected in 1858. The Swiss style was a popular one at the time, following the fashion set by Prince Albert as he redesigned the grounds and gardens of the royal residence, Osborne House, on the Isle of Wight, after he and the Queen had purchased it in 1845 with a view to establishing a permanent holiday home there. The architect for the lodge here in Devonport Park was the same man, Alfred Norman, who designed the Royal Albert Hospital which within a year or two was to border onto the park around by 'Newpassage-hill'.

'Tastefully laid-out flower gardens, in which are fountains and figures, a rockery and other pleasing embellishments' were set out to the side of the lodge along with 'the principle fountain . . . erected to the memory of Sir Charles Napier, by seamen and marines'.

A great British naval hero, Charles Napier had volunteered for the navy in 1799 when he was just thirteen and rapidly made his way through the ranks. He received command of his first ship, the 18-gun *Recruit*, in 1808. He served for a time during the Peninsular War as a volunteer in the army and was, like his cousin, Charles James Napier, wounded at Busaco. Employed 'on particular service' on the coast of Portugal in command of the *Galatea* in 1829, he was given the command of the young Portuguese queen's fleet and by defeating the Miguelite fleet he helped restore constitutional order there and was made admiral-in-chief of the Portuguese navy. Thwarted by the internal corruption of that navy he soon returned to England where he continued his rise through the ranks. Promoted to vice-admiral in 1853, he was, the following year, sent out to command the Baltic Fleet in the Crimean War.

By this time Napier and many of his commanders were really considered too old for such tasks and when he came back to England he was asked to 'strike his flag' – relinquish his command. Napier was unhappy about this, though, and consequently refused the GCB – Knight Grand Cross of the Bath. His involvement with the navy didn't end there, though, and right up until his death in 1860 he continued to work towards the reform of naval administration.

Just beyond this fountain and garden was the first of two bandstands the park was to have over the years, (seen here just in front of the line of buildings that was the original St Michael's Terrace) where the local military bands would often entertain large crowds. Hailed as 'a great boon to the inhabitants of Devonport and its suburbs,' Devonport Park was established by the Corporation as the result of public subscription which was supplemented by a grant of £500 from the Government. Further developed in the 1890s when the Park Pavilion was built, the story of the park in the twentieth century has tended to be one of bits lost rather than bits added, it still serves, together with the Brickfields and Mount Wise to remind us of the extent of the original town of Devonport.

Keyham Dock Yard

The advent of steam was to have major consequences not only for the ships of the Royal Navy but also for the Naval Dockyards themselves. The Devonport Yard soon fell behind Portsmouth and Woolwich and in the absence of adequate engineering facilities here there was often considerable delay and inconvenience as steam ships coming in for simple repairs and replacements had to be sent up to one of the other yards.

HMS *Lightning*, a wooden-paddle wheel-gun vessel was one of the Navy's first successful steam vessels and she was launched at Deptford in 1823. It was to be another eight years before the Admiralty ordered a steam fighting ship to be built down here and even then the 813-ton steam paddle-powered *Rhadamanthus* had to be sailed to Woolwich for engines to fitted. Nevertheless a large crowd assembled to see her floated out of dock one Monday afternoon in April 1832.

Twelve years later work began in Devonport Dockyard on the steam paddle frigate *Avenger* but once again after being launched, in August 1845, this ship was sailed off to have her engines fitted, this time in Deptford, where she was originally intended to have been built.

By now, however, work had begun on creating a dock-yard here where all this new technology could be fully embraced. After surveying both sides of the Tamar, a site had been chosen about half a mile upstream from the original dockyard and to that end 38 acres of land and 43 acres of foreshore were purchased from the trustees of the will of Sir I St Aubyn.

Just as Cornwall Street and North Corner had prevented a continuous development north, from the original dock-yard for the Admiralty in 1719, when they were looking for a site for a new Gun Wharf (Morice Yard), so now the slipway for the Torpoint Ferry necessitated another gap in their grip on the eastern shoreline of the Hamoaze.

The plans for the new site almost immediately put it on a par with the original yard which had grown steadily over the previous 150 years:

'Here it is proposed to construct two floating basins about six acres each, with entrances 80 feet wide, laid at a depth sufficient for the largest steamer to enter and depart at all times of the tide; there are to be three large docks besides the lock, which is to be constructed as to answer the purpose of dock when required. There are to be complete engine and boiler workshops, with the requisite tools and storehouses for fitting-out and repairing large fleets of steamers; the whole establishment will cover a surface of about 72 acres.' (Sir John Rennie).

Messrs George Baker and Sons were awarded the contract for the scheme and offered an estimate in September 1844 of £713,000 for the work. Originally Parliament had been given a figure of around £400,000, however, within four years the figure had gone up to £1,225,000 and by 1849 it had gone up almost another £100,000. Needless to say Parliament were unhappy with this state of affairs and it is possible that the new project would never have got under way had they known at the beginning, but of course they didn't and by then it was all too late.

To facilitate the building of the new yard an enormous coffer dam, 1,600 feet long and 26 feet wide, was built along the riverside to cut the site off from the tide and allow it to be pumped dry. Here steam power helped enormously to build towards a yard designed to meet the needs of a steam driven navy, for the world's first steam driven pile driver was used to drive piles home; James Nasmyth's hammer achieving in less than five minutes what would otherwise have taken more than twelve hours.

On Saturday 12th September 1846 the First Lord of the Admiralty, the Rt Hon Earl of Auckland laid the official foundation block, containing all the current coins of the realm, for what was to become the Keyham Steam Yard. This foundation block was incorporated into the South Lock entrance to the basin which in May 1850 was opened to admit water for the first time. However, water wasn't let into the docks and basins themselves for another three years, in May 1853. Five months later the Steam Yard was officially opened when HMS *Queen* was taken into the basin.

Situated immediately behind the large north basin can be seen the storehouses and offices that made up the front elevation of the impressive quadrangle, the vast 'Factory' containing the hub of the Engineering Department. Encompassing an area of about six acres under one glass roof, the complex was designed by Charles Barry, the celebrated London architect, whose other works include the Traveller's Club, the Reform Club and most notably the Palace of Westminster (the Houses of Parliament), all in London, the City Art Gallery in Manchester and Cliveden House in Buckinghamshire (subsequently acquired by William Waldorf Astor and some years later handed over to his son and Nancy Astor in 1906 as a wedding present). Barry won the competition for the new Houses of Parliament in 1836, he was knighted in 1852 as Keyham Steam Yard was being completed.

Dominating the skyline of this particular view, apart from the yard's foundry chimneys and the gate towers to the far right, is St James's Church at the west end of what was then Navy Row (now where St Leo Place meets Keyham Road). This Morice Town church was built at the same time as the Steam Yard, the foundation stone was laid in July 1849. It was designed by James Piers St Aubyn and the Lords of the Admiralty contributed £4,000 of the projected £6,000 costs incurred in its construction, 'in consideration of a great number of sittings being free for the use of the numerous workmen employed in the Government Steam Yard, &c.'.

Keyham Steam Yard

Over 1,200 men, 100 horses and 70 boats were employed in the construction of Keyham Steam Yard and the eventual cost of the project was said to be over £2,000,000. Its principal features were the two extensive basins which could be entered from the Hamoaze 'by locks of such magnitude that the largest ships may enter three hours before high water.'

The south lock, meanwhile, was special because it could be converted into a dry dock 'when a line of battle ship is brought to have her bottom examined or cleansed'. In addition to which were three large docks projecting off the eastern side of the south basin each 'capable of accommodating the largest steamers afloat'.

On the buildings' side, as well as the storehouses and offices forming the seaward frontage of the Quadrangle, there was a Boiler Shop, Boilersmith's Shop and Plater's Shop on the northern side; the Coppersmiths and Blacksmiths were on the southern side while to the east (our right in this view) inside the great wall was the Millwright's and Pattern Shop, the Brass Foundry and, of course, the Iron Foundry.

There were also a number of smaller buildings; the Fitting and Erecting Shops; the Leather Shop (where driving belts could be maintained and where plunger washers were prepared for the great hydraulic pumps used in heavy gun mountings); the Bottle Test Shop (for testing containers and reservoirs for compressed air or gasses); the Lagging Shop and even a Laundry.

By the time the yard was finished it was not only 'considerably larger than the one at Woolwich' but it was reckoned to be 'the finest and most extensive establishment of the kind in the kingdom' and to attest to its importance this grand gateway was constructed as its main entrance.

Based on a design drawn up by William Scamp of the Admiralty Department of Works, the gate stood at the bottom of Navy Row. Described by Whitfeld as at one time being 'the only pretence to a street in Morice Town', this thoroughfare later became Albert Road and the gate was named after it.

The Yard's Call Bell was originally sited just inside the gate mounted on the top of a spar, unfortunately, however, the bell's rope broke from time to time making it necessary for a duty constable to climb the pole and ring the bell. This, combined with the fact that the exposed bell, which was cast in the yard in 1859, was deemed to be 'unsightly', led to its

being placed behind the slatted shutters of the right hand tower. The other tower, as can be seen here, housed the clock.

At that time the Keyham Yard was still being run as a completely separate yard from Devonport, it had different hours of work and different rates of pay and conditions. It wasn't until 1876 that Keyham became fully integrated with the rest of the Dockyard.

Despite that the two yards had been provided with a direct physical link as early as 1857. Parliament had passed an Act 'to empower the Commissioners of the Admiralty to construct a tunnel between HM Dockyard at Devonport, and HM Steam Yard at Keyham' back in 1854, the year after Keyham opened. In the event, the 946 yards long tunnel, which linked the two Yards, without making use of the intervening Corporation property, was first used by pedestrian traffic in April 1857, exactly two years after work on the project had begun. Two hundred and seventy men were employed in the excavations which were carried out at nine points along the line.

Initially troubled by up to a foot or so of water at times when a heavy rainfall coincided with a high tide, the tunnel was improved in 1876 with the laying of a concrete bed, a raised footpath and the installation of a narrow gauge railway, which enabled rail communication to be made with the Dockyard from the main line system.

Towards the end of the 1870s the changes in naval warfare, as ships were equipped with newer engines, more sophisticated weapons and better protection (a far cry from the wooden sail-powered gun platforms they had been earlier that century and for many years before that), meant

there was a demand for a more sophisticated sailor and so in 1879 work began, on the edge of the Keyham Yard, on the 'Devonport Training School for Engineer Students'. Later restyled the 'Royal Naval Engineering College', it took over from the first 'Engineering College' which had been set up just three years earlier in Portsmouth on board the wooden hulk of HMS *Marlborough*.

Designed by EM Barry, son of Sir Charles who was responsible for the magnificent Keyham Quadrangle, the new college received its first students on the 1st July 1880. Sadly of course the College, having been superceded by RNEC Manadon in 1958, was demolished a few years ago.

Keyham Yard underwent further major extensions at the end of the nineteenth century which were to greatly alter the view from this vantage point particularly as some 80 odd acres of the new development was on land previously below sea level.

Extensions this century have rendered this view almost unrecognisable. Long since gone is Sparrow Park to the left of the gates and, in 1950, the site from which this view was sketched itself became part of the Yard. The Foundry towers and the clock tower of the gate (which closed in 1966), however, remain to fix the spot chosen by the artist W Hake. The view, though, is now very much dominated by the three massive covered docks of the frigate complex. Built across the site of No 2 basin and Nos 5,6 and 7 docks, the decision to construct the new complex was announced in January 1970 by the then Parliamentary Under Secretary of State for Defence (Navy), Devonport MP, Dr David Owen, and it was officially opened by him in September 1977.

Royal Naval Barracks, Devonport

'The Royal Naval Barracks at Devonport consist of a fine and substantially built group of stone buildings, and as viewed from the higher ground on the right of the road by which they are approached – as in the illustration – present a pleasing picture. Anyone not acquainted with the locality would search in vain for the barracks in Devonport; as a matter of fact they lie at the present extremity of Keyham Dockyard, which however, is in the process of being considerably extended, the ground between the barracks and the harbour being just now – and likely to be for a few years to come – a wilderness given over to the tender mercies of the inexorable contractor, whose plant and crazy-looking little waggons are very much in evidence.'

So began an account of the new barracks published on the 6th August 1897 in the *Army and Navy Illustrated*. At that time the barracks themselves were also in the process of being greatly expanded and indeed the view shown here is a slightly earlier one than that used in the journal, and therefore does not show the recently completed clock tower complete with 'the inevitable semaphore', the vantage point is similar though.

Said to have been designed by Sir John Jackson, the barracks were first occupied in 1889 although they had in fact been ready for some time before that. It is thought that delay was probably due to the 'scruples existing in the conservative minds of some of the authorities, who were loath to see bluejackets berthed on shore and the time honoured depot-ships relegated to the past'. There was even a rumour going around that the buildings were to be handed over to the War Office and used as a cavalry barracks.

In the event, however, it seems to have been generally agreed that the move was by no means as disastrous as anticipated and if anything a depot on shore was actually preferable to a floating depot. Which is as well as the barracks were built to replace the old depot-ship system ... 'performing a precisely similar function, being the centre to which all seamen belonging to the port return at the expiration of their leave, and from which they are drafted, in strict rotation, as crews required for ships being commissioned'.

Certainly the new conditions were a great improvement

for the British sailor, particularly from a sanitary point of view and 'certainly tend to emphasize the conviction that, when Jack is not wanted at sea, he is better off in a building of this nature than in some obsolete hulk where space and light are reduced to a minimum'.

The barrack rooms, nevertheless, were still laid out as much as possible like a ship's mess deck. There were four barrack rooms in each of the two main blocks then in existence and each barrack room had accommodation for 125 men, 'that is to say for hanging that number of hammocks'.

In 1891 all the rooms in the barracks were occupied for the first time, following the amalgamation with the *Indus* which had hitherto served as the steam reserve depot.

Perhaps in some way to celebrate this move, a grand wardroom ball was held in January 1891, in honour of the Commander-in-Chief, Admiral HRH, the Duke of Edinburgh (Prince Alfred) and which, despite being held on a day of abysmal weather, attracted some 1,200 guests. Interestingly enough records of the event show that the guests between them consumed amongst other things 576 bottles of champagne, 540 bottles of spirits, 3,000 bottles of soda and 6,800 oysters, all for 7/3d (about 36p) per head.

At this stage the impressive wardroom building we know now had yet to be built, it was begun in Victoria's Diamond

Jubilee year, 1897, and formally opened in January 1903 with another celebration ball.

Other completed buildings that we can see, however, in this mid 1890s view, though, include the corner of the drill shed, to the far left and to the right, beside the entrance to the barracks, the 'commodious residence for the captain'.

Captain Charles Johnstone, a hero against the French in Madagascar in 1883, was appointed commander of the barracks in May 1896 and it is perhaps no coincidence that the first houses built in this area were those shown on the right here that made up what was known as Johnston Terrace.

Opposite these buildings, just inside the railings of the barracks, is a small slate hung building that had stood here when all around was open fields and market gardens. This was the 'Sportsman's Arms', originally said to be in Stoke rather than Devonport, it was set on the side of the Keyham Road (Saltash Road), well to the north of Keyham Lake but close enough to the waters of the Hamoaze to be visited by boat at high tide.

The extensions to the Keyham Yard between 1895–1907, of course, extended the shoreline some way out into the Tamar, including the area in front of the barracks, however, the strip of water that is the mouth of Westonmill Lake, seen here as the band of white below the open fields of Barn, remains today.

As for the 'Sportsman's Inn', it ceased trading here in 1897 and its licence and licensee, William Williams, moved to the newly built No 1 Keyham Road, otherwise known as the 'Avondale Arms' opposite the site of what was to become the new northern entrance to the Keyham Yard, the St Levan Gate.

It is of course hard now to imagine the barracks being, as they were described in article in the *Army and Navy Illustrated*, 'rather out of the way', but they were and consequently a 'dockyard train' ran past here at stated hours from a small platform by the Captain's house (it met up with the Great Western Railway line, running behind Johnston Terrace, some little way beyond it). That platform is still there today beneath the bridge over which the barracks is entered, so too indeed are the other barrack buildings depicted here.

Torpoint Ferry

It would appear that there was some kind of ferry in operation from Torpoint to Devonport as early as 1730 as a document dated November 1760 contains the following; 'about 30 years Since a passage or fferry being Established at a place Call'd Tarrpoint . . .'

At this time the tiny community of 'Tarrpoint' was very much in its infancy, and there was probably no more than a handful of buildings there, if that. A reference in 1748 to the Torpoint Passage House however gives credence to the idea that a ferry service was already underway then. The name 'Tarrpoint' or 'Tarpoint' incidentally is said by some to be the original name for this place, deriving from the early practice of tarring boats on the shore there.

The growth of Torpoint was undoubtedly prompted by the development of the Dockyard on the opposite bank of the Tamar and the idea of setting up a regular ferry service had been the subject of serious debate for some time before such a service was finally achieved in 1791–100 years after the Dockyard had been established.

The ferry issue had been given added impetus after the 1760 Liskeard Turnpike Act had paved the way for a turnpike road from Torpoint into Cornwall potentially providing a much more direct and quicker southern route into Cornwall than that via Tavistock and Launceston.

Reginald Pole Carew, whose family estate included much of the surrounding land on the Cornish side, as well as Torpoint Field itself (the hub of the new development area) and who was one of the major employers in the area, was the principal protagonist of the bid to establish a regular ferry service here. In conjunction with George, Earl of Mount Edgcumbe and owner of the Cremyll Ferry, it was proposed that at their own charges they 'were willing and ready to build and provide, maintain and keep a competent number of substantial boats for the use of the said ferry, with a sufficient number of capable and experienced ferrymen.'

They also committed themselves to constructing wharves, landing places and all related buildings. In 1790, despite a certain amount of opposition from the people of Saltash, an Act was passed in Parliament enabling Pole Carew and the Earl of Mount Edgcumbe to go ahead with their proposals and on Monday 4th July 1791 the new service began.

Essentially there were two services, one for foot passengers and one for horses, carriages and cattle. The horse boats were a catamaran-like construction whereby two hulls were set side by side slightly apart and joined by a wooden platform. Three men worked these vessels which crossed more or less along the line of the present ferries. The foot passengers however were transported across to North Corner as this was closer to destinations of most passengers; there was at that time little or no development above that point, hence the name 'North' Corner.

Although somewhat at the mercy of the weather Pole Carew answered critics of the service in 1815 by stating that the horse-ferry had never been prevented from crossing for a whole day and 'the Foot-Boats pass at all Hours without interruption' – the service was a half-hourly one.

Not all wayfarers travelling under horse power chose to cross with their horses; novelist Charlotte Yonge recalled that her mother did not like this option and chose instead to go in a foot-boat . . . 'I remember our rowing once under the *San Josef*, one of the Trafalgar prizes, and looking up as it rose, like a mighty castle above us . . .'

Similar great wooden hulled warships can be seen in this picture but Miss Yonge's memories were from the days just prior to the advent of the steam powered ferry when sail and oarsmanship were still the order of the day.

The first Torpoint steam ferry was launched amid great excitement and watched by huge crowds, on 29th September 1829. Named *Jemima* in honour of Reginald Pole

Carew's daughter Jemima, and his daughter-in-law Lady Jemima Eliot it wasn't until 1831 that the vessel went into regular service. The *Jemima* however almost immediately failed to live up to expectations and, prone to being blown off course and being turned broadside on when about to be unloaded, she was soon relieved of her duties.

Thus it was that the proprietors of the service approached the great civil engineer James Meadows Rendel with a view to his designing a new means of crossing the river. Rendel had also been asked to look at the Saltash ferry and to provide a crossing of the Laira (he designed the bridge there – completed in 1827) in addition to which he had successfully designed ferries at Dundee and Dartmouth.

In the event Rendel, having considered the problems, came up with the new 'Torpoint Floating Bridge', a steam driven, chain guided ferry operating on the same principles as the present day ferry. The first was introduced in 1834 the second in 1835 and both are shown here. With a lamp on each corner the new ferry crossed the river four times an hour, taking 8 minutes at high tide and 7 minutes at low.

Each capable of carrying 3 four horse carriages, one pair horse carriage, 7 saddle horses and 60 foot passengers these both ran until they were replaced in the 1870s by two new craft of a similar design. Together the new ferries took the service from the 19th century into the 20th, both being replaced in the 1920s with models that had the now familiar design of a central traffic deck.

St Michael's Terrace

'The village of STOKE, situated at a short distance from Devonport, has rapidly increased in extent and population since the close of the late war. It contains some handsomely built houses, chiefly occupied by naval and military officers, and retired tradesmen. Elegant villas are scattered through this pleasant suburb, and among them the residences of John Norman, and R Bromley, Esqrs. stand pre-eminent.' (Carrington 1828)

John Norman's house, Belmont, was designed by John Foulston; it was not by any means the only contribution to this area by the man, who almost single handedly is credited for establishing Plymouth 'as one of the foremost provincial classical towns' (PH Mann 1975). Foulston is also thought to have been the man responsible for the designs of Albermale Villas, Penlee Gardens and this fine block here, St Michael's Terrace.

Foulston had come to Plymouth in 1811 as a result of winning the competition held for the design of the new Theatre Royal, subsequently hailed as Plymouth's first truly classical building, and it would appear that he produced the design for St Michael's Terrace as the Theatre was being built in 1812.

In the event St Michael's Terrace was constructed over a period of about 25 years and the Theatre was completed in 1813, the similarities between the two buildings are nevertheless striking. Both owe a great deal to the style Inigo Jones introduced into this country in the 1630s when he designed London's first regular square of terrace houses in Covent Garden. Not that Jones himself was the real innovator here for he was merely modeling his work on the Italian Renaissance style of the great Italian architect Andrea Palladio.

The proportions that make a building 'Palladian' are clearly seen in both the Theatre Royal and St Michael's Terrace, they are, essentially, a medium-sized ground floor, a high first floor with its windows twice as high as they are wide and a smaller third floor. Another common feature of the Palladian style was the rustication (the use of external blocks of stone around the window arches and doorways) on the ground floor level, with a line at the top of this level appearing to form a baseline for the unusually high main floor above; this is particularly well illustrated in the St Michael's Terrace block. The extensive use of pilasters (the flat decorative columns against the walls) here is also typical of that classical architectural style.

In designing buildings like these, Foulston and various celebrated English architects before him appeared, on the face of it, to be embracing a distinctly European type of elegance but in truth no other country in the world has opted for this particular style of regularity in its general housing to the same extent as the English have.

Terraces on their grandest scale were undoubtedly designed to look like a large mansion, a palace even, rather than just a row of identical houses. As Anthony Quiney observed in his book *House and Home* '. . . That is the point of the terrace. The whole adds up to more than the sum of its parts.' However, to quote another authority, Stefan Muthesius, in *The English Terraced House* '. . . there is no equivalent to the grand English terraces anywhere – except perhaps for the occasional imitation'.

It is very hard though, particularly in Plymouth, not to take terraced housing for granted, but it is peculiarly English . . . and it is a product of a variety of different considerations. In Europe the need to squeeze the population of an area in behind town walls died out far slower than it did over here, consequently the idea of living in an apartment or a flat was, and still is, far more widespread in Europe than it is in England where the house came to be seen as a home for only one family.

In addition to this the English were far more interested in pursuing a notion of class separation and creating 'up-market' areas, indeed the English were increasingly keen not to live over their shops and there was an early separation of work and trade from living areas. It would have been unthinkable to have placed a shop front in St Michael's Terrace.

The attractive aspect of the terrace, of course, was that no matter what its size a row of neatly ordered houses has an architectural unity which confers a positive social image and 'speaks of a special achievement on the part of those who planned it or built it and those who bought it or rented it' (Muthesius).

By the dawn of the twentieth century almost 90 per cent of the population of this country was living in terraced housing of one kind or another (some of the larger London terraced houses had rooms big enough to accommodate four small two up two downs!).

Today the terrace is still a popular type of house, although many particularly the larger buildings, perhaps originally occupied by a family with servants, are now multi-tenanted. Some have even fallen by the wayside; St Michael's Terrace was in a somewhat sad condition when it was acquired by the St Aubyn Estates in the early 1960s and, although there was talk of restoring it, it was eventually demolished to make way for the three-storey modern housing which now stands on this site and still bears the same name.

A neatly laid-out lawn still stands in front of it, however, and the building seen here to the right, St Michael's Lodge, also designed by Foulston, survives today.

Albermarle Villas

'Nearly at right angles with St Michael's Terrace, but on a rather lower site, are the ALBERMARLE VILLAS, which like the Terrace, were designed by Mr Foulston, and have been completed within these three years. They are of light and cheerful architecture, with verandas, &c. and so ingeniously contrived as to command, from each dwelling, a most beautiful prospect of Plymouth Sound and its vicinage. On the right is seen Mount Edgcombe and the town of Stonehouse; and the left, the haven of Plymouth, with Staddon Heights, and the distant Mewstone rock mingling its blue tints with the ocean.'

This description of Thomas Allom's much reproduced view of Albermarle Villas was printed next to it in Britton and Brayley's *Devonshire and Cornwall Illustrated*, the drawing itself being first published in 1830, two years before the book was completed.

There were not a lot of buildings in Stoke at that time, indeed Albermale Villas were erected on the site of the 'Cake Houses' which according to Whitfeld (1899) were the only dwellings between Dock and Stoke Church. A look at a contemporary map shows us that all the new Foulston developments in Stoke would have enjoyed fairly spectacular and relatively unbroken views across undeveloped fields.

These new and impressive houses were all part of a general move, by the growing middle classes, away from the hustle and commercial bustle of the towns, 'ignoring the real squalor of the labourer's dwellings which these wealthy families, and their servants did not have to endure' (LF Cave *The Smaller English House*). This move, coupled with an 'enthusiasm for the picturesque, produced villas in the most unsuitable places, provided the view was romantic, and the houses were perched on hilltops or other exposed sites ... areas near the coastal resorts of Devon and Cornwall ... have many villas with names like Prospect House, Bellevue, Mount Pleasant, Montpelier, Belmont, and 'Groves' of various kinds, unknown before the last century'. (Cave)

Beaumont, of course, should be added to this list and certainly Plymouth was full of examples of this tendency as many of the impressive new detached residences on the outskirts of town, occupying lofty sites, were given these names. Indeed Plymouth's 'Belmont' was another of Foulston's developments in Stoke, built for John Norman who was a wealthy Devonport banker and art connoisseur. A grand structure which retains many original features today, it was built in the classical tradition and the architect appears to have borrowed certain major external features from the Parthenon and the Monument of Thrasyllus.

Foulston, of course, made no great claims to originality 'except as regards construction and adaptation'. He was, like the other influential architects he was following, impressed by the classic architecture style of the Greeks 'the only one which reconciles grandeur with regularity and proportion' a style which was at its peak in the fifth century BC. Foulston's own particular favourites which he specifically cited as reference points for his public buildings were 'the Doric Portico at Athens, the Ionic of Ilissus, and the Corinthian of Lysicrates' (Foulston 1838). Of his domestic buildings in Stoke, Belmont is undoubtedly the best example of the architect's attempt to 'create a more general feeling for Architecture in the West of England' by imitating the 'paramount beauty' of the ancient Greeks.

Occupied today by Plymouth Youth Hostel, who acquired the house from the St Aubyn Estates in 1948, Belmont's views have been to a certain extent restricted by the subsequent surrounding developments, here at Albermarle Villas, however, the views are still impressive. The design of these buildings, however, are as Mann observed 'a definite departure from his (Foulston's) Neo-Grecian style and their form recalls the warm Mediterranean'.

Built at a time when the villa was in vogue and the term itself was being applied to almost any detached residence, they are notable for their interesting applications of cast iron work.

Prior to the late eighteenth century, houses were protected from the road by walls or wooden posts, only a very grand house would have expensive wrought-iron railings. Gates were sometimes added and occasionally these would contain the more elaborate patterns of shaped iron work, but this was always the work of individual smiths and beyond most people's pockets. But then as the industrial revolution made its presence felt the founder, with his ability to mass produce in cast-iron, meant that ironwork became somewhat more affordable. There followed a national outbreak of iron; railings, gates, lampstands and other street furniture but most conspicuously perhaps elaborate window balconies, of which Albermarle Villas still provides some excellent examples.

In many ways the early nineteenth century witnessed the beginning of the second great Iron Age with national production of pig-iron increasing from around 70,000 tons a year in 1790 to over 250,000 tons by 1806 and 1,500,000 tons by 1850. Over half of this latter figure was for the railways but the use of iron was becoming increasingly more widespread generally and according to Mann (1975) in his thesis on Foulston, the 'constant use of cast iron is perhaps the most interesting feature of his work .. He not only used it decoratively for railings and balustrades but also practically for windows and doors and structurally for roofs, floors and supports .. His extensive use of the material for the roof and auditorium of the Theatre Royal and the fact that they were designed to be factory-made and easily assembled on site make him an innovator in the constructional use of cast-iron.' Mann then added 'surprisingly his achievements are not widely known and often overlooked.'

Fortunately, however, here at Albermarle Villas there are still many examples of Foulston's 'state of the art' iron work from that period. Other domestic buildings, incidentally, that Foulston is credited with designing in Plymouth are houses in Athenaeum Street, Windsor Villas in Lockyer Street, No 1 The Crescent and Wyndham Place.

Weston Mill

'Leaving Devonport by the Saltash road, we speedily arrive at Weston Mill, a little hamlet deeply seated in a thickly foliaged vale, at the head of a creek of the Tamar. Its turnpike house, overshadowed by trees – its lichened bridge – its leafy lanes, stealing away into haunts of sylvan lovliness – and lofty hills which rise around form an interesting picture of peaceful seclusion, seldom found in the immediate neighbourhood of a populous town. The creek presents an extremely gratifying scene when the tide is up, and is gently rippling round the rock-edged promontories. It then possesses all the charms of a sequestered lake, and is seldom without a rude boat, or perhaps a rustic barge, to add to the general effect.'

This rather poetic prose introduced Henry Carrington's *Excursion from Devonport to Buckland Monachorum* in 1828; it was one of several such colourful descriptions of the hamlet written at the beginning of the nineteenth century just as this was one of several published prints of the same scene.

Weston Mill was then one of the more picturesque stops on the turnpike road from Plymouth to Saltash as it crossed Ham Brook running down through the woods to meet Weston Mill Creek which then had its head here. The spot is still remarkably rural today and has yet to be tarnished by overdevelopment, but the creek been greatly in-filled and the bridge, greatly reinforced under its arch, has lost part of

its original charm. The toll house which stood astride the road has long since gone, as has the mill which for centuries was worked here.

The Saxon, Ulnod, held Weston at the time of the Conquest, the manor as described in the Domesday survey stretching across Ham Brook from Manadon as far south as the Saltash road and as far west as Weston Mill. The name 'Weston' itself, a very common one in this country, suggests the west tun, that is the tun – enclosure or homestead – to the west of another tun or perhaps in this case 'ham' which has a similar meaning and here has long been known simply as Ham.

In a deed dated 1155 there is mention of Geoffrey of Weston and the land of Ham 'on the west side of the road from the mill'. This road, now primarily pedestrian, is still known as Ham Lane and runs from Weston Mill through Ham Woods to the western end of Weston Park Road, in Peverell. Peverell in turn being named after a former owner of Weston, Hugh Peverell, whom we know was in possession of the estate back in 1241. The name Weston Peverell was subsequently used to describe what we now know as the Pennycross area, then stretching from Hyde Park to Burrington and as far south as Camel's Head.

The creek of the Tamar at Camel's Head is still properly known as Weston Mill Lake and it's hard now to imagine

that not only did quite large vessels use this water but they were also able to come as far up as Weston Mill itself. Barges being sailed up to unload corn for the mill which was still being worked in the late 1890s.

In those days Ben Petherick was the miller here but he was perhaps better known as an engineer and wheelwright and for the carts and wheelbarrows he made. The road to Weston Mill had by then been greatly improved but back at the beginning of the nineteenth century, despite being a comparatively major thoroughfare there were still those who would rather avoid the cross country roads, indeed the artist William Payne who painted so much of this part of the world and who came here to sketch this scene around 1789, is thought to have been one who preferred to take the coastal routes and travel up estuaries.

Whatever form of transport though that the weary traveller took, he was always sure to find refreshment here at Weston Mill, indeed reporting for the *South Devon Monthly Museum* in 1835 GP Hearder, writer, artist and self confessed member of the temperance society, noted there was a 'snug little domicile, on the immediate right after the bridge has been crossed' where 'as the writer has more than once proved, 'a nice drop of tea', and thanks to our favored county, a basin of cream may at any time be procured, for a trifling sum, to assist in wiling away any thing but tedious hours'.

'Tea finished, or, perhaps, instead, the junket' (possibly here meaning a picnic party, although it could of course also then have referred to a cream cheese dish or any sweatmeat), 'the pedestrian is invited to descend to the margin of the creek, above the stone arch before mentioned; here, on a primitive bridge, consisting of a single stone thrown across it, the other bank may be gained; then, having walked about half-way up the hill side , a most pleasant path is discovered, overshadowed by trees, running towards the east, for nearly a quarter of a mile, this walk belongs to the Ham Estate.'

Home of the Trelawneys for over 300 years the estate, with its once pheasant filled woods was sold to Plymouth City Council in 1947 by the Rev WT Trelawny-Ross and today those woods are open to all.

St Budeaux

'St Budeaux is a parish and village, 4 miles north from Plymouth railway station, 4 from Devonport, and 1 from the river Tamar. . . . The church is a handsome stone building, erected in 1563–4, of ancient style, kept in good repair; it has a tower containing 4 bells, nave, north and south aisles, and porch . . . The parish register records the marriage, in 1569, of Francis Drake and Mary Newman; and, in 1583, the burial of Mary Drake, wife of Sir Francis Drake, Knt. The living is a perpetual curacy, of the value of £120 per annum, with a good residence, in the gift of the vicar of St Andrew's, Plymouth, and incumbency of the Rev. B.W.S. Vallack, B.A.'

So ran part of an account of St Budeaux published in 1856; at that time the population of the parish had just reached 1000, of whom only 30 or so were entitled to vote. The parish itself stretched over 2500 acres of land and included the hamlet of King's Tamerton, half a mile away; Salt Ash Passage, 1 mile west; Honicknowle, Knackers-knowle (Crown Hill) and Whitleigh to the east. Of this land around 100 acres of it had recently been reclaimed from the bed of the river. This land, which adjoined Newland cottage, residence of William Elliott, had been tidal up to 1840. Previously marshy and now 'rich and productive', its development threw back the two Ernesettle farms 'some considerable distance' from the Tamar, which they had both earlier enjoyed direct access to via Cliff-lane. This lane ran down to meet the Saltash ferry at Saltash Passage which was then described as being in the Cornish Patch.

The Cornish Patch was a roughly square area of land on the Devon side of the river which, it was said, had always belonged to the Duchy of Cornwall; on the 1840 tithe map St Budeaux was described as a Parish 'in the counties of Devon and Cornwall'. At the end of last century, however, this patch was handed over to Devon under the terms of the Local Government Order 32169 dated 1st April 1895.

The two farms, Great Ernesettle and Little Ernesettle, were both named after William Ernstell, a freeholder of Budshead who owned land here in 1428. In the middle of last century there were more than ten farms in St Budeaux, almost all of which have since fallen foul of the developer. For many centuries there was little major development in the parish, as late as 1781 there were less than 400 people living in the area, occupying only 77 households between them. Even then that was a comparatively high figure and

was doubtless due to its being located on the main southern route into Cornwall. Certainly this was true once the railway arrived. The building of the Royal Albert Bridge heralded a new era of expansion for St Budeaux, changes that would all have been witnessed by the Reverend BWS Vallack who was vicar of St Budeaux Parish Church from 1832 until his death in 1875. Benjamin William Salmon Vallack was born in 1803, his father, William, was the vicar of Maker Church while his mother, Judith, was the daughter of William Smith who had been vicar of St Budeaux Church in 1798; he would therefore have been no stranger to the area in 1832 when he took up his appointment here and moved in to the adjacent vicarage. Up until 1827 this building had been a modest affair, 'a mere cottage containing only two rooms on the ground floor', it was then enlarged and renovated, the original building, thought to have been built at the same time as the church, being preserved to as great an extent as possible. It was as well that the vicarage was then enlarged for the Rev Vallack had quite a large family, at least four daughters and one son. Around 1860 however a new vicarage was built by the Government in the wake of the proposals to meet the French invasion threat and the old vicarage was scheduled to go in the ring

of defences that was planned. The Rev Wollaston Goode, who followed Vallack here, moved into this new building in 1875. In 1962 that 'new' vicarage was reopened in a new role as the Cornwall's Gate Hotel.

It would appear that the Rev Goode used to regularly make the journey from the vicarage to the church in his buggy, a two-wheeled cart pulled by a shetland pony. During his incumbency the church underwent a major restoration and at the reopening a new organ was unveiled; it being played for the first time by Mr Hele, of Hele and Co who had installed the instrument.

It was also during Goode's time that the St Budeaux Foundation Church of England School was moved from its old site on the village green to fine new limestone buildings that until recently stood on the southern side of the Crown-hill Road, not far from the church. Founded as early as 1717, in the middle of last century this school had about 48 boys and 40 girls; these children were for the most part supported by subscriptions and money paid by their parents, although there was provision for twelve boys and twelve girls to be educated and clothed out of funds put aside for that purpose. For those who could afford to pay, the fee was at one time 2d (less than one new penny) per week.

Royal Albert Bridge

'Cornwall was practically a region 'beyond railways' with the exception of the short West Cornwall line running from Truro to Penzance . . . The project of a railway through Cornwall, to unite the western county in iron fellowship with the rest of England, has had its discouraging and costly history. In 1844 the Cornwall Railway Company was formed, and in the excess of speculation, if not the exuberance of capital, a rival scheme soon started upon the stage. The struggle was obstinate and expensive, and the result was the rejection by Parliament of both sets of plans. Eventually, after an expenditure by the Cornwall Company of no less a sum than £100,000 it succeeded in passing its bill through both Houses, and on the 3rd August 1846 it received the Royal assent.'

In this way the scene was set to describe the *History of the Royal Albert Bridge*, published by Wood and Tozer of Fore Street, Devonport, soon after its completion (the History cost one penny and was available from 'all booksellers and at the railway bookstalls' or 'post free on receipt of two stamps').

Such is not to say, however, that work began on the bridge as soon as the Act of Parliament was passed or that the work, once it had begun, went smoothly. The Act broadly concerned the establishment of a line between Plymouth and Falmouth and the man given the task of solving the problem of how to cross the Tamar at first came to a similar conclusion to that reached by his father some years earlier, that the river here was too wide to bridge.

Exiled Frenchman Marc Isambard Brunel had come to Britain in 1799 after six years working as an engineer in New York. He quickly made a name for himself here after the government adopted his plans for making ship's blocks and he was soon appointed to effect other innovative schemes around the various government dockyards. Such work brought him to Plymouth, where he was approached by a body of Saltash merchants to devise some way of bridging the Tamar but his answer was that it couldn't be done.

In 1831, the year that JM Rendel produced designs for a chain guided steam ferry across to Saltash, Marc Brunel's son Isambard Kingdom Brunel, (who had joined his father's office three years earlier) had his plans adopted for the construction of the Clifton suspension bridge. Sadly, due to lack of funds, that work wasn't completed until after Isambard's death, however, in 1833 he was appointed chief engineer for the Great Western Railway and it was in this capacity that he came here in 1846.

The young Brunel's first inclination was for a steam train ferry, however, the Act only provided for a fixed crossing and so Brunel, who had already perfected the art of constructing wooden bridges, came up with a scheme for a seven span timber bridge. The Admiralty rejected this plan, though, as they also did a subsequent one for a four span wooden construction, on the grounds that there should only be one pier standing in the river. It was at this point that Brunel abandoned all ideas of a double-tracked timber bridge and worked instead on a single-track, wrought-iron structure.

Once again his first thoughts, this time for an impressive single span structure, were rejected. The cost of such a project was prohibitive. So it was then that he went on to draw up a design for a two-span iron bridge with one central pier in the fairway and seventeen much smaller land spans, the finished track being the necessary 100 feet above high water that the Admiralty required.

This won the approval of both the Admiralty and the Cornwall Railway Board and so now, two years after the Act had been passed, work could begin. Test borings were made of the river bed, there was a great deal of mud below the water, mud which over the years had yielded for the people of Saltash a healthy oyster industry, and this had to be penetrated to find the rock bed.

Borings were made with an 85 foot long, 6 foot wide, iron cylinder, it was moved 35 times and 175 tests were carried out. However, despite the satisfactory conclusions provided by this information the impossibility of raising the necessary capital led to a suspension of work on the line from the beginning of 1849 through to 1852.

In that year Brunel had an even bigger cylinder made, a large water-tight tube which, like its predecessor, was constructed in two halves on the eastern shore. Measuring a massive 35 feet in diameter and 95 feet long and 'constructed with air tight chambers and a cupola about one third from the bottom' this was 'to the surprise of the uninitiated, easily floated off from the work-shops, and by the simplest contrivance, was sunk perpendicularly in the very spot, in the centre of the Tamar, where Mr Brunel had intended'.

Work now began on the excavations for the foundation of the central pier inside this great cylinder, the top of which can be seen surrounded by pontoons in the middle of this picture, which incidentally, bears the date October 1854.

It was not easy work, however, such a structure had not been used before in civil engineering work and there were problems of seepage. Brunel had plenty of experience working in this sort of situation though, having helped his father on the construction of the famous Thames tunnel back in the late 1820s and so gradually the early difficulties were overcome. This included having to keep the working environment 80 feet down, at an air pressure of 35lb per square inch, a situation that turned out to be too much for men working seven hour shifts. Consequently shifts were reduced to three hours and this stopped the problems of temporary paralysis in the men, although it meant increasing the workforce on this operation to 40.

Brunel Bridge

By the time the granite column to support the central pier of the bridge had been completed, much work had already been done on preparing the first great tube and roadway section that was to be the western span.

Designed to combine the principles of arch and suspension bridges, the great arched tubes counteracting the inward pull on the suspension chains when a large weight passes over the supported truss, the suspension chains themselves were those intended for the bridge at Clifton. The chains, which had originally been made in Hayle, in Cornwall, were, however, slightly too short for the bridge here and had to be taken to London to be lengthened.

By the summer of 1857 the western tube and truss section was ready to be floated into position and Brunel chose Tuesday 1st September for the great event. And what a great event it was too, for this was to be a major landmark in the history of the two counties, especially for Cornwall. It was also to be a major achievement in engineering history.

Across the Three Towns the event was treated as cause for a general holiday. The Saltash Steam Packet Company brought all their steamers into operation, and borrowed more, 'but though they ran up and down every half-hour they could not accommodate all applicants, notwithstanding the vessels were at times crammed with living freights, to an extent that caused them to roll about and dip in a manner that was truly alarming'.

'Every cab was engaged to take parties to Saltash, the fare being increased from 5s to 30s (25p to £1.50), and even at that high rate of charge the supply fell short of the demand.' People poured into the area from far and wide . . . 'and the intermediate towns, Exeter and even London, sent their thousands to swell the immense throng'.

As the time approached the appointed hour of one o'clock, when it was thought the tide would be right for floating the 'monster tube', every vantage point on both sides of the river was packed. In Saltash itself the flags were out and the bells were rung:

'. . . tents and marquees were erected in private gardens for the accommodation of friends, while for the accommodation of strangers, the various houses of entertainment had laid in enormous stores of edibles and drinkables. The provision, however, fell short of the demand, and we hear that before the evening closed, Saltash was regularly cleared out, there being scarcely anything edible left in the whole town. To estimate the numbers that were present is impossible, but at a low computation we should say that it amounted at least to from 30,000 to 40,000.'

No-one was injured and no-one was disappointed. At 1.15pm the immense load, weighing over 1,100 tons, was seen to float and the large workforce gradually moved the pontoons and their burden out into the river. 'The assembled crowds saw with astonishment this huge mass moving without the slightest sound. Not a voice was heard, not a direction was spoken; a few flags waved, a few boards with numbers on them were exhibited, and, as by some mysterious agency, the tube and rail borne on the pontoons travelled to their resting-place, and with such quietude as marked the building of Solomon's temple'.

Brunel himself directed the operation on a specially constructed platform in the middle of the truss, using his special arrangement of coloured flags. About 30 inches high and held up against a blackboard, they were appropriately red, white and blue, the red signalling 'heave in', the white 'hold on' and the blue 'pay out', the speed of waving determining the speed of action.

By three o'clock, when the tide was at its highest, the truss had been secured in its desired position 30 feet above high water, and as Brunel stepped down from the platform the band of the Royal Marines, on a nearby vessel, struck up 'See the conquering hero comes' and then 'God save the Queen' after which the crowd broke into long and loud applause.

It was to be another month or two before the truss was lifted a stage further and it wasn't until May 1858 that it reached its final resting place. By this time the second truss was ready and that was floated on the 10th July and lifted for the first time four weeks later. Brunel was at this time ill and resting in Lausanne and was unable to be present as these events took place. Indeed he even missed the opening ceremony itself, on the 2nd May 1859, when His Royal Highness Prince Albert made the six hour train journey down from Windsor to officiate.

The Prince Consort had given permission for his name to be used in this way six years earlier and on the day his train came down as far as this point so that he could see this panoramic view of the bridge for himself.

The first train to Truro from Plymouth had actually run three weeks earlier but it wasn't until the end of the summer of 1859, when this view was sketched, that Brunel was able to see the bridge for himself. Even then he was so ill that he could only view it from a couch mounted on a flat wagon, drawn slowly across the bridge by one of Daniel Gooch's locomotives, doubtless similar to the one depicted here (Daniel Gooch was appointed Locomotive Superintendent for the Great Western by Brunel in 1837 when he was only 20 and spent over 27 years in the position).

Isambard Kingdom Brunel sadly never recovered from his illness and on 15th September 1859 he died at his home in London, he was 53. The great engineer left the world with a number of notable memorials, however, and this bridge still standing today is one of the finest.

Blind Institution

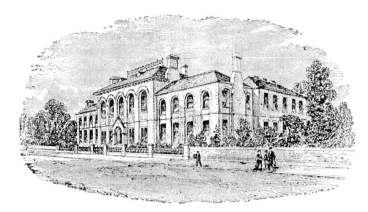

On the 19th April 1876 the Earl of Mount Edgcumbe laid the foundation stone to these buildings here on North Hill. Eighteen months later, on 26th October 1877, 'The South Devon and Cornwall Institution for the Instruction and Employment of the Blind' occupied these premises for the first time – it was to remain here for another 87 years.

Up until the nineteenth century little provision had ever been made for the blind in Plymouth, in Britain or anywhere else in world. The blind were, to a large extent, treated as a useless burden and families often resented them and grudged them their keep. In poor families blind children were often sent to the local workhouse, or sold as freaks to fun fairs or simply just turned out onto the streets and left to fend for themselves. Consequently, homeless blind people of all ages could be found begging on the pavements of most large towns, with many able people, even well educated people finding it amusing to watch these blind people struggling to get about.

The situation did distress some, however, in Paris there was a school that is said to have its origins in the middle ages when it was founded by St Louis for 300 of his soldiers who lost their sight in the Crusades. This Institution was much expanded in the late eighteenth century by Valentin Hauy who was disgusted at the way some of the Parisian common folk treated the pauper blind. Determined to find ways in which the blind could be rendered less helpless, it was Hauy whose work led to the production of the first book for the blind (1784), printed in relief so that the letters could be read by touch. Louis XVI was given a demonstration of the school's achievements in 1786 and gave royal support and

Hauy was later invited by the Russian Emperor to establish a similar institution in St Petersburg. Braille was later a pupil at the school and it was here he devised his language for the blind.

In 1791 and 1793 similar schools were set up in Liverpool and Edinburgh and over the next 90 years or so other major towns followed suit. In 1858 the Rev J Adams of St Paul's, together with a group of Devonport gentlemen, set about raising funds to establish a base for 'The Devonport and Western Counties Blind Association', while in Plymouth a young man in his mid twenties, James Gale, was trying to gain support for a blind institution.

Gale was blind himself; he had banged his head while playing on some railings when he was fourteen and within three years had lost all his vision. Born in Crabtree, the son of a prosperous coal merchant, James Gale determined to overcome his handicap and initially became involved in the family business, then came the desire to establish a blind institute. However, despite the enlightened attitude that was gradually spreading across the country it was no easy task, many wealthy and influential local people appeared unsympathetic. Eventually though, through the efforts of several individuals, notably Dr Tanock, vicar of Tavistock and Isaac Latimer, proprietor of the *Western Daily Mercury* (an ancestor paper of the *Evening Herald*), part of Plymouth Workhouse was rented and opened, on 2nd January 1860, as 'Plymouth's Institution for the Instruction and Employment of the Blind'.

The enterprise was a great success and just over a year later the Institution had expanded into new premises in Coburg Street. The move was marked by the change in name, from the 'Plymouth Institution . . .' to the 'South Devon and Cornwall . . .', and by the reception of the first resident inmate on the opening day, 2nd May 1861. The syllabus was now widened to include piano and organ playing and early in 1862 the new premises was further extended. It was still not enough though as the numbers of those seeking places here carried on growing and so the Institution started to look for a site on which they could construct their own purpose built establishment.

In 1872 the freehold for this site on North Hill was acquired and plans were subsequently drawn up by the local architect, described as a 'renaissance classicist', HJ Snell.

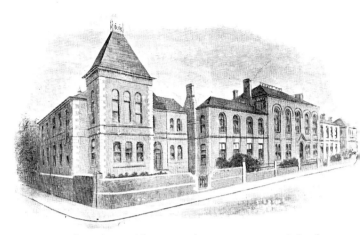

Messrs Palk and Partridge were the contractors and the first phase was finished in 1877, the same year that the neighbouring Plymouth High School for Girls was completed. An additional workshop was added two years later and then in 1891 the south wing was built onto the St Lawrence's Road corner of the building. This wing was destroyed in the Blitz of 1941 and later rebuilt.

The passing of the Education Act prompted further expansion in 1893, so that blind children could be accommodated and educated. Despite the various changes in emphasis over the years, though, basket making and coconut mat manufacture have always been among the principal activities of the Institution from the beginning and indeed continue to be at Stonehouse, where the Institution was moved in 1964, the old buildings here having since been annexed by Plymouth High School.

James Gale, incidentally, went on to become one of Plymouth's more famous sons, for not only did he go on to found the Royal National Institution for the Blind in 1869, he also was responsible for a number of enduring inventions; including a safe means for storing gunpowder which saved many lives (and after an audience with Queen Victoria in 1865 earned him the nickname 'Gunpowder Tamer' from Prince Albert), he also developed an electric alarm clock, a fire alarm a burglar alarm and the Ammunition Slide Gun believing that the time was rapidly coming 'when new inventions will make war such a scene of carnage that nations, as by one consent, will drop their weapons with a shudder'. What would he have thought of the bombs that shattered part of the building he did so much to realise.

Green Bank House

In 1837, in Exeter, a 23-three-year old Cornishman, Edward James, set up a small business with a man called Rowe and a silent partner; who took no active part in running the business called Rosewall, who also came from Cornwall. For ten years all went well and Edward James and his young bride, Joanna, started their large family. Then for some reason the two men decided to split the business, Edward James came to Plymouth and started 'James and Rosewall' afresh. Rowe meanwhile formed Rowe and Company. Both businesses thrived and it is only in recent years that Rowe and Company were bought out by the Graham Group while the James and Rosewall concern was taken over, first in 1971 by Associated Lead from London, and then the following year by Nicholls and Company who today occupy the old site in Octogon Road.

James and Rosewall weren't always in Octagon Road, however. They moved to this part of Plymouth (there was another premises in Rendle Street) around the turn of the century from their previous base in the erstwhile Woolster Street on the Barbican. This in turn was their second home having started out in George Street. There it was that James and Rosewall started up in Plymouth as 'Artist and House Painters' Oil and Colourmen; Crown, Sheet and Plate Glass Merchants'. These were the days before one could walk into a DIY store and buy a can of non-drip gloss or emulsion. Back then do-it-yourself meant buying linseed oil, raw ground colours (of which there might have been a range of

twenty or so) and some turpentine, then mixing the lot into a workable solution with a pestle and mortar or grinders – making up the paint yourself before you could even start to apply it. This was the lot of all painters and decorators until the late 1920s early 30s. Another of James and Rosewall's main lines was supplying lead and glass for windows, in those not so long gone pre-PVC days.

In 1870 the firm set up their own lead works and by this time Edward James was sufficiently affluent to move into Green Bank House. This splendid Victorian villa was built towards the end of the century and set magnificently in eleven acres, surrounded by trees, paddocks and this great sloping lawn (which could well be the original Green Bank that has since given its name to many parts of this area of Plymouth). The family moved here around 1865 and in 1871 the James household consisted of sons John 25, William 16, Charles 12 and daughters Mary 26 and Jessie 23, a live-in cook and parlour maid. The drawing room alone was thirty feet by twenty and the stables could accommodate ten horses.

John worked with his father and elder brother, also Edward, in the family business (the initials JJ and EJ grace the horse trough, given by the family, which still stands at the southwestern extremity of the land). John, like his father, entered local politics and while Edward James senior was twice Mayor of Plymouth (1877–78, 1884–85) John Bright James was twice Mayor of Devonport (1894–95 and

1895–96). Younger brother Charles, with whom he did not appear to get on too well, set up his own firm, James Brothers, and concentrated on the timber side of the Building business at Richmond Walk. This business again, has been taken over in comparatively recent years by Jewsons.

After a long and successful life, Edward James passed away just before the turn of the century and by 1897 the house had been demolished and almost all of the land sold for housing. Woodland Terrace had long since been built on the paddocks to the north west of the house and Greenbank Terrace and Villa constructed inside the original northern boundary, along from the gateway there to the stables. Now though, with the house itself gone, Diamond Avenue was built and the houses along the top side of Lipson Road to Woodside. Woodside was the earlier name for this area and Woodside itself was the original eastern boundary of Green Bank House.

Today there is but a tiny part of the old grounds undeveloped. Behind the old wall behind the horse trough is a site that has been empty some 50–60 years. However, soon housing units will fill this fraction of an acre (about one ninth) and there will be little left to recall the grand villa and its grounds. Green Bank House, incidentally, would have stood halfway up Diamond Avenue, its front door right in the middle of the road!

Mannamead

Just as Foulston, in 1811, had extended people's perception of the boundaries of Plymouth with the choice of location for his first public building in the area – the Theatre Royal, at the western end of town – so, ten years later, he prompted his more affluent contemporaries to consider pushing out the boundaries in a northerly direction when it came to looking for sites for new residential developments.

Foulston himself had a house built on Townsend Hill, a house which he modestly called 'Athenian Cottage', with a smaller, more cottage-like cottage close by for his coach-man. Sadly it did not prove to be one of the great architects' more enduring developments and by the end of the century it had been knocked down and replaced by Wilderness

Villa. Nevertheless, with its classically inspired gardens, Athenian Cottage had been an important development in its day.

At about the same time a Mrs Mangles had Mutley House erected a few hundred yards away, however the move out of town to this corner of Compton Gifford was by no means rushed and until the 1830s dawned Foulston had few neighbours. Mutley Plain was little more than an open road with little or no development on or off it.

Townsend House was built just up from Foulston in 1833 and the following year work was begun on the villas around Ford Park (almost all of which are now part of the Plymouth College complex). Maisonette Cottages followed

a few years later and Hyde Park Terrace was put up in 1849. The major move, however, came in the following decade when (in 1856 according to Worth) Messrs Edward Crispe Ellery, Francis Fowler, and John Nicholas Bennett acquired the two fields known as the Mannameads from the Seymour Trustees.

Having bought East and West Mannamead these gentlemen had the two fields 'laid out by Mr Damant for a series of villas'. So successful was the venture that in time the whole area was to become known as Mannamead. Strictly speaking, however, the Mannamead fields were bounded on the west by Tavistock Road, on the south by Hell Lane (later Elm Road) and by other privately owned fields to the

north and east (the BBC currently occupies the most easterly villa of the original development).

Among the earliest occupants of these fine new residences were the young boys of Mannamead School, which according to contemporary newspaper accounts, opened here on 25th July 1854. The school was run by the Rev Peter Holmes MA, who left the headship of the Corporation Grammar School to found his own institution.

Seymour Villa became the site of the main school, while Holmes and his boarders were resident in Wellington Villa. In later years Moorfield School came to occupy Seymour Villa, Mannamead School having joined forces with its erstwhile adversary, Plymouth College (founded at Ford Park in 1877), in 1896.

But to return to the 1850s, this is the vista that Peter Holmes, his pupils and neighbours would have enjoyed. To the east, there were uninterrupted views of the Plym, Saltram Woods and the open fields of the farms and villages that we now know as Plymstock. Looking towards Staddiscombe the great green expanse had but one major interruption, the relatively newly built block that was, and is, Lipson Terrace, then enjoying unbroken sea-views on the brow of the hill to the left of what is now Freedom Fields Park.

To the south, just west of Woodside, can be seen the recently completed exercise yard of the new Borough Prison, soon to be hidden from this angle by Longfield Terrace as Plymouth stretched out its boundary to meet the southern part of the rapidly expanding Mutley Plain. As we see it here though what little there was of Mutley was blocked by the villas to the middle and right of the picture. Only Chester Place (which had the leat curving around this side of it) was clearly visible. Although it was soon to be screened by Nottingham Cottages.

Stonehouse, Mount Wise and parts of Devonport are also to be seen here as indeed are the unmistakable heights of Maker and Mount Edgcumbe, constant features in this scene then and now.

The Laira

'May it please Your Majesty that it may be enacted . . . in this present Parliament assembled . . . that upon Payment of the Sum of Two hundred Pounds of lawful Money of Great Britain into the Bank of England, by the said John Lord Boringdon to the Cashier of the Bank of England . . . all that Creek, or Plot or Parcel of Mud Land, known by the Name of Chelson Bay, otherwise Shilston Bay, part of the said Tract of Land called The Lairy, situate within or adjacent to the said Parish of Plympton Saint Mary in the County of Devon, bounded on the North and East by Saltram Lawn, on the South by Lands in the Parish of Plymstock, and on the West by other Part of The Lairy, and containing by Estimation One hundred and five Acres . . . is hereby granted and confirmed unto, and shall be vested for ever, freed and absolutely discharged from all Claim, Right, and Title whatsoever of His Majesty in Right of His Crown, His Heirs and Successors, in the said John Lord Boringdon, His Heirs and Assigns, to the Use of the said John Lord Boringdon . . .'

So ran part of the text of one of the sentences contained in the Act dated 10th July 1805 which resolved the disputed ownership of some of the mud land here in the Plym Estuary. In this Act George III relinquished his rights to part of this 'tidal' land in return for a payment of £200 from John Parker, Lord Boringdon, who deemed the land to be his in his capacity as Lord of the Manor of Plympton.

Having paid the £200 Lord Boringdon almost immediately began embanking Chelson Creek. Work commenced in the spring of 1806 and was eventually completed by the autumn of 1817, by which time it was estimated that some £9,000 had been spent on the project and some 175 acres of land had been reclaimed, land which was then valued to be worth upwards of £20,000.

For his work the Saltram based nobleman was awarded a gold medal by the Society of Arts, but this was by no means his only contribution to the Laira waterfront. Under the auspices of the Plymouth Embankment Company he promoted, through Acts of Parliament dated 1802 and 1803, the embankment of the Western side of the Laira and the formation of the New Eastern Road which at long last by passed the steep old route over Lipson Hill.

'Sirs for the road on the Laira's banks / Accept the weary horse's thanks'.

That was one of the rhymes coined for the procession at its opening.

Lord Boringdon had of course already done his own horses a favour, back in 1794, when he constructed a fine embanked carriage drive from Longbridge at Marsh Mills to his residence at Saltram. This also had the effect of keeping the Plympton marshes free of tidal intrusions (there was a time when Plympton St Maurice itself was a working port on the waters edge).

With little or no development to be seen around the waterfront of the Laira, in the middle of last century when the Exeter based artist W Spreat produced this restful scene (around 1845) it is easy to imagine that Saltram was still very much a country seat with unspoilt views in every direction. Well might the Victorian historian RN Worth have suggested that it would be difficult to find a piece of land in the whole of Devonshire better suited to the staging of horse races than at Chelson Meadow, the land Lord Boringdon had reclaimed from the mud.

Incidentally, the mud banks here are reckoned by some to be another possible explanation of the name Laira, this school of thought claims that it comes from the Old Norse *leirr* meaning clay, hence leira 'a clayey place'. Expert opinion, however, appears to be divided and there is strong backing for the Celtic derivation, the suggestion here being that it has the same origin as the Welsh *llaeru*, to ebb or grow shallow.

Chelson or Chilson, meanwhile, is said to have the same origins as Chivelstone, that is it comes from the farm or 'tun' belonging to *Ceofel* which in turn comes from the Old English name *Ceofa* and so we are left to imagine someone of that name having a homestead here over a thousand years ago when Chelson was a substantial creek.

Horse racing began at Chelson Meadow in 1828 when an annual meeting was moved here after being staged for three years at Crabtree. Laira bridge had not long been completed and people came from all around, as much for the stalls and fairground atmosphere as for the racing itself, which was principally the domain of the local gentry. Lord James Fitzroy, Mr J Bulteel, Mr Charles Trelawney, Mr H Molyneaux, Mr T Lechmere and Colonel Gilbert were the leading gentlemen 'mounts' in the main event, a ten-sovereign sweepstake, held at that first meeting.

'The meetings continued from year to year and presented the same animated groupings – peers in their chariots of fours, with glittering outriders, booted grooms and powdered lacqueys; dashing equipages from neighbouring country houses and barracks; the same outlandish bustle and confusion – neighing and trampling of steeds, rattling of carriages and donkey carts, lusty laughter and perpetual clamour' (Whitfeld).

In the 1880s gate money, 6d for the public, £1 1s 0d for a Carriage and Four, was charged to try and keep away the 'worst class' and it was observed that although numbers were undoubtedly down, no disturbance took place during the meeting; which was just as well for the owners of Chelson Meadow had let it be known that had there been a disturbance they would have 'seriously considered the advisability of closing the Race Course for the future' (the *Western Figaro*).

In the event the mile and a half course was closed down in 1926 and although there were many ideas for the site, including, in the early 1920s, an airport (abandoned because it was too boggy). Little happened here until November 1961 when Plympton acquired the land, by a compulsory purchase order, for use as a tip. However, later in the same month the land was sold by the Earl of Morley to Plymouth City Council who wanted it for playing fields. The subsequent ownership dispute was resolved in 1963 by a joint ownership arrangement and the land has since been used as a refuse tip.

New Bridge

The caption on this picture when it appeared in the May 1835 edition of the *South Devon Monthly Museum* read simply 'Long Bridge on the Plym', unfortunately as was explained in the June edition of this same periodical this was incorrect. The bridge shown here was called 'from its birth to its destruction New Bridge; our 'devil', by accident, whipped in the name of Long Bridge ... though Long Bridge is not to be taken down or altered, and will remain the same as it has ever been.'

There has always been confusion over this issue and thanks indeed to their 'devil', that confusion was compounded in May 1835 despite the author's attempts to explain the situation. Writing of the bridge shown here he said:

'It has, absurdly enough, continued to be called New Bridge, in contradistinction to the older bridge across the Plym, higher up on the river, and called Plym Bridge. Those who ought to have given it a name, neglected to do so, but it is hoped that a name will now be given; though it must be acknowledged that the bridges in its vicinity have superseded the more obvious names of Plym and Plympton.'

Then he went on to add '... This name has been sometimes confused with Long Bridge, which is properly applicable only, to the raised road or bridge over the marshes; extending from the bridge over the stream that flows by the side of Marsh House to New Bridge.'

The original Long Bridge appears, therefore, to have been a bridge in the other sense of the word, that is 'a structure affording passage between two points at a height above the ground'. Thus we read that before the turnpike road was constructed here in 1758 'there was merely a beaten track leading across these marshes (subject therefore to inundation, and other impediments) communicating on one side with the road leading by Leigham Gate to Knackersknowle Village (Crownhill), and on the other with Plympton by a ford across the river, and thence by a narrow lane to Plympton.'

This raised embankment appeared as a result of the bill for 'the inning of Plympton Marsh' which had the effect of reducing the width of the Laira at this point thereby enabling, in 1618–19, a causeway to be driven across the Marsh Mills mud-flats.

Some 20 years or so later this new route into Plymouth was the scene of great activity and blood was spilt here as the Royalists and Roundheads battled it out. In December 1642 we read of Lord Grey de Ruthven, then in command of the men in Plymouth, and having been pushed back from his outposts holding 2,500 of the King's men, under Sir Ralph Hopton, for over three hours, on the narrow passage of Long Bridge, before Hopton fell back.

Then later on the 19th April 1644 we learn that Colonel Martin, in charge of Plymouth's Parliamentarians beat up the enemy's quarters at 'New Bridge on the way to Plympton'. Worth, in his *History of Plymouth*, suggests that this New Bridge was somewhere between Long Bridge and Marsh Mills, but could it be just an earlier example of the confusion as Long Bridge would still have been comparatively new then?

Five years before the end of the seventeenth century, Celia Fiennes, on her side-saddle tour of England, crossed the Plym on her way into Plymouth. Passing a very large house (presumably Saltram) she went down the side of a hill to the head of the river, 'which is filled with the tide from the sea', too far down river to be Plym Bridge, Miss Fiennes nevertheless records that 'here I crossed on a stone bridge'.

According to our writer in the *South Devon Monthly Museum*, New Bridge, as shown here, was built in 1753. At that time 'the wants of the increased population required better accommodation, and an act of parliament was applied for to constitute the gentlemen of the country, and adjacent towns, a body of trustees; authorizing them to collect tolls from all persons using the road, and to widen and improve the then almost impassable highways.'

The choice of the new route was by no means automatic, the Earl of Morley, John Parker of Saltram, backed a campaign for a crossing from Crabtree via a bridge to a spot inside his grounds at Blaxton, however, after a lively dispute he was thwarted by the successful bid of Sir John Rogers.

And so to these two bridges at right angles with each other, 'thrown over the two Rivers Plym and Torey which here unite their streams' (Rev John Swete 1795). By 1835 it was no longer deemed big enough to cope with modern traffic demands, having been erected 'when such a vehicle as a stage-coach was unknown in this part of the kingdom, and when carriages and carts of every description were very few.'

The idea of widening the bridge was considered but in the event the decision was taken to rebuild. James Green a civil engineer from Exeter, who was also Surveyor of the county bridges in Devon, was given the job of designing the new bridge and William Dwelly of Plymouth, the task of building it. The contract price was £1,050; it was scheduled for completion by the end of September 1835 and as of May of that year travellers were already using a temporary wooden bridge in place of this bridge which had been demolished.

The new bridge still stands today; it has survived thanks to the addition of a relief bridge a few feet away and, since 1973, the Plympton By-Pass. As to the naming saga, our writer of 1835 would doubtless be unamused today by the confusion that sees it now called Longbridge. But at least he would be pleased that it is not called New Bridge, 'to call it New Bridge is like calling a man John Smith, which everybody admits is no designation'.

Boringdon

Boringdon takes its name from the ancient British or Celtic camp or fort that was created in Saxon times and is to be found a little to the north of Elfordleigh, and hence that much further from the house depicted here, which was rebuilt a few years ago as Boringdon Hall.

The original Boringdon, literally 'bury down' – earthwork on the hill (hence also Burraton, Burrington, Burradon, Boraton, etc.) – was a simple castle ring, a rampart and ditch about 500 feet in diameter. The house depicted here is 'a little more than half' of what is supposed to have been largely an Elizabethan building, a typical 'E'-shaped structure, erected probably during the lifetime of Edmund Parker who died and was buried at Plympton St Mary's Church in 1635. It is thought that Edmund Parker's time at Boringdon saw the house through its finest period.

Parts of the building, however, are thought to have been older than late sixteenth century. Sometime after the twelfth century the Priors of Plympton erected a substantial grange at Boringdon which was appropriated by the crown following Henry VIII's Dissolution of the Monasteries. The gable ended structure seen here to the left of the surviving two parts of the 'E' formation is regarded as being fifteenth century while other areas show traces of fourteenth century work.

The Parker family acquired Boringdon through the marriage of John Parker, Edmund's son, to Frances Mayhew the heiress of Jerome Mayhew who had inherited Boringdon manor from his uncle who died in 1558, ten years after acquiring the property himself. Jerome had apparently had problems with the mortgage on Boringdon and Edmund Parker, who was originally from North Molton, had ensured that the estate would stay in his family by paying Jerome £3,000 as part of his son's marriage settlement. In the event, John Parker died in 1610 and his father remained in possession of Boringdon until his death, when he was succeeded by his grandson also named Edmund.

Boringdon remained in the hands of the Parker family, along with Colebrook, right down to the twentieth century. Like so many of the big country houses around, it was staunchly Royalist during the Civil War. The impressive fireplace in the hall bore the now faithfully reproduced Royal Coat of Arms and originally appears to have dated from 1641. The parapet on the main frontage, which was embellished with the arms of Mayhew and Parker is also

thought to date from this period, however, Boringdon wasn't always used as the family seat.

Said to have been ransacked by the Roundheads during the Civil War, when the eastern wing was damaged and not subsequently repaired, in the late seventeenth and early eighteenth century first Edmund Parker (great grandson of the first mentioned Edmund) and then his grandson, turned back to North Molton. Then following the purchase of Saltram in 1712 interest was turned in yet another direction.

The move to Saltram three years later marked the beginning of the end of Boringdon's days of true glory as a Parker residence. However, when John Parker was elevated to the peerage on the 18th May 1784 it was as Baron Boringdon, of Boringdon, Devon and significantly it appears to have been around this time that the Triumphal Arch was built marking the start of the grand carriageway that joined the two properties.

The evidence of the view depicted here, however, suggests none of the finery associated with contemporary views of Saltram. Published in 1809 and engraved by William Wolnoth, from a drawing by JR Thompson after a sketch by the celebrated Plymouth born artist Samuel Prout (some years before he made his reputation with his series of continental scenes), the foreground is rough and uneven, there are no well kept lawns, no elegantly dressed figures walking or on horseback, no huntsmen and no coaches, instead in their place we find two rustic figures by a farmyard cart.

The dedication on this print reads: 'The ancient Seat of the PARKER FAMILY & now belonging to LORD BORINGDON to whom this plate is respectfully inscribed'. Six

years later Lord Boringdon (of Boringdon) was further honoured with the title of Viscount Boringdon and Earl of Morley, significantly this time, however, the full title is now Viscount Boringdon of North Molton.

Throughout the nineteenth century Boringdon was let to a succession of local farmers, including James and John Thomas Butland, James Adams and in the 1880s and 1890s George and Alfred Gillard. Within the estate the deer park was still maintained and used by the Parkers but the house itself was adapted to its new use as a farmhouse. One of the many consequences being the removal of the grand staircase 'to suit the requirements of farmers'.

Meanwhile, over at Saltram, life was not all roses; in 1864 Albert Edmund Parker had succeeded to a 'severely encumbered estate' and part of Saltram itself was let to a tenant, James Hartman esq., for a number of years. Albert Edmund himself spent much time at his London address in Prince's Gardens. Born in 1843, Albert was a lord-in-waiting to Queen Victoria between 1868 and 1874. For the first half of the 1880s he was Under-Secretary for War and from 1889 to 1905 he chaired various committees in the House of Lords where he also sat as Deputy Speaker. Active also in the affairs of Devon as the 3rd Earl of Morley, he saw Saltram and Boringdon into the twentieth century.

Boringdon remained a Parker property until the 1920s and in the decades that followed, despite a number of ambitious plans for the place, it was allowed to all but fall completely down. Fortunately, however, it was saved in 1987 and, now extended and open as a hotel and restaurant, has had much of its former dignity restored and has become one of the city's more impressive historical landmarks.

Plympton Station

It was in 1848 that the South Devon Railway first brought trains this far west. Originally called the Plymouth, Devon and Exeter Railway Company, that title was restyled back in 1843, some seven years after Brunel had first been asked to survey a suitable route from Exeter to Plymouth. The idea of providing Plymouth with a rail link using steam locomotives had first been discussed the year after the country's first such line, from Stockton to Darlington, was opened in 1825, however, little was done about it over the next ten years.

By the summer of 1847 the difficult coastal stretch around Dawlish and Teignmouth had been negotiated and South Devon's atmospheric railway had reached Totnes. Work on the line west of Totnes had already begun but the atmospheric railway was destined to go no further and, once the Plym had easily been bridged, the first test train from Totnes to Laira ran past this point on 27th April 1848.

Laira Green was at that stage the end of the line, as there were problems negotiating the path of the railway north of Plymouth itself. For the people of Plymouth itself, though, none of this mattered, they turned out in their thousands to see the *Pisces* at rest at Laira and when, a week or so later, on Friday 5th May, the line was officially opened for passenger traffic, tens of thousands arrived to witness the spectacle as the *Pisces*, this time driven by its designer Daniel Gooch, steamed down the west bank of the Plym.

The day was declared a public holiday in Plymouth but there were no civic celebrations, the authorities somewhat sullenly perhaps choosing to wait until the line into Millbay, and therefore Plymouth itself, was open. In the event this

was to be another year away and in the meantime Plympton (or Colebrook) Station had been completed and was up and running.

Opened to passenger traffic on Thursday 15th June 1848 it took in its first goods train three months later on the 13th September, exactly one week after the last atmospheric train ran, further eastward along the South Devon line.

In the early days the locomotives on this line were mainly of the Leo class, like the *Pisces* with its five foot drive wheel, engines like the one depicted here with its small wheels were more usually used for shunting, although possibly this is a piece of 'artistic licence'. Certainly the figure with the flag must either have been a giant or drawn out of scale and the platforms would not have been above carriage level. The carriages would, however, have been box-like in their design, rather similar to the old horse drawn carriages and like the South Devon goods vans painted a deep chocolate brown.

The livery for the locomotives, as directed by the company, was different, though, here the frames were brown but the boilers and wheels were green and the lining black, picked out with red. The nameplates were not painted, they were brass as was the finishing on the splashers and handrails. Another of the details this picture affords us, and again one which is out of scale, is the positioning of the signals. It was common practice for each station to be protected by two signals, one at each end, one for 'down' trains, one for 'up' trains (the one here coming from Exeter is therefore a 'down' train). The signals were very simple affairs with a crossbar mounted on a revolving pole, a disc

on the crossbar at right angles to it. If the disc was facing the oncoming train all was clear, while danger was indicated by the crossbar being fixed full face.

On the locomotives themselves two whistles were used to give signals, one with a deep tone was used by the driver to indicate that he wished the guards to apply their brakes, the other, the higher pitched whistle, was used for everything else, including the two short blasts that was the instruction to release the brakes.

Generally the South Devon line was a fairly smooth running one, Plympton Station was, however, the scene of two of the more serious incidents that occurred on the line. In June 1849 the *Goliah* had just passed through the station and begun to climb Hemerdon Bank when its boiler blew up. The explosion was heard three miles away and the driver was thrown several feet into a neighbouring garden. He was dazed but otherwise alright. Unfortunately the fireman, fireman Evans did not escape as lightly, there were no other casualties though.

The other incident, also recounted in RH Gregory's book on the South Devon Railway, occurred 17 years later. On the night of 13th September 1866 the *Brutus* was halted at Hemerdon because it had a bearing which had run hot, a relief train was summoned and the *Brutus* was uncoupled from its night goods vans and left at Plympton. Some time later the night mail train, not due to stop here, steamed over Hemerdon Bank and saw the danger signal (a red light at night) but was unable to stop in time to avoid a collision. Meanwhile the crew of the *Brutus*, sensing that a collision was inevitable, released their brake, set the engine in motion and jumped clear.

The first coach of the mail was derailed along with the locomotive *Falcon* meanwhile the *Brutus* steamed towards Plymouth, unmanned. A message passed down the line by telegraph ensured that it had a clear run and it eventually came to rest embedded in the station cloakroom. The driver of the mail train was fined £5 and his fireman was dismissed.

The South Devon Railway era ended when it amalgamated with the Great Western Railway in 1878, Plympton Station, meanwhile, continued to serve the area until March 1959 although it played only a very minor role in later years. Still used for goods traffic until 1964, today there is nothing left of this small station, however, the view from the bridge above this site remains little changed from Hake's depiction of it sometime around 1850.

Plympton St Mary

Plympton St Mary 'is an extensive parish, on the east side of the vale of the river Plym, from 3 to 5 miles N.E. of Plymouth. It has no village of its own name, but includes those of RIDGEWAY, UNDERWOOD, and COLEBROOK, and the hamlets of Hemerdon, Sparkwell, Venton and part of Lee Mill Bridge. It includes the seats of Saltram, Newnham Park, Furzdon, Beechwood, Hemerdon House, Goodamore, Chaddlewood &c., and many scattered farm-houses some of them about four miles N.N.E. of the church, among the hills on the southern borders of Dartmoor Forest.'

So began a description of Plympton St Mary published in 1850 when a little under 3,000 people lived within this parish. The South Devon Railway had only just cut its path through Plympton and there were signs that a new element of prosperity was following in its wake. The Boringdon Hotel was built right opposite the station entrance, Mill Street was renamed Station Road and at Higher Ridgeway there were the newly built houses of South Devon Place. Houses which for the most part were occupied by elderly people with private means who could afford maidservants.

The Railway brought local employment of all kinds, there was a rail policeman (in the early days of basic mechanical signalling, traffic control was aided by men with flags giving hand signals) living with James Yabsley and his wife in Beechwood Lodge and in Dark Street Lane lived John Andrew and his family. Founder of the firm Andrew and Denning, John Andrew had mapped a long section of the South Devon Railway for Brunel.

One of Andrew's neighbours in Dark Street Lane (believed to be one of the oldest thoroughfares in the area) was the Reverend Coppard, vicar of St Mary's Church. Originally from the south east of England, William Isaac Coppard MA, had taken up his appointment at St Mary's back in 1817 when he was just 31. A popular local figure, he married a Plympton girl and stayed here, watching more than one generation grow up in the 48 years he served until his death in 1865.

In the later years of his incumbency the church underwent a major restoration, however, amongst the local community, the Reverend William Coppard was principally remembered for his unflinching work during the Cholera epidemic of 1832. At its height, in the summer of that year, in Underwood alone, 200 out of the 300 people living there were affected and some 30 of them died.

William Coppard kept a diary throughout this sorry time and it paints a very dark picture indeed of the lives of some of his parishioners. One family he visited were in cottage which no one else could be persuaded to go near; in it William Parsons lived with his wife and five children, between them they shared a room, measuring about 16 by 14 feet, and two beds. Parsons was lying ill, there was a terrible stench in the room, the overall condition of which the vicar described as 'truly appalling'. Upon examination, Coppard found a drain 'choked with every description of filth' under the slate floor and arranged to have a mason come and clean the drain and whitewash the walls of the rooms.

Other accounts sound equally squalid but everyone worked hard to minister the ad hoc medicines which included castor oil, tincture of rhubarb and laudanum, to the afflicted. Meanwhile, others willingly agreed to participate in blood transfusions to help save their neighbours. In those days the donor and recipient had to lie side by side as the transfusion took place.

By the end of October it was reported that the disease had now left the parish and the Rev Coppard arranged for a slate headstone to go on the graves of the victims simply bearing the date – 1832.

In contrast, of course, to the areas of poverty within the parish, there were the aforementioned comfortable country seats and it was the families who occupied these that played a large part in the internal refurbishment of the church.

During the restoration in 1860 Harriet, the wife of the second Earl of Morley gave a new pulpit to replace the old stone one in the chancel, then the third Earl, Albert Edmund Parker, of Saltram, donated the East window in memory of his father, the second Earl.

One of the richly stained windows in the north aisle was given around 1865 in memory of Admiral Woollcombe of Hemerdon, while the other was given five years earlier in memory of Katherine and Barbara Treby of Goodamore. Meanwhile, in the south aisle chapel, the Strode (or Courtenay) Chapel, the window above the ancient tomb of Richard Strode, was given by GS Strode of Newnham Park in 1863, in memory of his parents. Another nineteenth-century donation was the reredos given in 1845 by Colonel Symons of Chaddlewood.

There were of course other gifts to the church, from people other than the local gentry; WH Osmond, who had amassed a fortune in Australia, gave a window in the south wall and the Lewis organ, which cost almost £1000 in 1850. There is a window too to William Coppard in the tower and the later reredos was given in memory of the Rev Merton Smith, the well respected vicar who arrived here in 1873 and whose incumbency ended tragically when he was killed in an accident in the Pyrenees in 1884.

Merton Smith, incidentally, succeeded Edward Hunt who made his home in the Ridgeway, Smith's successor meanwhile, J Mercer Cox was the first to enjoy the purpose-built vicarage at Colebrook.

Plympton Priory

'In the churchyard are some remains of the Priory of Plympton St. Mary worthy of notice; among them, on what was the north side of the building, is a small door of beautiful workmanship, having on each side a twisted column; and on the south side in a garden, nearly enveloped with foliage, is a round-headed door, having a broad band of chevron work, and resting on two slender columns with ornamented capitals. ... Besides these the churchyard is strewn with fragments of clustered columns, rich capitals, embattlements, and various other pieces of sculpture, which give inadiquate idea of the original splendour of the building.'

'But where now is the venerable pile?
Where all his skill the architect display'd
Alas! in wrecks it lies.'

So ran part of the description of Plympton that appeared in an edition of a journal called the *Antiquarian and Topographical Cabinet* published in 1809. On the title page appeared this accompanying illustration. Sixty years later this same doorway, apparently now without any door was discovered 'after a diligent search ... encased with many coats of fine plaster' by a local architect, James Hine.

Hine identified this doorway as being the original entrance to the cellar of the priory, which, he said, was located under the refectory, and the refectory was, he pointed out, by no means an unimportant portion of the priory '. . . Here the monks, according to the seasons, had their one or two meals a day; the usual allowance being 'one white loaf, another loaf called Trequarter, a dish called General, another dish of flesh or fish called Pitance, three potells of beer daily, or three silver half-pence' for the teetotallers. And among the many distinguished guests entertained here over the years – Edward the black Prince, who dined here in 1348.

A victim of Henry VIII's Dissolution of the Monasteries, the last Prior, John Howe, surrendered the Priory and its possessions to one of the King's commissioneres on 1st March 1539. A few years later Leland, one of Henry VIII's chaplains, reported that the priory had been destroyed 'the lower and the first buildings almost clean choked with the sand that the Torey brook bringeth down from the tin works.' Thus ended a tradition of monastic use that stretched back over six centuries. The long serving Victorian Vicar of St. Mary's, J. Mercer-Cox, speculated that a

religious house was probably founded here sometime during the ninth century, the century that 'Devon was added by conquest to the Kingdom of Wessex. Previously it formed a part of what was then known as West Wales.' In his subsequent handing out of land the conquering King, Egbert, took care to keep Plympton for himself.

Founded soon afterwards, for over two centuries Plympton Priory was conducted along secular lines. Then in 1121 Bishop Warwist, supposedly unhappy that members of the clergy here were contracting clandestine marriages, decided to enforce stricter discipline and replace the secular clergy with regular canons.

Bishop Warwist's new Priory was dedicated to the Blessed Virgin Mary and St. Peter and St. Paul. The Priory arms simply feature the keys of St. Peter crossed with the sword of St. Paul. An old stone bearing these arms can today be seen above a Norman arch which now serves as a window in a part of the quaint 100-year-old twelve-house developement known as Old Priory. This archway has been identified as the old refectory doorway and is to be found in the first of the houses of Old Priory. Known as Tower House, this building features many 'bits' of the old priory refectory in and around it and indeed Mercer-Cox, writing towards the end of last century, claimed that this structure – 'upwards of twenty five years ago' had its roof raised and was 'altered in other respects to suit modern requirements.' Before the alteration 'it was' he said 'possible to make out the outline of the old refectory with its original fireplace, windows and roof, all of an Early English character ... Below it a Norman undercroft or cellar, sixty one feet six inches in length by fourteen feet in breadth.'

Today a great grand-daughter of the man thought to have effected these alterations and also to be responsible for building the other dwellings of 'Old Priory', Herbert Williams, lives in 'Tower House'. Her sister and a nephew, both trustees of 'Old Priory' live in two of the other houses.

Quite how long a Tower House has stood here, though, is unclear. There is record of the 'New Tower' in 1562 and mention of 'Towre House' not long afterwards. In truth there are many mysteries surrounding Plympton Priory and many look set to remain unsolved, however, it is just possible that a dig being carried out immediately to the east of the 'Old Priory' developement may just reveal something of note before the developers move in and obliterate completely another part of one of the most historic sites in the area.

Mount Priory

Here lived, 100 years ago, John Moolenburgh Minter MD, FRCS 'honorary physician to the Queen, surgeon to HRH Prince of Wales and inspector general of Hospitals.' However, although he still styled himself thus, Dr. Minter had in fact been retired for some years and indeed had only moved to Plympton after his retirement in 1875.

Sixty years old when he retired, John Minter had joined the Navy earlier, the year Queen Victoria came to the throne. As assistant-surgeon of the *Implacable* the young doctor saw first taste of action in 1840 on the Coast of Syria and was awarded a medal for his efforts. Eight years later he saw active service again as surgeon of the *Medea* when the ship was involved in an attack on 'three large piratical prows' in Tytham Bay, on the China Station. However, probably the most significant action he was involved in took place in 1852. Dr Minter was then surgeon of the *Fox* a vessel which witnessed the capture of Rangoon, an event which led to the British annexation of Lower Burma. The whole development of Burma, which was under British Rule from 1824 to 1948, really dates from this action. A troubled country in the early part of the nineteenth century, there had been an earlier Anglo-Burmese conflict between 1824 and 1826. Burma was at this time being ruled by one of two successive kings deposed for insanity; while the king on the throne in 1852 when the British took Rangoon was more interested in watching cock fights than dealing with affairs of state. Dr Minter was honourably mentioned in despatches for his services to the wounded at Rangoon, both on shore and at sea.

He was later promoted to deputy inspector general in 1859 and then inspector general of hospitals in 1872. In the meantime he had been appointed honorary physician to the Queen. By this time the last of Victoria's nine grandchildren had been born, the last being Beatrice (born 1857).

John Minter lived at Mount Priory for almost 16 years until his death on 15th December 1891. Mrs Minter, who remained at Mount Priory for sometime afterwards,

received telegrams from Her Majesty the Queen and His Royal Highness the Prince of Wales and also from the Duke of Edinburgh (Victoria's fourth child and second son, Alfred) who sent his carriage. It was Alfred who had earlier unveiled the foundation stone for the resiting of Smeaton's Tower on Plymouth Hoe in 1884.

The funeral service was conducted in the church overlooked by Mount Priory, St Mary's, by the vicar, the Reverend J Mercer Cox and a great number of local dignitaries attended the service, including the deceased's son Ernest, a naval surgeon like his father.

Following the Minter's occupation of Mount Priory, the house changed hands a couple of times prior to the outbreak of the First World War, during which time it was, strangely enough, used as a Red Cross Hospital. At the end of the War this extended Georgian mansion was 100 years old. For the first 50 years or so of its existence it had served as the home of the first William Evens senior, then William Hole Evens junior, his son. In 1870 the son sold the house 'with its garden, coach house, stables, lawn, field etc.', to William Derry of Plymouth and Ernest Derry lived here until the Minters moved in.

Home for over 30 years this century to Lt Col Frank Roff Phillips, DSO, in more recent times it served as an hotel and for the last 15 years or so it was known as Rentokil House, as it was adopted as the local headquarters of this national pest control firm. In 1968, Old Priory School was built in the grounds and now, 20 years on, twelve four-bedroomed self build detached houses are being constructed on the site of the house itself as just a few months ago Rentokil moved out and the house itself was demolished.

Plympton St Maurice

'The evening being on the wane I quitted Kitley and, passing through Brixton . . . I made my approach to Plympton Earl: from the descent of a long and steep hill I had presented to me the most extensive and beautiful view. The more distant countryside was finely wooded – and the towns of Plympton, Ridgeway and Plympton Mary lay beneath me, so that I could discriminate every feature they possessed. I saw at one spot the remains of a monastery and its richly ornamented tower, at another those relics of an old castle tottering with age, and nearer to me the archades of a building which is a schoolhouse, rose by the munificence of Elizeus Hele about the middle of the last century.'

In this way the Rev John Swete, the cleric who liked to travel with his sketch book and watercolours, described his visit to Plympton one summer evening in 1792. The scene that confronted him that day would have been much the same as that drawn by William Westall 36 years later and shown here after it had been engraved for publication by E Finden in 1828.

Plympton Earl was then a compact little community housed within just 200 acres of land, unlike its sprawling neighbour Plympton St Mary which was spread across some 10,000 acres of this corner of Devon. For all that, though, Plympton Earl, with a population of a little under 600, was bigger than any of the villages found within the larger parish – Ridgeway, Colebrook or Underwood.

As Swete described it: 'the town of Plympton consists principally of one street of no inconsiderable length' then he added 'it hath more good houses in it than almost any private town in the county and in point of situation it will yield to none.'

The Reverend Swete spent that night in Plympton, which at that time sported two inns – the 'London' and the 'Devonshire' – which, like so much of the property in Plympton St Maurice, was owned by Paul Ourry Treby. Indeed the four orchards in the foreground of this view – Marsh, Alcock's, Cistern and Higgin's were also Treby land; as was most of what lay east of George Lane and Longbrook across to what was then the boundary of the parish, Cherry Park Lane and which has since been renamed Yeoman's Way.

In those days this was all open fields, meadows, woods and orchards but now built-up streets, with names that have their origins in the history of the area, occupy much of this land. Here are Treby Road, Hele Gardens, St Thomas Close, St Maurice Close and Erle Gardens to name but a few.

The thirteenth century church here was originally dedicated to St Thomas but for some reason it was rededicated after 1538 to St Maurice. In addition to being known as Plympton St Maurice, this area has also been called Plympton Earl, in time corrupted to Erle, on account of this being the town belonging to the Earl of Devon.

Richard de Redvers, a descendent of Sieur Reviers Baldwin of Moeles, who was in turn related to and a companion of William the Conqueror, acquired Plympton and other lands in the county and was made Earl of Devon by Henry I soon after he had succeeded to the throne in 1100. Much of Devon had been in the family since the conquest and Richard appears to have been a court favourite of the king.

Although the mound is believed to pre-date Norman times, Plympton castle itself is thought to have been completed in Richard's time. Sadly, however, the castle was sacked sometime around 1135 after Richard's son Baldwin had taken up arms in Exeter and declared for Henry's only surviving, legitimate, offspring, Matilda. Standing against Stephen, Henry's nephew had usurped the throne, because, it is said, there had been a disagreement with the king over a manor which Baldwin had asked for. It was a disagreement that was to cost him dearly, for ultimately Baldwin, although spared his life, was banished from the kingdom.

The name Hele, of course, brings us back to the school which was established as consequence of the will of Elize Hele. Born around 1560, Elize Hele had the misfortune to see his only child, Walter, die at the tender age of twelve, some twelve years before he himself died in 1636 and it is thought that this was what prompted his charitable bequests. The school was founded by the two surviving donees of the will, John Maynard and Elize Stert and it was built between 1663–1671. Plympton's most famous son, Joshua Reynolds (1723–92) was a pupil here, while his father, the Reverend Samuel Reynolds was a headmaster of the school.

In the middle of the nineteenth century the Reverend George Patey was headmaster here and, although a capable scholar, he seems to have been unable to maintain the high reputation of the school and it was over-taken by local developments in education. It did, however, limp on until 1903 when it was, for the first time, closed. A fine building with its original character still in tact, it has since seen service in a number of educational and other related capacities.

The character of Plympton St Maurice itself also still survives, although now on three sides the area has now been greatly developed leaving only the southern aspect unspoilt.

Plympton St Maurice

It was just to the left in the foreground of this view, off Dark Street Lane, that the Honourable George Treby intended to form an entrance to his grand house, seen here to the left of the castle remains on the mound. The path of this new road was to cut through the Castle Hayes fields, across what is now George Lane to the house. In the event George Treby died before this could be done and his successors left things as they were.

The Trebys were the major landowners in Plympton St Maurice, at the end of the eighteenth century they owned half of the land in private hands within the parish, most of which had not been built upon; although in order to lay out the house and grounds George's father, Lord Chief Justice Sir George Treby, had bought and cleared a number of houses on either side of Maudlyn Street (George Lane).

Sir George Treby spent some time prior to his death acquiring land from various local landowners with a view to creating a mansion on a site he understood to be near his birthplace (the old house of the manor of Plympton Grange). Unfortunately, however, Sir George died in 1700 when he was 58 before he had made much progress with the actual building and it was left to George jnr to complete the work.

George Treby was only 16 when his father died and it was some time before the threads were picked up in earnest, the house eventually being completed around 1720 when the stables were finished, trees were planted and walkways laid out. Constructed with Portland stone and brick, it is interesting to note that many of the bricks used in the house and grounds, particularly those making up the boundary walls and garden walls, were made on site; the clay coming from a field east of Longbrook Street. Long afterwards known as Brick Field, Buller Close now stands on its site.

The Honourable George Treby died in 1841 leaving two sons, George and George Hele both of whom died without leaving a successor and so the house and the many Treby lands passed on to the three surviving sisters Charity, Dorothea and Anne. Plympton House and its immediate surroundings passed to Charity who had married Paul Ourry Ourry by whom she had a son, Paul. This Paul took the name of Treby and therefore became Paul Ourry Treby and, although by far the major landowner in the area, chose not to live at Plympton House instead opting, after his mother's death, to move to Goodamoor in the neighbouring parish of Plympton St Mary, where his mother had lived for many years.

So it came to pass that when Samuel Prout sketched this view in 1809 the great Treby residence was in the state of being let. No-one stayed here long, however, and for some forty years it stood empty until a Dr Duck took on the lease and opened it as a private lunatic asylum.

In 1876 the heirs of Paul Treby sold the house to Copleston Lopes Radcliffe who bought the land like the Trebys before him with the intention of clearing the site and building afresh, this time, however, the plan was to develop the site and the adjacent lands as a housing estate. Once again fate intervened and Radcliffe died before he could execute his plans and his son, Copleston Lopes Pollexfen Radcliffe, sold the house to Dr Charles Aldridge who continued to operate a lunatic asylum there. Today it is run by the Sisters of St Peter's Convent as a nursing home.

There were about 700 inhabitants of Plympton St Maurice in 1809, when this view was produced; doubtless they all knew or at least were aware of each other and doubtless most of them would have turned out for 'Games, Pastimes and Diversions' held on the castle each year to coincide with the election of the new Mayor. A handbill of 1807 advertising the programme for 14th and 15th July (Tuesday and Wednesday) included, boasted such attractions as 'Wrestling for a Purse of Guineas', 'Cudgel-Playing for a Silver Cup', 'A Jingling Match' plus 'Grinning, Bobbing and Diving with other innocent amusements producing fun and merriment'.

Seven guineas were to go to the wrestling champion, two to the runner up and seven shillings (35p) to every 'stander'. The rewards for cudgelling, fighting with short thick sticks, were more modest, only three guineas to the winner and a pound to the runner up; while whichever of the 'thirteen smart dashing lads' emerged successful from the jingling won himself a hat worth a guinea.

One wonders who would have taken part and who would have won, certainly Jack Russell, remembered as the hunting parson and breeder of the dog that bears his name, was at the Grammar School around this time and amongst his early achievements he describes himself as being 'Cock of the walk' after beating one of the Bulteel boys in a fight.

Life was, of course, a little different in those days, it is said that the newly elected Mayor traditionally supplied a bull for baiting on the castle and we also read that cock-fighting was a feature of Easter Monday celebrations on the castle until it was made illegal. Another illegal diversion in those days was duelling and it is said that one of the first persons to be buried in the newly consecrated grounds of the church yard was Lieutenant William Hindes, who was mortally wounded on Saturday 8th March 1817 after unsuccessfully fighting a duel with Lieutenant Gilbert Conroy near St Mary's bridge. An unhappy tale all round, Conroy and his second were found guilty of wilful murder at the subsequent inquest.

Fore Street

The fortunes of Plympton St Maurice appear to have gone into decline somewhat around the middle of the nineteenth century, the slide apparently beginning with the passing of the Reform Act in 1832.

There had been MPs representing Plympton in the very first Parliament about which full information exists, back in 1295 under Edward I and a full list survives giving details of the borough's representation over the next 500 years, a list that includes the celebrated architect Sir Christopher Wren. It was however very much a classic 'rotten borough' and it is likely that many of Plympton's MPs never even saw the place they were supposed to represent, Wren included.

Having said that the local gentry, in whose pocket the borough invariably was, regularly had themselves elected and the list features various Strodes, Heles, Drakes, Slannings and Fortescues in the seventeenth century and Edgcumbes, Ourrys and Trebys in the eighteenth and early nineteenth century.

The election process was very simple, only freemen had the vote and the freemen themselves were elected by the mayor and aldermen. No qualification was required, rather the privilege was a gift and those selected were chosen from among the friends and acquaintances of the mayor and his council companions and from the local gentry and magistrates extending well out into parts of Devon and Cornwall. Inevitably of course such freemen could be relied upon to vote in line with the wishes of the patrons of the borough and it is no surprise to learn that in the eighteenth and early nineteenth century there was a member of the Treby family in the mayoral seat on 24 occasions (14 times between 1807–1854).

From time to time sons of freemen endeavoured to assert their supposed rights but each time the mayor would turn them down, and the number of freemen who actually voted was never very great. In the 1803 election the candidates were Edward Golding, of Maiden Early, Berkshire, Paul Treby Treby and Thomas North, Lord Graves. Lord Graves was nominated by Captain Palmer, a prime mover in the case for sons of freemen, and in the event Lord Graves polled the same number of votes as the other two candidates – 23 – but the mayor refused 22 of Lord Graves's votes on the grounds that they were those of the sons of freemen and had therefore never been admitted.

Not only did the Reform Act go some way to eliminating this corrupt process it also redrew many constituency boundaries and Plympton lost its Parliamentary representation and with it some of the prestige and important financial patronage ebbed away from the mayor and his council. Without it the impetus for maintaining and looking after the guildhall also seems to have waned. The situation was compounded when the various acts were passed establishing a county police force and the Court of Aldermen and Common Council felt that they no longer had 'any franchises or immunities granted by the borough charters of any value to the inhabitants of Plympton' and that therefore 'the interests of the inhabitants would be best consulted by suspending operations of the charter, by refraining from the election of a chief magistrate in the year 1860'.

And so from that year to this no mayor has been elected for Plympton and two years later the old court, cells and other rooms were removed and a new hall capable of seating 300 people took its place. A far cry indeed from the heady days of this building at the beginning of the century when the young Duke of Clarence, the future William IV, used to come here to the guildhall and stay overnight in Plympton for the grand balls held here.

The situation in the corridors of lost power was echoed elsewhere in St Maurice, the grammar school was also struggling and even the population figures themselves went into decline. Generally over the century the population of St Maurice all but doubled from 604 in 1801 to 1,117 in 1901 but this was by no means a steady growth pattern. The 1841 census return showed 933 people living here in 195 houses, but ten years later that figure had dropped by exactly 100 and it was to be more than twenty years before there was any increase on that 1841 statistic.

In the middle of the nineteenth century parts of St Maurice, like Higher Ridgeway were already showing signs of becoming a popular retirement haven and this slight swing towards the more elderly perhaps partly explains the lack of population increase around this time.

In addition to which St Maurice did not have the same proportion of farm workers, quarrymen and general tradesmen as neighbouring Colebrook and Underwood and there were only two sizeable industries here, brewing and tanning. The aptly named Tom Brown, who lived further along Fore Street, employed twelve men in his tannery, while Henry Crews, Maltster and Brewer, who lived in one of the houses opposite the guildhall, was nominally the largest employer in the town with a staff of thirteen.

Saltram

'Saltram, the very beautiful demesne of John Parker, Viscount and Baron Boringdon, and first Earl of Morley, extends its 'pensile woods', along the eastern shore of the Lara, about four miles north-eastward from Plymouth. Here, 'Every step':

Awakes a varying scene, by Nature's hand
Fair sketch'd, of leaf crown'd hills, and flowery vales,
And lawns of fadeless emerald:-
'But on those groves
Of Saltram rests the eye, which fringe thy flood,
Sweet Lara.' (Carrington's Dartmoor)

In the reign of Charles the First, this estate was the property of Sir James Bagg, Knt. of Plymouth; but having become forfeited to the crown under an extent, it was purchased in 1712, after one or two intermediate ownerships, by George Parker, Esq., a forefather of the present Earl of Morley. John, his eldest surviving son and successor, married Catherine, daughter of John, Earl Paulett (secretary of state to Queen Anne), and was induced by that lady to transfer the family seat from Boringdon to Saltram, and to erect the expansive mansion now standing there. 'Great improvements have been made in the interior by the present Earl, who has likewise considerably improved the entrance front by the addition of a portico, (as shewn in the accompanying print) from a design by Mr Foulston. On the ground floor is the principal suite of apartments, which is most elegantly fitted up, and contains a very choice collection of paintings, by the best masters ancient and modern.' (Britton and Brayley 1828).

The stately mansion 'shewn here' was erected in the middle of the eighteenth century and was constructed around the manor house that the infamous James Bagge had built here at the beginning of the seventeenth century.

Quite what was here prior to that is unclear; the name 'Saltram' dates back to at least 1263 and fourteen years before that we find reference to the fuller title 'Salterham'. This name suggests that whatever buildings there were here, one or other of them was occupied by salt workers.

As Plymouth, or Sutton as it was then, was a community that relied fairly heavily on fishing for its livelihood, Leland described as being an 'Inhabitation for Fischars' around the time of Henry II (1154–89), and as it appears that often more fish were caught than were needed to serve local needs, then the rest would ideally have been salted down to help preserve it, prior to transportation or whatever.

Saltworks were recorded at Bere Ferrers and, across the water from Saltash, at Tamerton in the Domesday survey; even closer, for Plymouth and Saltram, was the saltworks, recorded at the same time, at Eggbuckland.

Salt was collected by holding back sea water in shallow pans and waiting for the sun to evaporate the water (such practices are still employed in parts of Brittany where the sun is stronger than here. Indeed in the middle ages consignments were brought into Plymouth from La Rochelle) and although it is now difficult to imagine it, tidal waters used to reach along what is now the Parkway to within 400 yards or so of Eggbuckland Church.

Perhaps some of those salt workers lived across the Plym at Saltram – there was also a Little Saltram, a farm which stood where Salisbury Road School now stands. Coincidentally perhaps, the main route to Saltash used to pass through what is now part of the grounds of Saltram across the Ebb Ford (Efford) of the Plym up the road behind Crabtree and it was known, even in recent years, as Saltash Lane.

But to return to the nineteenth century when this view was sketched, the first Earl of Morley had only recently received his title (1815) only 31 years after his father had been raised to the peerage as Baron Boringdon (1784). As if to commemorate his newly acquired status, as a symbol perhaps of this further honour, the Earl had the Three Town's most acclaimed architect of the day transform the entrance of the house with the addition of this now familiar portico and the family coat of arms carved in the gable above.

Foulston's work was executed in 1818 and the two sphinxes that formerly stood either side of the door were moved to the orangery entrance where they stayed until 1976 – they are currently outside the west door of the mansion.

Given to the National Trust in 1957, members of the Morley family still reside at Saltram although the Earl himself (the 6th) lives at Yelverton. Parts of the house, little changed over the years, and the delightful gardens, are now open to the public, however, the gardens, which at one time were designed to offer as spectacular views as possible of the surrounding countryside, have more recently been redesigned so that the new developments that have taken place all around this great country house are obscured by trees, hedges and other natural devices available to the landscape gardener.

Laira Bridge

'At the head of a branch of the sea, called the Catwater, which forms the westernmost inlet of Plymouth harbour, is a lake-like expanse named the LARA; probably form the "larus", or gull, by which bird its lucid waters are still numerously frequented, though not so abundantly as in the "olden times", ere the massive tors of Dartmoor were subjected to the iron grasp of commerce, and the rail-way and granite works were established on the northern banks of this estuary. Into the upper Lara, the "sylvan Plym" pours its "vagrant stream," the south side is fringed by the groves of Saltram, the splendid seat of the Earl of Morley, to whose public spirit and sagacious mind the Lara, or Lary Bridge, is indebted for its erection: this structure crosses the western part of the strait, at a short distance from the noble limestone cliffs of Oreston, and along its northern shore extends the Plymouth embankment road, which unites with the old road to Exeter, by Ivy Bridge and Ashburton.'

So began Britton and Brayley's glowing account of the new bridge here over the Plym, written for *Illustrated guide to Devonshire and Cornwall* published in 1832. Certainly they had every reason to be full of enthusiasm, the bridge was after all only a few years old and was at that time the second longest iron bridge in the country.

The debt acknowledged to the Earl of Morley was not only one of vision but also a financial one, for he it was who funded the project. The credit for its construction, however, should go to the young engineer who had also drawn up plans for a suspension bridge across the Tamar at Saltash, James Meadows Rendel. Indeed the original plan for 'Lara' too was for a suspension bridge, however 'different circumstances led to an abandonment of the first site proposed' and the 1823 Act of Parliament that approved the construction of this proposed suspension bridge was amended the follow-

ing year to allow for the building of the structure shown here.

Doubtless this all would have come as quite a surprise to Mr. Alexander whom the Earl of Morley first approached about building a bridge here back in 1807. Described as a 'successful engineer', Alexander concluded that because of the unfavourable bed of the river the erection of such a structure would, if it was practical at all, be so enormously expensive that the idea was then abandoned.

In the meantime the Earl, being the proprietor of the ancient ferry between Oreston and Cattedown, concentrated his efforts on improving this mobile link which he achieved by the introduction of his 'flying bridge'; a ferry boat open at both ends which was impelled across the water by an iron chain. Capable of carrying wagons, carts, carriages and other vehicles with their horses attached, this greatly improved Plymouth's link with Wembury, Brixton, Yealmpton and the South Hams.

The 'Flying Bridge' was nevertheless susceptible to spring tides and bad weather and in 1822 Lord Morley commissioned the young Rendel, who had worked with Thomas Telford and who had settled in this area, to consider the practicality of constructing a bridge across the Laira.

Like his predecessor, Rendel found that the river bed indeed posed the major problems '. . . On boring in several places, it was found that the substratum was schistos, or slate rock, lying nearly horizontal, at a depth of 80 feet below high water. The superstratum consists of a mixture of granite and sand, deposited by the Plym, and alluvial matter brought in by the tides, which having accumulated to the depth of 60 feet on average, a considerable portion of the basin is, at low water, left dry' (JM Rendel *Particulars of the Construction of the Lary Bridge*).

In order to combat this problem, Rendel created a false bottom to the bridge which ran to a depth of 70 feet below the bridge. Piles hammered into the ground ended nine feet below the spring low tide mark and these were levelled off underwater by labourers working in a wooden diving bell, said to be the first instance of its kind, with light being through lenses fixed at the top. The men then paved the spaces between the pile heads with masonry.

The limestone used in the construction of the bridge, incidentally, all came from the neighbouring quarries which then belonged to the Earl of Morley, Messrs Johnson of the Plymouth Granite works were the contractors. The main ironwork meanwhile came from Coalbrookdale where the first ever iron bridge was made. The total cost of the scheme in the end was around £10,000 and the bridge was opened on the 14th July 1827, 'on which day her Royal Highness the Duchess of Clarence [afterwards Queen Adelaide], and suite, first passed over it on her way to Plymouth'.

Such was the spirit of the time and the sense of classical achievement that the inscription, carved in granite, commemorating the completion, was in Latin. But well the Earl and his architect may have had reason to congratulate themselves for the bridge stood for over 130 years ultimately handling all manner and volume of transport that doubtless no one could have foreseen all those years ago.

In the end, however, the strain on the framework and problems of settlement brought about a 10 mph speed limit and a 12 ton load restriction on the bridge. In 1957 the City Engineer was instructed to design a new bridge and work began on it two years later. The new bridge was opened by Lord Chesham, Parliamentary Secretary to the Minister of Transport, on the 1st of June 1961, two months after the Tamar Road bridge.

Oreston

This view of Laira Bridge from Oreston was drawn in the middle of the nineteenth century by Philip Mitchell and subsequently produced as a lithographic print by the artist William Spreat. The hills beyond the bridge show no signs of development. In the foreground, however, Oreston appears as a crowded little village on the water's edge and although the community was much smaller than it is now it was nevertheless a thriving area.

Writing in 1859 for the *Geologist* about the *Ossiferous Fissures* (bone caves) at Oreston, W Pengelly described this place as 'essentially a limestone village, being based on, built of, and surrounded by limestone; its chief prospect consists of the limestone-hills and quarries whence the stone for the celebrated Plymouth breakwater was hewn, and its only trade is the exportation of limestone.'

The Oreston quarries had been opened to furnish the materials for the Breakwater on the 7th August 1812 and that this development had a considerable impact on the size of the local population is evidenced by the membership registers of the Oreston Methodist society. First recorded in 1798 when there were 14 members, up until 1813 the numbers fluctuated mainly between 14 and 22, although in 1811 they dropped as low as seven. By 1816, however, they had risen dramatically to 74 and this provided the impetus to build the first church here on land purchased from the Duke of Bedford.

Known as the old Chievely Hall it was built, at a cost of £816 and to seat 306 persons, in 1818, the year after a similar construction at Turnchapel had been erected. Registered for 'Religious Worship of Protestant Dissenters' in 1854, in 1886 it was described by the Plymouth Methodist Circuit as 'the most weather beaten building in the weather beaten village'. The decision then was taken to erect a new church for which

the Duke of Bedford again provided the land in part exchange for buying back the old one. This, the present Oreston Methodist Church, was opened on Wednesday 15th August 1888 . . . 'a fine summers day'.

As you might expect, like so many Oreston buildings, the stonework came from a neighbouring quarry (Radford) and the stonemasons were mainly members of the local church.

It wasn't just the quarries that supported the community here though. Oreston had been the principal arrival and departure point for the lowest crossing of the Plym since the middle ages at least and like so many ferry linked villages this had long since sustained related businesses. At one time there were as many as four or five inns in the village including the 'Ferryboat', the 'Old', the 'King's Arms' and the 'Forester's Arms'. The 'King's Arms', appropriate enough for a village which appears to have served as Royalist stronghold in the Civil War, is the only one open today. The 'Forester's', though, was open around the time this view was recorded and you can see the great tree which stood in its courtyard towering above the houses on the right of the picture. The tree has long since gone but the fine three storey building itself still stands, set back a little from the road.

Also clearly visible, just to the left of the building in the foreground, are two of the windows of Oreston's Anglican church, The Church of the Good Shepherd. A daughter church of St Mary and All Saints Plymstock, this delightful little building is probably the smallest Anglican church in the Plymouth area but it nevertheless has a very sizeable congregation. Standing on the same spot today, at the end of Marine Road with your back to Marine Villas, you can no longer see the church from here; the boatyard which has since been constructed out over the water to a point just

beyond the nearest sailing vessel in the picture, now obscures most of this scene. Many of the buildings shown here, though, are still standing; the side wall and window of the house on the end of Town Quay, or Turn Quay as it is now, stands out clearly even now, as does East End House, the tall building behind the mast of the sailing boat in the foreground.

Of course, boat building and ship building was another local source of employment and here in the latter half of the nineteenth century William Lapthorn, George Underhill and William Lucas all operated such businesses here. The sea link also led to the establishment of other industries; fish and fuel (coal) were two obvious ones, timber was another and Bayly & Fox had one of their bases, a steam saw mill and timber yard, here.

In those days, many were the men in Oreston referred to as 'captain' and many were they who lived overlooking the water. Park Lane had barely been developed, Thornable Lane (now Thornyville Terrace, Villas and Road) was just a lane leading to Pomphlett, there were no dwellings along it until after the school was built. Meanwhile, the only other major thoroughfare not on the waters edge was Plymstock Lane (now Road). Plymstock Lane then had a number of buildings leading up to the burial ground (behind the Methodist Church) but only the odd scattered dwellings beyond it.

Perhaps the biggest change to Oreston since this time, though, isn't so much the housing development but the quay side development which in recent years saw the infilling of the old Quay and the grassing over of the land that was 'reclaimed'.

Davey, Sleep & Co.

'In this era of exhibitions and test competitions, agricultural engineering has been brought to such a pitch of excellence that in few branches of the trade is the struggle for supremacy better maintained. Makers of machinery who from lack of intelligence or want of perseverance, have failed to keep pace with the times, have been forced out of the race, until the trade has become practically confined to a very limited number of firms. In the Western Counties no firm enjoys, or has enjoyed, a higher reputation than that of Messrs DAVEY, SLEEP & Co., of 'Excelsior' Works, Embankment Road (later Laira Bridge Road), Plymouth, who hold a leading position in their own line of operations, maintained by a consistent application of the latest scientific improvements to all the work for which they are responsible.'

So ran the opening lines of an article about this firm in the 1894 *Commercial Guide to Plymouth* and well may they have been entitled to boast back then. Just two years earlier they had been awarded first and second prizes for their turn-wrest ploughs at the Warwick trial, organized in conjunction with the Royal Agricultural Society of England; awards which brought William Sleep's tally of prizes and medals to a figure that was 'upwards of 3,116'.

William Sleep was born in 1837, orphaned by the age of ten, and started working as a farm boy in Mevagissey. After some time he took up an apprenticeship with the village blacksmith where 'not content with shoeing horses, he occupied a scanty and hard earned leisure by teaching himself 'the three R's . . .'

Once his five years as an apprentice had been served, he got a job working with another smith, and it was in his time here that he brought out a new plough. The plough was well received and from then on young Sleep set about looking for ways in which he could improve the 'somewhat primitive types of agricultural implements with which the British agriculturalist was then content.' Among the many implements that Sleep later produced versions of at his 'Excelsior' works were – rakes, cultivators, rollers, distributors, cutters, elevators, cake-breakers, horse gear and whippletrees. Whippletrees were the same as swingletrees, basically they were a device fitted to ploughs and carriages which gave the horse or ox freedom to move its shoulders. The turnwrest plough, incidentally, referred to above, was a plough in which the furrow slice always shifted over by itself when turned around, so as to be facing the right way when starting a new furrow.

With all these lines produced at the works here, though, (and some can be seen in the yard between the main building and the showroom) the emphasis is clearly on machinery that was pulled, rather than anything that was doing the pulling and in the event it was with mechanization that the real future lay at the end of last century.

Although there were over one million working farm horses in Britain as late as 1939, early steam engines began to appear on British farms from the middle of last century and while they were slow to spread initially, the first petrol driven tractor was developed in 1889.

William Sleep, with his great bushy beard extending fully six inches below his chin, was then very much a man of his age, but it was a brief, albeit significant era in farming. Up until the beginning of the eighteenth century farming had changed little in thousands of years. Then it was revolutionised by such innovations as Jethro Tull's seed sowing machine and Lord Townshend's system of crop rotation. In the nineteenth century another major boost came with the introduction of chemical fertilizers but it was the introduction of mechanical power steam, then petrol and electricity that was to have the biggest impact on farming practices. Horses and farmworkers generally were laid off in great numbers and the old machinery cast aside.

The firm of Sleep, Davey and Co continued to operate here in Embankment Road, next to the Great Western and London and South Western Railway lines (which transported their goods far and wide) well into the twentieth century. In 1935, however, the business was moved to Millbay where it was amalgamated with Bickle and Co and in the same year taken over by Willoughby's, although the firm continued to trade as Bickle and Co.

In 1930 the newly formed (Jan 1929) Western National Omnibus Co Ltd built their Laira Bridge Garage next door and started operating their green and cream liveried vehicles from this base, a fleet, incidentally, which included all GWR's road passenger vehicles. In 1935 Western National took over the whole site.

Passage House Inn, Cat Down

'This Old Inn still stands at Cattedown, and doubtless was, in olden times, a place of considerable importance, as before the erection of the Laira Bridge, and the introduction of steamboats plying across the Cattewater, the little village of Cattedown was the chief connecting link between Plymouth and the villages on the other side of the water. In fact, long after the erection of the Laira Bridge, foot passengers journeyed to Cattedown to take the ferry for Oreston, Turnchapel, Plymstock and elsewhere.'

That was written by WHK Wright in 1901 to accompany this drawing by Charles Eldred of the inn. Sadly the account went on to say 'We have nothing particular to say about this old inn. It has no history as far as we can discover. It was merely, as its name implies, the house of call for persons crossing the Cattewater at this point.'

'Picturesque it is to a certain extent, and there were several other picturesque houses at Cattedown, but these are all gone and have made room for the wharves and manufactories which form at the present time the chief characteristics of the village on the Cattewater.'

Before the Laira Bridge was completed, in 1827, Cattedown was indeed a distinctive little village and although there were only a dozen or so buildings here, it was a very busy thoroughfare. Nestled on the southern most shore of Cat Down (as it was then always referred to on maps) it spread out in a straight line immediately to the west of the 'Passage House'. Just behind it a sizable part of the Down had been quarried and hard by the Inn on the eastern side was the end of a horse drawn railway. Further quarrying extended from here as far as the bridge site just south of which was a small terrace of cottages on the water's edge which in time became known as Prince Rock.

The Prince Rock cottages, which included at one time the 'Robin Hood' and 'Little John' public houses, were pulled down in the 1890s to make way for the electricity generating station and now the area chiefly known as Prince Rock centres around what later became Prince Rock farm which stood approximately where River View meets Risdon Avenue. Originally, however, Prince Rock, like Cattedown, was just a tiny riverside community.

Cattedown itself was the least isolated of the two because of the ferry and the road link. By road it was approached by Cattedown Lane, which became Cattedown Road, and which ran from the old turnpike, now buried under Catte-

down roundabout, across the then open Down to the inn. Certainly this would have been a busy route long before the quarrying began and the lane actually split the quarries in two. Extensively plundered for stone for the Breakwater, the nearest buildings to Cattedown Village on the Plymouth side in 1827 were the 'Breakwater Inn' and Fareham Place. Doubtless built to house the quarry workers, Fareham Place was demolished as gas works were developed around there from 1846 onwards.

During the course of the nineteenth century there were enormous changes on and around the Cat Down, the quarrying continued as the Victorians delighted in the use of limestone … 'the rumble of the Cattedown stone carts through the streets was a familiar Plymouth sound for decades' (Crispin Gill). Inevitably as these waterside areas were levelled by the quarrying so they became ideal sites for development themselves and a number of chemical works were begun to the north and west of the village. Mainly focussed around the production of the newly invented superphosphate fertilizers, these works included those of Charles Norrington in 1846 (Norrington became Mayor of Plymouth in 1863), James Gibbs in 1870 and in 1878 Messrs Burnard, Leak and Alger, whose firm had been established 24 years earlier.

Initially the village appears to have thrived on all this development and in the middle of the nineteenth century you would have found Elizabeth Chapman doing good

business in the 'Passage House Inn'; meanwhile in Cattedown's second inn, the 'Three Crowns' (later it was the 'Freemason's Arms') Thomas Joslin was pouring the pints. Later succeeded by Francis then William Joslin, also in the village was Samuel Joslin who kept a shop. Cattedown also had at this time its own Wesleyan Methodist Chapel.

There was, however, no real room to expand the village here, what little land there was was fast becoming too valuable for just housing and as the various wharves were constructed and more industrial plants moved in, so the accommodation necessary to house those who were likely to man all these factories and depots was built on the other side of Cat Down. The heart of Cattedown moved with the construction of the Church of St John Sutton on Plym in 1855, built to serve the parishes of Coxside and Cattedown. Gradually new terraces sprang up, spreading along what is now Exeter Street towards the roundabout, until by the late 1890s almost all the remaining housing in Cattedown today had been laid out across the great green estate that had been fields just forty years before.

The old houses of Cattedown village have now all been pulled down, the 'Passage House Inn' itself was all but demolished a year or so after this sketch was made and a new inn constructed upon its original thick cellar walls, the name remains the same however, a reminder of those very different days when the water was closer and provided a living for the little community of Cattedown.

Turnchapel and Oreston

Up until the end of the eighteenth century Oreston was by far the busiest settlement in recent times on the eastern bank of the Cat-Water. Around that time, however, Turnchapel began a transformation from being little more than a quarry with a small waterside shipbuilding interest to being a thriving Victorian village.

In 1770 John Parker, the future Baron Boringdon, set up a landlady on a peppercorn rent in the 'New Inn', Turnchapel. Twenty seven years later his son, the second Baron Boringdon and also called John Parker, enclosed part of Turnchapel as a dry dock. It is not therefore surprising that we find the main thoroughfare in the village is called Boringdon Road or that it sports a pub that has always been known as the 'Boringdon Arms'.

Doubtless the Parkers were responsible for many other developments in the area at the same time and in this view, sketched around 1830, you can see the eastern side of Boringdon Road enjoying an uninterrupted view of the Cat-Water (as it was then called). The original 'New Inn', incidentally, was behind the building on the right hand side of the road at the foot of 'The Hill', the road into Turnchapel, seen here running down from the top of the quarry face.

John Parker in some ways probably lessened a lot of the smaller boating traffic with the building of Laira Bridge in 1827 and this, combined with the growing importance of Turnchapel, did much to by-pass the old main route from Plymouth to Plymstock and the surrounding villages, which was via the Cat Down to Oreston ferry.

As a short and direct route, this clearly had much to commend it to the oarsmen who worked the ferry. However, as steam became a viable means of power for small vessels as well as larger ones, it no longer mattered that ferries took the shortest water crossing, but rather that they started and finished at the shortest distance possible from houses and workplaces of people who, in those pedestrian days, wanted to use the ferries. Cattedown, in these terms, was a long way from Plymouth, which was then mainly built up around the western side of Sutton Harbour, and stretched little further than a half a mile beyond St Andrew's Church in any other direction.

So it was that when the Oreston Steamboat Company announced the commencement of the running of their new service using their brand new steam-boat *Little Pet*, on Monday 3rd May 1869, its route was from Oreston to the Barbican Pier and back, calling at Turnchapel each way. The fare was one penny each way and the proprietors wished to make it known to 'Inhabitants of Plymouth and its vicinity', that the arrangements afforded 'a favourable opportunity for visiting the beautiful scenery at Radford, Hooe, Staddon Heights, &c., &c.'

The first ferry left at 5.30 every weekday morning and was in Plymouth by 5.45, thereafter the service was on the hour right through to 9.00pm. On Sundays it ran 9.00am till 9.00pm. 'Persons going from the Country to Plymouth can be accommodated with good Stabling at Oreston.'

Clearly the service flourished, as by August of that year a new saloon steamboat, the *Favourite* had been brought in to run in conjunction with the *Little Pet*. Furthermore, the route had now been extended to take in 'the much frequented and picturesque village of Hooe, from which place the *Little Pet* will leave at 6.30am'. The *Favourite* left Oreston half an hour later. The new route also took in stops at Cattedown and Mount Batten (tide permitting). 'These arrangements will thus give half-hourly communication between the above mentioned places'.

This wasn't the only steamboat ferry company in the area though, and in 1871, in order to regulate the traffic, a joint committee was set up of the Oreston Company and the Turnchapel Steamboat Company. The regulations were strict. The crew were to be fined 1/6d (7p) if they started more than five minutes late, which was a considerable amount in terms of their wages which were then 23/- (£1.15p) per week for the skipper, 21/- for the engineer and 3/- (15p) per week for the boys. The crew also had to pay for any damage caused by the steamers.

Certainly this new age of ferryman could not afford to be complacent. In the 1880s Henry Elford's red funneled steamers of the Oreston and Turnchapel line faced stiff competition from Greaney's rival yellow funneled ferries. Indeed it was in order to see off this challenge that Elford had the old wooden pier at Turnchapel built at a cost of £1,000. The measure worked and within two years Greaney sold his boats to the Oreston and Turnchapel Company. New technology was in time to present new threats to the ferry service, however, as the advent of the bicycle and the car slowly made their impact felt. The railway came first though and in 1896 Oreston and Turnchapel were linked into the London and South Western Railway. It is hard to gauge the effect this had on the ferry service and in the event the ferries here outlasted the trains, the last engine running between here and Friary in 1951.

It was the motor vehicle, however, which ultimately saw off the ferry here, in particular the omnibus. There were many complaints, though, that while a bus service was provided to the top of Turnchapel there was no good bus link between the Barbican and the town centre. But the complaints went unheeded. In the mid 1960s the ferries stopped but maybe not forever. As parking becomes an increasing problem and as plans are on hand that could transform the whole Mount Batten peninsula who knows what the future may hold?

Burrow Hill

It is still possible to stand on Burrow Hill and locate the vantage point that Henry Worsley must have taken in 1830 when he came here and completed the drawing that Floyd later engraved. Although there have been great changes over the intervening years the foreground is still open grassland and runs for some distance until you reach the properties that make up Simon Close and Lippel Drive (the latter being named after the local estate agent, Billy Lippel, who developed the land in the late 1950s/early 1960s, the former after his son).

The healthy expanse of fresh water in Radford Lake is still clearly visible, as is the folly – the Castle – that sits by the weir. Newly built when this view was recorded, the castle appears somewhat larger in real life than it is shown here but otherwise the weir is much the same. The salt water and thus tidal, Hooe Lake still presents a similar appearance but is almost devoid of water these days at low tide, the silt mud flats being a good forty feet deep in places.

The trees and clear green spaces of Radford Park still give the area a rural feel as do the woods around lower Hooe and Hexton, where clearly much quarrying had already been done at the beginning of the nineteenth century. One building is visible here at the bottom of Turnchapel, today though Turnchapel stretches much further back to meet Hooe, and the houses of St John's Drive line the top of the high ridge shown here. This is of course the very ridge that gives its name to the area as Hooe, like Hoe, means simply 'high place'.

Beyond this point Mount Batten tower can be seen standing proud on that famous peninsula, while beyond it to the right at the mouth of the Tamar the artist has drawn Drake's Island, possibly on this occasion employing a bit of artistic licence. Other features, however, have been recorded here with remarkable accuracy, sweeping across from Maker Heights and Mount Edgcumbe, past the undeveloped Devil's Point, Millbay and West Hoe to the Hoe itself with its rugged coastline awaiting the later decoration that was to transform it into one of the most visited public spaces in the West Country.

Plymouth at this time extended little beyond the two parish churches of St Andrew and Charles, the towers of both being clearly depicted here above that large, high, flat area – Catte Down. Today a large gasometer obscures all but the spire of Charles Church from this standpoint, while the tiny village of Cattedown itself has been swallowed up as commercial wharfs and quays spread around the waterside from Sutton Harbour.

In the middle distance Dean Park Road now curves around from Oreston to meet the ancient thoroughfare (now Radford Park Road) that ran from Radford House past the recently restored Lodge up to Dean Cross. While just out of sight, then as now, is the land upon which Quarry Park Road, Drake Way, Mountbatten Way, Berry Park Road, Gower Ridge and Princess Crescent and Avenue have all been constructed, for the most part in the last thirty years.

Back in the early twentieth century though this was still all very rural, but such is not to say that there were no significant changes in the previous century. Writing in the 1850s Dr Bellamy has left us with a fine account of the ancient byways in this area:

'Among the less ancient monuments of former times, the roads by which our forefathers of the rural districts mostly travelled, may claim a passing record. Many of them remain in this primitive condition, and are found not much above 6 feet in diameter, being thus clearly unsuited for the vehicles now in general use, having rather been formed only for the foot passenger, the horse with pack, pannier, saddle and pillion, butt, slide or crook, in the transfer of manure etc., between cultivated plots or of man and produce between farms, villages and towns.

These ways were frequently united by paths crossing the intervening fields and a high peculiarity which must strike any of their present visitors, was their great and quaint crookedness, implying perhaps, that the country being formerly cultivated in patches, these lanes so traversed as to visit in their devious way a number of such enclosures. We find them proceeding without the study of convenient construction or of easy travel, from high to low ground with the most sudden ascents and descents.

One of the connecting path-fields in question, occurring in the parish began in the narrow lane at Dene Cross, proceeded to take Burrow Hill at its steepest angle, crossed the very summit, intersected the lane there and descended in a similar abrupt fashion to the farm at Goosewell.'

Today that road, Burrow Hill, despite having been somewhat altered still remains as one of the most rural roads negotiable by car in the whole of Plymouth and it is just off it that this scene was captured, the views here being just as spectacular in other directions as they are in this one.

Messrs. Burnard & Alger

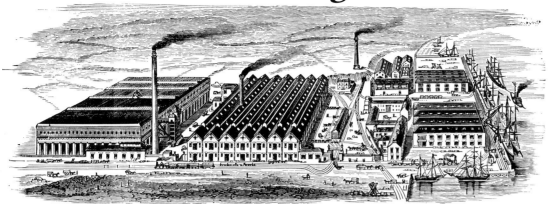

Messrs Burnard and Alger Limited were 'Manufacturers of Sulphuric Acid, Chemical Fertilizers, &c; also Metal Extractors, Wharfingers and Warehousemen', their works extended in front of and behind the old village of Cattedown. The main street or road off which most of the properties which made up the old village stood, ran in front of the building at right angles to the left hand ship in the foreground of the view here. Virtually all the development in front of this block had been carried out under the terms of an unopposed private Act known as 'Burnard and Alger's Cattedown Wharves' Act 1887'.

Charles Burnard had begun manufacturing fertilizer in Milbrook around 1840, his father, a farmer, had moved the family up from the Bodmin area some years earlier. In 1854 Charles went into partnership with a Mr Lack and they opened a works on Lambhay Hill, the business prospered and in 1860 they moved to Sutton Road. Sometime around 1870 another move began, to Cattedown, and Mr Lack was bought out for £44,000 and William Henry Alger became a partner in the firm. Over the years it grew quite spectacularly, but this was not altogether surprising as it was, as it boasted in 1894; 'one of the earliest of the firms for the manufacture of chemical fertilizers, and its reputation deservedly stands very high in the United Kingdom, as well as on the Continents of Europe and America'.

The link between chemistry and agriculture was a modern phenomenon in the nineteenth century, indeed one of the pioneers in this field, the great Cornish chemist Humphry Davy, was asked to deliver a series of lectures on the subject in 1802 by the newly established Board of Agriculture. Entitled *The Connection of Chemistry with Vege-*table Physiology, the series was extremely popular and was repeated over the next ten years. In 1812 Humphry Davy was knighted and in 1813 he published his work as *Elements of Agricultural Chemistry*.

Further research followed in his wake. In 1838 The Royal Agricultural Society was founded with its motto 'Practice with Science'. Two years later the epoch making book *Organic Chemistry in its Application to Agriculture and Physiology* by Justus von Liebig, was published and a new era in farming was under way. In 1842 a factory was established in Deptford to produce artificial fertilizers and in the same year the foundations were laid for an experimental farm at Rothamstead to monitor the success of the new products.

As knowledge of plant needs increased, so the demand for new fertilizers grew, superphosphates, bone dust and Peruvian guano were among the early favourites and at one stage Britain was importing as much as 300,000 tons of guano (sea bird manure) per year. Burnard and Alger themselves had a massive guano warehouse. But the scientific advances were rapid and by the 1870s the demand for guano began to fall off and superphosphates of lime had become 'the most largely used artificial manure'.

Burnard and Alger (as they were then) were abreast of all these developments and armed with the 1887 Act, which gave them powers to levy rates on goods deposited or warehoused with the firm, they acquired the site of what had become Hill's shipbuilding yard in the middle of the tiny village of Cattedown and constructed these extensive wharves in front of it. Fifty-year-old William Alger, was, interestingly enough, enjoying his second term as Mayor of Plymouth at this time, he held office in 1885–6 and 1886–7;

Charles Burnard had held the office himself in 1881–2.

In the course of all this activity the old quarry at the back of the shipyard was reworked to a level twelve to fifteen feet beneath the level of the old floor. This now brought the quarrying to over 70 feet below the height of the original surface of the Cat Down.

Before it was called Cattedown, this area was known as Hingstone, which Worth suggested possibly indicated the existence of a hanging stone here at some time. However, while there are records of executions here over the centuries, it is perhaps more likely that like one of explanations of the name Hinton it comes from Hean tun, that is an enclosure or homestead on high land. Certainly 'Henstone' or 'Hingston' as it has also been referred to, is on the same limestone ridge as the Hoe and directly opposite that of Hooe both of which owe their names to their being high points.

The idea that there may, long long ago, have been some kind of settlement here at Hingston or Cattedown received an enormous boost as Burnard and Alger extended the quarry for 'soon after the excavation commenced, in the autumn of 1886, the men broke through the east wall of a fissure containing earth and a few stones, and ere long found a few bones, of which they took no heed' (Worth 1890). Before long, though, yet more bones were found and Robert Burnard (Charles's son, now running the business) was called in and he in turn brought RN Worth in to investigate. Eventually this led to the discovery of further infilled cavities and deposits that contained the remains of some 15 humans of both sexes young and old, plus various animal remains including those of rhinoceros, lion, hyena and other extinct British animals. Also uncovered were ashes of fires and 'a rudely-chipped flint nodule' all of which, 'carries back the residence of man on the site of Plymouth itself to paleolithic times' (Worth).

Further remains were discovered nearby in 1964 and 1973, and a bone of a reindeer found then was dated by the Radiocarbon Laboratory at the British Museum to be around 15,000 years old, well within the late stone age.

The firm of Burnard and Alger, meanwhile, sold their fertilizing interests and name to the Anglo Continental Guano Works Ltd in 1920. At the same time Cattedown Wharves Ltd was formed and it continued to be managed by members of the Burnard and Alger families until 1957 when they sold out to FT Everard and Sons. Today all the great storehouses built on the wharves shown here survive and the 'new' offices of Cattedown Wharves stand in the foreground on the edge of the nearest store.

The New Patent Candle Company

'The Plymouth Steam Candle Company was inaugurated about 35 years ago, when several old-established chandleries were absorbed. The works, at that time situated in Manor Street, were utilized chiefly in the manufacture of tallow dips, moulding and rush candles. Originally, composites were moulded by means of hand frames, but with the adoption of patent moulding machines the manufacture quickly developed into proportions wholly unanticipated, and, more recently, paraffin and mineral wax candles have been added to the list of qualities previously made . . . some idea of the magnitude of the business may be gathered from the fact that, at the time of writing, from 25,000,000 to 30,000,000 candles are annually distributed, showing that modern inventions have simply added to our resources, and while the new forms of illuminations are widely adopted, the old still have their uses.'

The 'time of writing' was 1894 and the above quotes are taken from an article publicizing 'The New Patent Candle Company' in Sutton Road. The modern inventions, of course, were gas and electricity. Gas lighting around that time was becoming increasingly widespread and back in 1868 a new national standard had decreed that the amount of light from a gas burner should be increased from the equivalent of 12 to 16 candles. However, the real threat was just about to make its presence felt for, coincidentally, it was in 1894 that the town's main artificial lighting moved away from oil or coal gas to electricity – under the terms of the 'Plymouth Electric Lighting Order' of that year. To give some idea of scale to the Company's statistics, total British consumption of candles at the beginning of this century was around 50,000 tons. By 1939 this figure had been halved; at the end of the fifties it was down to 7,000 and last year total British candle production was about 2,500 tons. Given that you might get two or maybe three candles to the lb that would mean that the entire British candle out-put last year was about a half of the annual production of this Coxside factory in 1894. Furthermore, today there are only four major candle manufacturers in the United Kingdom; one hundred years ago there were four in Plymouth alone with others in Stonehouse and Devonport.

However, just a few years earlier there had been still more and in the 1850s there were seven to eight operating in the town. There was John Hawks, Ann Lear, Nicholas Rowse, Robert Snow, Mary Fry, William Smerdon, Ponsford Fisher and GE and EP Doudney all operating their own

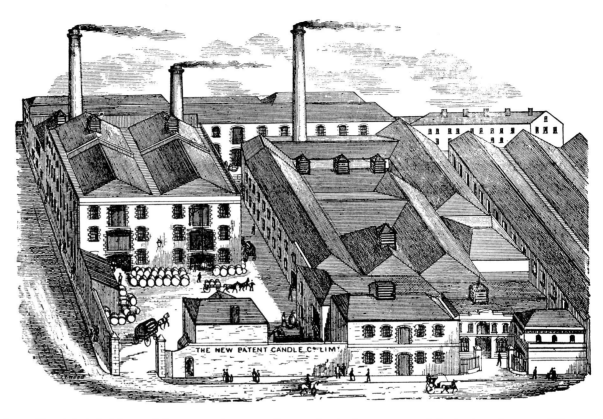

THE NEW PATENT CANDLE C⁰ LIM⁰

'Tallow Chandeleries'. Many of them were long standing family businesses. Samuel Rowse had been going in 1812, the Snow's in 1823, advertising themselves as 'Tallow Chandler and Soap Boilers'. William Snow later merged his interests with the New Patent Candle Company and in 1859 when the new company was established it was based around the Manor Street premises of the Doudneys. It is likely that the Fisher, Fry and Smerdon interests were among those 'old established chandleries' which were 'absorbed' at the same time. Of the local independent concerns, it was Lear and Company who lasted longest, operating until just after the turn of the century. Then by 1910 we find that 'Millbay Soap' had moved in with the New Patent Candle Company in Sutton Road. Twenty years later the factory closed down.

Part of the old premises can still be seen adjoining what was known as Candlework Lane, and reading WJ Powers

intriguing account of the business houses of Plymouth we learn that Candlework Lane was 'a favourite spot for the boys from the nearby St John's School to 'settle their differences'.'

Today tallow is little used in candle production; neither is beeswax. However, until about 1830 these had been the principal ingredients of candles since the middle ages. Tallow comes in two forms, from the seeds of Chinese Tallow Trees or, more commonly, it is animal fat derived from beef or mutton suet. Good quality tallow can be eaten. Beeswax has a more obvious derivation and in Roman Catholic Churches even today altar candles are required to consist 'in the Greater part' (usually about 65%) of beeswax. Most candle burning these days, however, is done in restaurants or at the dining table. However, they are also popular on anniversary cakes and useful in power cuts!

Mount Batten

It has been suggested, by Professor Barry Cunliffe of Oxford University (1989), that Mount Batten could well be Britain's oldest port. Evidence, he believes, supports the notion that international trade, with Brittany, Spain and possibly even the Mediterranean, was conducted here as early as the eighth century BC.

Certainly various finds here from the nineteenth century onwards indicate that people were probably living here, in comparative comfort, long before major settlements were established around Sutton Harbour, or anywhere else in the immediate vicinity. In the last 150 years over 300 pieces of prehistoric metalwork and pottery have been found at Mount Batten along with more than 2,000 fragments of ancient animal bones.

Easily defensible from the land and once regularly cut off from the mainland at high tide, this would have been a very sensible area in which to settle in the days before anyone feared an attack from the sea. However, once such an attack became a real threat Mount Batten was soon found to be vulnerable and its population left in favour of safer havens.

It is nevertheless conceivable that this was the peninsula known to the ancient world as Ictis, on the edge of the known world, with 'natives' who were 'extremely hospitable and who lived in a civilized way because of their contact with foreign traders' (Diodorus Siculus around 10BC).

The earliest recorded name we have for it, though, is Hostert or Hawe Stert or some similar version of these two old words which we can fairly confidently take to mean 'end of the hoe', that is the end of the high place or ridge.

Used as a defensive post by Plymouth's Parliamentarian forces during the Civil War this area not only witnessed plenty of action during those troubled times it also acquired a new name, being rechristened in honour of the man whom Parliament came to appoint Governor of 'Batten's' Tower, Captain, afterwards Admiral, Batten.

Although Charles II subsequently ordered the construction of the substantial tower that we still see here today, Mount Batten by that time, no longer had an indigenous local population and as the nineteenth century dawned there was nothing on this 500-yard peninsula except this little round fortification.

The social changes of the nineteenth century, however, brought a new lease of life to the area as great numbers of day-tripping Plymothians flocked here on high days and holidays. Most people then were not in a position to have anything more than the odd day off and certainly such wheeled transport as existed was not always within the means of those looking for an exciting excursion. Mount Batten, being but a short stretch of water away from almost everyone who lived in Plymouth, quickly became a much frequented spot and on a quarried site on the northern side of the headland, in the shadow of the tower, the 'Castle Inn' was built.

Here for many years at the end of the nineteenth century, George Hine was the landlord, and doubtless among his more regular customers were William Kelly and John and Isaac Darton, all boat builders who had their premises at Mount Batten. Doubtless too the coastguards who lived in the seaward-facing, purpose-built row of cottages at Mount Batten, would also have found their way to the 'Castle' from time to time.

There was competition for custom, though, for a while with the construction of the 'Breakwater Inn' at the head of the Batten Breakwater in the 1880s. Like the other 'Breakwater Inn' at Coxside, which was designed to meet the requirements of the men quarrying for the main Breakwater in the Sound some 70 years earlier, this was presumably built to serve the needs of the men who built the 300-yard-long structure on the Batten Reef.

The idea of a breakwater on the reef had first been mooted some hundred years earlier but in the event nothing was done until after the formation, in 1874, of the Cattlewater Commissioners. There had long been concern about protecting the Cattewater, particularly against potential breaches of the Batten Isthmus; indeed there was an order passed that 'every Plymouth lighter and sand barge should yearly carry a load of rubble, &c., from the Cattewater, and deposit it on the southern part of the Batten Isthmus'.

The Batten Reef itself had also been a major threat in the past and many old sailing ships came to grief on its rugged rocks. Among the more horrific tragedies here, in 1811 HMS *Amethyst* was lost in a gale on Mount Batten rocks with the loss of some 600 lives and six years later the brig o' war HMS *Jasper* came to grief here with the loss of all but two of the 67 people on board. Long after the completion of the main Breakwater in the Sound there were still many wrecks here.

The new Breakwater, designed by JC Inglis and made of concrete, not only helped alleviate this problem it also, of course, afforded a good deal of protection for Sutton Harbour and the Cattewater. Following its construction new deep water wharfs were quickly established at Turnchapel, by Messrs Bulteel and at Cattedown by Burnard and Alger.

A new chapter opened in the history of this headland in September 1913 when yet another development in transport and thus in the means of waging war led to the establishment of a flying base at Mount Batten. The coastguards and the few civilians living here were obliged to leave and the 'Castle Inn' was commandeered as the residence for the first Station Commander and renamed Greenleaf House in the process.

Now, as a new century looms, it looks as though the role of this peninsula is set to change again, and given the fine views it has always had to offer it would be nice to see it once more used as a place for leisure and pleasure.

Bibliography

Abbreviations: WEH – Western Evening Herald; WMN – Western Morning News; Trans PI – Transactions of the Plymouth Institution; Trans DA – Transactions of the Devonshire Association; ALC – Arthur L Clamp, Publisher; PLHL – copy in Plymouth Local History Library. Dates when known are those of editions referred to.

Barbican, The, and its People Remembered, Arthur L Clamp, ALC (1985)

Biographia Navalis, John Charnock, London (1798)

Boniface of Devon, John Cyril Sladden, Jarrold (1975)

Borough of Crabtree, A History of the Mayor & Corporation, John Webb, *Doidge's Almanac* (1882)

Brunel's Royal Albert Bridge, Thomas Bowden & Bernard Mills, Peter Watts (1983)

Business Houses of Plymouth Vols 1 & 2, WJ Power, typescript PLHL (1982)

Burrow Hill, Ivy Langdon, *Plymstock Chronicle* (April 1972)

Chamber of Commerce First Report, Henry Woollcombe (1814)

Citadel – A History of the Royal Citadel, FW Woodward, Devon Books (1987)

City of Plymouth, European Architectural Heritage Year, City Planning Officer (1975)

Cookworthy, A Man of No Common Clay, Douglas Selleck, Baron Jay, Plymouth (1978)

County of Devon, Survey of the, Tristram Risdon, Rees & Curtis (1811)

Crabtree Limeworks, JW Perkins, *Devon & Cornwall Notes & Queries* (1960–70)

Crownhill, Reflections, Arthur L Clamp, ALC (198-)

Days in Devonport, Parts I-VII, Gerald W Barker, ALC (1982–5)

Devon and Cornwall, Early Tours in, ed R Pearse Chope 1918, David & Charles (1968)

Devonport, History of, RN Worth, W Brendon (1870)

Devonport, Stoke and Morice Town, Stonehouse & Plymouth, John Sanford (1830)

Devonport, Official Guide to, Burrows (190-)

Devonport, Inns and Beer Houses of, 2 vols, Henry Horwill, manuscript PLHL (1975)

Devonport Dockyard Story, KV Burns, *Maritime* (1984)

Devonport, Hail and Farewell to, FS Blight, *Trans PI*, xii (1951)

Devonshire and Cornwall Illustrated, J Britton & EW Brayley, H Fisher, R Fisher & R Jackson (1832)

Drake's Island, Mayflower Centre Trust (198-)

Drake's Island, a Brief History of, PJ Mowan, Old Plymouth Soc (1951)

English Terraced House, Stefan Muthesius, Yale University Press (1982)

Floating Bridge at Saltash, IM Rendel, Plan (1831)

Gardens of Saltram House, Mary Crosse, *Devon Life* (May 1983)

Grand House on the Hoe That Few People Use, Veronica Horwell, *WMN* (26 11 1965)

Ham, An Account of, GW Copeland, Plymouth (1947)

Ham, the Oldest Inhabited House in Plymouth, Audrey Hawkins, *WEH* (30 4 1939)

Higher Stoke & Milehouse, a Short History of, David Ayres, Plymouth (1965)

HM Naval Base Devonport, Historic Architecture of, Jonathan Coad, National Maritime Museum (1983)

HMS Drake, Wardroom Mess (Dec 1973)

Hooe and Turnchapel Remembered, Arthur L Clamp, ALC (1981)

Hooe, The Story of, RHC Fice, *South Devon Times* (26 2 1960)

John Kitto, Gerald KS Edwards, *WEH* (22 9 1934)

Kelly's Devonshire Directory, also published by White & Billings (1856–1928)

London and South Devon Railway vol 2, RA Williams, David & Charles (1973)

Lord Morley's Flying Bridge, Keith S Perkins, *Rendel's News* (1982)

Making of a Cornish Town, Gladys & FL Harris, Torpoint Town Council (1976)

Mannamead School, Story of, CR Serpell (1945)

Memories of Southside Street, RD *Western Independent* (30 5 52)

Mount Edgcumbe Park, William Crossing, Hoyten & Cole (18--)

Mount Edgcumbe, A Walk Around, W Byers (1836)

Mount Edgcumbe, Duprez's Visitors Guide to, WHK Wright, Duprez (1871)

Mount Batten, Archaeology of, Cynthia Gaskell-Brown (1985)

Mount Edgcumbe, Survey, Colin Griffin, Cornwall (1983–84)

Mount Batten, the Story of, Arthur L Clamp, ALC (198-)

Mr Rawlinson's Report on the Sewerage, Drainage... of Plymouth, PD&S Herald (12 3 1853)

Nineteenth-Century Britain, Intigration and Diversity, Keith Robbins, Clarendon Press (1988)

Old Plymouth, Nooks and Corners of, John MacDonald (1883)

Old Plymouth, Sybil Jerram, *WMN* Book (1913)

Old Plymouth, Ecclesiastical History of, J Brooking Rowe (1876)

Old Devon Bridges, Charles Henderson & E Jervoise (1938)

Old Plymouth, Views of, Sarah Foot, Bossiney Books (1983)

Old Plymouth, Streets of, C Eldred & WHK Wright (1901)

Old Plymouth, New Light on, James Barber, Plymouth Athenaeum, Vol IV (19--)

Ordnance Land at Devonport, *Western Daily Mercury*, (May 1857)

Oreston and Its People Remembered, Arthur L Clamp, ALC (198-)

Palmerston's Follies, John Babbs, manuscript PLHL (1980)

Pennycross, Story of, Robert Groves (1964)

Pictorial Plymouth, Robert K Dent, JJ Allday (1900)

Playbill, A History of Theatre in the Westcountry, Harvey Crane, McDonald Evans (1980)

Plymouth and Devonport in Times of War and Peace, H Whitfeld, Plymouth (1900)

Plymouth Through the Lens, Vols 1–5, Brian Moseley, Plymouth (1985–87)

Plymouth, Story of, RAJ Walling, Westaway (1950)

Plymouth, Stonehouse & Devonport, Nettleton's Guide to, George Wightwick, E Nettleton (1838)

Plymouth, Stonehouse & Devoport Illustrated, Handbook to WHK Wright, WH Luke (1879)

Plymouth Steam 1954–63, Ian H Lane, Ian Allen (1984)

Plymouth, A Portrait, JC Trewin, Robert Hale (1973)

Plymouth Old and New, Owen A Baker, EP Publishing (1976)

Plymouth Municipal Records, ed RN Worth, Plymouth (1893)

Plymouth Memoirs, Dr James Yonge (1647–1721), ed John J Beckerlegge (1951)

Plymouth Libraries, Arthur Maddison, The Municipal Review (June 1965)

Plymouth Institutions in the 1861 Census, WN Bryant, *Devon & Cornwall Notes & Queries*, Vol XXXV (1982–86)

Plymouth, Industrial Architecture of, ed Cynthia Gaskell-Brown, Plymouth City Museum (1980)

Plymouth in Old Picture Postcards, Mary M Devonport, European Library (1985)

Plymouth, History of, RN Worth, William Brendon & Son (1890)

Plymouth Friaries, New Light on the, Jennifer Barber, *Trans DA*, Vol 105 (1973)

Plymouth Dock Guide Etc, The Hoxland, Dock/Devonport (1792)

Plymouth Division Royal Marines, Col RD Ormsby, Globe Laurel (1930)

Plymouth, Story of, for young and old, WHK Wright, A Wheaton & Co (18--)

Plymouth, Devonport, Stonehouse & South West Devon, various editions, Ward Lock (18--)

Plymouth, Devonport, Stonehouse etc, Handbook of, Henry Besley (186-)

Plymouth Bygones, Sixty Years of Memories and Pictures, Guy Fleming, Devon Books (1991)

Plymouth, Devonport & Stonehouse, The Strangers Handbook to, (1842)

Plymouth Dartmoor Etc, Place Names of, W Best Harris, W Best Harris (1983)

Plymouth Churches, Layman's View of Same, 2 vols, WJ Power, typescript PLHL (1977)

Plymouth Buildings of Architectural & Historical Interest, City of Plymouth/DOE

Plymouth, Devonport & Stonehouse (Post Office) Directories of (between 1812–1955) various publishers

Plymouth, Book of Reference, FE Sach, FE Sach & Co (1916)

Plymouth, Devonport, Stonehouse, Wood's Handbook to, various editions, W Wood (18--)

Plymouth Blitz, SM Green & RFO Cock, Western Independent (194-)

Plymouth, A New History of, Vols I & II, Crispin Gill, David & Charles (1979)

Plymouth and District Illustrated Commercial Guide, WHK Wright

Plymouth in the Late 'Forties, My Personal Recollections of, Samuel Weekes, William Brendon & Son, (1925)

Plymouth and Plymothians more Photographs & Memories, Andrew Cluer, Lantern Books (1975)

Plymouth and Plymothians Photographs & Memories, Andrew Cluer, Lantern Books (1974)

Plymouth Blitz, The Story of the Raids, F Crisp & HP Twyford *WMN* (194-)

Plymouth in Pictures, Crispin Gill, David & Charles (1968)

Plymouth and Devonport Guide with Sketches, HE Carrington, Byers & Son (1838)

Plymouth and the West, Early Newspapers in, James L Palmer, *Trans Pl* Vol XIX (1944)

Plymouth, Ancient Heraldry of, some notes, RN Worth, Journal PI (1877)

Plymouth Library, Architectural Notes, HJW Stirling, (1956)

Plymouth, A History of, CW Bracken, SR (reprint) (1931/70)

Plymouth, The Ancient Buildings of, GW Copeland & EN Masson-Phillips, Old Plymouth Soc (1958)

Plymouth, History of, Llewellyn Jewitt, WH Luke (1873)

Plymouth – 100 Years of Street Travel, RC Sambourne, Glasney Press (198-)

Plymouth Blitz, the Story of, Frank Wintle, Bossiney (1981)

Plymouth, History of, John Harris, typescript PLHL (1808)

Plymouth's Past Through Postcards, Guy Fleming, ALC (1985)

Plymouth's Historic Hoe, Arthur L Clamp, ALC (1985)

Plymouth's Historic Barbican, Arthur L Clamp, ALC (1985)

Plymouth's Ships of War, Lt Com KV Burns DSM RN, National Maritime Museum, (1972)

Plympton St Maurice Guide, Audrey F Mills, Civic Association (1981)

Plympton St Mary, J Mercer-Cox, Plympton (19--)

Plympton, History Beginnings of, RN Worth, Plymouth (1887)

Plympton Erle, A History of, J Brooking-Rowe, James G Commin (1906)

Plympton 1851, Extracts from Census Returns, J Stevens

Plymstock in Perspective, Arthur L Clamp, ALC (1982)

Plymstock Area, Recollections of, Dorothy Warley Pitt, Plymouth (1985)

Radford House, Vanished Glories of, GW Copeland, *WEH* (1954)

Raglan Barracks, feature *WEH* (1 8 1936)

Raglan Barracks, Godfrey Wycisk, *WMN* (13 4 1970)

Raglan Barracks, *Navy and Army Illustrated*, (1 5 1896)

Regiments of Foot, Godfrey Wycisk, *WMN* (15 11 1971)

Royal Naval Hospital Plymouth, History of, Surg Capt PD Gordon Pugh (1972)

Royal Citadel, Arthur L Clamp, ALC (198-)

Rule Britannia, The Victorian World, Times Newspapers Ltd (1974)

Seaside England, Ruth Manning-Sanders, Batsford (1951)

Selevan, the Fisherman Saint, Richard Angove, *Cornish Life* (Feb 1985)

Sherwell Story, Stanley Griffin, Plymouth (1964)

Sir William Morice, CW Bracken, *Devon & Cornwall, Notes & Queries*, Vol 21 (1940–41)

Smeaton's Tower and the Breakwater, LM Merrett, Graphritre (19--)

South Devon Railway, RH Gregory, The Oakwood Press (1982)

South Devon & East Cornwall Hospital, *Western Daily Mercury* (July 1884)

South Devon & East Cornwall Hospital, George Wightwick, *Architectural Magazine*, Vol VII (1836)

St Budeaux, Yesterday's Village, Marshall Ware (1982)

St Budeaux, the Ancient Parish of, Marshall Ware, ALC (1983)

St Budeaux, Historic Treasures, Rev TA Hancock, *WEH* (16 2 1934)

St Budeaux, Growth of Through Peace & War, Rev TA Hancock, *WEH* (23 1 34)

St Budeaux, H Montagu Evans, *Trans Pl* (1913)

Stoke Damerel, Ann Chiswell, *WEH* (20 11 1980)

Stoke & Morice Town, FS Blight, *Trans Pl* Vol XXII (1951)

Stonehouse, Early History, RN Worth, *Journal of the Plymouth Institution* (Nov 1886)

Stonehouse, Archaeological Survey, Cynthia Gaskell-Brown, Plymouth (1975)

Street Trader's Lot, The, Mayhew & Rubinstein, Reader's Union (1851)

Sutton Harbour, Crispin Gill, Sutton Harbour Improvement Co (1976)

Tales of Old Pomphlett, Dorothy Warley Pitt, *Plymouth Times* (1982–83)

Technical Colleges in the Three Towns, Terry J Bickford and Digby Hole, Learning Resources (1976)

The Libraries, Public and Private, of Plymouth, WHK Wright, Library Assoc (190-)

The Drainage of Town, A Hamilton Bampton, Plymouth & Devonport (1849)

The Hoe, Chatty Joe, *Doidge's Almanac*, Plymouth (1882)

The Bear's Head and Queen Anne's Battery, *The Perambulator*, South Devon Monthly Museum (1 12 1835)

The Obsolete Plymouth Manors of Sutton Pyll, CW Bracken, *Trans DA* Vol 74 (1942)

The Inn, Explorer's Guide, Frank Bottomley, Kaye & Ward (1984)

The English Inn, Thomas Burke, Herbert Jenkins (1948)

Transport Bygones in the Plymouth Area, Sydney VC Goodman, ALC (1984)

Turnchapel, Gordon Hines, *South Devon Times*, (21 1 1965)

Twelve Men of Plymouth, Gerald Hamilton Edwards, Plymouth (1951)

Tything of Compton Gifford, RN Worth, *Trans DA* Vol 28 (1896)

Vanishing Street Furniture, Geoffrey Warren, David & Charles (1978)

Vanishing Plymouth, Brian Moseley, BS Moseley (1982)

Victoria, The Life and Times of, Dorothy Marshall, Book Club Associates (1972)

Victoria's Heyday, JB Priestley, Heinemann (1972)

Victorian Pubs, Mark Girouard, Studio Vista (1975)

Victorian Children, Eleanor Allen, Adam & Charles Black (1973)

Victorian Days and Ways, Mark Edward Perugini, Hutchinson

Water from the Moor, David J Hawkins, *Devon Books* (1987)

Western Morning News, History of, supplement *WMN* (4 1 1960)

White's 1850 Devon, William White, David & Charles (reprint) (1850/1968)

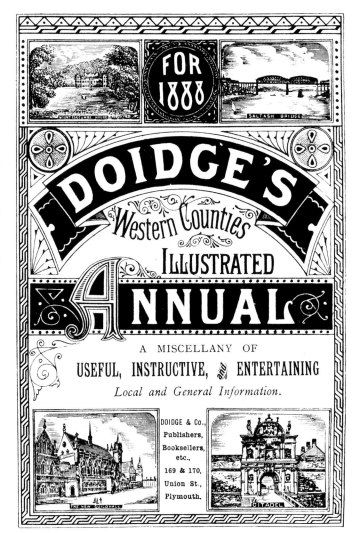

Unlisted but rich in information are: the many street and survey maps of Plymouth – several of which are available as prints from Plymouth Local History Library or Museum; various editions of *Doidge's Almanac* which were produced between 1868–1955 and the 'Christmas Cheer' booklets that followed it for some years; countless newspaper and magazine articles; souvenir programmes; advertising brochures; a variety of general reference volumes, books of facts and encyclopedias; census returns, old telephone directories and electoral registers, copies of which can generally be found in the local history or reference rooms of Plymouth City Library.

Index

Presentation Copies

Local Studies Department,
   Plymouth Central Library
Alan Cooper, Editor,
   Evening Herald
Desmond Robinson
Rob & Nita Warren
John Dudley
John Turner, Bill Bugler,
   The Latimer Trend Group
Crispin Gill
Plymouth City Museum
Laurence & Patricia Greathead

Subscribers

Phyllis Porter
Ronald ER Taylor
John James
John Terence Nichols
Phil and Carol Love
Mrs Sylvia M Boulden
JC Evely
Robert Broughton Vickery
SJ Rendell
Peter Lawrey
Paul Anthony Watson
Gerald Hooper
Mrs REA Ladd
Mr and Mrs MA Cass
Mrs JE Henwood
Ann Beer
Michael Judge
Pauline Frances Buckland
Gareth S Dempster
John A Pitts
Maxine Arnold
PD and VJ Vittle
Denzil Lush
Ann and John Mulinder
FA Hosier
GL Johnson
LP Smerdon
Anthony and Marion Banbury
Dr and Mrs AWG Rees
Charles M Thompson
Mrs Doreen Johnson
Mrs Gillian M Williams
FJ Jeffery
Peter Spriddell
Jeannie Parker
Neil Johnson
Alan and Jennifer Goode
Tony Miller
Mr and Mrs AR Cann
Mr QB Spear
RS Foweraker
Ronald Edwin Heath
Dr and Mrs AW Lambert
Dr Michael Grayson

John and Ena Prior
Keith Woodward
FG Clemits
TE Hardy
Mrs JG Taskis
Philip John Perraton
Mrs PA Lillicrap
Mr and Mrs A Jones
John Penwill Hodge
Mrs Rita Barrett
Maureen P Selley
Sheila Noronen
Roy Davis
George H Horn
Revd KG Horswell
'The Pezey Family'
JJ Henderson
Patricia Goodden
RD Spear
Brian L Veale
Pamela M Wingett
Kevin Merry
Brian Bird
Mr and Mrs JT Veale
Brian Knox
WGM Jones
Rt Rev C Budd
PJ Swallow
Nigel Taylor MRCVS
Devon Library Services
Plymouth Central Library
JC Stabb
Mr and Mrs CH Smith
Michael John Hanrahan
Harold Young
PG Parsons
Keith A Mills
Mr RG Tozer
David Elliott
Mr and Mrs FG Russell
Cyril and Henry Champion
Moira Billing
William John Maher
DAF and Mrs JK Bryant

John Beatson
Peter W Gill
DCI Powell
Mr DGJ Burch
Peter Billing
Linda Maguire
Mr B Sullivan
Derrick Venn
Phillip Ley
Graham Knight
Peter Body
Phillip Allen
Mr IF Carn
Den and Shirley Smith
JB Rundle
Olive McMahon
AJ Cooper
Cynthia Wharton
Mr DJ Cliffe
Len Hocking
Roger J Helmore
Mrs Pat Woodhouse
Rhonda Wootten
SLR McGinnes
Mr G Atkinson
Plymouth Athenaeum
H Robins
AH Doughty
Kim Palmer
Mrs CE Douglas
Susan Davie
Jean Hambly
John and Dianne Ball
John Edward Kirk
John Templeton
Philip W Luscombe
Matthew P Brown
David Cluard
Chris and Cherrill Hall
Paul Davies
Victor R Cavill
Margaret O'Hagan
FA Hogg
Roy S Algar

Malcolm H Grant
Douglas James Bishop
Roger Compton
Keith Raymond Loze
Western College
   Preparatory School
J Batt Dingle
Derek WF Robinson
David FH Goldie
Peter Smerdon
Mr and Mrs J Trotter
Dennis WJ Wilmshurst
Mrs DP Bowles
Edward W Luscombe
Mr CC Banbury
Mrs Joan I Butland
Mrs Beryl Hunt
Matthew Webber
Graham Martin
Anthony Hughes
Mr N Peters
Mr V Mitchell
Ray Pashley
Bob Bishop
Ernest James Pearn
Norman Gilliam
Rose Fuzard
Norma L McTighe
Larry Girling
David G Gilmour
William Coombe
Florence Rivers
Barry and Norah Woon
Janet Bingham
Douglas S Hocking
Owen Hanmer
David Buckingham FRCS
Brian Stocker
Dennis Flack
Phylis Compton
Pam Brown
Katharine Bates
Bill Fox-Smith
Helen Greathead